KW-284-004

Transnational Classes and International Relations
Kees van der Pijl

Gender and Global Restructuring:
Sightings, Sites and Resistances
Edited by Marianne H Marchand and Anne Sisson Runyan

Global Political Economy
Contemporary Theories
Edited by Ronen Palan

Ideologies of Globalization
Contending Visions of a New World Order
Mark Rupert

The Clash within Civilisations
Coming to Terms with Cultural Conflicts
Dieter Senghaas

Global Unions?
Theory and Strategies of Organized Labour in the Global Political Economy
Edited by Jeffrey Harrod and Robert O'Brien

Political Economy of a Plural World
Critical Reflections on Power, Morals and Civilizations
Robert Cox with Michael Schechter

A Critical Rewriting of Global Political Economy
Integrating Reproductive, Productive and Virtual Economies
V. Spike Peterson

Contesting Globalization
Space and Place in the World Economy
André C. Drainville

Global Institutions and Development
Framing the World?
Edited by Morten Bøås and Desmond McNeill

Global Institutions, Marginalization, and Development
Craig N. Murphy

Critical Theories, International Relations and 'the Anti-Globalisation Movement'
The Politics of Global Resistance
Edited by Catherine Eschle and Bice Maiguashca

Routledge/RIPE Studies in Global Political Economy is a forum for innovative new research intended for a high-level specialist readership, and the titles will be available in hardback only. Titles include:

1 Globalization and Governance*
Edited by Aseem Prakash and Jeffrey A. Hart

2 Nation-States and Money
The Past, Present and Future of National Currencies
Edited by Emily Gilbert and Eric Helleiner

3 The Global Political Economy of Intellectual Property Rights
The New Enclosures?
Christopher May

4 Integrating Central Europe
EU expansion and Poland, Hungary and the Czech Republic
Otto Holman

Criti[...]nal Relations and 'the Anti-Globalisation Movement'

90 0633457 0

7 Day

1 2 JAN 2006

University of Plymouth Library

Subject to status this item may be renewed
via your Voyager account

http://voyager.plymouth.ac.uk

Exeter tel: (01392) 475049
Exmouth tel: (01395) 255331
Plymouth tel: (01752) 232323

resistances
iscipline of

obalisation
l capturing
ices consti-
ised power
e claims to
daments of
ould be of
sed on the
istance. Yet

edge of the
' struggles.
ntributions
ement' and
movement
y Marxist,
t-anarchist.
approaches
The book is
an ongoing
ractice, and

University

Bice Maiguashca is a Lecturer in the Department of Politics at the University of Exeter.

WITHDRAWN
FROM
UNIVERSITY OF PLYMOUTH
LIBRARY SERVICES

RIPE series in global political economy

Series editors:

Louise Amoore   University of Newcastle, UK
Randall Germain   Carleton University, Canada
Rorden Wilkinson   University of Manchester, UK
and Wellesley College, USA

Formerly edited by Otto Holman (*University of Amsterdam*),
Marianne Marchand (*Universidad de las Américas-Puebla*), Henk
Overbeek (*Free University, Amsterdam*) and Marianne Franklin
(*University of Amsterdam*)

The RIPE series editorial board are:

Mathias Albert	Bielefeld University, Germany
Mark Beeson	University of Queensland, Australia
A. Claire Cutler	University of Victoria, Canada
Marianne Franklin	University of Amsterdam, the Netherlands
Stephen Gill	York University, Canada
Jeffrey Hart	Indiana University, USA
Eric Helleiner	Trent University, Canada
Otto Holman	University of Amsterdam, the Netherlands
Marianne H. Marchand	Universidad de las Américas-Puebla, Mexico
Craig N. Murphy	Wellesley College, USA
Robert O'Brien	McMaster University, Canada
Henk Overbeek	Vrije Universiteit, the Netherlands
Anthony Payne	University of Sheffield, UK
V. Spike Peterson	University of Arizona, USA

This series, published in association with the *Review of International Political Economy*, provides a forum for current debates in international political economy. The series aims to cover all the central topics in IPE and to present innovative analyses of emerging topics. The titles in the series seek to transcend a state-centred discourse and focus on three broad themes:

- the nature of the forces driving globalisation forward
- resistance to globalisation
- the transformation of the world order.

The series comprises two strands:

The *RIPE Series in Global Political Economy* aims to address the needs of students and teachers, and the titles will be published in hardback and paperback. Titles include:

Critical Theories, International Relations and 'the Anti-Globalisation Movement'

The Politics of Global Resistance

Edited by Catherine Eschle and Bice Maiguashca

Routledge
Taylor & Francis Group

LONDON AND NEW YORK

University of Plymouth
Library

Item No.

9006334570

Shelfmark

First published 2005 by Routledge
2 Park Square, Milton Park, Abingdon, Oxon OX14 4RN

Simultaneously published in the USA and Canada
by Routledge
270 Madison Ave., New York, NY 10016

Routledge is an imprint of the Taylor & Francis Group

© 2005 Catherine Eschle and Bice Maiguashca for selection and
editorial matter; individual contributors their contributions

Typeset in Times by Taylor & Francis Books
Printed and bound in Great Britain by MPG Books Ltd, Bodmin

All rights reserved. No part of this book may be reprinted or
reproduced or utilised in any form or by any electronic, mechanical, or
other means, now known or hereafter invented, including
photocopying and recording, or in any information storage or retrieval
system, without permission in writing from the publishers.

British Library Cataloguing in Publication Data
A catalogue record for this book is available from the British Library

Library of Congress Cataloging in Publication Data
Critical theories, international relations, and "the anti-globalisation
movement" : the politics of global resistance / edited by Catherine
Eschle and Bice Maiguashca.
        p. cm.
Includes bibliographical references and index.
1. Anti-globalization movement. 2. International relations. 3. Political
participation. 4. Political violence. I. Eschle, Catherine. II.
Maiguashca, Bice, 1965-III. Title.
JZ1318.C754 2005
337.1-dc22

        2004019117

ISBN 0–415–34390–9 (hbk)
ISBN 0–415–34391–7 (pbk)

Contents

Contributors

Vicki Birchfield is Assistant Professor in The Sam Nunn School of International Affairs at the Georgia Institute of Technology and Director of the Brussels Summer Program. Her research and teaching interests include comparative politics, international political economy and European integration. She has published in the *European Journal of Political Research* and the *Review of International Political Economy* and is currently completing a book manuscript entitled 'Institutions, Values and Income Inequality in Capitalist Democracies', which presents a comparative analysis of the institutional and cultural roots of income inequality in sixteen countries.

Roland Bleiker is Reader in Peace Studies and Political Theory at the University of Queensland in Australia. He is the author of *Popular Dissent, Human Agency and Global Politics* (Cambridge University Press, 2000); *Rethinking Korean Security: Towards a Culture of Reconciliation* (University of Minnesota Press, forthcoming 2004); and essays on political theory, social movements, aesthetics, international relations and Asian politics. He is currently pursuing a research project that engages key dilemmas in global security through a range of neglected aesthetic sources, such as literature, visual art, architecture and music.

Irasema Coronado is Assistant Professor of Political Science and academic advisor of the Center for Inter-American and Border Studies at the University of Texas at El Paso. She is the co-author of *Fronteras No Mas: Toward Social Justice at the U.S.-Mexico Border* (Palgrave, 2002) and co-editor of *Policy and Politics on the Texas Border* (Kendall-Hunt, 2003). She received a Border Fulbright scholarship for the academic year 2004–5, during which time she was teaching border politics at the Universidad Autonoma de Ciudad Juárez. Her research interests include environmental and gender issues on the border.

Catherine Eschle is a Lecturer in the Department of Government, University of Strathclyde. Her teaching and research interests lie at the intersection of feminist theory, IR theory, (anti-)globalisation and social movement politics. Recent and forthcoming publications on these topics include articles in *Signs: Journal of Women in Culture and Society*, *Global Society* and *Alternatives*. She is also the author of *Global Democracy, Social Movements and Feminism* (Westview, 2001). She is currently working with Bice Maiguashca on a book project tentatively entitled 'Making Feminist Sense of "the Anti-Globalisation Movement"'.

Annette Freyberg-Inan teaches world and European politics at the University of Amsterdam. She is the author of *What Moves Man: The Realist Theory of International Relations and Its Judgment of Human Nature* (SUNY Press, 2004) and a range of other publications in the fields of international relations, foreign policy, political economy, and Romanian studies. Her main current research interests are the evolution of the European Union, EU enlargement, Romanian politics, and the transnationalisation of democratic dissent.

Branwen Gruffydd Jones is Lecturer in International Relations at the University of Aberdeen. She was previously ESRC Post-Doctoral Research Fellow at the University of Sussex. Her research interests are in the areas of the international political economy of global poverty and development, imperialism, Africa and social science methodology. She has written articles in *Portuguese Literary and Cultural Studies*, *Journal of Critical Realism*, *Review of African Political Economy* and *Portuguese Studies Review*. She is currently writing a book on global poverty.

Nick Higgins is an independent documentary film-maker and part-time lecturer in global politics at the University of Glasgow. He has published in the academic journals *Alternatives*, *Global Society* and *International Affairs*, as well as in the film publications *Roughcuts* and *DOX* magazine. His book, *Understanding the Chiapas Rebellion: Modernist Visions and the Invisible Indian*, is published by the University of Texas Press (2004). His first commissioned film, *Scotland's Women in Black*, was screened on Scottish Television in 2004, and his second, *Hidden Gifts*, broadcast throughout Europe later in the same year.

Bice Maiguashca is a Lecturer in the Department of Politics at the University of Exeter. Recent publications include 'Theorising Politics in "No Man's Land": The Fourth Debate and Feminist Theory', in B. Neufeld and M. Ebata (eds) *Confronting the Politics in International Relations* (Macmillan, 2001) and a sole-authored introduction to a co-edited special issue (with David Armstrong and Theo Farrell) of *Review of International Studies* on the topic of 'Governance and Resistance in World Politics'. Bice has been co-editor of the *Review* since 2002. She is currently working with Catherine Eschle on a book project tentatively entitled 'Making Feminist Sense of "the Anti-Globalisation Movement"'.

Marianne H. Marchand is Professor of International Relations at the University of the Americas, Puebla, Mexico. Her research demonstrates a great concern with the politics of change and (global) restructuring. In her work, Marchand looks to feminist and postcolonial theory and engages in critical explorations of the narratives and practices of development, globalisation and regionalisation/regionalism. She addresses the politics of change and how global restructuring often leads to increased marginalisation and social exclusion. In 2004, she completed the national report to the Dutch parliament on the implementation of the UN Convention on the Elimination of all Forms of Discrimination against Women (CEDAW).

Ralph Pettman holds the foundation Chair of International Relations at the Victoria University of Wellington. A graduate of the University of London (LSE), his previous appointments include teaching and research posts at the University of Tokyo, Princeton University and the Australian National University. He has also held posts in the Australian Human Rights Commission and its foreign aid bureau. His published works include: *Reason. Culture. Religion. The Metaphysics of World Politics* (Palgrave, 2004), *Commonsense Constructivism, or the Making of World Affairs* (M.E. Sharpe, 2000), and *Understanding International Political Economy, with Readings for the Fatigued* (Lynne Rienner, 1996). He is currently writing a phenomenology of world affairs.

Mark Rupert has been teaching in the areas of international relations and political economy since 1988. He is the author of two books: the first, entitled *Producing Hegemony* (Cambridge University Press, 1995), is a study of the politics of mass production and American global power; the second, *Ideologies of Globalization* (Routledge, 2000), examines ideological struggles over the political significance of globalisation. Together with Scott Solomon, he is co-author of a forthcoming book entitled *Globalization and International Political Economy* (Rowman and Littlefield).

Kathleen Staudt, who received her PhD from the University of Wisconsin in 1976, is Professor of Political Science and Director of the Center for Civic Engagement at the University of Texas at El Paso. She has published twelve books, focused on women/gender, international 'development' institutions, and the US–Mexico border. She is a community and cross-border activist.

Sian Sullivan is a Research Fellow in the Centre for the Study of Globalisation and Regionalisation at Warwick University (www.csgr.org). Her research explores discourses and practices that contest the assumed subjectivities of modernity in contemporary resistance to global corporatism. Previously she worked to interrogate disjunctions between discourses and practices regarding 'the environment' held at local, national and transnational levels with fieldwork conducted over an eight-year period in Namibia. Her publications include *Political Ecology: Science, Myth and Power* (co-edited with Philip Stott, Edward Arnold, 2000), articles in a range of journals, and chapters in several edited volumes. She also dances.

Series editors' preface

With this book, Catherine Eschle and Bice Maiguashca make an important intervention in the contemporary debates on critical IR theory and the implications for concrete 'anti-globalisation' politics. In our view, their provocative and stimulating book will mark a departure from IR and IPE accounts of 'anti-globalisation' that take the theory and empirical realities as a given. Motivated by a desire to explore the intersection of critical theory and anti-globalisation practices, this book draws together insights from approaches as diverse as Marxism, Gramscian theory, feminism, poststructuralism, constructivism and postcolonialism. As such, the perspectives on power and movement that are taken in the volume cannot be easily captured under a single rubric. Eschle and Maiguascha have sought to engage their authors in an ongoing dialogue that stimulates open debate, rather than closing down possible insights into the anti-globalisation movement. Indeed, the reader will find that there are many more questions raised and explored than definitively answered in this volume. What does it mean to be 'anti-globalisation'? Is it possible to identify a singular entity we might call the 'anti-globalisation movement'? How can we best understand the politics of movement in an era of globalization? Who speaks, and who is silenced in international relations and international political economy accounts of power and resistance?

If the reader is looking for an unambiguous answer to these kinds of questions, then they will not find it here. For, rather like the very politics of social movements, Eschle and Maiguashca's book is a body of work by virtue of its differences, debates, tensions and contests, and not simply by a common stance on an emergent global civil society. Indeed, one of the common threads that is to be found woven through the contributions is the desire to root the understanding of an anti-globalisation movement in the interrogation of actual and situated social practices. As the editors explain: 'we pay close attention to the concrete political practices of those involved in the "anti-globalisation movement". What are their tensions, exclusions and violences, and what political possibilities do they offer?' The chapters of the volume explore the discursive and concrete making of an anti-globalisation movement through diverse contexts and political practices: through spaces and places (from Seattle and Mozambique to Japan and Mexico); via different media (poetry, film, struggles at the border); drawing on distinct perspectives (cultural theory, neo-Gramscian IR, feminist theory, poststructuralism); and with situated movements as their subjects (from ATTAC and the Hemispheric Social Alliance, to the Zapatistas). The effect is to reveal different sites of the playing out of the anti-globalisation movement, and thus to enquire into the nature of politics itself: to intervene in a terrain that is too often taken for granted, and to expose the difficulties and possibilities for the making of a better world. We invite the reader to enjoy this refreshing take on a phenomenon that has come to be known as 'anti-globalisation' and, we are confident, will continue to provoke what Eschle and Maiguashca refer to as an 'ongoing and fruitful dialogue'.

Louise Amoore
Randall Germain
Rorden Wilkinson

Preface and acknowledgements

The seed of this book on critical theories and 'the anti-globalisation move-ment' was planted in an animated conversation at the annual conference of the International Studies Association in New Orleans, February 2002 (in the women's toilets!). We were rediscovering both a friendship that had become dormant and the fact that we share remarkably close research and political interests. At that time, we discussed the possibility of a distinctively feminist book on 'the anti-globalisation movement' but, labouring under the profoundly mistaken assumption that there wasn't enought to be said on this topic from a feminist perspective, we decided to focus our efforts instead on this edited volume of diverse critical approaches. It was while working on and arguing over this edited book, however, that we became persuaded of the rich-ness offered by feminist insights and embarked on a parallel feminist book project. For us, the journey through the creation of this edited book has been a necessary one, instructing us on the range of approaches, interventions and insights that are possible in International Relations, and on the depth of the challenges we face when combining critical theorising with an empirical focus on movement politics. As we make clear in the Introduction and Conclusion, we think that discussion on this conjuncture and its implications is only just beginning. For us, then, this book is part of an ongoing engagement with crit-ical theorising and 'anti-globalisation' politics – for many of our contributors too and, hopefully, for our readers.

We organised two conference panels directly related to this book at the annual meetings of the British International Studies Association in London, December 2002, and of the International Studies Association in Portland, Oregon, March 2003. We would like to thank all of the participants in those panels, and those who joined the discussion from the audience, for their contri-butions. Specifically, we would like to thank Charlotte Bretherton and Karena Shaw for chairing the panels, and also Shirin Rai for her presentation at BISA and for the long and extremely helpful discussion afterwards. In addition, we thank all the contributors to the book for their hard work, patience and co-operation with the editorial process. Special thanks are due to Roland Bleiker, whose friendly emails and forbearance revived our spirits in moments of gloom, and to Branwen Gruffydd Jones and Sian Sullivan, who came on board near to the end of the project and who worked extremely hard to produce wonderful pieces in very little time. We are particularly pleased that Branwen and Sian were able to join us given that the former brings with her an empirical focus on Africa (specifically Mozambique) and the latter a background in anthropology, ethnography and 'militant' activism. Usually, these barely feature in IR as a discipline, let alone in IR discussions of 'the anti-globalisation movement'. Furthermore, we would like to thank Louise Amoore, one of the editors of the RIPE Series in Global Political Economy, for her boundless enthusiasm for this project in its early stages and for shepherding us into the Routledge fold. We are also grateful to Grace McInnes at Routledge for her patience and helpfulness.

On a more personal note, Catherine would like to convey her gratitude to her parents, John and Sheila Eschle, for their ongoing support and for looking after her during her frequent trips to Exeter to work with Bice on this book. It is not very often that academic research actually brings families together! Conversely, she would like to thank Denis Donoghue for bearing her frequent absences with stoicism and humour.

The chapters presented here are original pieces for the majority, specially commissioned for this book. A couple have already appeared elsewhere. Accordingly, we would like to thank Lynne Rienner for permission to reprint 'The Zapatista Uprising and the Poetics of Cultural Resistance', by Nick Higgins, from *Alternatives: Social Transformation and Humane Governance*, vol. 25, no. 3, 2000, pp. 359–74, which appears here as Chapter 5 with the addition of a new epilogue. Chapter 2, by Catherine Eschle, was originally published in the *International Journal of Peace Studies*, vol. 9, no. 1, spring/summer 2004, pp. 61–84, and we reprint it here with grateful thanks to the journal. Finally, we thank Taylor & Francis for permission to reprint parts of Chapter 11 by Roland Bleiker, although it should be acknowledged that the version here is substantially changed from the original: 'Activism after Seattle: Dilemmas of the Anti-Globalisation Movement', *Pacifica Review: Peace, Security and Global Change* (Australia) 14 (3): 191–207 (http://www.tandf.co.uk).

Abbreviations

AFL–CIO	American Federation of Labor–Congress of Industrial Organizations
ASC	Alianza Social Continental
ATTAC	Association pour la Taxation des Transactions Financières pour l'Aide aux Citoyens (Association for the Taxation of Financial Transactions for the Aid of Citizens)
BCM	Banco Commercial de Moçambique
BSE	Bovine Spongiform Encephalopathy
CISEN	Centro de Investigación y Seguridad Nacional
DAWN	Development Alternatives with Women for a New era
DSEi	Defence Systems and Equipment International
ECLAC	Economic Commission for Latin America and the Caribbean
EU	European Union
EZLN	Zapatista National Liberation Army
FINRRAGE	Feminist International Network of Resistance to Reproductive and Genetic Engineering
FLN	Fuerzas de Liberación Nacional
FMLN	Frente Farabundo Martí para la Liberación Nacional (Farabundo Martí Liberation Front)
FTAA	Free Trade Area for the Americas
F15	15 February 2003 (worldwide anti-war demonstration)
GABRIELA	General Assembly Binding women for Reform, Integrity, Equality, Leadership and Action
GATS	General Agreement on Trade in Services
GJM	Global justice movement
GOM	Government of Mozambique
HSA	Social Hemispheric Alliance
IADB	Inter-American Development Bank
IAS	Inter-American system
ICFTU	International Confederation of Free Trade Unions
ICPD	UN Conference on Population and Development
IMF	International Monetary Fund

IR	International Relations (the discipline)
IWHC	International Women's Health Coalition
IWHM	International Women's Health Meetings
MAI	Multilateral Agreement on Investments
NAFTA	North American Free Trade Agreement
NATO	North Atlantic Treaty Organization
NGO	Non-governmental organisation
NSM	New social movement
OAS	Organization of American States
OECD	Organisation for Economic Co-operation and Development
OGD	Observatoire Géopolitique des Drogues
PNAC	Project for a New American Century
PRI	Partido Revolucionario Institucional
RMALC	Red Mexicana de Acción Frente al Libre Comercio
SAPRIN	Structural Adjustment Participatory Review International Network
TNI	Transnational Institute
UN	United Nations
UNCTAD	United Nations Conference on Trade and Development
UNDP	United Nations Development Programme
UNESCO	United Nations Educational, Scientific and Cultural Organization
UNODCCP	United Nations Office for Drug Control and Crime Prevention
UPJ	United for Peace and Justice
V-Day	Organisation/commemorative day striving to end violence against women and girls ('the V stands for Victory, Valentine and Vagina' (V-Day n.d.))
WGNRR	Women's Global Network for Reproductive Rights
WMDs	Weapons of mass destruction
WOMBLES	White Overalls Movement for Building Libertarian Effective Struggles
WTO	World Trade Organization
9–11	11 September 2001 (attack on the World Trade Center, New York)

Introduction

Catherine Eschle and Bice Maiguashca

> To my mind, no-one has yet improved on Marx's 1843 definition of critical theory as 'the self-clarification of the struggles and wishes of the age'.
>
> (Fraser 1995: 21)

> the [Seattle] protests form part of a worldwide movement that can perhaps be understood in terms of new potentials and forms of global political agency.
>
> (Gill 2003: 218)

> The powerful want us silent. When we were silent, we died. Without the word we did not exist.
>
> (Subcomandante Insurgente Marcos 2001: 80)

This book explores the interface between social movement resistances to neoliberal globalisation and a range of critical theories in the discipline of International Relations (IR).

Since the late 1980s, mainstream theories in IR have come under sustained attack from a range of critical perspectives. Indeed, many commentators see the rise of these perspectives as challenging the very constitution of the discipline (see e.g. Hoffman 1987; Lapid 1989; Linklater 1992; George 1994; Smith *et al.* 1998; for a more sceptical view see Navon 2001). Critical theorists share the notion that, in Robert Cox's famous phrase, '[t]heory is always *for* someone and *for* some purpose' (Cox 1986: 207): that is, the act of theorising is always political. Given this, critical theorist interrogate the relation between power and knowledge production; they expose and denaturalise power hierarchies and relations of domination more generally; and they seek out immanent possibilities for disruption, resistance and transformative change. In this context, all acknowledge the importance of exploring social struggles and resistances, whether conceptualised as social movements or not, as crucial sites of world politics. This is true of neo-Marxist, Gramscian, Habermasian, poststructuralist and feminist theorist, among others.[1]

One recent, high-profile instance of collective resistance is what we refer to here as 'the anti-globalisation movement'. It is ten years ago at the time of writing, in 1994, that the Zapatistas launched their insurrection in the Lacandon jungle in Mexico to coincide with the launch of the North American Free Trade Agreement (Marcos 2001; Higgins, this volume). Five years later saw the high-profile 'Battle of Seattle' in November 1999, when anti-'free' trade activists successfully blockaded negotiations for the World Trade Organization (Cockburn *et al.* 2000; Bleiker, this volume). Many commentators and activists have argued that the Zapatistas and Seattle are iconic representatives of one of the most important social movements to emerge on the world stage in recent years – what has been called, amongst other things, 'the anti-capitalist movement', 'the global resistance movement', 'global backlash', 'the global justice movement' or 'the anti-globalisation movement' (e.g. Bircham and Charlton 2001; Broad 2002; Kingsnorth 2003; Klein 2002; Notes from Nowhere 2003; Starr 2000).[2]

In bringing this movement and IR critical theorising together, this book has both empirical and theoretical aims. In terms of the first, we seek to provide a map or rather several maps of 'the anti-globalisation movement', collecting accounts of resistances in different parts of the world while simultaneously questioning whether such resistances constitute a unified and coherent 'movement' that is unproblematically 'anti-globalisation' in identity and orientation. In terms of the second, theoretical, aim, we strive to extend the application of a variety of critical perspectives in IR to this distinctive form of movement politics. We ask: what can these different perspectives tell us about the nature and significance of 'the anti-globalisation movement'? What are their strengths and weaknesses, convergences and divergences? And what can the study of this movement contribute to critical theorising? In sum, by combining empirical study and the construction of theory, and reflecting on the dialectical relationship between theory and practice, we hope to reveal new insights into both 'the anti-globalisation movement' and critical theorising in IR.

Given the preoccupations of critical theorising with social struggle and resistance, it is somewhat surprising to find that, as yet, relatively little work has been done on 'the anti-globalisation movement'. Amongst critical theory scholars, it is the Marxists who have paid it most attention, with some being optimistic about the counter-hegemonic potential of the movement and others offering a more sceptical assessment. In the former camp, the pioneering collection of Barry Gills (2000b) brings together diverse theorisations and case studies of what Gills calls the 'politics of resistance' to 'neoliberal economic globalisation'. However, these resistances are not framed as a single social movement and Gills does not offer a sustained Marxist theorisation of them. Such a theoretical framework can be gleaned from the work of the 'new Gramscians' (Germain and Kenny 1998), who insist that resistance needs to be understood as a response to globalised hegemonic structures maintained by and for a transnational capitalist elite. The counter-hegemonic potential of resistances associated with 'the anti-globalisation movement' has recently received attention from theorists working with this perspective. Thus Adam Morton (2000, 2002) offers a cautiously optimistic assessment of the political possibilities offered by the Zapatistas. Inspired by the Seattle protests, Stephen Gill (2000) argues for the emergence of a new global movement while Mark Rupert analyses the 'increasing threat' to neoliberal ideology posed by 'progressive social forces' (Rupert 2000: 154–5). From a distinctive focus on 'transnational practices', Leslie Sklair reaches similar conclusions, seeing the defeat of the Multilateral Agreement on Investment (MAI, see Birchfield and Freyberg-Inan, this volume) and Seattle as the 'two defining campaigns' of 'the anti-globalisation movement' (Sklair 2002: 277–93). Firmly in the more sceptical Marxist camp, Fred Halliday (2000a) is concerned to dampen down what he sees as unrealistic expectations following Seattle, while Alejandro Colás criticises protests and networks 'dedicated to the contestation of "globalization" ' (and theories which eulogise them) for being anti-statist in orientation. He goes on to characterise movement networks as dependent on Internet communications and thus more virtual than real (Colás 2002: 82; see also 2003).

'The anti-globalisation movement' has also caught the attention of a handful of non-Marxist scholars in IR. For example, Richard Falk has characterised the actions of movements in 'global civil society' as 'globalisation-from-below', counterposed to elite-driven 'globalisation-from-above' (Falk 1999: 2–3 and ch. 9; cf. Brecher *et al.* 2002). Also using the trope of global civil society, Marlies Glasius *et al.* chart the growing significance of what they call 'the anti-capitalist movement', focusing on events such as the World Social Forum in Porto Alegre, Brazil, and mass street demonstrations against international institutions, including protests subsequent to Seattle (Glasius and Kaldor 2002: 6–11, 19–22; also 387–8).[3] Moving away from a global civil society approach, Robert O'Brien *et al.* (2000) are concerned with the impact of movements on 'global governance', specifically 'multilateral economic institutions'. Finally, there is also an interdisciplinary feminist literature of relevance here with at least one foot in IR, or perhaps rather international political economy. Feminist work focuses on women's activism in local communities against globalising forces and/or on the implications of globalisation for transnational feminist organising (e.g. Marchand and Runyan 2000; Rowbotham and Linkogle 2001; Wichterich 2000; Naples and Desai 2002).

Although all of this work offers interesting insights into 'the anti-globalisation movement', in our view it is as yet rather underdeveloped. Starting with the Marxist literature, we think that the practices and significance of 'the anti-globalisation movement' remain undertheorised. Arguably, this is due to the more general propensity of IR Marxists to focus their efforts more on mapping structural relations of power and domination than on theorising the logic and nature of resistance or counter-hegemony. Making a similar point about the 'new Gramscians', Randall Germain and Michael Kenny tell us that:

> hegemony [is seen] largely as a one-directional power relationship …
> fashioned by the elite transnational class on its own terms and then
> forced or imposed on subaltern classes. These subaltern classes in turn
> either resist such frontal assaults as best as they can or capitulate.
> Hence, the rather pessimistic tone of many new Gramscian analyses.
>
> (Germain and Kenny 1998: 18)

Although the Zapatistas and the Battle of Seattle have prompted some 'new
Gramscians' to adopt a more optimistic attitude about the potential of resistances and thus to pay them more attention, in our view, their
conceptualisations of these resistances have yet to be fully integrated into
their theoretical frameworks. For example, Gill's discussion of the counter-
hegemonic potential of the nascent movement manifested at Seattle, which
is appended to the end of his recent book, does not cause him to rethink his
prior analysis of the hegemony of 'market civilisation' (Gill 2003). Further,
while Morton and Rupert for their part are more centrally concerned with
resistance, in the form of the struggles of the Zapatistas and the conflicting
ideologies of globalisation in North America, there is more work to be
done on the implications of these case studies for theorisation of 'the anti-
globalisation movement' specifically (for steps in this direction see Morton
2004 and Rupert, this volume).

Turning to the non-Marxist approaches identified above, we would want
to sound a note of caution about the extension of 'global civil society'
approaches to the analysis of the 'anti-globalisation movement'. On the
whole, such approaches have positioned movements as operating in a
distinct realm between the state and economy, and as primarily concerned
with self-organisation and the constraint and contestation of state and
economic power. As many critics have pointed out, this framing has the
effect of masking the role of multiple power relations within civil society
and social movements, and of representing movements as intrinsically and
uniformly progressive (Walker 1994: 679–84; Pasha and Blaney 1998; Colás
2002: 9–17 and ch. 5). While Glasius *et al.* and Falk respond to some of
these difficulties in their application of the global civil society approach to
anti-globalisation activism, they remain wedded to this basic framework. In
contrast, O'Brien *et al.* focus more centrally on the interactions of movements with state and interstate institutions. The difficulty here, however, is
that social movement politics tends to be reduced to the activities of NGOs,
thereby downplaying other forms of movement activism and marginalising
those social groups already excluded from political institutions (as acknowledged in O'Brien *et al.* 2000: 58). It should also be noted that the book by
O'Brien *et al.* was produced before Seattle and therefore, unsurprisingly,
does not engage with 'the anti-globalisation movement' as such. This is not
the case with the feminist scholarship on resistances to neoliberal globalisation,
which has largely been produced subsequent to Seattle but which has nonetheless not yet engaged with the notion of an 'anti-globalisation movement' *per*

se or assessed its implications for feminist politics. Indeed, feminist and anti-imperialist scholar Chandra Talpade Mohanty recently highlighted the political costs of this neglect, insisting that 'the theory, critique, and activism around antiglobalization has to be a key focus for feminists' (Mohanty 2003: 230).[4]

In addition to these difficulties with specific theoretical traditions, we would draw attention to two problems that cut across current critical theorising on 'the anti-globalisation movement'. The first is the fact that much of this theorising has not been built upon sustained empirical investigations of 'anti-globalisation movement' practices. It has relied instead either on brief and rather general references to Seattle and similarly iconic movement manifestations, or on more extensive empirical work on phenomena associated with 'the anti-globalisation movement' but not directly equivalent to it.

The second, related problem has to do with the conceptual language used to frame social movement politics. On the one hand, those who use the terminology of 'social movement/s' tend to do so inconsistently and unreflexively, without reference to the established and diverse literature on social movements that already exists in sociology and politics (for an exception see Colás 2002; also Walker 1994).[5] On the other hand, those who avoid the language of social movements altogether in favour of 'the politics of resistance', 'social forces' and the like, also deploy their preferred terms largely unreflexively. Although we would not deny that there are problems with the concept of social movement (see e.g. Shaw 1994), we would argue that substitute terms also carry theoretical baggage that needs to be unpacked. Little of this kind of analysis has yet been done (for an exception on 'the politics of resistance', see Chin and Mittelman 2000; on resistance and 'dissent', see Bleiker 2000). Further, the relationship of such terms to the notion of social movement has to be explored rather than assumed or ignored. In other words, the ways in which we talk about social struggle and resistance, and the theoretical implications of our chosen conceptual languages, have not yet become the subject of serious conversation among critical theorists in IR.

Curiously, poststructuralists in IR, who perhaps have paid the most attention to the question of language and the power moves involved in labelling and constructing political practices, have contributed the least to discussions about 'the anti-globalisation movement'. Indeed, at the time of writing we are not aware of any poststructuralist IR work on this subject. This is doubly curious given that movements more generally have received some attention from IR poststructuralists as sites of 'a new politics altogether, a politics in which the institutions of the liberal state are denied their status as fora within which human liberation is possible' (Brown 1994: 233). It is in such a spirit that Walker has explored the possibilities of a 'politics of movement' and a 'politics of connections' (1994: 700; Maiguashca, this volume); William Connolly has focused on the role of movements in the reconceptualisation of democracy as 'an egalitarian constitution of cultural life' (1991b: 476;

Bleiker, this volume); and Christine Sylvester (1994) has discussed the practices of Zimbabwean women's collectives and of Greenham Common anti-nuclear protests. One possible explanation for the lack of interest in extending such analyses to 'the anti-globalisation movement' may lie in the fact that it can all too easily be seen as an 'older' form of politics, rooted in class, concerned with material redistribution and not speaking directly to poststructuralist interests (see below). However, we would suggest that post-structuralist approaches potentially have much to offer the theorisation of 'the anti-globalisation movement'. After all, there is a growing body of post-structuralist-influenced work, perhaps more securely located in social and political theory, that has theorised 'anti-globalisation' politics in ways that have strongly resonated with many movement activists (Hardt and Negri 2000; Deleuze and Guatarri 1988 [1980]; Bourdieu 1998; Sullivan, this volume). In our view, there is an urgent need for poststructuralists in IR to engage with this literature and with the theorisation of 'anti-globalisation' politics.

Indeed, the above discussion has demonstrated the limitations of critical IR theorising on 'the anti-globalisation movement' and thus the pressing need for further enquiry into this subject. This book strives to respond to this need and to offer a more systematic empirical exploration of 'the anti-globalisation movement' and a more sustained interrogation of what critical theories can tells us about the political practices of this movement. To this end, we have brought together chapters that draw on a range of critical perspectives, including Marxism, Gramscianism, feminism, postcolonialism, post-anarchism, constructivist social movement theory and poststruc-turalism.[6] The empirical cases discussed are similarly diverse and encompass not only the usual suspects of the Zapatista uprising and mass protests at Seattle and elsewhere, but also women's organising against violence on the US–Mexico border and for reproductive rights, journalists mobilising against corruption in Mozambique, French and German campaigns to regu-late global finance, and efforts to construct regional counter-hegemonic identities in the Americas, amongst others. In our Conclusion, we reach for a more comparative perspective on these chapters, analysing the ways in which the different theoretical and empirical accounts speak to each other and where they conflict. We also seek to identify questions that still need to be answered.

We have organised the chapters into three parts, each focused on an inter-linked cluster of themes that provides a distinctive entry point into thinking about the relationship between critical theorising and 'the anti-globalisation movement'.

The first part focuses on *power/resistance/movement*. As noted above, the relationship between power and resistance is crucial not only to several of the recent IR interventions into debates about 'the anti-globalisation movement' but also to critical theorising more generally. However, we have argued that much critical theorising of this relationship is actually rather underdeveloped and that its implications for thinking about social movements in general and 'the anti-globalisation movement' in particular have not been fully elaborated. In addition, we have pointed out that labels such as 'the politics of resistance' or 'the anti-globalisation movement' are often used in an uncritical, unreflexive way, without consideration of their theoretical baggage or of the specific empirical entity to which they refer. This first part of the book, then, seeks to bring 'the anti-globalisation movement' into full view and to subject it to sustained scrutiny, exploring in what sense we can consider it an actor in world politics and whether diverse resistances can be seen as constituting a movement as such. What structures of power shape this form of politics, who is included and who is excluded? We are also interested in exploring how we can characterise this kind of resistance.

The second part focuses on the themes of *discourse/identity/culture*. It is undeniable that the last couple of decades have seen a marked rise in interest across the arts and social sciences in culture and identity as key sites and sources of power and resistance. This 'cultural turn' has to some extent been led by poststructuralist theorists with their focus on discourses as productive of culture and identity, power and resistance.[7] In IR, there has been a rather belated proliferation of critical theorising on these issues (Zalewski and Enloe 1995; Krause and Remnick 1996; Lapid and Kratchowil 1995; Halliday 2000b; Connolly 1991a; Der Derian and Shapiro 1989; Campbell 1992), with poststructuralists, in particular, interested in exploring social movements in terms of discourse and identity (see Maiguashca, this volume). As noted above, however, poststructuralist IR theorists have not yet extended their framework to 'the anti-globalisation movement'. What is more, the critical IR theorising on the movement that does exist has not interrogated the relation of the movement to discourse, culture and identity. This part of the book seeks to address this rather startling lacuna. In so doing, it interrogates the ways in which 'the anti-globalisation movement' is constituted discursively and asks in what ways it operates on the terrain of culture and what kinds of identities are mobilised and contested.

The third and final part focuses on issues of *politics/strategy/violence*. Notwithstanding the strong assertions made about the political character and significance of 'the anti-globalisation movement' by some critical theorists in IR, more work needs to be done to flesh out such claims. To what extent does this movement represent a 'new politics' and what kind of politics is this? Could it, for example, be described as a 'postmodern' politics (Burbach 2001; Kingsnorth 2003), a 'counter-hegemonic' politics, or perhaps a 'politics of resistance'? Moreover, how might such efforts to conceptualise the movement encourage critical theorists to rethink the nature of the political more generally? We agree with Karena Shaw when she urges us to avoid 'global' generalisations and to pay attention to the context-specific understandings and strategic practices of activists (2003: 215). In such a spirit, the chapters in this part of the book pay close attention to the concrete political practices of those involved in 'the anti-globalisation movement'. What are their tensions, exclusions and violences, and what political possibilities do they offer? What kind of challenges do they pose to the structural and intentional violences involved in 'politics as usual'?

We begin with a chapter by one of us, Catherine Eschle, which directly interrogates the claim that a transnational 'anti-globalisation' social movement has emerged. Eschle draws on constructivist social movement theory, globalisation studies, feminist praxis and activist websites to make two main arguments, mapping onto the two parts of the chapter. First, she claims that a movement has indeed emerged, albeit in a highly contested and complex form with activists, opponents and commentators constructing competing movement identities. This chapter – and book – is itself complicit in such a construction process. Second, Eschle claims that the movement is not 'anti-globalisation' in any straightforward sense. Focusing their opposition on globalised neoliberalism and corporate power, activists represent their movement either as anti-capitalist and/or as constructing alternative kinds of globalised relationships. Threading through these two arguments is a normative plea to confront the diverse relations of power involved in both globalisation and movement construction in order that globalised solidarities be truly democratic. This is to challenge hierarchical visions of how best to construct 'the anti-globalisation movement'.

Chapter 2, by Mark Rupert, maps the transformation of what he calls 'the global justice movement', particularly in the United States, in the light of the current 'neo-imperial moment'. Resistances to the project of neoliberal capitalist globalisation have been developing in various locales for decades but this 'movement of movements' has faced serious challenges since the attack on the World Trade Center of 11 September 2001, with the subsequent reinvigoration and remilitarisation of US imperialism. The chapter puts forward a Gramscian analysis of the neo-imperial moment and examines the extent to which the US global justice movement has allied with or transformed itself into an anti-war movement, charting its successes and failures. Although Rupert may be rather sceptical of the future potential of the movement, he nonetheless concludes that resistance in some form will continue as 'the structures of global capitalism and their current imperial instantiation remain deeply contradictory and cannot be permanently normalised' (p. 51).

Rather than documenting a particular, identifiable strand of 'the anti-globalisation movement', Branwen Gruffydd Jones' chapter is concerned with 'prior questions about the conditions of possibility for social change' (p. 54). Gruffydd Jones argues from a Marxist perspective that 'globalisation' must be understood as a process that necessarily produces an endlessly nuanced variation of concrete effects, including particular instances of anti-globalisation resistance. For this reason she insists that any analysis of such resistances must be context specific and pay particular attention to the structural *limits* to social struggle. Her chapter then goes on to explore the condition of globalisation in the context of Mozambique and the consequent structuring of, and constraints upon, resistances and struggles there. She identifies two very different kinds of struggle: the campaigns of journalists and others against corruption and the daily efforts of the majority to survive in conditions of crisis and deprivation. This analysis points to a real problem for theorising the nature and potential of 'the anti-globalisation movement'. As Gruffydd Jones concludes, it is the poor of Mozambique 'who need most urgently the reform, taming and, ultimately, transformation of the forces of globalisation. Yet they are least likely … to engage in collective political struggle, to join the "anti-globalisation movement" ' (p. 69).

The fourth chapter, by Ralph Pettman, continues to expand the geographical scope of the empirical work in the book by examining 'anti-globalisation' discourses in Asia. Pettman begins with a very different analysis of globalisation than that put forward by Rupert and Gruffydd Jones, drawing attention to the neglected politico-cultural and politico-spiritual dimensions of the phenomenon. He argues that 'the modernist project, rooted in a specifically Euro-American tradition, is spreading ever more worldwide. As it does so, it encounters very different politico-cultural and politico-spiritual traditions and generates a variety of critical responses' (p. 77) The chapter briefly examines 'anti-globalisation' claims that remain rooted in the modernist paradigm before focusing on claims that step at least partially outside of that paradigm, drawing on alternative Asian traditions. Specifically, Pettman examines the complex combination of modernist and non-modernist approaches to culture found in Japanese state policies on heritage and the challenge to market economics posed by the spiritual teachings of the Buddha. His analysis indicates that critical theorists must develop a more multidimensional and historicised approach to the phenomenon of globalisation and must not become blinkered by the rationalist preconceptions of the modernist project when searching for resistance politics.

Chapter 5, by Nick Higgins, shifts our geographical and substantive focus yet again, this time to Chiapas, Mexico, and to the Zapatista insurgency that is so frequently seen as emblematic of 'the anti-globalisation movement'. Like Pettman, Higgins is less concerned with applying existing categories of analysis to this case than with highlighting the potential for resistance of alternative discourses. To this end, he explores the poetry of Subcomandante Insurgente Marcos, 'not out of any desire to reify, mystify or romanticise its author, but rather to treat him and his words as living bridges between the Indian world of the Mexican south-east and the ever more pervasive world of global politics' (p. 88). The narrative that Higgins weaves around this poetry makes it clear that Marcos arrived in Chiapas with a pre-formed theoretical framework in place, specifically the Marxist–Leninist model of resistance, which was systematically challenged by the local Indians he was attempting to lead. In collaboration with them, Marcos has developed an alternative imaginary and language representing a 'cultural humanism' which, according to Higgins, may provide a fruitful starting point for conceptualising alternative forms of politics and ethics.

Marianne Marchand's contribution in Chapter 6 also explores discourses in the Americas but deploys a very different approach. Drawing on the insights of postcolonial theory, she offers a comparative analysis of the discourses involved in constructing competing regional identities. More specifically, she juxtaposes the very different historical discourses of regional identity provided by the Monroe Doctrine and by 'the liberator' Simon Bolívar, before exploring the extent to which these competing discourses are marshalled in contemporary negotiation and contestation of the Free Trade Area of the Americas (FTAA). The representative of 'the anti-globalisation movement' on which Marchand focuses is the 'Hemispheric Social Alliance' (HSA). She argues that the HSA has selectively discarded the anti-democratic element of Bolivarian discourse, elaborating instead on his anti-colonialism and internationalism in order to formulate a democratic alternative to profoundly anti-democratic contemporary processes of 'corporate-led globalisation/regionalisation' (p. 113). Marchand clearly sees the HSA as a potentially counter-hegemonic force in the Americas.

In Chapter 7, Bice Maiguashca continues Marchand's focus on the discursive construction of identity but seeks to interrogate its operations in the discipline of IR. More concretely, Maiguashca is concerned with the ways in which critical IR theorists have conceptualised movements as exemplars of the 'politics of identity'. She identifies two prevalent conceptions of this politics in IR, one emphasising the cohesive nature of identity and pointing to a 'politics of solidarity', the other emphasising the divisive nature of identity and pointing to a 'politics of difference'. Maiguashca develops her critique of the operations of these discourses of politics in the work of critical IR theorists Walker, Connolly, Andrew Linklater and Jan Aart Scholte, by analysing them in their own terms and then in the light of an empirical case study: that is, women's reproductive rights activism. Noting that in IR women's movements are often seen as exemplifying the 'politics of identity', while 'the anti-globalisation movement' is positioned in terms of a more materialist politics, she claims that women's reproductive rights activists have been striving increasingly to integrate themselves into 'the anti-globalisation movement'. Maiguashca concludes with a plea for the abandonment of the notion of the 'politics of identity' altogether.

Irasema Coronado and Kathleen Staudt in Chapter 8 also offer a case study of women's organising, specifically the bi-national 'Coalition Against Violence toward Women and Families at the US–Mexico Border', in which they are both participants. As they acknowledge, this group 'would not generally be considered part of the "anti-globalisation movement"'. Why? Theorists and activists rarely link the issue of violence against women to globalisation processes. It is our view that this is a major limitation of established discourses on resistance to globalisation' (p. 141). Writing from a feminist perspective, Coronado and Staudt strive to show how violence against women in the region is interconnected with processes such as trade liberalisation and the internationalisation of the Mexican state also highlighted by Marchand and Higgins. They offer an insider's account of Coalition strategies before reflecting on the relationship between resistance and academic knowledge. This relationship is for them rooted in the concept of *compromiso*, 'which compels us in our study of globalisation and resistance to move beyond the collection of data and to work with others to connect theory with practice in the struggle for justice' (p. 141). Coronado and Staudt end by discussing the implications of *compromiso* for their own academic and activist work.

The strategies of what they prefer to call an 'alternative globalisation' group, ATTAC, are the subject of Chapter 9, by Vicki Birchfield and Annette Freyberg-Inan. Founded in France in 1998 to contest the structuring of international finance, ATTAC now has associations in forty countries and has also helped to found the World Social Forum, the high-profile annual meeting of 'alternative globalisation' activists. By any measure, ATTAC is an important group whose strategies deserve careful evaluation. Birchfield and Freyberg-Inan adopt Gramscian concepts for this task, placing particular emphasis on Gramsci's theorisation of the role of the 'organic intellectual'. They describe the origins of the movement in terms of the contemporary crisis of capitalist hegemony before examining organisational structures in two of the largest national associations, ATTAC France and ATTAC Germany. They go on to discuss the ideology and normative agendas of these associations and then analyse ATTAC's activities as an international movement. Their final section explores ATTAC's mission as a movement of popular education, highlighting its congruence with a Gramscian concept of the 'organic intellectual'. They conclude that Gill's (2000) characterisation of the anti-globalisation movement as what he calls the 'post-modern Prince', i.e. the potential leader of a counter-hegemonic shift in social relations, is most applicable to ATTAC.

Chapter 10 by Sian Sullivan shifts our attention to more confrontational modes of politics, specifically the rise of 'militancy' in the street protests of what she calls 'the (anti-)globalisation movement/s'. Like Coronado and Staudt, Sullivan is a declared participant in the politics of which she writes. Her analysis is grounded in an ethnography of recent protests in Thessaloniki and London, and also draws upon diverse sources of critical theorising that force the doors of the IR discipline wide open, including poststructuralism, psychoanalysis, 'post-anarchist' political theory and anthropology. Seeking to move beyond dominant analyses that focus on whether tactical destruction of property and confrontation with the police is 'strategically "good" or "bad" for "the movements" ' (p. 176-7), Sullivan instead offers a contextual framing of the rise of these practices in terms of globalised structural violence. She then discusses the ways in which individual subjectivities and political agency are constituted through complex processes of depression, desire and anger. She concludes that, although militant practices may generate exclusions and closures, they also involve a 'conscious transformation of the felt experience of rage in relation to the glue of structural violence' (p. 190) and point towards alternative ways of being human.

Roland Bleiker in Chapter 11 also examines the ramifications of street protest, focusing particularly on Seattle, November 1999 (thus ending our volume where most accounts of 'the anti-globalisation movement' begin). Like Sullivan, Bleiker is concerned with violence and agency, but he discusses these themes in the context of how and to what extent '[a]nti-globalisation protests can be seen as a crucial element in the establishment of a global democratic ethos' (p. 196). To develop an answer, Bleiker draws on 'international political theorists' such as Connolly 'who have sought to demonstrate that an ethical approach to politics must be based not on a fixed set of rules, but on a fundamentally open attitude' (p. 196). Bleiker discusses two hard questions facing theorists and activists, both of which are key to a global democratic ethos: the representative character of the movement, that is who speaks for whom, and the dilemmas of violent versus non-violent strategy. Although he reaches very different conclusions on the latter than Sullivan, he echoes her closing insistence on the political potentialities of street protest, which 'engender the very idea of productive ambiguity that may well be essential for the long-term survival of democracy' (p. 211).

Taken together, we suggest that these contributions substantially advance our understanding of the connections between 'the anti-globalisation movement' and critical theories in IR. We do not pretend here to offer complete solutions to the political dilemmas and theoretical issues raised along the way. It is important to remember that we are at an early stage of debate on this topic in IR and that we have encouraged our contributors to be speculative, to take risks and to ask questions. While the Conclusion takes some steps to map out the similarities and differences between our chapters in terms of the key themes around which the book is organised, it also points to questions that remain unanswered and to further research agendas. The book is intended to facilitate a dialogue between 'the movement' and IR, between theory and practice, and between different critical theory perspectives. There is rich insight in what follows, which suggests that the dialogue will be fruitful and ongoing.

Notes

1 It should be noted that in much contemporary IR literature the term Critical Theory (upper case) refers exclusively to theory drawing on the Frankfurt School and particularly to the work of Jürgen Habermas (see e.g. Hoffman 1987). Our use of the lower case is meant to indicate our broader understanding of the term, which includes Critical Theory but also other approaches such as poststructuralism (for a similar understanding see Brown 1994; for an alternative which excludes 'postmodern scholarship', see Gruffydd Jones, this volume, p. 71: note 4).

2 We, the editors, use throughout 'the anti-globalisation movement'. It should be stressed that we recognise that this is a highly political and contested term, which is even offensive to some (see e.g. discussion in Graeber 2002; Callinicos 2003a: 13–14). We use it mostly for pragmatic reasons: because it is accepted in some quarters; because in our experience it has been the label that academics, activists and publishers find most instantly recognisable and because it indicates a link to disciplinary concerns about globalisation and global politics. We also use the term in the knowledge that it indicates a claim that diverse resistances to some of the impacts of globalisation have come to be seen as in some sense a coherent force for change. We have put the term in quotation marks here and elsewhere to indicate its contested character. Indeed, we have encouraged our contributors to explore the politics of naming and many of them opt for alternative terms. The deconstruction of the label is particularly central to the next chapter by Eschle.

3 Peter Waterman also uses the global civil society trope and has written extensively on the reshaping of movement solidarities within it, increasingly with regard to what he calls 'the global justice movement' (2000; 2002a). His work is notable for its concern with building and conceptualising solidarities between movement strands, particularly labour and others.

4 For tentative steps in this direction see Marchand 2003 and Eschle 2005. Further, it is worth noting that many feminist activists beyond the academy have been striving for years to engage critically with 'the anti-globalisation movement' (see discussions in Eschle 2005).

5 Turning momentarily to this sociology and politics literature, we find some useful extensions of social movement theory to globalised contexts (see Smith *et al.* 1997; Hamel *et al.* 2001; Della Porta *et al.* 1999; Melucci 1996a; Guidry *et al.* 2000). Jackie Smith and Hank Johnston (2002) have sought to apply their framework specifically to resistances associated with 'the anti-globalisation movement'; in so doing, they draw on North American social movement theory, including theories of political opportunity structures and resource mobilisation. This work is trail-blazing but, as with the work of O'Brien *et al.*, it is limited by its mainly institutional focus and also by the rationalist and instrumentalist view of politics that underpins the variant of social movement theory on which it draws.

6 We recognise that we have not exhausted the variants of critical theory here: we would also have liked to include contributions from Habermasian Critical Theory, ecological thought and constructivism (some versions of which, not all, have affinities with critical theorising; however, constructivists have focused their attention thus far almost exclusively on the state rather than alternative sources of power and resistance (see the overview provided by Reus-Smit 2001)). Clearly, these perspectives could also have very interesting things to say about 'the anti-globalisation movement'.

7 Another exemplar of the 'cultural turn' is new social movement (NSM) theory, which redescribes contemporary social movements as operating on the terrain of culture, civil society or the 'lifeworld' and as centrally concerned with the collective contestation of symbols and identities. This is in implicit (and now much criticised) contrast to 'old' movements such as labour and nationalism, which are seen as organised hierarchically and as concerned with material redistribution and gaining state power (see e.g. Melucci 1989; 1996a; Cohen 1982; Touraine 1985; Scott 1990). It is interesting to note that most accounts of 'the anti-globalisation movement' in activist-oriented texts imply that it is not typical of 'new' movements, but rather represents a return to an older, more materialist politics (e.g. Klein 2001). This is in danger of replicating the neglect of the cultural dimension of 'anti-globalisation' politics found in IR.

Part I

Power/resistance/movement

1   Constructing 'the anti-globalisation movement'

Catherine Eschle[1]

Introduction

This chapter asks a deceptively simple question: is there a transnational anti-globalisation social movement?

Some critics of the movement have already produced its obituary. They point to the failure to rival the spectacle of the Battle of Seattle and, more fundamentally, to the ramifications of the September 11 attacks. The space for protest is understood to have closed down and the movement thrown into an identity crisis (see discussion in Martin 2003; Callinicos 2003a: 16–19). I am not responding in this chapter to such contentious claims, nor to the undoubtedly changing conjuncture for activism. Rather I want to interrogate the more basic proposition that there has ever been such a thing as 'an anti-globalisation movement'.

This is not a particularly original course of enquiry but it is not one that has yet been undertaken in the discipline of International Relations (IR) in a systematic way. As made clear in the Introduction to this book, phenomena associated with 'the anti-globalisation movement' have been discussed by IR scholars (e.g. Falk 1999; Gills 2000b; Sklair 2002; Glasius *et al.* 2002; Held and McGrew 2002; Gill 2003). Activist tactics, ideologies and organisations may be assessed (e.g. Halliday 2000a) but generally the focus is on non-governmental organisations or civil society; global power and governance; or the politics of resistance. This tendency to avoid the concept of 'movement' could stem from a tacit agreement with those who fear it imposes totalising and hierarchical assumptions about anti-globalisation identity and organisation (e.g. Esteva and Prakash 1998: 13; Whitaker 2003). I will argue below that it is more accurate to think of movements as heterogeneous and continually reconstructed. More pertinently here, I think avoidance is more likely to derive from the general neglect in IR of 'social movements' and social movement theory. Movements have traditionally been seen as located not in the international but in the domestic, and not in the political but in the social (Walker 1994). They are, therefore, doubly invisible in IR and the proper subject matter of sociology. In addition, they disrupt the usual categories of state-centric, pluralist or structuralist IR and are difficult to assess through the dominant IR methodologies of empiricist quantification, analysis of historical continuities or Marxist materialism (Eschle and Stammers 2004).

This chapter does not provide a straightforward empirical (and empiricist) response that recounts evidence of activism in order to trace the outlines of 'the anti-globalisation movement'. There are many surveys by activists and commentators that can be consulted for that purpose, of which I will provide a short summary later. I want to focus more on conceptual, methodological and political issues: what do the labels 'social movement' and 'anti-globalisation' mean? On what theoretical and empirical resources could we draw to find out? On what basis have some interpretations become dominant over others? What are the ramifications of intervening in such debates, for IR theorists as well as activists?

In what follows, I adopt an eclecticism which is both pragmatic (given space constraints and the lack of similar work in IR) and principled (derived from a belief in the importance of paying attention to multiple discourses of activism and anti-globalisation). I draw on various theories, including constructivist social movement theory and feminism. I also foreground activist representations of themselves, from publications and from the websites of the following groupings: Peoples' Global Action, an anarchistically inclined network of local organisations, founded in Geneva in order to expand the transnational solidarity work begun by the Zapatistas in Mexico; the World Social Forum, a vast gathering of diverse activists held parallel to the World Economic Forum, the culmination of a rolling process of national and regional activist meetings intended to generate visions of alternative worlds; and the British group Globalise Resistance, a membership organisation run predominantly by activists associated with the Socialist Workers' Party.

In the first part of what follows, I focus on the notion of a 'social movement'. I argue that a movement has indeed emerged, albeit in a highly contested and complex form with activists, opponents and commentators constructing competing movement identities. This chapter is itself complicit in such a process – and seeks to further a particular construction of the movement as a site of radical–democratic politics. In the second part, I examine 'anti-globalisation'. Focusing their opposition on globalised neoliberalism and corporate power, activists represent their movement either as anti-capitalist or as constructing alternative kinds of globalised relationships. Threading through both parts of the chapter is a normative plea to confront the diverse structures and relations of power involved in both globalisation and movement construction, as many commentators and activists are already doing, in order that globalised solidarities be truly democratic. This is to challenge hierarchical visions of how best to construct 'the anti-globalisation movement'. I conclude by emphasising the importance of the self-understanding of movement activists for theorising globalisation and resistance in IR.

Constructing a movement

> I couldn't escape a growing conviction that what I was seeing was the fumbling birth of a genuinely new political movement – something international, something different and something potentially huge.
>
> (Kingsnorth 2003: 8)

Many activists and commentators have remarked upon what they see as the emergence of a new movement in recent years. Surveys typically include some variation of the following: the armed rebellion of the Zapatistas against NAFTA and the Mexican state; high-profile protests against corporate power, free trade and international financial institutions; environmental groups; campaigns against Third World debt; student anti-sweatshop activism in North America; struggles against the privatisation of utilities and basic resources; organised labour and trade unions (e.g. Bircham and Charlton 2001; Danaher and Burbach 2000; Cockburn *et al.* 2000; Globalise Resistance 2002a). Paul Kingsnorth (2003), quoted above, also includes West Papuan struggles for independence, and Amory Starr (2000), whose account remains perhaps the most thorough, adds small-business campaigners, peace activists and religious nationalists. There is certainly plentiful evidence here of the proliferation of resistances. But the question remains: how can such radically diverse activities be taken as evidence of the existence of a – single, new – movement?

In part, this depends on what is meant by a 'movement'. Here the field of social movement theory may be helpful. The earliest systematic approach in this field defined its subject as 'crowd psychology' and 'collective behaviour', focusing on large-scale mobilisations in the streets as a sign of social dysfunction and irrationality (e.g. Smelser 1962). More recently, 'resource mobilisation' theorists have interpreted social movements as the rational result of individuals coming together to pursue collective interests. This approach focuses on the enabling effect of available social resources, particularly the role of movement 'entrepreneurs' in formal organisations (e.g. McCarthy and Zald 1977). Developing on these foundations, 'political opportunity structures' theorists emphasise changes in the political context and particularly in state structures (e.g. Tarrow 1998). The impact of globalisation on the state and thus on movements has received some attention recently in this approach (Tarrow n.d.; Smith *et al.* 1997). Indeed, it is here we find a few analyses of 'the anti-globalisation movement' itself (Smith and Johnston 2002). The focus generally remains on organisations oriented towards political institutions, and/or on the material and cultural resources used by such organisations to 'frame' their goals and mobilise supporters. This focus is challenged by the 'new social movement' (NSM) school, which begins from the assumption that there have been profound changes in recent activism, responding to structural shifts in late modernity. Movements are depicted as organised in socially embedded, diffuse, horizontal networks; as primarily concerned with culture and identity; and as aiming to constrain state and economic power rather than to gain access to it (e.g. Cohen 1982; Melucci 1989). This movement form is seen to be spreading around the world in conditions of cultural globalisation (Melucci 1996a).

There are problems with all of these approaches, but the key thing I want to point to here is the perhaps rather surprising fact that there is no agreement about what a social movement actually is (Diani 2000). Some theorists include mobilisation on the basis of identity, others emphasise shared interest; some emphasise irrationality, others rationality; some emphasise formal organisation, others horizontal networks; some institutionally orientated lobbying, others extra-institutional activism. I want to suggest that all these forms and orientations can be part of movement activism; this is to say that they can, and do, co-exist within the same movement. Mario Diani makes it clear that, although 'social movements are not organisations', organisations may well be part of a movement. Indeed, 'bureaucratic interest groups and even political parties' can be included (2000: 165–7). But he also insists that a social movement need not give rise to any formal organisations at all. Jean Cohen and Andrew Arato argue that movements typically have 'dual faces' and adopt a 'dual strategy': 'a discursive politics of identity and influence that targets civil and political society and an organized, strategically rational politics of inclusion and reform that is aimed at political and economic institutions' (1992: 550). In sum, the claim here is that movements are *typically* diverse in organisational form and orientation.

Thus the diversity apparent amongst modes of 'anti-globalisation' activism does not exclude the possibility that a movement has emerged. However, if we cannot judge when a movement has emerged by recourse to empirical evidence of a specific ideological or organisational formation, how can we identify one? In other words, on what basis can it be asserted that 'an anti-globalisation movement' has in fact emerged? I suggest that *we know that movements exist when activists claim that they are part of one and participate in efforts to define 'their' movement in particular ways.* This requires attention to activist representations of themselves.

I adopt this idea from social movement theorist Alberto Melucci's 'constructivist' approach (1989; 1996a)[2.] Melucci's starting point is a critique of the assumption that movements act as 'unified empirical datum' or 'personages', each with a coherent identity, pre-formed interest and single will. He defines a social movement as 'a composite action system, in which differing means, ends and forms of solidarity and organization converge in a more or less stable manner' (1989: 28). In other words, movements are ongoing processes in which diverse actors construct a common frame of reference. One element in this construction, or one result of it (Melucci is elusive on this point), is the formation of a collective identity through which participants establish relationships to each other, locate themselves in their environment, differentiate themselves from others, and gain recognition as a collectivity. Approaching 'the anti-globalisation movement' in the light of this claim, it becomes evident that common identity themes can be found on the websites of Peoples' Global Action (n.d.), the World Social Forum (2002) and Globalise Resistance (2002a). All insist that participants share opposition to free trade, corporate power and international financial institutions. They all claim to support extra-institutional, direct action as a key mode of struggle. Further, they all state that they recognise the diversity of the movement as a strength. Significant differences remain, of which more below, but Melucci's framework implies that identity is forged through a *continuous* process of ongoing communication, negotiation and decision-making among participants; total agreement and closure is thus not to be expected. The key point is that activists have to participate in a shared process through which identity is (re)negotiated. The websites of Peoples' Global Action, Globalise Resistance and the World Social Forum all indicate that their participants see themselves as part of a wider struggle and explicitly appeal to others identified with that struggle.

For Melucci, identity-formation processes occur largely within 'subterranean' networks through which people meet face to face in everyday life, with movements only occasionally surfacing as visible, public actors. It is this subterranean dimension of activism that should thus be the focus of those studying movement construction (1989: 70–3; 1996a: 113–16). However, this approach needs modification when considering the possibility of 'an anti-globalisation movement'. First, there is the widely recognised significance of the Internet in constructing networks among geographically dispersed activists who may never actually meet. There needs to be more critical interrogation of the limitations that a reliance on the Internet for networking, and for studying the movement, brings with it. It is possible that a 'geekocracy' is emerging (Klein 2002: 18); many groups are excluded from access to the Internet and thus from many conceptualisations of the movement; and 'virtual' connections may remain rather weak.

Second, it would seem that collective identity has also congealed in the face-to-face, but highly visible, public gatherings at Seattle, Prague, Genoa, Porto Alegre and elsewhere. These have received an extraordinary emphasis in much activist commentary as well as catching the eye of some academics (e.g. Cockburn *et al.* 2000; Smith 2002). They may be particularly key in transnational movements in which subterranean networks are otherwise 'virtual' or stretched very thinly over great distances. In the case of 'the anti-globalisation movement' they have also functioned to construct the movement in ways that foreground the travelling protestor and the politics of the spectacle. Again, this means that other kinds of activism are marginalised within the movement and our understandings of it, particularly ongoing community-based struggles (Dixon n.d.; Crass n.d.).

Third, Melucci's exclusive emphasis on the role of participants in movement construction can be criticised for ignoring the possible role of exterior social processes, public discourses and other actors. In the case of 'the anti-globalisation movement', it has been suggested that the limited and largely negative representation of the movement in the mainstream media is one factor behind the proliferation of alternative, independent media. These aim to represent movement activism to its participants and to the public in a more positive, nuanced, light (Rodgers 2002). Or see Naomi Klein's book of 'dispatches from the front lines of the globalization debate' (2002). Klein is centrally concerned to respond to elite, police and media representations of the movement as violent, as the politics of the spectacle, and as 'anti-globalisation', and to put forward alternatives. Evidently, representations of the movement by external actors have political implications and can act as a spur to new identity constructions by movement activists.

This brings me to the possibility that academic analyses may also play a role in movement construction. Indeed, Alex Callinicos argues that '[o]ne reason we can talk about a global *movement* is that it has found ideological articulation in a body of critical writing produced by a variety of intellectuals' (2003a: 9, emphasis in original). Callinicos draws attention to the high-profile figures crossing between academia and activism, directly intervening in movement construction. However, I want to extend this point and make the case that even those apparently external to a movement, engaged in study of it for solely academic purposes, are also engaged in its construction. Melucci (1996b) and others are critical of the empiricist assumption that we study movements as pre-existing objects 'out there'; rather, it is the researcher who constructs the social movement they are studying by interpreting activism through a particular lens. This is a strong version of the post-positivist view now widespread in IR that academic study is both shaped by and constitutive of the world around it: we approach the world from a particular perspective and our work can have concrete effects upon it. It means that social movement theory is implicated in the interaction through which a social movement is constructed and should thus be self-consciously interrogated in the process of research.

Further, I suggest that the study of social movements is a political act. In taking the possibility of a particular movement seriously, social movement scholars are helping to call it into existence. They are using the label persuasively, in an effort to give scholarly and political legitimacy to their research and its subject matter. This chapter, for example, is contributing to an academic discourse that claims diverse moments of 'anti-globalisation' activism do indeed constitute a movement that should be taken seriously. What is more, I seek in this chapter to encourage the construction of a particular kind of movement. I want to draw attention to a strand of activism that aims to confront hierarchical power relations in the movement and to reconstruct it as a site of radical–democratic politics.

Now, Melucci's framework does not pay sustained attention to the structures and relations of power through which some movement identities become dominant over others. Most approaches to social movements, and most activists, focus rather on the power structures in the wider social context, which may enable effective mobilisation or present a target. Movements themselves are typically presented as somehow outside or below power: as intrinsically counter-hegemonic or emancipatory; as part of a power-free, global civil society; or as new movements unconcerned with claiming power. In my view, this idealised view of movements has been challenged nowhere so thoroughly as within feminism, and we can find resources here to modify further the constructivist framework. Feminists argue that power is pervasive in social life, including in intimate relationships. They have reflected extensively on their marginalisation within radical movements. They also continue to struggle to take on board the differences and inequalities between women (Eschle 2001: chs 3 and 4). The interventions of black and Third World feminists have been particularly key here, exposing and challenging racist hierarchies within feminist organising (Collins 2000; Mohanty 2003). It has thus become a central concern for feminists to pay attention to the structures and relations of power at work within movement organising; to work out who is included and excluded.

This encourages me to search for the women and the feminists in 'the anti-globalisation movement'. Although women, particularly young women, are heavily involved and there are also a few, high-profile women leaders (see Egan and Robidoux 2001), such women rarely speak as feminists. Further, there is only limited recognition beyond explicitly feminist groups that gender is a source of power. Peoples' Global Action is an exception, including a rejection of patriarchy in its hallmarks and a critique of gender oppression in its manifesto (Peoples' Global Action n.d.; 1998). The World Social Forum has a more ambiguous, if improving, record. At the first forum, held in Porto Alegre, Brazil, in January 2001, feminist groups had to fight at a late stage to get their perspectives onto the agenda. At the second forum, in 2002, feminist lobbying resulted in the naming of patriarchy as a source of oppression in key forum declarations and in themed panels on the connections between domestic violence, militarism, gender inequality and fundamentalism. However, the Organizing Committee was still male dominated and the supposedly more radical Youth Camp remained impervious to analysis of gender inequality. Further shifts occurred at the third forum, in 2003, with a visible feminist presence emerging in the Youth Camp to fight against the sidelining of women and their concerns (see DAWN 2002a; 2002b; Grzybowski 2002; Vargas 2002; Burrows 2002; Beaulieu and Di Giovanni 2003). Globalise Resistance appears most resistant to feminism, with some women members claiming they face gender hierarchies in both political organising and personal relationships, and lamenting the secondary status of resistance to such hierarchies (Hoyles 2003; Rodino 2003). Such feminist critiques of 'the anti-globalisation movement' are paralleled by those of anti-racist organisers who have asked, for example, why the Battle of Seattle was so white (Martinez 2000), and called for further work to be done by the World Social Forum to integrate black, African and indigenous perspectives into the agenda-setting process (Marin 2002). In short, some activist voices and struggles are systematically privileged over others.

Clearly, 'the anti-globalisation movement' does not operate outside glob-alised economic, gendered, racialised and geopolitical power relations but is bound up within them and reflects them. It is also possible – as many white, Western, middle-class women have been forced to admit within the feminist movement – that those in a more structurally privileged position reinforce their position by promulgating a movement identity and strategy that fails to challenge and even reproduces hierarchies that shape the lives of those less privileged than themselves.

I would suggest that there are two, interrelated, efforts to construct 'the anti-globalisation movement' currently taking place that are particularly problematic from this point of view. The first aims to reorientate the move-ment as primarily and above all else an anti-capitalist movement, rooted in working-class organisation and Marxist ideology. As the feminist laments within Globalise Resistance show, this can have marginalising effects. The ideological basis of this move will be discussed in the next section. The second, related, effort to construct the movement in ways that function to marginalise others can be found in attempts to create unity along formally structured, centralised and ultimately hierarchical lines. On this point, Marxist vanguardists and social democratic reformists are in tacit agree-ment. For example, critics of the World Social Forum have pointed to the influence of both the campaigning group ATTAC France and the Brazilian Workers' Party over the organisation of the forum, and to the resultant priv-ileging of the 'big men' of the left and of a lecture-based, hierarchical, plenary format (Coletivo Contra-a-Corrente 2000; Milstein 2002; Klein 2003). The criticisms have been sharper with regards to Globalise Resistance. It should be acknowledged that the website of this organisation has links to many different groups and its newsletter makes some effort for dialogue with non-affiliated voices (e.g. Globalise Resistance 2001). But there is also a consistent stress on the need for 'acting in unity' (Globalise Resistance 2002b) and the organisation has been attacked for its apparent attempt to take on the leadership of the movement in the UK (see, e.g., discussion in Kingsnorth 2003: 232–3).[3]

Although such attempts may have had some success in shaping the move-ment in the UK, they have not succeeded in achieving dominance over the movement on a transnational scale and are widely challenged. As Klein puts it:

> At the moment, the anti-corporate street activists are ringed by would-be leaders, eager for the opportunity to enlist activists as foot soldiers for their particular vision. ... It is to this young movement's credit that it has as yet fended off all these agendas and has rejected everyone's gener-ously donated manifesto, holding out for an acceptably democratic, representative process to take its resistance to the next stage.
>
> (Klein 2002: 26–7)

Klein and others point to the existence of a resilient, radical–democratic strand within the movement. This can be attributed to the influence of anarchism, which reaches far beyond self-declared anarchist groups like Ya Basta! and the Black Bloc to encompass groups that are not explicitly anarchist such as Peoples' Global Action and large-scale actions like the Seattle protest. These share an emphasis on direct action and civil disobedience; on non-hierarchical, decentralised, self-organised modes of activism centred on affinity groups; on participatory, inclusive and consensus-based decision-making processes; and on 'prefiguring' ways of living and acting in a transformed world (Graeber 2002; Epstein 2001; Klein 2002: 17–21, 34–6; Rupert 2003). Some commentators claim that this strand of the movement defies old political categories and is instead symptomatic of a new, 'postmodern' politics (Burbach 2001; Esteva and Prakash 1998). The Zapatistas seem to be the most important source of such politics. There are clear affinities between the Zapatistas and anarchism in the emphasis on local autonomy and participatory democracy, rooted in a belief in the need to decentralise and devolve power (e.g. Kingsnorth 2003: 31, 44–5). But in addition, attention is drawn to the displacement of modern ideology by story-telling emphasising the absurd, the poetic and the everyday (Higgins 2000). Culture and the media are identified as key terrains of struggle. Further, it is argued that the notion of transnational solidarity has been reconstructed to include an emphasis on the need for a diversity of ways of life to flourish – what Gustavo Esteva calls 'one no, many yeses' (interviewed in Kingsnorth 2003: 44) or a 'pluriverse' (Esteva and Prakash 1998: 36). Whether or not the postmodern categorisation is widely accepted by activists, the principles and practices implied by it certainly are – witness the refusal of the World Social Forum to issue a final declaration on which all participants have agreed. Taken together, proponents of this postmodern-cum-anarchist politics are attempting to construct 'the anti-globalisation movement' in radically democratic, non-hierarchical and inclusive ways, in direct opposition to attempts to organise the movement more hierarchically through centralised, representative procedures.

It is here that we reach an important ideological affinity with more radical feminist approaches to movement construction. Of course, not all groups based on anarchistic principles are friendly to feminism or to women, particularly versions emphasising militarised confrontation with the state. Conversely, not all feminism is friendly to anarchism (or to postmodernism). Note for example the critical commentary on the 'NGOisation' of transnational feminism and the limitations of its turn to 'mainstreaming' within international institutions (e.g. Alvarez 1999). There is some evidence that this has constrained feminist participation in the more anarchistic sectors of the World Social Forum (Waterman 2002b: 6). But the more radical elements of feminism have long emphasised the need within their own movement to equalise power between participants, enabling diverse voices to be heard; to achieve consensus through participatory dialogue; to treat other participants in the dialogue holistically and empathetically (see Eschle 2001: chs 4 and 6). So there does seem significant potential for overlap here. Peoples' Global Action appears to have combined feminist analysis of gendered hierarchies with a radically democratic, devolved framework and feminist elements within the World Social Forum continue to push for a fuller integration. The further consolidation of the position of feminism within a radical–democratic strand of 'anti-globalisation' activism is surely to be encouraged if feminism is to maintain its radical edge and if 'the anti-globalisation movement' is to be constructed on a truly democratic, inclusive basis.

However, experience within the feminist movement does urge a final qualification. It has been argued that overly idealised applications of the radical–democratic model generated hidden, informal hierarchies and suppressed difference and dissent in the name of consensus. Such problems were one factor in the subsequent splintering of feminist organising on the basis of more distinct ideologies and identities. This in turn generated its own problems of factionalism and exclusion. Out of this experience, a feminist politics of coalition or alliance has emerged (e.g. Reagon 1998). Black and Third World feminists in particular have insisted that struggles for social change need to connect with one another on a strategic basis in recognition of the need to tackle multiple and 'shifting currents of power' (Sandoval 1995: 218). This connection needs to be based on transparent, developed mechanisms of participation and open dialogue, which recognise that consensus is limited to specific issues and specific times (see Eschle 2001: chs 4 and 6). Arguably, this approach does not entail abandoning the radical–democratic approach to movement construction but refining it. It insists on the need to build connections as well as to celebrate diversity; to do so on a strategic and democratic basis rather than to work towards complete consensus; and to think through concrete procedures for democratic movement construction. There are important practical lessons here for the radical–democratic strand in 'the anti-globalisation movement'.

This first part has examined the concept of 'social movement'. I have pointed out that there is no agreement on a definition of the concept and outlined a constructivist approach that emphasises the importance of activists' representations of themselves. My examination of 'anti-globalisation' activist commentary and websites has confirmed the possibility that a movement exists, albeit in a highly contested and complex form with activists constructing overlapping and sometimes contradictory movement identities. I have also put forward a normative argument, informed by feminist praxis, for the need to be aware of the structures and relations of power through which some activists are marginalised. Further, I have drawn attention to the fact that the accounts of opponents and commentators, including academic social movement theorists, are implicated in movement construction. I have sought explicitly here to highlight and support one particular strand of 'the anti-globalisation movement', one which resonates with anarchist, 'postmodern' and feminist organising and which seeks to construct movement activism on a radically democratic basis, in opposition to more hierarchical forms of movement organising. I want now to turn in the second part of the chapter to what it means to be 'anti-globalisation'.

Globalise this!

> My concern with terminology is to do with the role that differing discourses of 'globalization' play in the taking up of political positions. The discourse of being pro- or anti-globalization is a case in point.
>
> (Brah 2002: 34)

The 'anti-globalisation' label became widespread after the Seattle demonstration, apparently 'a coinage of the US media' (Graeber 2002: 63). However, it is important to realise that the term is strongly contested amongst activists – and that many, if not most, reject the label 'anti-globalisation' entirely.

So what is it, exactly, that activists oppose? Although there has been significant attention recently to militarism in the context of the wars on Afghanistan and Iraq, it seems to me that most activist accounts in recent years have focused more centrally on phenomena associated with *economic* globalisation: the increasing power of corporations, the growing role of international financial institutions, and the neoliberal policies of trade liberalisation and privatisation propounded by the latter and from which the former benefit. These are seen to produce economic inequality, social and environmental destruction, and cultural homogenisation. They are also accused of leaching power and self-determination away from people and governments – of being anti-democratic. Such an interpretation of 'the enemy' chimes with many commentaries on the movement (e.g. Starr 2000; Danaher and Burbach 2000; Burbach 2001; Klein 2002). It can also be discerned on activist websites. The Charter of Principles of the World Social Forum (2002) declares participant groups 'opposed to neoliberalism and to domination of the world by capital and any form of imperialism'. The declaration of principles on the Globalise Resistance site (2002a) indicates that it is primarily against the extension of corporate power over people's lives under the heavy hand of international financial institutions like the WTO and IMF. The group's newsletters then target the exploitative practices of particular multinational corporations as well as drawing attention to problems of debt and financial restructuring. Finally, the Peoples' Global Action manifesto (1998) articulates opposition to the extension of the role of 'capital, with the help of international agencies' and trade agreements.

There are important resonances here with academic depictions of globalisation. I have argued elsewhere that an 'economic-homogenisation' model of globalisation is becoming increasingly dominant, in both academic and popular usage, which focuses attention on the increased integration of the global economy and its homogenising effects on state policy and culture (Eschle 2004; see also Robertson and Khondker 1998). Such a model is widespread in IR. It is characteristic of liberal IR approaches that support globalisation, sceptical refutations of globalisation as exaggerated and ideological, and critical IR theories that condemn globalisation as profoundly damaging. It is with this last, critical, approach in IR that we find the strongest resonance with activist discourses. Both activist and academic critics share the assumption that globalisation equates with the neoliberal economic developments described above. Then, in a highly significant move, these developments may be linked to the underlying structures of the economy and globalisation reinterpreted as the latest stage of capitalism. According to Klein, 'the critique of "capitalism" just saw a comeback of Santana-like proportions' (2002: 12).

I would add that it is Marxist critiques of capitalism in particular that are making a comeback. Marxism, after all, offers a ready-made template for theorising the workings of the global economy. It is expanding in influence in IR in recent years, in tandem with the growth of interest in globalisation. Much Marxist writing in IR tends to adopt a nuanced Gramscian framework, which draws attention to the interaction of economic shifts with ideologies and institutions in global or national civil society (Cox 1997; 1999; Rupert 2000). There has also been some effort to integrate Foucauldian insights on surveillance and disciplining (Gill 2003). Neo-Gramscianism can be criticised for tending towards a totalising account of globalisation in which the role of agency is circumscribed (Eschle 2001: 166–70), although the events of Seattle and beyond seem to have inspired a greater emphasis on the capacities for resistance (e.g. Gill 2003: 211–21). However, neo-Gramscianism has not, to my knowledge, gained currency amongst activists. It seems to me that activist commentary relies rather on an ad hoc, strategic appropriation of elements of Marxism (e.g. Starr 2000) or on a more structuralist, reductive version of Marxism that depicts globalisation as driven by changes in the mode and relations of production and as generating political forms that reflect class conflict and struggle. This last involves not only a reframing of globalisation as capitalism, but a reframing of 'the anti-globalisation movement' as 'the anti-capitalist movement', a shift increasingly evident in the newsletters of Globalise Resistance (e.g. 2002c). In the most developed articulations of this perspective, there is an insistence that the organised working class plays, or ought to play, a pivotal role (e.g. Bircham and Charlton 2001; Callinicos 2003a).

I see several interrelated problems here. The first is economism. The argument that the mode and relations of capitalist production are causal of all other developments associated with globalisation implies that gendered and racialised hierarchies, cultural processes, etc., are superstructural and that struggles focusing on them are distractions or deviations from the more fundamental struggle against capitalism. This brings me to a second problem, the consequent privileging of class as the locus of resistance. Some effort may be made to redefine working-class-based resistance in a broad and inclusive manner (Barker 2001: 332). However, it still tends to be strongly emphasised as *the* emancipatory vehicle, given the structural position of workers within capitalism, and either its role is talked up or political effort is focused on the need to strengthen it (e.g. Callinicos 2003a: 96–101). A third problem is the lack of attention then paid to how to construct relationships between workers' organisations and others on a democratic basis. Callinicos asserts that autonomy and diversity can still be preserved (2003a: 98), but gives no details of exactly how, instead lambasting the preoccupation of much of the movement with radical–democratic processes as an evasion of more fundamental strategic questions posed by the struggle against capitalism. Given the structural primacy afforded to organised labour, the danger is that the relations pursued with other groups will be hierarchically organised and many groups will simply be excluded, as discussed in the first part of this chapter.

Some non-Marxist activist strands are also highly critical of capitalism but the relationship with globalisation is explained differently. The convergence of corporations, international financial institutions and neoliberalism may still be interpreted as the latest stage of capitalism, but not equated with globalisation per se. Rather it is labelled neoliberalism, 'capitalist globalisation' or 'economic globalisation'. Further, the anti-capitalist label may not be adopted, or not exclusively. See, for example, the Call of Social Movements (2002), on the World Social Forum site, which pledges to 'continue our struggles against neoliberalism and war ... against a system based on sexism, racism and violence, which privileges the interests of capital and patriarchy over the needs and aspirations of people'. This is critical of the dominance and over-extension of capitalism in its neoliberal form; it thus implies the possibility of living with a more contained version. This is perhaps a strategic move, generated by a desire to stay open to more reformist elements ('Declaration of a Group of Intellectuals' 2002). However, I think there is a principled element also in terms of giving equal weight to militarism and patriarchy as globalised structures of oppression. As for Peoples' Global Action, this has shifted from simply opposing neoliberal policies to an explicitly anti-capitalist stance. Its 'five hallmarks' now emphasise 'a very clear rejection of capitalism' as well as of 'all forms and systems of domination and discrimination including, but not limited to, patriarchy, racism and religious fundamentalism' (Peoples' Global Action n.d.; 2001). Like Globalise Resistance, this group thus opposes the capitalist system itself. But like the World Social Forum, it gives considerable weight to other global hierarchies. There is no danger here of a blurring with reformism, which is explicitly rejected in favour of a 'confrontational' approach. This appears to be an anarchist-influenced formulation that is critical of power hierarchies in any shape or form, including but not reducible to capitalism.

Taken together, I suggest that what we are seeing emerging from these groups is an 'intersectional' approach to globalisation. To my mind, this has again been developed most explicitly in feminist theory and practice (Eschle 2004). Feminist movement texts and debates have long insisted that there are multiple global structures and relations of power, which intersect in complex, context-specific and contingent ways, and which require context-specific resistances in a diversity of forms. More recently, this analysis has been explicitly linked to academic arguments about globalisation (see e.g. Afshar and Barrientos 1999; Marchand and Runyan 2000; *Signs* 2001; *Feminist Review* 2002). Further, feminist groups have sought to bring such an analysis into 'anti-globalisation' activism. The acknowledgement of patriarchy, sexual violence and their interconnections with neoliberalism on the websites of the World Social Forum and Peoples' Global Action, and the accompanying emphasis on facilitating contextual specificity of struggle, is a direct result of feminist influence. There is some overlap with this intersectional understanding of global power and sociological theories of globalisation that emphasise multiple structures, the interplay of the local and the global and the open-ended and contingent character of globalisation (Eschle 2004). However, I can find no evidence that such sociological theories have informed movement discourses, which are in any case much more alive to the power relations involved in global processes and to the need for resistance. One common source may be the fact that both the academic and activist discourses described here evolved, to some extent, in opposition to more reductionist Marxist formulations.

Like their Marxist colleagues, most activists working with some kind of intersectional approach desire to move away from the 'anti-globalisation' label. Both movement strands recognise that globalisation is being used as a code word for neoliberalism and corporate power, and they wish to bring these into sharper focus. For Marxists, this is because the connection can then be made to more fundamental underlying structures of capitalism and the movement reorientated from anti-globalisation to anti-capitalism. For those adopting a more intersectional approach, it is because neoliberalism needs to be exposed as the specific version of globalisation to which they are opposed – and attention drawn to the alternative versions of globalisation put forward by, and embodied in, the movement. Some activists/commentators are concerned that 'anti-globalisation' is being used persuasively by critics keen to label the movement as isolationist, parochial and protectionist (e.g. Klein in Thomas 2002). Although some activists/commentators do emphasise the necessary devolution of economic decision-making (e.g. Starr 2000), most of the activist texts that I have read foreground the fact that the movement is or should be global in scope, extended through globalised communications, transport and social networks. Further, the movement is characterised as globalist or internationalist in orientation, concerned to construct more humane, just and democratic interconnections between people on a worldwide scale (see also discussion in Callinicos 2003a: 13–14). The precise details of this positive vision of globalisation are still being thrashed out at the World Social Forum and elsewhere. But, in general, this effort has led many activists and commentators to abandon the 'anti-' label altogether and rename the movement on the basis of what it is *for*.

Thus we find labels along the line of 'the global justice movement', 'the global justice and solidarity movement', the 'global democracy movement', or even, simply, 'the globalisation movement' (Graeber 2002: 63; Klein 2002: 77–8; introduction to Danaher and Burbach 2000; Waterman 2003). This last is a bold attempt to turn the popular meanings of globalisation and anti-globalisation on their heads: to claim that the movement is the 'true' defender of globalisation. I think it is probably too ambitious a discursive shift – and also rather too simplistic. After all, we are left here with a highly complex and differentiated picture of the movement's relationship to globalisation: opposing elite efforts to globalise the economy around the interests of corporations; bound up within and reproducing other aspects of globalisation; and creating its own forms of globalised social relationships. I find the label 'critical globalisation movement' more helpful: used by several activists at a recent conference I attended in Austria, it conveys the fact that the movement is not simply rejectionist but embodies a developed critique of current patterns of globalisation and, by implication, that it points to an alternative.[4] Or perhaps some sort of composite title might emerge, such as the 'global social justice and democracy movement'. This is a mouthful but it is also, usefully, a largely 'empty signifier' that can be filled in different ways by activists with differing concerns. It foregrounds the need to challenge iniquitous global economic relationships and that this involves not simply redistributing material resources but also enforcing popular control over those resources. Further, feminists have shown that the projects of justice and democracy can be extended beyond strictly economic concerns in opposition to hierarchies of power and resources in other areas of life. Finally, such a label highlights the radical–democratic element of the movement: the attempt to construct relations between participants on an egalitarian and participatory basis that prefigures the wider possibilities for society.

It should be stressed again that this project of democratic movement construction is not complete and the movement should not be idealised. I have emphasised ongoing struggles over the construction of the movement, highlighting the divide between those urging unity through hierarchical organisation and those defending participatory horizontal networks; and between those reframing the movement as anti-capitalist and those seeing globalisation in intersectional terms and the movement as thus developing alternative forms of globalisation. I have indicated that feminist and anti-racist critics continue to struggle against their marginalisation within the movement. Certainly, it seems to me that more work needs to be done on how best to counter the ways in which the movement is bound up within, structured and compromised by dimensions of globalisation. I have already hinted at gendered and racialised hierarchies, and at the exclusions that can emerge from a reliance on internet networks and on international gatherings. Peter Waterman (2002b: section 7) adds that attention needs to be paid to the financial power of northern funding bodies over international gatherings like the World Social Forum. The discursive reframing of the movement as 'pro-democracy' rather than 'anti-globalisation' would seem an important step in raising awareness of such issues amongst activists and thus in tackling them. The democratisation of globalisation is not simply something that has to happen 'out there', in the offices of the WTO or Nike. As many activists and commentators realise, democracy has to be nurtured within the movement itself if it is to offer a genuine, radical, alternative.

Conclusion

This chapter has interrogated the proposition that there is a transnational anti-globalisation social movement. In the first part, I discussed the term 'social movement', pointing out that there is no agreed meaning. The term is applied to a diversity of phenomena and used persuasively to legitimise them. Drawing on a constructivist approach, I argued that a movement exists when activists claim they are part of one and participate in processes of collective identity formation. Such processes do appear to be ongoing amongst diverse groups opposed to aspects of globalisation, particularly at international gatherings and in Internet networks. I also suggested that external forces, including academic theorising, can contribute to the construction of the movement – which makes this chapter complicit in the construction process. I have sought explicitly to further a particular view of the movement, one that confronts the structures and relations of power at work within it and supports its democratic potentials. Drawing on feminist praxis, I have highlighted some exclusionary implications of efforts to reorientate the movement as a class-based, anti-capitalist movement, unified through hierarchical organisation. I have also drawn attention to resistances posed by more participatory practices grounded in anarchism and 'postmodern politics'.

In the second part of the chapter, I focused on the concept of 'anti-globalisation', by looking at activists' representations of what it is they are against. Although there is substantial agreement on the need to oppose the neoliberal convergence, this has led activists in very different directions. I contrasted a Marxist reorientation of the movement as anti-capitalist and class-based with an intersectional view that recognises the multiplicity of forms of global power and the need for context-specific resistances. The intersectional view encourages a complex understanding of the relationship of the movement to globalisation: as opposed to some dimensions, bound up with others and embodying alternative globalised relationships of solidarity and democracy. This has led many activists and commentators to criticise the 'anti-globalisation' label and to argue for a new name based on what the movement is for. I suggested that a name highlighting the democratising impetus of the movement may be useful. However, I also stressed that the democratic element of the movement should not be taken for granted: the struggle to make the movement more inclusive continues and there is a need for further work on the ways in which it is bound up within and compromised by broader processes of globalisation. Thus the second section ended by reinforcing my normative plea for further democratisation in movement construction.

I want to close by drawing out some of the implications of this analysis for the construction of *theory*, particularly with regards to IR. First, I would stress that the neglect of movements in IR, and the consequent lack of attention to the detail of so-called 'anti-globalisation' activism, is not adequately redressed by an empiricist strategy that provides evidence of that activism and weighs its significance against criteria already established within the discipline. For a start, if it is accepted that a range of organisational and ideological orientations are possible within a movement then there is no easy empirical test that can be applied to check when a movement has emerged. In this chapter, I have insisted on the need to focus on activist self-understandings as a source of knowledge about the movement – and about global processes more generally. This still involves empirical study, in the sense of attention to practices in the world. However, it also involves a move away from an empiricist model of knowledge based on impartial observation of external objects, towards a more interpretative model based on interaction with subjects who are producers of their own knowledge. This is predicated on the assumption that knowledge is situated, finite, socially constructed and discursively mediated. Further, this chapter strives to go beyond an argument for 'grounded theory', whereby theoretical categories are developed on the basis of empirical study, in the direction of what Noel Sturgeon (1997) terms 'direct theory', whereby movements are taken seriously as agents of knowledge generating their own theoretical categories. For example, I have drawn attention here to the analyses of globalisation put forward by activists. The overlaps and divergences with globalisation theory in IR and sociology are intriguing and point to ways in which academic frameworks, as well as activist practice, might need to be further refined or rearticulated.

In some ways, my approach here meshes with a 'postmodern' IR emphasis on the knowledge claims of subordinated discourses. Yet, and this is my second point, a rigorous postmodernist, or poststructuralist, approach is also likely to be insufficient for further research of the kind I have presented here. I have made additional moves that slide more towards standpoint epistemology: casting activists as agents not just subjects of discourse; privileging discourses produced by activists as fundamentally constitutive of the movement; and evaluating movement discourses in relation to normative criteria generated by a feminist-informed commitment to radical–democratic practices. However, I have also taken on board postmodernist criticisms of standpoint epistemology in terms of deconstructing the movement as a unitary subject. I have insisted throughout the chapter that the movement has diverse and shifting identities and that attempts to 'fix' its identity in ways that discourage diversity should be resisted. This is for epistemological as well as political reasons: the diverse voices within the movement generate distinctive insights about the operations of power and resistance in different contexts, and democratic dialogue between those voices needs to be encouraged to gain a fuller picture of reality and to build stronger oppositional struggles (Collins 2000). I cannot attempt here to resolve the tensions between postmodern and standpoint epistemologies – but I would note that many other feminist scholars work with both and find the tension between the two to be fruitful.

My third and final point concerns the issue of power and its relation to theory construction. This chapter shifts away from simplified celebrations of movement diversity to explore the ways in which some movement strands become dominant over others. Such an approach needs to be extended within IR and social movement theory more generally in order to challenge idealised accounts of movements as beyond power. There is also a particular need to pay closer attention to the power of academic analysis. Some academic accounts have more constitutive power than others, for complex reasons of ideology, class, gender, nationality, social resources and media dissemination that demand further investigation. This chapter may not have any representational authority beyond a small circle of IR scholars, but the possibilities and limitations of this still need to be taken seriously. I have argued that theorists should overturn long-established epistemological hierarchies by acknowledging movements as a source of knowledge in and about the world. I have also striven to be explicit about my support for, and thus privileging of, certain kinds of movement activism. This seems to me to be a start, but it still skirts lots of problematic power-laden issues to do with co-optation, translation, representation and authority. So I want to end this chapter with a slightly different question from the one with which I began: how do we gain understanding of the transnational anti-globalisation social movement in ways that both increase knowledge and challenge globalised relations of power? The answer to this is surely of crucial importance for the future development of both activist politics and critical IR theory.

Notes

1 This chapter was originally published as 'Constructing "The Anti-Globalisation Movement"', *International Journal for Peace Studies*, 9 (1), Spring/Summer 2004, pp. 61–84. I would like to thank the editors of the *IJPS*, particularly Howon Jeong, Karen Andrews and Charles Snare, for their encouragement to submit the paper, for their impressive efficiency, and for granting permission to reprint. An earlier draft was presented at a panel entitled 'The Power/Knowledge of Practice: Activism and the Politics of International Relations', at the International Studies Association annual congress, 25 February–1 March 2003, Portland, Oregon, USA. Thanks are due to all those who participated and particularly to Jayne Rodgers and Bice Maiguashca for their detailed feedback. This chapter is part of an ongoing project with Bice on 'the anti-globalisation movement' and owes much to our conversations together. Any shortcomings with the argument presented here remain, of course, entirely my own responsibility.

2 This is not to be confused with constructivism as invoked in IR, which usually focuses on the intersubjective practices between states that shape identity and interest within the international system. The constructivist label is also sometimes applied to poststructuralist approaches in IR. Even more confusingly, in the field of social movement theory, the label may be used for North American frameworks that emphasise 'framing' and cultural factors. The common assumptions in all these versions of constructivism, including Melucci's, seem to be the following: actors are not unitary; interest and identity are constituted through social interaction, not prior to it; and empirical study should focus on changes in interaction, self-understanding, symbols and ideas.

3 My own, admittedly limited, experience of Globalise Resistance in action gives me some sympathy with these criticisms. For example, I attended a conference in Glasgow in January 2001 at which many different groups were welcomed. Yet most of the chairing and opening and closing speeches were undertaken by members of the Socialist Workers' Party and there was a strong drive for recruitment to the Party throughout. This was an attempt to pull diverse resistances into a hierarchical structure under the control of one particular group.

4 The conference was organised by feministATTAC Austria and held in Graz, Austria, 11–14 September, 2003. The Association for the Taxation of Financial Transactions for the Aid of Citizens (ATTAC – *Association pour la Taxation des Transactions Fiancières pour l'Aide aux Citoyens*) was founded in France, originally to campaign for the Tobin tax on financial speculation. At the time of writing, there are over 100 national ATTAC groups worldwide, campaigning on a range of related issues. My thanks to Karin Lukas and Evamaria Glatz of feministATTAC Vienna for drawing the label 'critical globalisation movement' to my attention. The label appears to be unique to German-speaking activists. At the more recent European Social Forum, held in Paris, 12–16 November 2003, the majority of ATTAC France and other francophone activists appeared to prefer instead the label 'alterglobalisation movement'.

2 In the belly of the beast
Resisting globalisation and war in a neo-imperial moment

Mark Rupert

Introduction

The years 2000 and 2001 were for me, as for many others around the world, a time of excitement and optimism. A new kind of social movement was emerging. Inspired by the diverse and dialogical networks of resistance imagined by the Zapatistas (Marcos 2001), a variety of grassroots mobilisations and activist-oriented non-governmental organisations – perhaps predominantly but by no means exclusively from the global North – were coalescing into 'a movement of movements' resistant to neoliberal globalisation. Among them could be found critics of the International Monetary Fund, World Bank and World Trade Organization; advocates of debt relief for developing countries; proponents of re-regulation and taxation of global finance capital; groups critical of the heightened power of multinational firms; movements of and for small farmers and landless peasants; environmentalists; women's groups and lesbian activists; labour advocates; direct action networks; and anti-capitalist groups inspired by various articulations of anarchist and socialist ideologies (on the scope of the movement see *inter alia* Bircham and Charlton 2001; Fisher and Ponniah 2003; Notes from Nowhere 2003; Mertes 2004). Together, these groups seemed to be constructing a new form of politics premised upon transnational solidarity and emergent norms of collective responsibility and reciprocity (see discussions in Rupert 2000; 2003; 2004b).

The terrorist attacks of 11 September 2001 and their aftermath, however, have posed serious challenges to what is coming to be known as the Global Justice Movement (GJM). The social meanings attached to what is widely referred to as 9–11 in the United States, the empowerment of forces of militaristic nationalism and the attendant changes in the politics of global governance have combined to alter the political landscape in which the movement operates. The current conjuncture may be described as a 'neo-imperial moment' in which the balance of coercion and consent underlying US global supremacy has shifted towards greater reliance on directly coercive power, officially rationalised by the thinnest veneer of self-serving nationalistic moralism and double standards. In this context of terror and almost universally offensive displays of US power, processes of economic, social and political de-territorialisation which had supported the growth of transnational solidarity-building movements may be increasingly rearticulated in nationalistic terms. Whether the GJM is able to weather the neo-imperial storm, resist the gravitational pull of nationalisms both American and anti-American and thereby sustain its momentum towards a world of greater solidarity, self-determination, justice and peace is an open question.

In this chapter, I will trace the origins and contours of the neo-imperial moment, offering a Marxian–Gramscian analysis of the linkages between 9–11, the so-called 'Bush doctrine' and the broader neoliberal economic context (for an overview of my interpretation of Marxian–Gramscian analysis, see Rupert 2004a). Then I will show how the GJM, particularly as manifest in the United States (since that is the wing of the movement I am best able to observe), is responding to the neo-imperial moment by reorientating itself as a movement for global justice *and peace*, reaching out to new constituencies and building new organisational linkages. I will conclude by exploring the most pressing dilemmas facing those activists fighting globalisation and war from within 'the belly of the beast'.

Capitalism, imperialism and the Bush doctrine

The significance of 9–11, I think, has less to do with the magnitude of death and destruction caused by the attacks (horrifying as they were) and much more to do with the fact that these were visited upon Americans (and visitors from around the world) going about their daily business *in America*. What changed – in ways profoundly disturbing and threatening to Americans – was the sense that their lives were lived in a separate social space, uniquely privileged, largely immune to the troubles which (somehow) plague much of the rest of the world. What was lost, then, was the comfort and security afforded by the assurance – itself an unacknowledged effect of global structural power – that 'those things don't happen here' – a telling comment, expressed in tones of deep shock, which I heard often in the wake of the attacks. This I believe is what lies behind Americans' stunned sense that 'everything has changed'; the world may not itself have changed, but Americans' perception of the ways in which they live in that world surely have.

This realisation might have led to a questioning of the US role in producing and sustaining a world of inequality and of violence both overt and structural. But such questioning would have entailed moving away from collective self-understandings based upon American exceptionalism,[1] and an explicit acknowledgement of the economic and political power and privilege enjoyed by the United States, and this most Americans are not yet prepared to do. Instead, the shock of the terrorist attacks has given way to virulent reassertions of American exceptionalism and privilege, a hyper-patriotism profoundly suspicious of otherness, and a blatantly neo-imperial foreign policy sold to Americans on the grounds that the aggressive exercise of US military power can protect them from future terrorist attacks while preserving their position of (global structural) privilege. Although this view is not uncontested, most Americans see the reassertion of US military power as a defensive move, a response to unprovoked, unintelligible and unjustifiable terrorist attacks. As I will argue below, this involves a convenient forgetting of the history of US imperialism, its intimate connection to US global privilege, and the global inequalities that it builds upon and sustains.

Capitalism and US imperialism

As Marxists remind us, the conditions for imperialism are built into the historical social relations that constitute the core of capitalism (Rosenberg 1994; Lacher 2002; Wood 2003). Since capitalism entails a structural separation between the economic and political aspects of social life (i.e. the depoliticisation and privatisation of the economy which makes possible capitalist property and wage labour), the state in a capitalist context is generally dependent upon the economic activities of capitalists in order to generate resources which it can tax, and to create enough economic growth and prosperity within its territory to legitimate the government and the social order as a whole. The state has, therefore, a compelling interest in successful accumulation by capitalists whose operations are based within its territory. But since capitalist economic activity routinely overflows those juridical boundaries, the imperatives of capitalist competition and geopolitical rivalry may converge to generate imperialism – the deployment of military power in the service of capital accumulation.

Capitalist imperialism – as distinct from pre-capitalist tribute-extracting or commerce-controlling empires – has involved the use of coercive power in order to create and maintain the conditions necessary for capitalist production, exchange and investment to occur on a transnational scale (Wood 2003). This has entailed forcibly integrating new areas into the world market, destroying non-capitalist ways of life and commodifying social relations to create an exploitable proletarianised labour force, and/or enforcing the dominance of private property and capitalist access to important resources. Viewed from a world-historical perspective, the spatial expansion of capitalist social relations and processes has prepared the way for the recession of explicitly political coercive force into the background of global capitalism; while never entirely absent, it is not as a rule directly present or transparent in economic relations. When conditions of transnational accumulation have been more or less secured, capitalism can function without ongoing recourse to directly coercive exploitation. Rather than the sharp point of a bayonet, it relies on what Marx (1990 [1867]: ch. 28) called 'the dull compulsion of economic relations', the relentless pressure in a commodified society to earn enough to secure the material necessities of life.

As Ellen Meiksins Wood has forcefully argued, the contemporary capitalist world may be understood as a process of economic domination managed by multiple states:

> Neither the imposition of economic imperatives nor the everyday social order demanded by capital accumulation and the operations of the market can be achieved without the help of administrative and coercive powers much more local and territorially limited than the economic reach of capital.
>
> (Wood 2003: 154)

When local states and ruling classes are unable or unwilling to maintain the political conditions of transnational accumulation, coercive force may be brought out of the closet by the dominant imperial state in order to reimpose those conditions.

This conceptualisation sheds considerable light on the history of US foreign policy. From its colonial origins to its role in reshaping the twentieth-century capitalist world order, the United States has been intimately involved with imperial power. Among the more outstanding examples are: the forceful expropriation and near extermination of native Americans; the military conquest and absorption of substantial territories formerly belonging to Mexico; the establishment of domination over the hemisphere and the enforcement of capitalist property rights on a transnational scale through enactment of the Monroe doctrine and the Roosevelt corollary; the annexation of Hawaii and conquest of Cuba, Puerto Rico, the Philippines and other territories used as strategic bases in the pursuit of an 'Open Door' for expansionary US capital; global order struggles leading to the destruction of fascism and the subsequent reconstruction of the infrastructure of the capitalist world economy; and the 'containment' of a putative global communist threat which was invoked to justify numerous bloody interventions (both overt and covert) to secure a hospitable environment for US political and economic interests during the second half of the twentieth century (Kolko 1988; La Feber 1989; Blum 1995).

A foundational document of US postwar strategy, NSC-68, called upon the United States to assume a role of 'world leadership' in order 'to create conditions under which our free and democratic system can live and prosper' (May 1993: 26, 29). US strategists explicitly envisaged a symbiotic relationship between the vitality and robustness of the non-communist 'free world', 'an international economy based on multilateral trade, declining trade barriers, and convertible currencies', and globally projected US military power capable of defending 'any of several vital pressure points' where the 'free world' might be vulnerable to incursion or subversion (May 1993: 48; also 29, 41–3, 46, 53–4, 73). In a polarised, zero-sum world where 'a defeat of free institutions anywhere is a defeat everywhere', US national security and the survival of 'civilization itself' was thus seen to depend upon a liberalised and reinvigorated world capitalism and the possession of 'clearly superior overall power' by the United States and its 'free world' allies (May 1993: 26, 43). Though the relative balance between coercive and consensual aspects of US global domination may have shifted from one historical conjuncture to another, variants of this basic strategy governed US world order policy throughout the Cold War period, and continue to echo through the George W. Bush's *National Security Strategy* (White House 2002).[2]

With the end of the Cold War, the coercive aspects of US power were de-emphasised, fading into the background as ideological representations of spontaneous, voluntary and generally beneficial globalisation were highlighted. The neoliberal triumphalism which constituted the hegemonic ideology of the post-Cold-War era suggested that depoliticised market relations were natural and necessary products of human social evolution, and that with the extension of market-based liberalism and presumptively concomitant republican political forms would come a spreading zone of peace and prosperity potentially encompassing the globe. Exemplary of this perspective is Thomas Friedman, who comes as close to being an official spokesperson of the global capitalist bloc as anyone. Friedman's representations of globalisation contain a revealing contradiction: the dominant theme of his narrative suggests that global capitalism emerges spontaneously out of a universal interest in freedom, progress and prosperity. Lurking in the background of Friedman's story of natural and spontaneous capitalist global development, however, is a frank acknowledgement of the role of coercive force in maintaining this system: 'The hidden hand of the market will never work without the hidden fist. … And the hidden fist that keeps the world safe for Silicon Valley's technologies to flourish is called the US Army, Air Force, Navy and Marine Corps' (Friedman 1999: 373). This acknowledgement is accompanied by remarkably little reflection about *why* this is so, or what this might mean for the presumption of spontaneous and voluntary capitalist globalisation, thus leaving intact the simple and happy plot line of Friedman's story: globalisation is giving the world's people what they want. This has been, until recently, the official story of neoliberal capitalist globalisation (for analyses, see Rupert 2000: ch. 3; Steger 2002: ch. 3).

Although the market-oriented liberal vision continues to animate US global policy, it is no longer represented by key US policy-makers as presumptively natural or spontaneous – that is, voluntary, co-operative and multilateral. Rather, it is now portrayed more explicitly as the product of the global assertion of unilateral US power, especially military force. Coercion was never absent from neoliberal capitalism, of course, but to the greatest extent possible the exercise of power underlying this system was hidden or disguised. During recent decades, the most significant coercive mechanisms prying open the global South for neoliberal capitalism and (re-)subjecting working people to the discipline of capital were the structural adjustment programmes administered by multilateral international financial institutions, their exercise of power simultaneously mystified and legitimated by the scientificity of neoclassical economics. Now, however, there has been a shift in the balance of coercion/consent at the core of US global policy, with the unilateral and directly coercive elements officially brought to the fore.

The neo-imperial moment

This neo-imperial moment must be understood in the context of a particular vision of the post-Cold-War geopolitical environment, in which the United States appears as a global superpower of singular pre-eminence, facing historic opportunities and corresponding dangers. The current strategy for asserting, protecting and promoting this extraordinary global power and the neoliberal capitalist order which sustains it was born out of an alliance in the highest levels of the administration of George W. Bush (henceforth Bush II), between old-fashioned nationalist conservatives (Vice President Dick Cheney, Defense Secretary Rumsfeld) and 'neoconservative' or 'neocon' ideologues (scattered throughout the Bush foreign policy bureaucracy but most prominently represented by Deputy Defense Secretary Paul Wolfowitz and Cheney's deputy Lewis Libby).[3] These most hawkish and hard-line elements in the Bush administration have exploited the atmosphere of jingoism and fear in the United States following the terrorist attacks of 9–11 to put into effect their long-cherished vision of US global military supremacy, unilateral action and the pre-emptive use of military force, deployed to create a world in which the US model of capitalist democracy is unquestioned.

The neo-imperial strategy has its roots in the period when the Cold War was waning, along with the Reagan–Bush era.[4] Before the administration of Bush senior departed the White House, then Defense Secretary Cheney tasked Zalmay Khalilzad and Libby with drafting a long-term strategic vision under the administrative supervision of Wolfowitz. The resulting document, known as the 1992 *Defense Policy Guidance* (DPG), envisioned a post-Cold-War world in which the US position of power and privilege would be beyond challenge (Armstrong 2002; Lemann 2002; Mann 2004). The incoming Clinton administration, with its more multilateral neoliberalism, displaced the ultra-hawks from the executive branch, but they continued to build on the foundation laid out in the DPG strategy.

With the leadership of neoconservative publisher William Kristol in 1997, they formed an association called the *Project for a New American Century* (PNAC), dedicated to persuading Americans that 'we need to accept responsibility for America's unique role in preserving and extending an international order friendly to our security, our prosperity, and our principles' – all of which the PNAC understood to require 'a Reaganite policy of military strength and moral clarity' projected on a global scale (PNAC 1997).[5] PNAC principals have been clear and explicit that the American-centred world order they seek to strengthen is not just a matter of superordinate power, but also a superior moral order: 'The American-led world that emerged after the Cold War is a more just world than any imaginable alternative.' What the PNAC advocates, then, is 'preserving and reinforcing America's benevolent global hegemony', a policy based on 'the blending of principle with material interest' which takes 'its meaning and coherence from being rooted in universal principles first enunciated in the *Declaration of Independence*' (all quotes from Kristol and Kagan 2000: 6, 13, 23, 24). On this view, the principled exercise of extraordinary US power entails confronting potentially threatening authoritarian states with the aim of transforming them into putatively more pacific liberal democracies, as PNAC Executive Director Gary Schmidt explained: 'The hard truth is that unless you change some of these regimes, you're going to be hard-pressed to get rid of the threat. Liberal democracies don't go to war with one another' (quoted in Murphy 2003).[6] It is worth noting that as early as January 1998, PNAC's heavy-hitters were collectively and publicly calling upon the Clinton administration to use military force for regime change in Iraq (PNAC 1998).

Among the PNAC principals recruited into the Bush II administration were, as already mentioned, Cheney as vice president and Libby as his chief of staff, along with Rumsfeld and Wolfowitz at Defense. Other key figures given posts included Richard Perle at the advisory Defense Policy Board (on whom, see Drew 2003; Hersh 2003), John Bolton in the State Department (on whom, see Williams 2002; Daniel 2002), Khalilzad and Elliott Abrams at the National Security Council (on whom, see Powers 2003 and Lobe 2002b respectively). Even the Bush administration's Trade Representative, Robert Zoellick – whose portfolio includes management of US relations with arguably the most powerful multilateral global governance institution, the WTO – has signed on to the PNAC global agenda (PNAC 1998).

It is not altogether surprising, then, that the strategic response of the Bush II administration to 9–11 bears a clear resemblance to the policies advocated by the PNAC and envisioned in the 1992 DPG. Made public in September 2002, one year after 9–11, the so-called 'Bush doctrine' is exemplified in the *National Security Strategy for the United States* (White House 2002). This document clearly and explicitly outlines a long-term vision of US global predominance based upon military power, a vision in which the United States faces no serious military competitors and will tolerate no challenges to its interests and authority or to its putatively universal model of democracy, freedom and the market. Exploiting 'a position of unparalleled military strength and great economic and political influence', – a unipolar condition referred to as 'a balance of power that favors freedom' – '[t]he United States will use this moment of opportunity to extend the benefits of freedom across the globe. We will actively work to bring the hope of democracy, development, free markets, and free trade to every corner of the globe' (White House 2002: 1–2). In sum, the *National Security Strategy* represents a dangerous synthesis of commitments to unilateralism, military supremacy and the pre-emptive use of force, all justified by a messianic presumption of American moral superiority.[7]

The administration's rush to war in Iraq may be understood as an expression of this doctrine of global military dominance. Although I certainly don't discount US interests in Middle East oil as one of the key motivating factors behind the war in Iraq, I am sceptical of more reductive, instrumentalist explanations which point to the common background of Bush and Cheney in the oil industry and which focus on the desire of US-based oil companies to gain direct control of Iraqi oilfields. Rather I would argue for a more nuanced version of the relationship between capitalism, oil and war. In the first place, the state is structurally positioned within capitalist social formations in such a way that, while it is structurally dependent on the investment activities of the capitalist class as a whole and hence bound to seek the reproduction of capitalism, it is not reducible to a simple instrument of particular elements of that class (see e.g. Carnoy 1984). Moreover, the material interests of capitalists and state managers must be understood as ideologically mediated, in so far as it is only through ideology that people become conscious of, and actors in, fundamental social conflicts (Gramsci 1971: 162, 164, 377). On this view, US interests in Middle East oil do not directly determine state policy, but are rather interpreted through the ideological lens of the *National Security Strategy*, which suggests that US strategic dominance of this oil-rich region is crucial to the reproduction of both global strategic dominance *and* the form of energy-intensive capitalism within which that dominance is embedded (for roughly convergent arguments, see Callinicos 2003b; Dreyfuss 2003a; Judis 2003; Klare 2003a; 2003b; Panitch and Gindin 2003; Everest 2004). Moreover, in the moral universe of members of the PNAC, both of these conditions are identified with 'freedom' and hence are unambiguously in the general interest of humankind. Any direct benefits which may accrue to particular US oil companies are then icing on the cake. Further weakening a straightforward ruling-class instrumentalist account of the war is evidence suggesting that the global capitalist bloc was sharply divided over US unilateralism and jittery about the economic implications of war (Becker 2003; Cohen 2003; Dreyfuss 2003a; Freeman 2003; Landler 2003).

The Bush administration has not, of course, abandoned the longstanding US commitment to the deepening of neoliberal capitalist relations on a global basis. Indeed, the Bush doctrine explicitly elevates free trade to the status of 'a moral principle', handed down to us along with liberty and democracy as part of the heritage of Western civilisation (White House 2002: 13). All three principles are presumed to be universally valid and generally applicable as aspects of 'a single sustainable model for national success: freedom, democracy, and free enterprise' (White House 2002: 1). The institutional forms associated with neoliberal capitalism are explicitly integrated into US national security strategy: 'pro-growth legal and regulatory policies to encourage business investment'; 'lower marginal tax rates';

conservative fiscal policies (no small irony here); free trade and international capital flows (White House 2002: 12). Whereas for much of the preceding decade, the core rationale of neoliberalism had been to use (primarily if not exclusively) multilateral and co-operative means in order to separate politics from economics to the greatest extent possible and thus to mystify the workings of power within the global capitalist economy (Rupert 2000: ch 3), the *National Security Strategy* directly and explicitly links neoliberal capitalism with global US military dominance. The institutional concomitant of this shift in the balance of coercion and consent – as well as the underlying continuity of the US-led global capitalist project – is well summarised by Leo Panitch and Sam Gindin:

> Perhaps the most important change in the administrative structure of the American empire in the transition from the Clinton administration to the Bush II administration has been the displacement of the Treasury from its pinnacle at the top of the state apparatus. The branches of the American state that control and dispense the means of violence are now in the driver's seat; in an administration representing a Republican Party that has always been made up of a coalition of free marketers, social conservatives and military hawks, the balance has been tilted decisively by September 11th toward the latter. But the unconcealed imperial face that the American state is now prepared to show the world above all pertains to the increasing difficulties of managing a truly global informal empire – a problem that goes well beyond any change from administration to administration.
>
> (Panitch and Gindin 2003: 30)

In sum, the Bush doctrine thus entails both continuities and discontinuities in relation to previous US policy. Attempting to secure the political conditions of global capitalism in a world of multiple sovereign states, the new strategy shifts the balance of coercion and consent significantly towards the more coercive side of power. It is in this sense, I think, that the present conjuncture represents a 'neo-imperial moment' within the historical development of US-led global capitalism. As we are already seeing, this re-emphasis on coercive power may have the effect of rendering the power relations of the neoliberal world order (or some of them at any rate) more transparent and more difficult to legitimate effectively.

Resisting the neo-imperial moment

Unsurprisingly, repeated acts of self-righteous and militant unilateralism by the world's most powerful nation have provoked considerable disquiet almost everywhere (Farley and McManus 2002; Ford 2002; Becker 2003; Cohen 2003; Freeman 2003; Landler 2003). In a series of moves implicitly or explicitly affirming American exceptionalism and privilege at the expense of multilateralism and frameworks of international law and co-operation – and profoundly offensive therefore to much of world opinion – the Bush administration backed out of the Kyoto Protocol seeking to reduce global emissions of greenhouse gases, aggressively pursued National Missile Defense, scuttled the Anti-Ballistic Missile Treaty, obstructed the Biological and Toxin Weapons Convention, demanded special US exemption from the International Court of Justice and withdrew US consent from the Rome Treaty which founded the Court. Then, as if it had merely been warming up, the administration unveiled the *National Security Strategy* and prepared to besiege Iraq with or without the approval of the United Nations or even America's European allies.

Anticipating the imminent US attack upon Iraq, in early 2003 political activists around the world planned demonstrations of popular opposition. The most spectacular result was a series of nearly simultaneous protests on 15 February 2003 (widely known as F15), involving anywhere from 5 to 11 million persons in some 600 cities worldwide. Hundreds of thousands of Americans joined this mass global protest, taking to the streets in New York, San Francisco, Philadelphia, Chicago, Seattle, Miami, Detroit and many other US cities. In a number of particular places around the world the magnitude of the local demonstrations was historically unprecedented, but in their global totality they were a breathtaking show of the scope and intensity of popular opposition – not just to the war in Iraq, but also to the imperial pretensions of US power (Agence France Presse 2003; Ford 2003; Reuters 2003).

There are important connections, both direct and indirect, between the GJM and the recent transnational anti-war movement. First, much of the anti-war movement has adopted the highly successful network model of transnational grassroots political mobilisation characteristic of the GJM (on which see Rupert 2003). Second, organisers and organisations central to the GJM have become directly engaged in the anti-war movement and have articulated linkages between capitalist globalisation and US military power. Third, the ideological constructions of the movement, its representations of the world it wants to change, readily incorporate an account of US imperialism as integral to the structural inequality and anti-democratic powers at the core of global capitalism.

Numerous reports suggest that the anti-war movement has been remarkably diverse, encompassing not just the usual suspects – that is, the traditional left (which predominated early in the movement's emergence) or the direct action groups associated with the GJM – but also more mainstream religious groups, women's groups, labour unions, a variety of other organisations and large numbers of unaffiliated ordinary citizens, including many from the broad and notoriously bland middle class (on this socio-political diversity see Montgomery 2002; Alvarez 2003; Goldberg 2003a; Horsey 2003; Kaplan 2003; Tempest 2003; Treneman 2003). The large-scale co-ordination of political actions organised by geographically, culturally and socially disparate groups bears the hallmarks of political networking processes developed by the GJM, which has executed a dramatic series of such decentralised but transnational protests over recent years (see Rupert 2003). And indeed the great anti-war demo of F15 emerged out of plans first laid at the European Social Forum – regional counterpart to the GJM's World Social Forum held in Porto Alegre, Brazil. At least 25,000 people from over 100 countries, including delegates from some 475 civil society groups, attended the European Social Forum in Florence in November 2002. Opposition to US militarism was a central theme of discussion, and 15 February 2003 was designated as the date for Europe-wide protests against the impending war (Baker 2002a; 2002b; Vidal 2002). News of the plan quickly spread by e-mail to activists in North America and elsewhere, where organisers began work co-ordinating local protests.

In the rapid and dramatic emergence of a transnational anti-war movement, electronic mediation via the Internet has been crucial for co-ordination of widely dispersed nodes of political opposition – that is, for creating a sense of 'imagined community' (to use Benedict Anderson's (1991) famous terminology) among persons and groups who might otherwise feel relatively isolated and disempowered, and for facilitating their convergence at particular times and places for collective acts of resistance (see J. Lee 2003; O'Connor 2003; Packer 2003; Webb 2003a; 2003b). In this way, anti-war activists followed in the footsteps of the transnational Zapatista support networks of the 1990s who pioneered use of the Internet to construct an 'electronic fabric of struggle' (Cleaver 1998; 2003; Zapatista Net 1995), and the widespread network of Indymedia websites (112 sites located on six different continents as of April, 2003) which generated transnational flows of decommodified, dialogically formatted, grassroots-oriented information in order both to facilitate and report decentralized yet co-ordinated protests against neoliberal globalisation (Notes from Nowhere 2003: 228–43; Indymedia 2004; Sellers 2004: 189–90).

Using the Internet, United for Peace and Justice (UPJ) – one of the largest anti-war umbrella groups in the United States – organised the massive New York City F15 demonstrations in only six weeks. The group's national co-ordinator, Andrea Buffa, reported that their web page (United for Peace 1993) was receiving in excess of 1.5 million hits per day in March 2003. On the site were listed over 150 different local actions being co-ordinated in advance for whatever day the war began. In another indicator of the significance of electronic mediation, Internet-based organiser MoveOn.org claimed an e-mail list of about 2 million people (O'Connor 2003). More than a million people responded to MoveOn's appeal for a 'Virtual March on Washington' on 26 February 2003, bombarding Congressional offices with carefully timed e-mails, faxes and phone calls (Packer 2003). Win Without War, the self-consciously mainstream peace coalition with which MoveOn has been affiliated, told the *New York Times* that it raised over $400,000 in 48 hours through an Internet fundraising appeal. Further, the coalition was able electronically to organise around 6,800 candlelight vigils during the week the war started (Zernike and Murphy 2003). One of the major sources of information and critical analysis about imperial tendencies within the Bush administration has been a virtual think tank, the Foreign Policy in Focus project, co-founded by the Institute for Policy Studies and the Inter-hemispheric Resource Center, both long-standing participants in the GJM (Foreign Policy in Focus 2004). In the opposition to Bush's war, as in the GJM, electronically mediated networks of otherwise autonomous groups and coalitions have been vitally important.

Another crucial set of connections has to do with the persons and groups involved in the GJM who have actively participated in and facilitated the development of the transnational peace movement, and their ability to forge conceptual linkages between these political projects. I have already mentioned the origins of the F15 demonstrations in the European Social Forum in November 2002. Transnational opposition to the war was also propelled by the 2003 Porto Alegre World Social Forum, attended by perhaps 100,000 persons from 126 countries in late January: 'fighting militarism and promoting peace' was designated as a central theme of the grassroots activist extravaganza. In a statement entitled 'Resistance to Neoliberalism, War and Militarism', the 2003 World Social Forum denounced the 'permanent global war to cement the domination of the US government and its allies' as 'another face of neoliberalism, a face which is brutal and unacceptable. ... Opposition to the war is at the heart of our movement' (in Fisher and Ponniah 2003: 347). After Porto Alegre, author–activist George Monbiot suggested a genetic connection between the GJM and the nascent global peace movement:

> the anti-war campaign has, in large part, grown out of the global justice movement. This movement has never recognised a distinction between the power of the rich world's governments and their appointed institutions (the IMF, the World Bank, the World Trade Organization) to wage economic warfare and the power of the same governments, working through a different set of institutions (the UN security council, NATO) to send in the Bombers. ... the impending war has reinforced our determination to tackle the grotesque maldistribution of power which permits a few national governments to assert a global mandate.
>
> (Monbiot 2003)

The distinguished Egyptian scholar Samir Amin was more direct: 'As long as the aggressive, fascist strategy of the United States is not defeated, an alternative globalisation will not be possible' (quoted in Ehrenreich 2003). Despite the clear and explicit focus on neoliberal capitalism and militarism as forms of global power in which the United States continues to be deeply implicated, activists from the United States were embraced at Porto Alegre in a spirit of transnational solidarity that did not succumb to divisive nationalisms. Indeed featured speaker Tariq Ali stressed the importance of carrying the struggle into 'the heartland of the empire' (quoted in Ehrenreich 2003). At the same time some participants in the World Social Forum reminded the US delegates that, as a consequence of US global power and attendant privilege, American activists bear a special responsibility to 'democratize your own country' (quoted in Ehrenreich 2003).

Intimate connections with the GJM are clearly apparent within the US wing of the anti-war movement. While early opposition to the impending war was organised by International ANSWER – a coalition associated with a tiny party of the sectarian left – large, diverse and non-sectarian anti-war coalitions emerged and played key roles in organising the massive turnouts for F15. Representatives of more than seventy different social movement groups and NGOs met in Washington on 25 October 2002 and formed a more ecumenical coalition with the simple and broadly appealing message 'Say NO! to war'. Among the founders of the United for Peace and Justice coalition were persons and groups deeply involved in the GJM: prominent among them Jon Cavanagh of the Institute for Policy Studies and Medea Benjamin of Global Exchange. Both organisations contributed substantial staff time and resources to the rapid creation of a broad-based anti-war movement. In addition to the seminal involvement of the Institute for Policy Studies and Global Exchange, the United for Peace and Justice coalition of more than 200 member groups contains names familiar to anyone who has followed the GJM: Anti-Capitalist Convergence, Greenpeace, Ruckus Society, the Student Environmental Action Coalition, and United Students against Sweatshops, among others. Almost simultaneously, a somewhat overlapping constellation of groups founded Win Without War as 'America's mainstream antiwar coalition', explicitly oriented towards 'patriotic Americans' who 'reject the doctrine that our country, alone, has the right to launch first-strike attacks' (Win Without War 2003). In addition to a constellation of celebrity spokespersons, Win Without War affiliates included the National Council of Churches, the Lutheran, Methodist and Unitarian Churches, the United Church of Christ, the Quakers (AFSC), the Sierra Club and Greenpeace, the National Association for the Advancement of Colored People (NAACP) and Jesse Jackson's Rainbow/Push Coalition, the National Organisation for Women (NOW), the National Gay and Lesbian Task Force, Oxfam America, and MoveOn. These were the coalitions which mobilised impressive numbers of protests across the United States in co-ordination with the F15 global day of action (see Kaplan 2003; Packer 2003; Zernike and Murphy 2003).

But despite its spectacular early successes, the US wing of the anti-war movement clearly lost its momentum after President Bush announced the start of the war amid wall-to-wall television coverage of the bombing of Baghdad on 19 March 2003. Within the movement there were divisions over tactics, with some arguing that since peaceful protests had been ignored in the halls of power, large-scale campaigns of non-violent direct action were called for. Others argued that it would be counterproductive for the movement to disrupt daily life and alienate more mainstream opponents of the war whose support would be required to build a broad-based, long-term campaign against the Bush administration and its militarist strategy (Garafoli 2003; Goldberg 2003b).

Relatedly, as US forces entered combat, the peace movement was put on the defensive by a surge in public opinion favouring the war (peaking at around 70 per cent) and the widespread demand that all loyal Americans must 'support the troops', implying that criticism of the war served Saddam's purposes and was a betrayal of those risking their lives for their country. Framing the 'war on terror' in terms of a 'prescriptive, militarist patriotism', conservative forces in and out of government waged a multi-front assault on political dissent (Platt and O'Leary 2003). The US peace movement saw this coming and attempted to incorporate patriotism and support for the troops into its message, but this was clearly a defensive strategy which did not succeed in sustaining the momentum of F15 (Campbell 2003; Farhi 2003; Salladay 2003; Younge 2003).

Finally, the peace movement failed to mobilise African–Americans in significant numbers, in spite of that community's deeper scepticism towards the war and despite the efforts of organisers such as Black Voices for Peace. Even as it invaded Iraq, the Bush administration was advancing the neoconservative agenda and attacking the domestic priorities of African–Americans by, amongst other things, undermining affirmative action; expanding military spending at the expense of public schools, health care and housing; and enacting tax policies overwhelmingly beneficial to wealthy (disproportionately white) Americans (Ciria-Cruz 2003; Montgomery 2003). Despite prominent black leadership in the anti-war movement, by failing early on to prioritise the connection between social justice issues and imperial militarism, the movement seems to have missed an opportunity to build relations of trans-racial solidarity – a possibility which might have contributed to overcoming a similar racial imbalance in the US wing of the GJM (on which see Rupert 2004b).

As the US military rolled through Iraq and the magnitude of demonstrations declined, peace groups responded by taking a more strategic view and asking how best to maintain some of the momentum of the largest peace movement in decades. The bigger, more broad-based coalitions – Win Without War and United for Peace and Justice – hoped to gather support for a more substantial multilateral role in rebuilding postwar Iraq, and to be ready to respond should the Bush administration target Iran, Syria or somebody else for military confrontation. The National Council of Churches and Working Assets and others are launching humanitarian assistance drives for Iraq. Win Without War, MoveOn, Working Assets and other groups are also emphasising electoral politics in hopes of effecting domestic regime change. Damu Smith of Black Voices for Peace planned voter registration and education efforts to dramatise the war's domestic costs and to mobilise

African–American voters in the next election cycle (see Campbell 2003; Ciria-Cruz 2003; Garafoli 2003; Nieves 2003). Phyllis Bennis and Jon Cavanagh of the Institute for Policy Studies suggested strengthening relations of transnational solidarity to counter Bush's imperial project: 'Building our ties with other parts of this international mobilisation will help strengthen our movement's "anti-empire" identity' and help to link opposition to US militarism to larger issues of central concern to the global justice movement (Bennis and Cavanagh 2003). Medea Benjamin, veteran activist with Global Exchange and co-founder of United for Peace and Justice as well as Code Pink, also saw the peace movement in a context of potential global transformation: 'It is through strengthening this global movement for peace and justice – a movement never before seen – that we can bring about sweeping changes in who makes decisions for our global community and in whose interests those decisions are made' (Benjamin 2003).

Conclusion: pessimism of the will, optimism of the intellect?

The neo-imperial moment poses great challenges to the nascent GJM, many of whose activists have been up to their elbows in anti-war work. Will they be able to articulate connections between neoliberal global capitalism and the coercive power of the US government in ways that resonate with 'popular common sense' and that are convincing to the broad publics which participated in the anti-war movement? Will they be able to mobilise opposition to US neo-imperialism in ways which do not simply degenerate into anti-Americanism (readily compatible with resurgent nationalisms), but which reach out in solidarity to progressive social forces everywhere – including in the United States? Will they be able to develop an agenda which challenges the strategy of empire but which goes beyond it to transform the structures of transnational inequality that enable empire and which empire is designed to defend? The answers to such questions will, I think, determine whether or not the GJM can survive in the neo-imperial moment, and whether or not it can combine with anti-war struggles to form a potentially counter-hegemonic force.

Based on my perspective in the 'homeland' of the empire, I find it hard to be optimistic. To the extent that building relations of solidarity across national boundaries is the *sine qua non* of the global justice and anti-war movements, the violent reassertion of US power in the service of US global privilege, the mobilisation of popular jingoism in support of this (re)militarised imperialism, and the suppression of alternative voices within the United States are likely to weaken these movements in significant ways. I do not mean to suggest by this that activists worldwide will not continue to oppose US neo-imperialism and global capitalism. On the contrary, I am sure that such opposition will continue to mount. However I suspect that movement activists will have great difficulty constructing social spaces of transnational solidarity – and emergent norms of reciprocity and collective responsibility – which potentially include many or most Americans. Further, I fear that global justice and peace activists will be perceived within US political culture as marginal malcontents, and the social spaces imagined by them are likely to be understood by most Americans as coming from 'outside', as un-American, implicitly flawed and potentially treacherous. If the GJM does in fact need American social movements to democratise the United States as an integral part of the project of global democratisation – the reciprocal responsibility inherent in transnational solidarity, as was pointed out to US activists at Porto Alegre – the onset of a neo-imperial moment and the powerful reactivation of longstanding and deeply rooted cultural tendencies towards American exceptionalism and privilege cannot but damage the culture of transnational solidarity which the movement has struggled to construct.

My feelings of discouragement within this neo-imperial conjuncture, however, are tempered by those intellectual arguments which convince me that the structures of global capitalism and their current imperial instantiation remain deeply contradictory and cannot be permanently normalised (Halliday 2002; Wood 2002; 2003; Callinicos 2003b; Panitch and Gindin 2003). The emergent political culture of transnational solidarity may be, for a time, disrupted or contained, but it cannot be extinguished.

Notes

1 American exceptionalism, articulating liberalism with a self-righteous and militant nationalism, has longstanding residence in popular common sense in the United States and has been profoundly influential in shaping US foreign policy for over a century (see Hunt 1987). This theme is also central to my analyses of ideological struggles implicated in the construction of US global power (Rupert 1995; 2000).

2 I am grateful to Diane Swords for calling to my attention some of the continuities between NSC-68 and Bush's *National Security Strategy*.

3 In the US political context, 'neoconservative' refers to a political tendency which had its roots in a band of Cold War liberals who, during the 1960s and 1970s, became increasingly disillusioned with welfare state policies and the perceived dominance of the anti-war McGovernite wing within the Democratic Party, and gravitated to anti-communist, free-market political positions overlapping (if not entirely congruent) with the emergent New Right. As a result of this ideological confluence, the neocons shared in the largesse of strategically targeted conservative funding from the likes of the Bradley, Scaife and Olin foundations (on which, see note 5 below) and became part of the Reagan revolution. The influence of the neocons was especially pronounced in Reagan's vigorously anti-communist foreign policy: 'Neoconservatives believed in the role of the United States as world leader: the defeat of communism was a first step toward spreading American-style "democracy" around the world' (Diamond 1995: 275; also chs 8–9). On the more recent, second-generation neocons and Bush II foreign policy, see Barry and Lobe (2002a; 2002b), Dreyfuss (2002), Lobe (2002b), Vest (2002), Carr (2003), Drew (2003), Hersh (2003) and Murphy (2003). On the sometimes uneasy alliance between the neocons and old-fashioned

conservatives (such as Cheney, Rumsfeld or Bolton) who may be enthusiastic about muscular exercises of unilateral military power but are sceptical towards the expansive state-building commitments implicit in the neocon agenda of 'democratic imperialism', see Daniel (2002), Baker and Fidler (2003) and Daalder and Lindsay (2003).

4 On the roots of this strategy, see Armstrong (2002), Keller (2002), Lemann (2002), Boyer (2003), Dreyfuss (2003a; 2003b), Purdum (2003) and Mann (2004). Useful analyses of its implications include Anderson (2002), Falk (2002), Ikenberry (2002), Callinicos (2003b), Panitch and Gindin (2003) and Everest (2004); compare the altogether more credulous and sanguine view of Gaddis (2002).

5 Kristol's New Citizenship Project (which served as midwife to the PNAC) and the PNAC itself have been supported by regular infusions of cash from the ultra-conservative Bradley, Sarah Scaife and John M. Olin foundations. These leading conservative foundations, along with a few others, have for decades strategically invested in the development of right-wing think tanks, quasi-academic institutes, conservative magazines and journals, researchers, polemicists and policy networks. All of this contributed mightily to the ideological infrastructure of the Reagan revolution and the ratcheting rightward of US political culture over the last quarter of a century (see People for the American Way 1996; Paget 1998; Chinoy and Kaiser 1999; Kaiser and Chinoy 1999; Barry and Lobe 2002a; Murphy 2003; Media Transparency 2003a; 2003b; 2003c; 2003d). It was this hot-house environment of conservative funding and ideas which, during the 1990s, sustained and nurtured the ultra-hawks and gave birth to their foreign policy vehicle, the PNAC.

6 Note that Schmidt is drawing on an ascendant tendency within American IR scholarship – the so-called 'democratic peace' literature – in order to rationalise the PNAC's neo-imperial project. For a critique of the democratic peace literature which broadens into a critical examination of the politics of US political science more generally, see Oren (2003).

7 It is noteworthy – especially on a Gramscian view – that the PNAC is deeply embedded with conservative organisations waging the 'culture wars' on American campuses, such as Lynne Cheney's 'American Council of Trustees and Alumni', William Bennett's 'Americans for Victory over Terrorism', and Daniel Pipes' 'Campus Watch'. Their leading personas are drawn from the incestuous tangle of right-wing political networks, the ideological visions they project are very nearly congruent, and they are funded by the Bradley, Scaife and Olin foundations discussed above. In the wake of the terrorist attacks of 9–11, these organisations have sought to pressure insufficiently loyal US academics into eschewing critical re-examination of the role of the United States in the world and instead to reaffirm what they refer to as 'traditional Western values' – axiomatically identified as 'the great heritage of human civilisation' (Martin and Neal 2002: 5) – which are understood to be embodied in the United States and for which US foreign policy is seen as a powerful evangelical vehicle. On the role of these organisations in the campus culture wars, see Eakin (2001), Healy (2001), Lobe (2002a), Goldberg (2002) and Platt and O'Leary (2003).

3 Globalisations, violences and resistances in Mozambique

The struggles continue

Branwen Gruffydd Jones[1]

Este é um tempo de exculsão social, o tempo de uma outra Internacional, a do Capital [This is a time of social exclusion, a time of another International, that of Capital].[2]

(Serra 1999: 119)

A sociedade do mercado livre vestiu-se com a roupagem da bandalheira [Free-market society has dressed in the shabby clothes of the shameless].

(Couto 2003)

[H]istory holds together and ... purported ruptures, although appearing as such to those who are close to them, are more like fissures or cracks when seen from a distance.

(Depelchin 1999: 157)

Introduction

Attention is being drawn with increasing frequency to the phenomenon of an, the or many anti-globalisation movement/s. While the term globalisation suggests some common process happening everywhere, exactly what that involves necessarily varies widely according to context – the world, as many have pointed out, is becoming 'globalised', but in most respects it is not becoming homogenised. What does this mean for our understanding of what constitutes struggles against globalisation? What kinds of struggles are now being waged, in different parts of our globalised world? What kinds of struggles *can* now be waged?

The term globalisation is used here to signify a specific period in the world-historical development of capitalism. The remarkable twentieth century began with much of the world controlled by European colonial powers, and ended with most of the world, whose peoples are now organised territorially in the form of sovereign states, accepting the imperatives of free trade, free markets and private property in a liberal world market order. In between, the twentieth century witnessed the rise and demise of Soviet and Chinese communism, state socialism in Eastern Europe, anti-colonial and anti-imperial revolutions in formerly colonised societies and, in many cases, subsequent attempts to follow a non-capitalist path of development, as well as the considerable strengthening of the organised labour movement in the West. It is following the weakening, co-optation, destruction or collapse of these various non- and anti-capitalist struggles of the twentieth century that the current phase of triumphalist capitalist hegemony – globalisation – has emerged (see Ahmad 2000; 2002: 96–106).

This chapter examines a part of the world that has suffered centuries of adjustment to the more general and much longer process of capitalist globalisation. It focuses on specific forms of resistance and struggle that have arisen in and against the condition of globalisation in the particular context of Mozambique. Mozambique is a modern state, located structurally and spatially in what is often termed the periphery of the global political economy. Its boundaries, social formation and social condition were shaped in part by the 'crucible of colonialism' (Ahmad 1992: 17–34); subsequently by the revolutionary armed struggle for independence and the beginnings of a quest for a non-capitalist path to development; then brutalised by a highly destructive war which, notwithstanding its internal dynamics, was also a fundamental moment in the global counter-revolution[3] that eventually issued in the current phase of globalisation. Mozambique is now seen in some quarters as a success story of globalisation. It has obediently followed the discipline of neoliberal reform, and has witnessed periods of remarkable economic growth. Indeed, according to recent figures from the UN Conference on Trade and Development (UNCTAD 2002: 4), Mozambique is among the 'high growth economies' of the least developed countries, near the top of the table, behind only Equatorial Guinea and the Maldives. The World Bank notes approvingly that 'Mozambique's growth rate has been well above the African average and among the highest in the world. ... Economic growth was 8.3% in 2002 and is projected at between 7% and 12% annually until 2005' (World Bank 2003: 1, 3). Yet underlying these widely celebrated figures, the concrete condition of globalisation in Mozambique is characterised by profound inequalities, enormous deprivation alongside enormous enrichment, corruption, fraud and violent, socially destructive forms of accumulation. What forms of struggle are arising in this specific context of globalisation?

Rather than documenting a particular, identifiable element of 'the anti-globalisation movement', this chapter is concerned with prior questions about the conditions of possibility for social change. It explores how forms of resistance and struggle in the particular context of Mozambique are structured *and limited* by the concrete conditions and social relations of globalisation. The problem of conceptualising resistance to globalisation is posed in the first part of the chapter. Two points are emphasised with regard to critical social enquiry: the need for a methodological approach which foregrounds the concrete specificity of empirical conditions; and the need to move beyond a focus on existing forms of movement organising to examine also the structural limits to struggle arising from concrete conditions and social relations. Accordingly the chapter then moves to examine the condition of globalisation in Mozambique, which is characterised by structural violence and insecurity. In the era of globalisation, the logic of capital is imposed through processes of 'adjustment' that are conceptualised here in the form of a dialectic between the 'adjustment of accumulation' and the 'adjustment of daily lives', each characterised by specific forms of violence. The third part of the chapter examines two very different forms of struggle and resistance generated by the dialectic: first, articulate professional struggles against corruption and primitive accumulation; second, the widespread but rarely examined and highly circumscribed resistances of the majority against daily-endured conditions of social crisis.

Critical theory and anti-globalisation resistance

This book explores the relationship between critical theories about world politics and social movement resistances to globalisation. Over the past two decades, critical approaches have developed in the discipline of international relations (IR) that are centrally concerned with the possibilities and trajectories of transformatory social practices and emancipatory goals (e.g. Neufeld 1995; Murphy and Tooze 1991; Gill 1993; for overviews, see Devetak 2001; Linklater 1996b).[4] Such critical approaches have much to offer enquiry into struggles against globalisation, and such an enquiry should be of central concern to them. The growing magnitude of organised protest and movements against globalisation and for social justice is a vital emergent feature of world politics in the current era. Many diverse and often conflicting groups and interests converge at the same points in time or space with, if not the same goals, at least apparently the same enemies. This phenomenon is quite properly receiving considerable attention from critical scholars, within and beyond IR (e.g. Wilkin 1999; Danaher and Marks 2003; Opel and Pompper 2003; Broad 2002; Kingsnorth 2003; Notes from Nowhere 2003; Fisher and Ponniah 2003).

However, if we are to gain a broader appreciation of the social contradictions and emergent struggles generated by capitalism in this historical phase of globalisation, we must also look beyond the most visible forms of social movement organisation. The combined legacy of twentieth-century social forms and struggles (especially those in the West) and twentieth-century social theorising has left an implicit image (at least among many Western academics) of 'resistance' as taking place on the streets or at the workplace (factory), organised through labour unions and popular movements. But practices of resistance and struggle emerge always in determinate forms, arising from, shaped and limited by historically specific, concrete conditions and contexts (material, economic, political, cultural, individual), structured and reproduced by specific sets of social relations. The concern of critical social enquiry with emancipatory practice must be conceived in a way that directs attention beyond already existing, visible forms of organised political activity, and that asks broader questions about the conditions of possibility for change and transformation in the current conjuncture. This entails two moves.

First, rather than beginning enquiry with already existing, visible movements, we should begin by exploring the concrete condition of globalisation in specific contexts and the possibilities of struggle to which this gives rise. Prior to the construction of movements in a particular context there must be forms of consciousness and diverse strategies of resistance and struggle from which a more directed and conscious collective movement for social change might emerge. The forms of resistance and consciousness that can and do emerge are products of the specific concrete conditions and experiences of globalisation in a particular context, and their underlying social relations. It is therefore necessary to adopt a method of analysis that comprehends the historical specificity and concrete detail of the condition of globalisation in different contexts. As Marx himself stressed:

> the same economic basis – the same in its major conditions – ... display[s] ... endless variations and gradations in its appearance, as the result of innumerable different empirical circumstances, natural conditions, racial relations, historical influences acting from outside, etc., and these can only be understood by analysing these empirically given conditions.
>
> (Marx 1991 [1894]: 927–8)

The globalisation phase of world capitalist development is producing endlessly nuanced and uneven conditions and corresponding struggles and resistances (Gills 2000b; cf. Marx 1993 [1858]: 193). Not all reach the streets in the form of an identifiable 'movement', nor are all necessarily labelled by participants as 'anti-globalisation'. Further, as Sivanandan emphasises, many are 'not necessarily working-class struggles against capital as such, but resistances to the political project of the global market – call it neo-liberalism if you like – as it impacts on people's lives and livelihoods' (1999: 15). Thus we should heed the observation of Chin and Mittelman that 'an ontology of resistance to globalization requires grounding' (2000: 43). We must ground the ontology of resistance to globalisation in the concrete experiences and struggles of peoples suffering the various 'empirically given conditions' of globalised capitalism in their concrete specificity.

Second, we should take seriously the ways in which the social relations of globalisation give rise to, but also constrain and limit, possibilities of political struggle. Critical social enquiry with a concern for transformation and emancipation must ask these prior questions about conditions of possibility. This requires exploration of conditions that *do not* give rise to explicit practices of organised resistance and political movement, in addition to examining social movements that already exist. The problem of political consciousness – how individuals and groups in different material, social and cultural conditions attain a certain consciousness of their condition and their interests, and how this informs the kinds of political action or support they engage in – underlies the *possibility and limits* of the emergence of collective movements for change. This was a central concern of critical theorists involved in two major historical struggles of the twentieth century – the international socialist movement and the anti-colonial struggles – from Lenin, Luxemburg and Gramsci to Fanon, Cabral and Nkrumah.

These two methodological emphases point us towards empirical study which foregrounds the actual conditions and structured social relations characteristic of the current conjuncture, and acknowledges the limits to real transformation, as well as celebrating and expressing solidarity towards 'the movement of movements' (Mertes 2004).

The condition of globalisation in Mozambique: a social order of structural violence

For many countries of the so-called Third World, globalisation signifies a process of adjustment to the requirements of global capital, enforced from outside and mediated by national bourgeoisies. This, the latest in centuries of enforced adjustment (Balogun 1997), is effected through the peculiarly technocratic form of power which is one of the defining features of contemporary imperialism: the imposition of economic policy reforms through the 'conditionalities' of International Monetary Fund (IMF) and World Bank lending to structurally indebted economies. The fundamental core of neoliberal policies is enforced reorganisation of the economy in the interests of global profit rather than local human need.

The abstract logic of profit can never actually overcome the concrete logic of human need, however. This is one of the fundamental contradictions at the heart of capitalism, and in this era of globalisation it is generating specific phenomena of individual, social and environmental crisis, exhaustion and violence, alongside cancerous forms of growth and accumulation (see Collier 1994; Brennan 2000; McMurtry 1999; 2002; Forrester 1999). The reorganisation of social conditions in the interests of enhanced and more rapid circulation and accumulation of profit implies the reorganisation of the conditions of real, concrete individuals, communities and societies, whose logics are quite different from those of capital. This process must be conceptualised as a form of structural violence. The routine and normalised structural violence of neoliberal reform characterises societies such as Mozambique, heralded as 'success stories' of economic growth.

In Mozambique, the neoliberal era followed in the wake of previous struggles against adjustment to capitalist globalisation: first, the long, armed struggle for independence from Portugal; and, second, the attempt to pursue a non-capitalist path towards social progress and justice. Orthodox accounts of 'postwar reconstruction' and 'development' in Mozambique assert, in a neutral and approving manner, the self-evident 'fact' that, during the mid-1980s, the Frelimo government abandoned its socialist values and state-planned economic policies in favour of market reforms and a transition to multiparty democracy (e.g. World Bank 1998: xiii–xiv; Government of Mozambique (GOM) 2001: 1–2). Such technical accounts remove from view the conditions under which this 'policy change' took place, thus contributing to the naturalisation and entrenchment of neoliberal ideology. In fact, the conditions of possibility for Mozambique's struggle to pursue a non-capitalist route to social development were deliberately destroyed through externally orchestrated war. Placing emphasis on the historical, structured conditions of 'agency' does not in itself entail an uncritical acceptance of all aspects of Frelimo's socialist/Marxist–Leninist project. However, it should be acknowledged that very significant gains were made in the first years of independence, especially in areas of health and education.[5] Further, it is hardly surprising that some aspects of economic policies were imbalanced and poorly managed and co-ordinated, given the conditions of Mozambican society after Portuguese colonial rule, especially the desperately low levels of education and professional, technical training among black Mozambicans. As Cardoso argued, 'the Mozambicans in 1975 were starting from scratch' (1987: 11). Finally, the attempt to create a non-capitalist society in independent Mozambique was relentlessly and deliberately undermined by the war of destabilisation initiated by Ian Smith's regime in Rhodesia and then, after Zimbabwe's independence, continued and intensified by the activities of Renamo, co-ordinated and funded by South Africa, with the tacit and material support of the West. The economic and social costs of this war (see e.g. Serra 2001: 7–8; Nhabinde 1999; Marshall 1990; Cammack 1987; Cliff and Noormahomed 1988), combined with rising oil costs, falling commodity prices in the world market and a severe regional drought, meant that by the mid-1980s the conditions for the very reproduction of Mozambican society were beyond the control of Frelimo. Under such conditions the only 'choice' was to turn to Western donors and financial institutions for assistance, and to accept the demands for reform which inevitably followed.

Neoliberal reform in Mozambique, which began in 1987 and increased significantly after the end of the war in 1992, entailed the standard recipe of currency devaluation, deregulation and liberalisation of trade, elimination of export and foreign exchange controls, privatisation, and reduction of social spending. These reforms were implemented during and after the war between Frelimo and Renamo. With the end of the war in 1992 soldiers were demobilised from both forces, and thousands of refugees and internally displaced people began to return. Further, regional and global processes of crisis, adjustment and reform resulted in thousands of Mozambicans returning from former employment in South Africa, and from the former GDR and Soviet Union. These overlapping conditions created a desperate societal need for order and security, through employment and provision of social services. Instead the social order was reorganised in the interests of the security of capital accumulation. Imposed on the material and social devastation of years of war, the combination of privatisation, liberalisation and reduction in social expenditure has entrenched and exacerbated already existing deprivations and insecurities, while creating new forms of accumulation and exclusion.

According to official statistics, 69.4 per cent of the population of Mozambique are 'absolutely poor'. Three out of four Mozambican women cannot read or write; the vast majority of the population do not have access to clean drinking water (GOM 2001: 14) and Mozambique's maternal mortality rate is among the highest in the world, estimated at 1,500 out of 100,000 live births (the figure in the UK is seven) (IRIN News 2002). The condition of globalisation in Mozambique is thus a social order of insecurity and structural violence for the majority, involving routine violation of human needs and values, and generating further forms of violence and insecurity. As Bourdieu observes:

> You cannot cheat with the *law of the conservation of violence*: all violence is paid for, and, for example, the structural violence exerted by the financial markets, in the form of layoffs, loss of security, etc., is matched sooner or later in the form of suicides, crime and delinquency, drug addiction, alcoholism, a whole host of minor and major everyday acts of violence.
>
> (Bourdieu 1998: 40, emphasis in original)

In Mozambique the structural violence of globalisation is exerted through the processes of 'adjustment'. This is manifest in a dialectic of two related but opposed logics of adjustment, and corresponding practices of struggle and resistance: the adjustment of accumulation and the adjustment of daily lives. The adjustment of accumulation enables vast enrichment for some, through parasitic and corrupt practices of dispossession. The corruption that has saturated Mozambican society is being resisted by members of the middle classes – journalists, lawyers, economists. These can, following Serra (2003), be conceived as struggles within the realm of the *mundo não problemático*.[6] The other face of the dialectic of adjustment, the concrete adjustments of daily lives of the poor and excluded, gives rise to very different forms of struggle and resistance: struggles not for social change but for survival; not against, but outside society. These are the struggles of the inhabitants of what Serra calls the *mundo problemático*.

The adjustment of accumulation

The imposed adjustment of accumulation in peripheral economies effects a reordering of social relations by reconstituting public and private spheres and processes of production, accumulation and social distribution. As Gowan explains, it

> involves a shift in the internal social relationships within states in favour of creditor and rentier interests, with the subordination of productive sectors to financial sectors and with a drive to shift wealth and power and security away from the bulk of the working population.
>
> (Gowan 1999: vii–viii)

It thus effects a basic adjustment of the balance of power from those social forces pursuing a broadly collective approach to social change to those pursuing an essentially private approach. Economic reform in Mozambique from the late 1980s, especially the process of privatisation, has aligned the interests of members of the political elite with the neo-colonial agenda of the international financial institutions and creditor countries. The creation of 'business-friendly environments' – the relentless endorsement of entrepreneurs and the private sector in pursuit of 'economic growth' – creates conditions in which practices of parasitic, primitive accumulation thrive.[7] Couto (2002) has observed that such adjustment of accumulation has created some very rich people in Mozambique, but it has not created a wealthy Mozambique.

The privatisation programme, 'bedevilled by lack of transparency' (Castel-Branco *et al.* 2001: 1), has been a causal process in the reordering of social relations. It is not only the fact of privatisation per se, but how it was achieved, which has created a structural condition conducive to parasitic, primitive accumulation. Privatisation was extensive and rapid, pushed through by the international institutions with no care as to regulation of the process, or implementation of appropriate regulatory or industrial policies by the state (Castel-Branco *et al.* 2001; Hanlon 2002). On one hand this enabled a systematic process of personal enrichment of members of the political elite, within or connected to Frelimo, Renamo and the army. Many companies were sold off cheaply and have not been rehabilitated, many loans have not been repaid and thousands of workers have been left without salaries for months or even years.[8] On the other hand the largest enterprises and utilities – gas fields and other mineral resources, water services, port and railway transport corridors – have been sold to external capital. Three closely related phenomena have emerged as integral to this process: financial fraud and money-laundering; organised crime; and corruption.

Hanlon (2002) has detailed the various practices of fraud which have been systematic in the banking sector since the early 1990s, through which significant sums have been removed from the banks. The rapid privatisation of Mozambique's commercial banks in 1996–7, forced through by the World Bank and IMF, served to entrench such practices. The tendering process transferred ownership of the banks to networks of businessmen who were members of or connected to Frelimo. The pace of privatisation allowed no proper audit of the banks before they were sold. Most notoriously, 144 billion *meticais* (around US$14 million at the exchange rate at the time) were removed prior to the privatisation of Banco Commercial de Moçambique (BCM). This was not an isolated instance, but a manifestation of systemic practice (Hanlon 2002). Through fraud, accumulation of 'bad debts' or simple mismanagement, the two privatised banks BCM and Banco Austral generated significant losses in the years following privatisation (see *Mozambiquefile* November 2000, 292: 4–6 and July 2001, 300: 15–17). Hanlon estimates that since the mid-1990s a total of around US$400 million has been 'siphoned off' from the two banks. Money-laundering has become integral to Mozambique's banking and foreign exchange system. The number of foreign exchange bureaux operating in Maputo has expanded enormously in recent years (Gastrow and Mosse 2002). It is widely suspected that one mode of money-laundering is investment in the many new hotels, restaurants and other building projects which have become such a prominent feature of Mozambique's cities in recent years (Gastrow and Mosse 2002: 9).

Under these conditions, Mozambique's towns and cities have witnessed a significant rise in the rate of violence and crime (Serra 2003: 15–16; Ética Moçambique 2001). The rise in gun crime includes 'car-jacking' and armed bank robberies (Massingue 1996; Vines 1998), in addition to other forms of armed robbery such as theft of mobile phones at knife-point. This is related to various factors, including levels of unemployment and poverty, and the availability of guns left over from the war. Some of this crime is committed by the poor and unemployed – individuals brutalised by war who face little prospect of regular employment. However, more significant are groups involved in 'organised crime': drug trafficking, smuggling stolen cars and other illegal trading, which have all increased significantly since the early 1990s and which are connected to the rise in money-laundering (Gastrow and Mosse 2002; Paulino 2003). Since the end of the war, Mozambique has become a new transit point on international drug-trafficking routes, from Latin America via Mozambique to Nigeria and on to Europe, and from South East Asia (in particular Pakistan) via Mozambique to South Africa and on to Europe (Observatoire Geopolitique des Drogues (OGD) Report 2001: 241; Paulino 2003; Laniel 2001; United Nations Office for Drug Control and Crime Prevention (UNODCCP) 1999).

Within Mozambique, what sustains the routine trafficking of drugs and stolen cars is the equally routine 'trafficking of influences' (Paulino 2003).[9] Practices of corruption range from direct involvement, close connections between criminal groups and members of the political elite, protection of criminals by senior officials in the government, police and judicial system (e.g. by delaying or preventing investigations and court cases, organising early releases or escapes from prison), to collusion, bribes and 'turning a blind eye' by lower level officials in the institutions of the police, prison services and customs (Gastrow and Mosse 2002: 8–10; Paulino 2003). Public despair and cynicism have grown in the face of such routine, high-level corruption. While the wealthy and well connected buy their protection or their escape, however, the crimes of the poor are punished, and suspected or convicted petty thieves languish in filthy overcrowded prisons.[10]

Adjusted lives

The celebratory language of economic growth masks the corruption and violence of accumulation detailed above. It also obscures the routine conditions suffered by those who, according to the language of orthodox economics, fall under the perverse categories of 'ultra-poor' (Ministry of Planning and Finance 1998: 58) or 'micro-entrepreneurs': the multiple violences of social exclusion in the *mundo problemático*. These conditions are related through the dialectic of adjustment, which gives rise to both accumulation and *dispossession*.

Economic adjustment in Mozambique has created two processes that underlie the condition of exclusion and dispossession suffered by the poor and 'ultra-poor'. First, the process of currency devaluation has entailed a massive increase in the cost of living for the majority in society. With the first devaluation, prices rose 200 per cent while salaries rose only 50 per cent; with the second, prices rose 100 per cent and salaries only 50 per cent (Serra 2003: 28). In 2001, the minimum monthly wage was around US$33.6 (665,706 *meticais*), enough for less than 40 per cent of the basic needs of an average-sized family of five, forcing families to send their children to work (*Mozambiquefile* June 2000, 299: 17–18). In 2003, the minimum wage increased to around US$41 per month (982,717 *meticais*), which still only covers about half the basic needs of workers (*Mozambiquefile* May 2003, 322: 21). Added to and exacerbating the effects of this has been the imposition of charges for education and health care.

Second, privatisation and liberalisation have entailed the loss of livelihood for thousands of people. Since 1987, more than 1,470 companies have been privatised, a third of which are now paralysed, their workers unemployed or with suspended contracts, and many other companies are in crisis with a risk of closure. Overall more than 116,000 workers had lost their jobs by 2001 (Sindicato Nacional dos Trabalhadores de Moçambique cited in Serra 2001: 10). It is not just the 'worker' who loses their livelihood when they lose their job, but the five, six or more members of their family. For some, the absence of possibilities of formal and secure employment is substituted by a return to the economy of subsistence in the countryside. Here they join the majority of the population who have never had the possibility of paid employment, except perhaps on a seasonal or migratory basis. Yet in the countryside, just as in towns, the imperatives of the market unleashed by neoliberal reform undermine the possibilities of making ends meet, through the falling value of crops compared with the goods in the shops, and the conditions of unregulated competition. The *camponeses*[11] in the countryside experience economic adjustment through the continuous increase in cost of goods they need to buy and the decreasing value of the crops they try to sell:

> you need to take large quantities of your produce just to buy one *kapulana*.[12] The prices are very low. Yes ... the prices in the shops are very high in relation to the price of our produce. When a *camponês* takes their produce there, to the market, in order to buy one *kapulana* you have to take a lot of your product, and when you get back home you remain hungry. Yes.
>
> (Interview with a group of nine women, Mutepo, Muecate District, Nampula Province, 3 July 1999)

In the cities, towns and suburbs, thousands struggle to survive through petty 'business', buying, making or acquiring goods to sell to anyone with coins in their pocket: second-hand clothing and shoes imported from Europe and North America, chocolate, chewing gum, boiled sweets, cigarettes, cooking oil, exercise books, pens, belts, hair clips, skin cream, bags, cotton thread, second-hand books, soft drinks, beer, fruit and vegetables, samosas, recycled metal and electrical parts. The sprawling, noisy *dumba-nengues* (informal urban markets), as well as the hard surface of city pavements, are the sites of the celebrated 'micro-entrepreneurs' in Mozambique's 'market civilisation' (Gill 1995). This extreme context of 'market civilisation', in which individuals are pitted against each other in the routine and relentless struggle for survival, gives rise to precisely the behavioural patterns and conditions which, centuries earlier, Hume and Hobbes mistakenly assumed to be definitive of human nature per se – the 'propensity to truck, barter and exchange one thing for another' in a context in which life is 'nasty, brutish and short' (Serra 2003). The propensity to sell anything for some coins which can be used to meet any need extends beyond the realm of the *dumba-nengues* to the *lixeiras* (city rubbish tips). The remarkable research of Carlos Serra's team has revealed in detail the lived world of *lixeiros* – those who survive by searching the city's rubbish dumps for items which can be sold or reused – old cans and bottles, scraps of metal and plastic, discarded items of food, remnants of clothing, old tyres, and so on (Chefo 2003; Colaço 2001).[13]

Struggles and resistances

What forms of consciousness, resistance and struggle have arisen in these concrete conditions of globalisation in Mozambique? What kinds of struggle *can* arise, and what are the limits of resistance in such circumstances? These questions will be explored through examination of two very different forms of resistance which, following Serra, can be located in the dialectically related but concretely opposed worlds – the *mundo não problemático* and the *mundo problemático*. On the one hand, the corruption and violence of primitive accumulation is resisted by the middle classes: journalists, lawyers and economists defend values of truth, integrity and the public good which have been increasingly eroded and abandoned in the process of economic adjustment. On the other hand, the conditions of exclusion and routine daily lack and suffering are resisted by the poor and dispossessed in ways that can be seen as the very antithesis of 'the anti-globalisation movement'.

The struggles of the middle classes in the mundo não problemático

For inhabitants of the *mundo não problemático*, the process of neoliberal adjustment has undermined and destroyed conditions and practices that, although already severely constrained and limited, nevertheless embodied some notion of collective societal progress and public interest. The fraud and corruption arising from the adjustment of accumulation are profoundly disturbing not only in themselves, and in the violent dispossessions they bring in their wake, but also in the very social order they signify. The rot of corruption in Mozambique is being resisted in different ways by journalists, lawyers, economists and other professionals and organisations, including some politicians. Corruption involves lies, deception, covering up, secret deals, turning a blind eye. Therefore one of the most important forms of resistance which can emerge to counter corruption is the process of public exposure. In liberal capitalist societies, this responsibility lies mainly with journalists.

The free and critical press in Mozambique is a crucially important and ongoing element of resistance to the social order of globalisation. Mozambique's press laws are recognised as among the most liberal in the world.[14] The Mozambican press constitutes an important forum for articulating resistance through critique and public exposure, by journalists, economists, lawyers, writers, and many others. Newspapers such as *Metical*, *Mediafax*, *Savana* and *Domingo* as well as the English-language monthly *Mozambiquefile* have, with greater or lesser frequency, expressed criticism of the entrenched culture of corruption in the state legal and police institutions. Harvey has identified the free press as a basic contradiction in liberal capitalist societies which contains inherent potential for transformative agency. This arises from society's division of labour where 'individuals with expertise in, say, the discursive realm or the political institutional realm, always have the possibility to exercise some kind of agency for change even within their own limited situations' (1996: 105).

Perhaps the foremost figure in this crucial moment of societal resistance was Carlos Cardoso – one 'individual with expertise in the discursive realm' who exercised very considerable agency for change. Through his journalism and political activity, Cardoso provided precisely the kind of 'relentless criticism' advocated by Marx, 'relentless in the sense that the criticism must not be afraid of its results and just as little afraid of conflict with the powers that be' (Marx 1983 [1843]: 94). In 1992, Cardoso and a group of others founded an independent journalists' co-operative, Mediacoop, and Cardoso edited the new daily paper *Mediafax*, 'the declared purpose of which was to produce investigative journalism, and in-depth articles on issues not normally touched by the other media' (Fauvet 2000). He later left and set up another paper, *Metical*. The writings of Cardoso and his colleagues in *Metical* provided a vociferous and insistent expression of public exposure and critique of neoliberal reform throughout the 1990s. For example, over months and years, the pages of *Metical* provided well-researched critical analysis of the World Bank's policies which destroyed Mozambique's cashew-processing industry, leaving thousands of workers without jobs. Cardoso was relentless in his defence of the common good, and drew explicit attention to the routine conditions of insecurity and disorder that characterise the lived experience of globalisation for ordinary Mozambicans.

Cardoso was not afraid of the results of criticism, and just as little afraid of conflict with the powers that be. He was relentless in exposing the other side of globalisation's cancerous 'economic growth' – the corruption, fraud, money-laundering and smuggling that have enabled a few private individuals to grow enormously rich through social theft. He denounced not only instances of crime but the total social order which enabled such practices to become routine. He conducted rigorous investigations of crime and fraud, making persistent demands to the state authorities to pursue suspects and bring them to trial. It was his refusal to let the BCM fraud case slide away from public attention, and his tenacious investigation, which led to his assassination on 22 November 2000.

Cardoso was not alone. This tragic assassination, organised by the same men responsible for the 1996 fraud, was one of a series of killings and attempted killings, threats and bribes through which organised crime in Mozambique has sought to eliminate, silence or remove inconvenient critics and incorruptible lawyers and police (Paulino 2003: 11). As many have observed, the struggle for social justice represented by Cardoso was a broader collective struggle, one that continues after his murder and the subsequent murder of economist Siba-Siba Macuacua in 2001. The editorial of *Mozambiquefile* commented after Cardoso's assassination:

> Such a public killing, on a major street in a central part of Maputo, is also meant to send a message to other journalists. As the general secretary of the Mozambican journalists' union, Hilario Matusse, put it: 'This is an attempt to silence us all'. But we will not be silenced. Although few of us have the talent of Cardoso, we can try and follow the morally upright and intellectually honest example that he set.
>
> ('Requiem for a murdered colleague', *Mozambiquefile*
> September 2000, 290: 3)

Similarly, economist Antonio Souto declared that the campaigns surrounding the murders of Cardoso and Siba-Siba were now one and the same campaign for justice and integrity (*Mozambiquefile* November 2001, 303: 5).

In November 2001, a year after Cardoso's death, hundreds gathered at the place of his murder (Figure 3.1) to celebrate his memory. Persistent public criticism of the ineffective police investigations, articulated within Mozambique and internationally,[15] meant that eventually the suspects were brought to trial in November 2002. The whole process was plagued by attempts at disruption. One of the key suspects mysteriously 'escaped' from the maximum-security prison; a series of threats were made to several witnesses and officials in the Public Prosecution Office, including the presiding Judge, Augusto Paulino; and mobile phones were routinely available to the imprisoned suspects. Such disruption ultimately failed because of the determination and integrity of individuals administering the case and a broader awareness that the very social legitimacy of the state in the eyes of Mozambican society was at stake. The trial lasted from the end of November 2002 until mid-January 2003 and became a central topic of conversation. People throughout the country followed the proceedings daily, broadcast live on television and radio. For weeks the whole country was gripped by accounts of the routine practices of Cardoso's murderers: practices of usury ('loan-sharking'), buying and selling stolen cars, money-laundering, contract killings, issuing threats of violence, murder, kidnap, handling weapons and vast sums of money without a shrug. Thus the trial, in publicly exposing the rot underlying the celebrated 'double-digit economic growth', served to galvanise broader societal awareness of Mozambique's condition of structural violence. Cardoso's widow, Nina Berg, commented after the trial was eventually over:

Figure 3.1 Memorial at the site of the assassination of Cardoso; Avenida Martires de Machava, Maputo, December 2002
Source: Branwen Gruffydd Jones, personal archive

Carlos is now known throughout the country, which he wasn't before he died. And I don't think it's only Carlos who's known throughout the country. It's all the issues that he worked on and these issues of essential importance for the development of Mozambique.

(Cited in Carte Blanche 2003)

Mia Couto has expressed in a particularly pertinent manner the broader social crisis and obstacles to struggle manifest in the particular instance of Cardoso's murder and the recent trial, a crisis and social tragedy resulting from the neoliberal triumph of private over public:

> Cardoso was not just a victim of fraud by the BCM (or by the *Banco Austral* or any other bank). Nor was he was the victim of a particular case that he had been investigating. He was murdered by a much bigger and more generalized fraud. Not a fraud perpetrated against a single institution. But rather against Mozambique. Against the future of Mozambicans.
>
> Carlos Cardoso was not just the victim of the gangsters who killed him or who ordered his death. He was the victim of an unwillingness to take action. The same case that withered our hopes also left our journalist alone against criminals. The very same people who did not lift a finger when Cardoso exposed the most serious irregularities are now singing the praises of a democracy proven to work in the trial of those who killed him. And they point with pride to the freedom of the press, a freedom they confuse with allowing anything to be written and taking absolutely no action. Such indulgence continues today.
>
> At the BO[16] trial there was more than one victim, more than one judge, and more than the half dozen defendants. The victim was not only Cardoso but an entire people sacrificed, all those unable to pull the strings of power, those condemned to live at the margin. The judge was not only Augusto Paulino. But all those who, tired of lies, want to believe again. And the defendants on trial were not only the suspects detained or waiting detention. A parade of swindles and crimes was on show. And something else appeared, but always as an absence: the faceless countenance of those who govern too little or who are governed too much.

(Couto 2003)

The struggles against the effects of globalisation in the *mundo não problemático* consist of efforts to defend the collective good and norms of justice and integrity, through public exposure via the media or the formal justice system. These efforts have been routinely confronted by more violence, bloodshed, threats, corruption and official inaction. Such violent limits to struggle arise structurally from the social relations of Mozambique's neoliberal social order. This is rooted in the fact that the social order which gives rise to corruption and parasitic social theft is the very social order conducive to 'economic growth', imposed and legitimised through the institutions of the international political economy and mediated by Mozambique's political elite.

The daily struggles of existence in the mundo problemático

The concrete condition of globalisation is manifest most fundamentally in the daily lived experiences of the poor and excluded – the majority of Mozambican society. Objectively it is precisely those who suffer most, whose circumstances are most undermined by the structures of globalisation, that most need the transformation of globalisation and the creation of a more just social and world order. Yet one of the most profound contradictions of contemporary world politics is the fact that the worst conditions of suffering created by a particular social order do not necessarily generate a response of collective, organised, political struggle to transform that order. In Mozambique, individual lives are adjusted in ways that encourage the development of strategies to cope and survive rather than engagement in collective struggle. The daily conditions of structural violence suffered by the poor and excluded are caused by the forces of globalisation, but the concrete experience of those conditions is, for most, intensely local, personal and individualised.

The *mundo problemático* is inhabited by many who struggle in different ways for daily survival – beggars, street children, the *lixeiros*, *vendadores da rua* (street vendors), demobilised soldiers, people who are disabled or mentally ill, prostitutes, drug addicts, money changers, street gangs, pickpockets (Serra 2003: 20, 29). In this world of adjusted lives, 'each day is a hard battle … [an] endless search for the bare necessities' (Serra 2003: 25). Without the stability of secure employment, the future of the inhabitants of the *mundo problemático* is highly insecure and 'they know that they have to struggle hard to sell at all costs because "hunger does not take holidays" ' (fieldwork diary of Coleti, cited in Serra 2003: 33). These celebrated 'microentrepreneurs' struggle in the intensely competitive markets to sell their goods in order to acquire food or exercise books for their eldest children (Serra 2003: 35).

What forms of resistance can arise in such conditions? What organised, political struggles can emerge among atomised individuals, excluded from the normal routines of society, unacknowledged, desperately struggling to buy and sell for daily sustenance, under constant fear of, on the one hand, petty theft and, on the other hand, the police and tax-collectors? Many

> are reluctant to speak of their life, of their circumstances, they fear being imprisoned at any moment and are terrified of the consequences of speaking out; they opt, resigned, for the law of silence; politics offends them, they have no confidence in the government.
>
> (Serra 2003: 35–6; see also Chefo 2003: 25)

In the *dumba-nengues*, *chapas*[17] and *lixeiras*, the rule is: each for him- or herself (Chefo 2003: 24; Serra 2003).

Some turn to traditional *curandeiros* (witchdoctors), seeking charms that will bring them luck and protection against evil spirits, or to evangelical churches such as *Igrega Universal do Reino de Deus*, which are increasingly ubiquitous throughout Africa. Such churches offer a feeling of belonging, identity and spiritual strength to those suffering the experience of rejection on the margins of society. But these churches promote the notion that social conditions of poverty and inequality are caused by God or supernatural forces – the antithesis of political consciousness. They offer salvation not through political struggle but through prayer, hard work and, of course, monetary donations (Serra 2003: 72–7). Some turn to alcohol, glue-sniffing and drugs for escape. For others,

> when they suffer too much, when the needs of life spur them on, they may try out a life of crime, turn to begging, take refuge in the churches, be thrown into psychiatric hospitals or, even, live from the rubbish thrown out by the *mundo não problemático*.
>
> (Serra 2003: 46)[18]

The adjusted lives of the excluded involve multiple daily struggles in and against the condition of globalisation, but are not recognisable as part of an 'anti-globalisation movement'. Arguably, participation in such a movement already presupposes a certain normality, stability, security – conditions necessary to be able to look towards the possibility of a better future and to co-ordinate with others in struggles for social change. For members of the *mundo problemático*, resistance and struggle is not a particular activity engaged in at certain times and places collectively, the result of a conscious decision, in order to protest against specific conditions or policies, to seek reforms and rearrangements in society. Daily life is routinely constituted by resistance and struggle – not to live, but to survive; not to change society, but to get through the days, to sustain mind and body or even to escape from reality; a continuous and individualised struggle outside society. These struggles indeed take place precisely 'on the streets'; but not in the form of marches, with no banners and slogans, rarely reported in the news, largely ignored.

Such daily-lived struggles can in fact be seen as the antithesis of an 'anti-globalisation movement'. They do not form part of an organised global, or even local, movement in quest of definite social change. Yet there is a contradiction which must be acknowledged by critical theorists concerned about transformatory possibilities in the age of globalisation. It is precisely the inhabitants of the *mundo problemático* who suffer most acutely the structural violence of globalisation, who need most urgently the reform, taming and, ultimately, transformation of the forces of globalisation. Yet they are least likely, given their concrete conditions, to engage in collective political struggle, to join the 'anti-globalisation movement'.

Conclusions

In response to current celebration of the 'movement of movements' against globalisation, this chapter has raised a note of caution, posing questions about prior conditions of possibility for and limits to the emergence of political consciousness and collective action. The social order of globalisation in the particular context of Mozambique is defined by concrete conditions of structural violence. Particular forms of struggle and resistance are emerging in this context, but they are constrained by obstacles and limits rooted in the very structures of globalisation. The dialectic of adjustment involves processes of accumulation and dispossession that are creating an increasingly unequal society composed of two worlds, within which different forms of resistance emerge. Journalists and others struggling to resist the violence, theft and corruption of globalisation are confronted by systemic inaction, which simply enables further violence. For others, resistance consists of daily individual adjustments to routine lack – lack of employment, food, education, shelter, recognition. Improvements are sought through prayer, charms, drugs, alcohol or petty crime, in a quest to change one's luck or consciousness, rather than to change society.

In the West, globalisation unravels previous conditions of stability, growth, rising living standards, mass consumption and high employment which were enjoyed during the golden years of the postwar boom. Here, mounting critiques of globalisation are in part rooted in awareness and experience of this transition from security to insecurity. Other regions of the world such as Africa, however, have never experienced periods of stable growth and mass improvement, while today's struggles in and against globalisation are only the latest of centuries of struggle. Perhaps we should question the 'purported rupture' of globalisation in the history of capitalism, and acknowledge the profound obstacles to, as well as possibilities of, transformatory practice. 'Globalisation' is only the latest phase in a long history of capitalist expansion, adjustment and violence, and surely is not going to be easily defeated. As Depelchin has pointed out:

> Ignoring the groans and denunciations of hundreds of millions of people from the slave ships of the sixteenth century to the homeless of Harlem today, capitalism has gone from triumph to triumph, consolidating itself and acquiring such a formidable armor that no existing counterweapon seems capable of disarming it, let alone destroying it.
>
> (Depelchin 1999: 157)

Do the multifaceted and growing movements against globalisation provide hope that capitalism, in this twenty-first century, can perhaps be disarmed? Or will the groans and denunciations of those struggling to survive the conditions of globalisation in their daily lives continue to be ignored? *A luta continua.*[19]

Notes

1 Thanks to Carlos Serra, Soila Hirvonen, Phillip Rothwell, Julian Saurin, Elly Omondi, and the Department of Politics and International Relations, University of Aberdeen, for discussions, support, and help with translation.

2 Translations from Portuguese into English are my own (with help from Phillip Rothwell), whenever provided in the text in brackets or whenever quotes originate from interviews conducted in Mozambique or Mozambican sources written in Portuguese.

3 The period of the Cold War is conventionally seen as a period of conflict between East and West. However, an integral part of the West's strategy of 'containment', especially on the part of the United States, was the containment or destruction of radical and leftist regimes in the Third World through counter-revolutionary tactics ranging from direct military assault, assassinations, covert financial and military support, training and direction of opposition groups and 'freedom fighters', to financial, military and police support to right-wing regimes. In some cases the West gave support to a regional 'policeman' instead of directly intervening, whether covertly or overtly. In the case of Mozambique, the West supported first Portugal and Rhodesia, and then South Africa, in two decades of military assault on Mozambique; but see Austin (1994) for details of more direct intervention.

4 I refer here to scholars who develop various forms of Critical Theory influenced by the work of the Frankfurt School, as well as the work of Gramscians or neo-Gramscians; but not to forms of postmodern scholarship which reject outright any notion of progress or emancipation.

5 In 1982 the World Health Organization

> singled out Mozambique as an example of a very-low-income country that had made "extraordinary" strides in rural health and education, having vaccinated 95 percent of the country's children within three years of independence and quadrupled the number of primary and secondary school graduates.
>
> (Ciment 1997: 65)

6 This and the phrase *mundo problemático* are borrowed from the important work of Carlos Serra and his colleagues (2003). He uses the phrases to foreground the existence of two social worlds in Mozambique. For the inhabitants of the *mundo não problemático*, the basic conditions of life are not in question. But for those in the other world, the *mundo problemático*, it is necessary to struggle on a daily basis simply to get by – each day is a hard battle (Serra 2001: 21).

7 The concept of 'primitive accumulation' was developed by Marx (1990 [1867]: Part Eight). It refers to a process of accumulation which has to have occurred already for *capitalist* accumulation – accumulation of surplus value in the sphere of production – to be possible. Primitive accumulation involves plunder, theft, slavery, dispossession, rather than production of surplus value. It is integral and necessary to the historical formation of propertied and propertyless classes. It is an analytical category that refers to a particular form of social change and reorganisation in the development of capitalism, rather than to a specific *period* of time. Actual forms and processes of primitive accumulation are therefore necessarily historically specific, and must be examined in their concrete and historical specificity, rather than read off from theoretical categories. See Depelchin (1981: 22) for an important discussion of the notion of primitive accumulation in neo-colonial social formations in Africa. The related term 'parasitic' is used to specify processes of accumulation which do not lead to or enable overall increases in productive capacity, but, rather, occur at the expense of society's productive capacity.

8 The editorial of *Mozambiquefile* remarks bitterly:

> Remember how much we were sold the benefits of privatisation? How we were told that private ownership was much more efficient than state ownership? ... Not so much was heard from the IMF and the Bank when some new owners of privatised companies broke their contractual obligations, stopped paying their workers, or even changed the very nature of the companies (in some cases turning productive units into warehouses). Not even a whisper of disapproval was heard from the mentors of privatisation when the privatised steel rolling mill, CSM, ground to a halt, after its Portuguese owners had acquired at least US$ 17 million in loans from the Mozambican treasury, supposedly to import equipment. The equipment was not imported and the money has never been repaid.
>
> ('The bitter aftertaste of privatisation', *Mozambiquefile* July 2000, 288: 3)

9 There has been a tendency to portray high-level corruption as a feature specific to so-called developing societies, but this is not the case. Corruption is a routine practice at the core of the current capitalist world order (see e.g. Palast 2003; Curtis 2003). The money-laundering services in Mozambique are employed not only by local networks of drug traffickers, but also, reportedly, by companies like British Aerospace, which transferred funds to the former South African defence minister to secure the £1.5 billion sale of BAE hawks to South Africa (*Guardian* 2003: 11).

10 Most notoriously and tragically, in November 2000 at least eighty-three people died of asphyxiation in a massively overcrowded police cell in Montepuez in the north of Mozambique. Recent studies have revealed that Mozambique's prisons are full of people who have not been sentenced; and the bulk of prisoners who have been tried

> were found guilty of fairly petty offences: 53 per cent were serving sentences of two years or less. Only 15 per cent had been found guilty of serious crimes for which the sentence is eight years or more. As might have been expected, poverty, illiteracy and unemployment are among the common paths to jail. Out of a large sample of the prison population questioned for the report, only 10 per cent said they had completed their primary education. 16 per cent had never set foot in a school. About half the prison population consisted of people who, at the time of their arrest, were either unemployed or working in the informal sector.
>
> (*Mozambiquefile* February 2001, 295: 18–19)

For a pertinent commentary on the 'penalisation of poverty' as an integral part of the neoliberal social order in Europe see Wacquant (2001).

11 The word *camponeses* means peasants, but I am deliberately using the Portuguese word here, not as a social-scientific analytical category, but because people in the countryside whom I interviewed refer to themselves as *camponeses*.

12 A large rectangular cotton cloth, printed with different designs, worn by women.

13 This brings to mind a scene witnessed recently in Kenya, where the social order suffers similar conditions of structural violence to that of Mozambique. Travelling by coach through the outskirts of the town of Nakuru, I saw painted on a wall the words:

WE REPAIR BROKEN EGGS

AND ROTTEN TOMATOES

14 'Press Freedom: an issue SADC must take up' (editorial, *Mozambiquefile* May 2000, 286: 3). After independence, with the establishment of a one-party state

under Frelimo, the media were controlled by the state. By the late 1980s, government interference in journalist writing, restriction of information and detention of journalists led to increasing criticism and calls for press freedom. In 1991, in the context of political liberalisation, new press laws were passed and the state monopoly of the media ended. See Fauvet and Mosse (2003: ch. 16).

15 The public campaign to bring the investigation to fruition was led by staff of *Metical* and the Cardoso family, and included a petition which was signed by more than 10,000 people, including prominent public figures, ordinary workers and students, and many outside Mozambique, from more than forty countries. An appeal was also issued by a group of foreign writers, headed by Günter Grass and including Noam Chomsky and Susan Faludi (United States); John Pilger (UK); Jan Myrdal and Henning Mankel (Sweden); Erik Hansen and Jon Michelet (Norway); Leif Davidsen and Pehr Ohrgaard (Denmark). See 'Little progress over Cardoso murder', *Mozambiquefile* (February 2001, 295: 4–7).

16 The maximum-security prison in Machava, where the trial took place, for security reasons.

17 Privately owned mini-bus taxis, which are the main means of transport in Maputo for those who do not have cars. See Matsinhe (2000).

18 Serra's team of researchers discovered a sharp and clear consciousness among the *lixeiros*, a consciousness that there are two societies in Mozambique (Serra 2003: 49). One society lives well, in comfort and security; the other lives in permanent insecurity and lack, forced literally to scrape a living from the unwanted detritus of those who enjoy a normal life of comfort. The discarded rubbish of one society constitutes the daily sustenance of the other (Chefo 2003: 25).

19 'The struggle continues' – the slogan of the Mozambican revolution.

Part II
Discourse/identity/culture

4 Anti-globalisation discourses in Asia

Ralph Pettman

Introduction

Today we see 'globalisation' proceeding apace. That is to say that the modernist project, rooted in a specifically Euro-American tradition, is spreading ever more worldwide. As it does so, it encounters very different politico-cultural and politico-spiritual traditions and generates a variety of critical responses. While the dominant voices of critique have been largely generated within a modernist analytical framework, alternative challenges are now starting to emerge that are not underpinned by the axioms that characterise the Euro-American mainstream. In other words, anti-globalisation discourses include not only critical discourses within the project of modernist world affairs but also discourses exogenous to and critical of that project.

This chapter discusses the ways in which globalisation and anti-globalisation are articulated in 'Asia'. What does it mean to call discourses and their proponents 'Asian'? Clearly an Orientalist concept, the particular construction and peculiar currency of 'Asia' directly result from European imperialism in this region. As the Malaysian critic, Chandra Muzaffar, says, 'the West is all around us. The West is within us. The West is us' (Muzaffar 1998: 457). Further, the region comprises large and highly diverse populations, several major religions and many different cultures. Thus to posit the concept of *an* 'Asia' seems absurd. Like the concept of globalisation, 'Asia' is multidimensional, multilayered, complex, imprecise and highly political. That said, the idea of Asia is widely employed now by many peoples in this part of the world to refer to their geographic region and to themselves. They have appropriated the term as part of the process of constructing identities of their own. It is in deference to this usage that the term 'Asia' is used here.

This chapter is concerned to identify those anti-globalisation discourses in Asia that provide alternatives to the politico-cultural and politico-spiritual fundaments of the modernist project. It will do so by contrasting the truth claims of what I will call 'modernist' and 'non-modernist' critics of globalisation in the region. More specifically, it will first examine the high-profile modernist discourse of Walden Bello on de-globalisation, before turning to the politico-cultural challenge posed by the Japanese policies on heritage and the politico-spiritual challenge offered by Buddhist economics. I will argue that the latter two offer potentially valuable discursive resources for constructing an alternative to globalisation and that they are a necessary supplement to dominant accounts of the anti-globalisation movement, accounts which have thus far been constrained by their modernist framing.

Globalisation and its discontents

The most common explanation for the phenomenon of globalisation is materialist in orientation. In its non-Marxist guise, this explanation highlights changes in the technologies of transport and communications. These changes are said to facilitate global connectivity, to put every part of the world within reach of every other part, a process that may or may not be linked to accounts of the spread of liberal markets (Held *et al.* 1999). In its Marxist guise, the materialist explanation focuses on the capitalist system and the social struggles that it generates (Sklair 2002; Colas 2002; Callinicos 2003a).

However, materialist approaches to globalisation are in my view inadequate. In this chapter, I treat globalisation more broadly, as a portmanteau term for the way in which the Euro-American modernist project is intensifying its worldwide reach. This modernist project is multidimensional: it is not only defined by the material relations of capitalism and the state forms related to it but it also has important politico-cultural and politico-spiritual elements. The politico-cultural dimension of modernity includes a focus on reason as the source of knowledge and way to truth, and an emphasis on the individuated human subject as the basis of social, political and moral life. In hegemonic, liberal articulations of the modernist project, this subject is assumed to be self-interested, calculating and autonomous with regard to social relations. The politico-spiritual dimension of modernity ostensibly involves the secularisation of social life but in fact is built upon a strong Christian heritage, which brings with it a conception of the sinful self, responsible for his or her own actions and for his or her own salvation.

It is worth noting that, understood in this way, the politico-cultural and political-spiritual dimensions of modernity reinforce each other. They converge on a view of the individual as a self-determining, autonomous agent. Within this framework, the nature of the individual has been conceptualised in varying ways: we find the self-interested but potentially co-operative individual of liberalism; the selfish, state-bound individual of realism, nationalism and mercantilism; the altruistic, cosmopolitan self of globalism, socialism and collectivism; and the historicised and perfectible self of Marxism. These different views of the self feed into and sustain the more materialist dimensions of the globalised modernist project, generating some variation in relations between state, economy and society. However, at the present time, the liberal version of the individual, and of its appropriate social, economic and political context, has become hegemonic worldwide.

This hegemony has not gone uncontested, however. In what follows, I will examine three challenges: the first remains within a modernist framing. It is the 'de-globalisation' argument of Walden Bello.

Modernist Asian anti-globalisation

Bello was born in Manila, and educated there by Jesuits. He did postgraduate studies at Princeton University and he subsequently worked in the United States as an academic and an activist (Anderson and Mertes 2002). Thus, although born and raised in an Asian country, Bello's formal education took place in the politico-spiritual context of Christianity and the politico-cultural context of modernist rationalism. During this time, he was profoundly influenced by Marxism and neo-Marxism, becoming at one stage a member of the Communist Party of the Philippines. Marxist principles continue to inform his reading of globalisation. He remains persuaded of the significance of political economy, for example, and of the importance of critiquing attempts to de-link international economics from international politics. He also continues to highlight the significance of corporate-driven capitalism and overproduction, drawing clear distinctions between the centre of the global capitalist economy and its periphery. Furthermore, he uses class as a key analytic category, arguing for the need to mobilise the working classes worldwide (Anderson and Mertes 2002; Bello and Bullard 2001). In addition to Marxism and neo-Marxism, Bello also draws upon other modernist analytical languages. These include mercantilism, nationalism and modernist forms of environmentalism.

This combination of modernist discourses can be seen in Bello's argument for 'de-globalisation', which involves a partial reversal of open-market principles and the implementation of protectionist state policies. He advocates, that is, the withdrawal of the state from the world economy, the reorientation of local economies towards local needs, and the radical redistribution of land and income (Bello 2002b: 23). For Bello, de-globalisation clearly means a move away from liberal internationalist institutions and their 'one-size-fits-all' formula for furthering economic development, towards a plurality of different kinds of development. It also means the establishment of regional financial institutions, such as an Asian Monetary Fund, as well as capital controls at both the regional and local levels, constant monitoring of the state and private sectors by civil society, and the exclusion of transnational corporations from poorer states. 'We are talking', Bello concludes, 'about a strategy that consciously subordinates the logic of the market, [and] the pursuit of cost efficiency, to the values of security, equity, and social solidarity' (Bello 2002b: 24; see more generally Bello 2002a).

Bello has become a high-profile figure in the struggle against globalisation and his ideas have reached both a national and an international audience. For example, he was commissioned to write a report for the

German Bundestag (Bello 2002b). Furthermore, he has become a key figure in the World Social Forum process, which brings together activists from all over the world to discuss alternatives to liberal globalisation. He regularly speaks at regional fora and at the World Social Forum itself. Closer to home, he set up his own non-governmental organisation, the Nautilis Institute, to look at the world politics of energy issues, and he also helped establish Focus on the Global South, which looks at regional affairs and actors in their global context (Anderson and Mertes 2002).

Bello is a trenchant in-house critic. That is to say that he offers an insightful analysis of the negative impact of economic and political changes associated with liberal globalisation, and articulates a compelling economic and political alternative. However, I would argue that his critique and alternative are limited by the fact that they remain within a modernist framework. They are predicated on a broad acceptance of the politico-cultural and politico-spiritual dimensions of the modernist project described above, which together project a rational, self-determining self. Bello does not pay attention to non-modernist Asian discourses that offer a very different approach.

Non-modernist Asian anti-globalisation discourses

In this section, I will explore two such non-modernist discourses. The first is the Japanese approach to heritage, which can be seen as exemplifying a politico-cultural challenge to globalisation. It contests the reification of the rationalist mind-gaze by supplementing the modernist concept of 'heritage' as a product, with the non-modernist concept of heritage as practice. The second discourse I examine draws on the teachings of Buddha to interrogate modernist economics, thus exemplifying a politico-spiritual challenge to globalisation. This discourse contests the egoistic and individuated character of the modernist subject through notions of the 'not-self'.

The Japanese state and the concept of heritage

The politico-cultural dimension of the modernist project not only objecti-fies, but also reifies. It tends to lead to an emphasis upon *products* rather than *practices*, as can be seen in the concept of 'heritage'. Hence the contemporary penchant for choosing particular items from the 'past', like historic monuments or relatively unspoiled parts of the countryside, and the many efforts to bequeath these items to the 'future' as representative of the past. Once selected, such items are conserved and preserved, more or less effectively, for the contemplation of generations to come. If they are portable, they may be put in special institutions (museums and galleries). The list established under the auspices of UNESCO's World Heritage Convention provides a universal reference point in this regard. It is particu-larly notable, therefore, that under the terms of this convention, the concept

of world heritage is crafted in such a way as to play up the cultural significance of particular natural or social products (UNESCO 1999).

This is in contrast to a non-modernist view of heritage as continuing
cultural practices, which relies upon a very different understanding of the
past as integral to a living present and future. Consider, for example, the
Japanese approach. On the one hand, Japanese culture promotes the
modernist penchant for reification. On the other hand, it manifests a non-
modernist orientation towards process. Representatives of the Japanese state
signed the World Heritage Convention in 1992, immediately nominating
Horyuji Temple and Himeji Castle for inclusion on the World Heritage List.
In doing so, they signalled their acceptance of the modernist definition of
heritage. Indeed, from the time of the Meiji restoration, the Japanese have
objectified their past and selected things from it for conservation and preser-
vation, the first official decree to this effect being issued in 1871. Yet this
focus on objects needs to be understood in the broader context of the
Japanese discourse on heritage. In the Japanese language, the word for
heritage is *isan*. This refers not only to the inheritance of family assets or
debts, but also to the achievements of one's ancestors. It is important to
understand that the Japanese seek to preserve memory in non-physical form
(Takashina 1996: 3). It is a key characteristic of Japanese culture to use
abstract cultural practices, like rituals and ceremonies, to preserve valued
communal memories. Thus the Japanese concept of heritage is complex and
nuanced. In Japanese cultural terms, both things and processes affirm the
nation's identity. Taken together, they represent a distinctive way of living
and constitute the country's heritage.

Amongst Asian states, Japan was the first to give explicit, official recognition to the co-existence of modernist and non-modernist approaches. As
early as 1950, the Japanese established a Law for the Protection of Cultural
Properties, which covered not only tangible cultural properties, like paint-
ings, buildings and beauty spots, but also intangible cultural properties, like
drama, music and the applied arts. In 1975 this law was amended to recognise the necessity to protect the skills required to conserve old and revered
things, as well as to preserve 'folk properties' in their more intangible form.
Under the auspices of this law, the Agency for Cultural Affairs gives support
to individuals who practise traditional crafts and theatre arts. This
programme is popularly known as the *ningen kokuho* (living national trea-
sures) programme, and is designed to honour particular artists and
craftspeople for their traditional abilities. It gives them an annual stipend so
that they may continue to practise and pass on traditional arts or crafts that
would otherwise be commercially non-viable.

This emphasis on non-modernist conceptions of heritage finds compelling
parallels in Chinese attitudes to the past, as one might expect given the
historic influence Chinese culture has had on Japan. Pierre Ryckmans notes,
for example, how the Chinese way of passing down ancient moral and spiritual values 'appears to have [been] most often combined with a curious

neglect or indifference ... towards the material heritage of the past', in contrast to Europe, where 'every age has left a considerable amount of monumental landmarks' (Ryckmans 1986: 1–2). The argument here is that the Chinese sense of the past seems to be enshrined more in the people and the language than in things

The distinctively Japanese combination of modernist and non-modernist conceptions of heritage is displayed in Table 4.1 below.

In the first quadrant of this matrix we find heritage construed in terms of tangible products. Since this is the most common form that the modernist conception of heritage can take, examples are legion. Japanese ones include ancient monuments like the country's feudal castles, and culturally esteemed natural assets like Mount Fuji. The second quadrant includes tangible practices. I would place here traditional rituals that have a reifiable outcome, like the Shinto shrine at Ise. In Japanese terms, Ise Shrine is one of the most significant heritage sites in the country. Because it gets rebuilt every twenty years, however, it is not allowed onto the World Heritage List. Mainstream Western modernists consider it a replica, thereby failing to appreciate the authenticity of the ritual practices that the reconstruction involves. Similarly, although mainstream Western modernists may appreciate the visible manifestation of a Japanese festival like *Okunchi*, the meaning of the ritual practices that this festival involves largely escapes them.

The third quadrant, that of intangible properties, is exemplified by traditional Japanese theatre forms like *Noh* or *Kabuki*. *Noh* stories have to be learned from generation to generation. They exist only while they are being performed and cease the moment the performance stops. Their expression is instantaneous, which means that *Noh* represents nothing more than what is experienced in its performance, by those present at its performance. The fourth quadrant, that of intangible practices, is exemplified by the practice of that dense network of reciprocal obligations (*giri*) that underpins the entire Japanese society. There are tangible artefacts involved in the performance of these obligations, but the obligations themselves are hard to objectify and reify. In sum, the table shows that the Japanese approach to heritage combines modernist and non-modernist cultural conceptions in complex and interesting ways.

So what is the significance of this Japanese example for our understanding of anti-globalisation? First, it points to the need to expand the scope of enquiry to include not only grassroots movement activism but also state practices. In discourses on globalisation/anti-globalisation, the state

Table 4.1 The Japanese conception of heritage

	Tangible (material)	Intangible (non-material)
Products (artefacts)	*Horyuji*	*Noh*; *Kabuki*
Practices (processes)	*Okunchi; Ise*	*Giri*

tends to be depicted either as irrelevant in the face of global forces or as complicit with them. Either way, it is not seen as currently taking on the role of challenger to globalisation: some activists and commentators call on state elites to take on board this responsibility while others seek to bypass the state altogether. The case of the Japanese state and heritage policy suggests a much more complex analysis of the role of the state is needed. Second, this example points to the need to pay attention to non-modernist, politico-cultural discourses as potentially significant sources of anti-globalisation politics. Finally, I would argue that there is a need to rethink the notion of anti-globalisation itself, which implies a dichotomy of 'for and against' and a politics of confrontation and opposition. The example of the Japanese state and its heritage policies shows that responses to the cultural homogeni-sation of the modernist project can be articulated in complex, even ambiguous, ways. Indeed, in this case, the Japanese state can be seen as embracing both modernist and non-modernist concepts of heritage as a way of conserving a distinctively Japanese cultural identity in a globalised world.

Buddhism and market economics

Having considered politico-cultural discourse above, I will now turn my attention to politico-spiritual discourse. There are many non-modernist politico-spiritual discourses originating in Asia, including various forms of communalism (Tai 1989) and Hindu challenges to Christian values (Vivekananda 1964). I will focus here on Buddhism, and more specifically the challenge that Buddhism poses for market economics. It should be acknowledged that Buddhism is a rich, contested tradition, with many varia-tions. Rather than engaging in the complex debates between these variations, I will draw here on my own interpretation of Buddha's teachings and on a number of recent texts on the social and economic implications of Buddhism (notably Payutto 1994), including some by non-Buddhists and non-Asians (e.g. Schumacher 1973; Batchelor 1990; Bubna-Litic 2000).

The fundamentals of Buddhism can be found in the Buddhist equivalent of Christ's Sermon on the Mount, namely the 'Setting in Motion [of] the Wheel of Truth'. There is no unmediated account of this sermon, not least because it was not written down until hundreds of years after the Buddha gave it. From what can be ascertained, however, the Buddha articulated two basic insights in this sermon, one of which was the Middle Way, the other of which was the Four Noble Truths. The Middle Way is Buddha's injunction to avoid the extremes of 'sensuality and self-torture' (Parrinder 1977: 29). The Four Noble Truths are: abiding sorrow (or suffering or pain); the roots of this sorrow in craving for pleasure and power; the possibility of bringing sorrow to an end; and the way to do so. This way is the Noble Eightfold Path, that is the exercise of Right Views, Right Resolve, Right Speech, Right Conduct, Right Livelihood, Right Effort, Right Mindfulness and Right Concentration (de Bary *et al.* 1958: 102; Armstrong 2000). Two insights, three ways and four truths (one of which involves eight kinds of behaviour) – this plurality can mask the fact that there remains a singular vision at the heart of the Buddha's sermon. What the Buddha ultimately sought to develop was a way of thinking and being that would create true human peace and ultimately *nirvana*, or spiritual enlightenment (de Bary *et al.* 1958: 102).

In more concrete, material terms, one can read Buddha's teachings as calling for integrated communities centred on monasteries. In these communities, monks and nuns try to become enlightened, while serving the spiritual needs of lay believers. Lay believers, meanwhile, engage in worldly pursuits, and seek a more limited form of spiritual progress by practising the Four Noble Truths, and providing monks and nuns with the necessities of life. Although many Buddhists live in such communities, it is difficult to gauge the extent of the application of this way of life.

At first glance, the Buddha's ideas would seem to prescribe a form of socialism, that is a global economy made to work in non-selfish ways, based on redistribution according to need and strong communities in which all members work for the collective good (Payutto 1994: 53, 62). Considered more closely, however, I would argue that the Buddha's ideas are much more radical. First, as should be clear from the above, his vision of community is ethically and spiritually based, involving a division of labour in which some serve the spiritual needs of the social group and others its material needs. Second, the Buddha's teachings offer a very different understanding of the individual self and its needs than that found in the modernist discourse of socialism and, more importantly, of liberalism. Third, and closely related, the Buddha's teachings also challenge the rationalism of the modernist project, shared by both liberals and their modernist critics, by emphasising that the path to truth and emancipation lies in meditation, spiritual reflection and right practice.

The Buddha taught that the individuated self is imaginary or illusory and he envisaged a world where an awareness of the not-self prevails. This does not mean that the self has no existence, but rather that the essence of its existence is impermanence (Morris 1994: 59). In Buddhist terms, therefore:

> The correct position ... is ... to try and see things objectively as they are without mental projections, [that is] to see that what we call 'I' ... is only a combination of physical and mental aggregates, which are working together interdependently in a flux of momentary change.
>
> (Rahula 1959: 66)

If the individuated self is imaginary, then its needs are imaginary too. This means that the production, investment and exchange systems that are dedicated to meeting these needs must be seen as monuments to the desire of the individuated self, rather than miracles of supply and demand. They are profound mistakes. This is not to say that markets do not alleviate some material misery, but from a Buddhist perspective we must question whether they deliver deep, abiding happiness. The Buddhist response to the illusion of the individuated self and its desires lies in repudiation of the 'I'. The Buddha counselled striving for clear inner vision through meditation, which would result in detachment, peace, enlightenment and, finally, *nirvana* (de Bary *et al.* 1958: 102). Further, the Buddha's own mediations led him to see that freeing ourselves from desire requires more than spiritual reflection; it also requires practising, among other things, Right Action and Right Livelihood. By Right Action he meant honourable and peaceful action, that is action that does not involve thefts or dishonest dealings. By Right Livelihood he meant blameless work, that is work that does not involve harm to others. In my view, this would militate against the pursuit of material wealth for its own sake and against participation in a range of industries, from tobacco to military armaments.

The implications of the Buddha's teachings for economics have not been widely institutionalised, even in Buddhist countries like Thailand or Myanmar, and they are not in evidence in regional social movements. Nonetheless, I would argue that they present an important discursive resource for thinking about alternatives to globalised liberal markets. Buddhism offers some concrete suggestions for ways to mitigate the worst effects of modernist marketeering and the worst effects of the rationalist, self-centred, self-maximising ethos on which liberal economics is based. It also offers a profound challenge to the rationalism and individualism underpinning the modernist project, and found both in hegemonic liberal forms of globalisation and in dominant discourses of anti-globalisation, such as that articulated by Bello. The politico-spiritual tradition of Buddhism rejects the very basis of the modernist project itself. As the alienating effects of the modernist project proliferate under conditions of globalisation, Buddhism could well become much more important in informing opposition in the Asian context, particularly given that it is already familiar to many Asian peoples.

Conclusion

This chapter has explored anti-globalisation discourses in Asia. It has contrasted the high-profile modernist discourse of Walden Bello to the politico-cultural discourse of the Japanese state and the politico-spiritual discourse of Buddhism. Thus it can be seen that discourses of anti-globalisation in Asia are articulated both within and outside the modernist project. It has been my contention that, given the global reach of this project, attempts to mount critiques within it are arguably not anti-globalisation at all, or rather they offer only limited opposition to globalisations. The rejection of one part of the globalisation agenda, like liberal economics, is combined with acceptance or lack of attention to other parts, namely the cultural and spiritual ones. In other words, Marxist and other critical discourses offer only a partial critique of the modernist project. They are only anti-globalisation if globalisation is defined reductively in terms of the global expansion of the market.

If globalisation is defined more broadly as a multidimensional project with important cultural and spiritual dimensions, then more profound challenges can be found in the Japanese discourse on heritage and the Buddhist discourse on economics. Even though the Japanese discourse on heritage accepts and works with certain aspects of the modernist politico-cultural discourses, namely the concept of heritage in terms of products, it nonetheless subverts the modernist project as a whole by combining it with very different politico-cultural values, namely the concept of heritage in terms of processes, or living memory. This complex hybrid of modernist and non-modernist aspects of heritage helps to create a culture that is distinctively Japanese and that offers an alternative to contemporary hegemonic cultural formations.

Likewise, I have drawn attention to Buddhist teachings as a politico-spiritual discourse offering valuable resources for the development of alternatives to globalised market economics. Going beyond a Marxist emphasis on redistribution and solidarity, Buddhist teachings direct us towards a more spiritually centred understanding of community and a radical rethinking of the individuated self. The Buddha counselled repudiation of the 'I' through meditation and the practice of Right Action and Right Livelihood. This points towards a very different relation of the individual to economic life and to truth than that found in globalised liberal economies. Rather than an economic order based on production, supply and demand, in response to rationalist assumptions about human needs and the profit imperative, we are presented with a vision of economic interaction subordinated to the quest for spiritual enlightenment, and the ethical injunction to live compassionately with others.

Finally, this chapter draws attention to the relationship between ways of knowing and the use of power in the discussion of globalisation and its discontents. It points to the need to consider faith-based paths to the truth rather than focusing exclusively on the modernist preference for rationalist epistemologies. It also points to the need to consider the ways in which these epistemologies have come to claim universal status and to dominate and subordinate non-modernist alternatives. Furthermore, it directs us towards a consideration of the ways in which power is manifested: not only in material but also in discursive ways; not only in economic and political domains, but also in cultural and spiritual domains; and not only in terms of confrontation and coercion, but also in terms of agenda-setting and consensus-building. Finally, this chapter is intended to remind a modernist audience that resistance to globalisation can be found not only in social movements and political parties, but also in the ideas and actions of culturally astute state-makers and the practitioners of enlightened faiths.

5 Lessons from the indigenous

Zapatista poetics and a cultural humanism for the twenty-first century

Nick Higgins[1]

Introduction

Subcomandante Insurgente Marcos, or *el sup* as he is better known, was born on 1 January 1994, or so the legend goes. There are of course those that deny this, not least among them the Mexican government and their national intelligence service (Centro de Investigación y Seguridad Nacional, or CISEN). They instead would have us believe that the masked figure who is both military commander and spokesperson for the rebel Zapatista National Liberation Army (EZLN) is none other than one Rafael Guillen, a Jesuit educated, ex-university lecturer born in 1957 in Tampico, northern Mexico (de la Grange and Rico 1997: 24–8). The story they wish to tell is of a man corrupted by the texts of Marx and Mao, a man so frustrated with the apathy of metropolitan campus life that he allowed himself to become embroiled in the more radical politics of violent subversion (Diaz 1995).[2] And to some extent they may in fact be right, but only, as academics might say, within the terms of their own discourse (Foucault 1991; Hacking 1982; Rabinow 1986). And it is with this discourse, the discourse of Mexican officialdom, the discourse of government knows best, of government has the legitimacy to represent, the discourse of fact over fiction, that Marcos, and the Zapatista rebels with whom his life is now so inextricably linked, take issue.

It is not so much that Marcos never came from the city to the countryside to preach the revolutionary doctrines of Marxist–Leninism, for this he freely admits, whilst still refusing to confirm his governmental identity. His own story, however, places greater emphasis on his encounter with Indian culture, an encounter that he claims changed him and the very principles upon which the thousands of Zapatista soldiers thought it necessary to fight. The nature of this change, and consequently the nature of the revolutionary movement to which Zapatismo gives its name, has thus become *the* principal focus of the speeches and texts to which he has dedicated himself ever since. That Marcos should often choose the narrative form of the short story, usually employing the 'literary' creation of a pipe-smoking beetle, *Don Durito*, as his alter ego, or the wise parables of the Indian elder, *el viejo Antonio*, or sometimes simply the direct enquiries of Mayan children, as his preferred means to illustrate the motives behind the 1994 New Year's Day uprising, should not be mistaken as the signs of a purely literary indulgence (a vice to which he is by no means immune; see e.g. Marcos 1997a; 1998a; 1998b; 1998c). Equally, his less copious but similarly telling choice of poetry as a favoured form of expression should not be acknowledged simply on the grounds of literary merit, but instead should be recognised as a conscious and *political* statement concerned with just how, and by whom, the realm of experience can best be communicated (see Marcos 1998a: 169).

His now famous communiqués to the national and international press are thus in and of themselves an attempt to disrupt and disturb the government's monopoly on truth and fact (see e.g. *Zapatatistas!* 1994; Marcos 1995). His texts seek to reveal everything that has been excluded from the realm of official discourse in a way every bit as vital to the Zapatista revolution as the unexpected physical apparition of thousands of armed Indians that first made public the thin veneer of an inclusionary and developmentalist rhetoric upon which governmental claims to legitimacy had previously been based. This chapter thus engages with the poetry of Subcomandante Marcos, but not out of any desire to reify, mystify or romanticise its author, but rather to treat him and his words as living bridges between the Indian world of the Mexican south-east and the ever more pervasive world of global politics.

La palabra dura – the hard word

Even now, few people live in the deepest, most dense parts of the Lacandon jungle.[3] Not even the Indians. So on 17 November 1983 when six individuals arrived in Chiapas to found the Zapatista National Liberation Army (EZLN), they knew that in terms of the clandestine, few places could compete with the seclusion of the Chiapan jungle.[4] Buoyed up on the intellectual opiates of Marxist–Leninist theory, the group were poorly armed, badly equipped, deficient in the practice of political conversion and lacking in anything but the most skeletal of local indigenous contacts upon which to base a guerrilla movement. Faced with the sheer severity of the jungle environment, their first battles were with the mountains, with hunger, with sickness and with the cold. In view of this, they named their first camp *la pesadilla* (the nightmare) and ironically the area in which it was located, in contrast to the intense volume of its vegetation, had long since been known as *el desierto* (the desert) (Le Bot 1997: 133). By all accounts it was not an audacious beginning.

In 1984, Marcos himself arrived. At this time the group consisted of only three Indians and three *mestizos* (non-Indians).[5] The Indians already had a long experience of political movements, they had also seen the inside of prison, suffered torture, and were only too familiar with the internal squabbles of the Mexican left. As a teacher Marcos was set the task to instruct them to read and write, and to school them in what it was they most demanded: *la palabra politica* (the political word). The word in this instance was history; history in general, and in particular the history of Mexico and its struggles. Still, for all the bookish knowledge Marcos may have had of the triumphs and failures of Mexican history, it soon became evident that his role as teacher would be limited only to the informal classroom of the camp. Outside, it was the Indians who taught him how to negotiate the jungle; how to walk so as not to exhaust himself, how to hunt and how to prepare and cook what he caught, how to make himself, as they put it, 'part of the mountain'. Even for the Indians, though, it was not an easy time, it was unusual for them to spend such a long period away from their communities, and whilst the jungle was completely alien to the urban-dwelling *mestizos*, for the indigenous, the fact that they were living in an uninhabited sector of the mountains had an added cultural significance.

Slowly Marcos realised that this desert of solitude was, for the Indians, a place far more culturally potent than he had ever imagined. It was, in his own words,

> the home of the dead, a place of spirits, and of all the histories that they populate, and that still populate the night in the Lacandon jungle, and of which the Indians of the region have much respect. Much respect and much fear.
>
> (Gilly *et al.* 1995: 133; on this period see also
> Duran de Huerta 1994: 83–98)

For Marcos, it was his first experience of an indigenous world of phantasms, of gods reborn, and of spirits that took the form of animals or objects. As he began to listen to the myths and stories of his Indian companions, it was, he would later reflect, the slow beginning of a process that he now calls the 'Indianisation' of the Zapatista National Liberation Army (Le Bot 1997: 150). First, however, there were more harsh lessons to be learnt.

Both the importance and the amorphous nature of Indian culture was to make itself painfully felt when the group made its first attempts to proselytise among the communities that lived closest to the jungle interior. In retrospect Marcos talks of entering these communities and trying to teach 'the absurdities that we had been taught; of imperialism, social crisis, the correlation of forces and their coming together, things that nobody understands, and of course neither did they' (Gilly *et al.* 1995: 137). The Indians responded honestly and when he would ask if they understood they would tell him straight.

> They would tell you that they had understood nothing, that your words were not understandable, that you had to look for other words [they would say] '*tu palabra es muy dura, no la entendemos*' [literal translation: your word is very tough, we don't understand it].
>
> (Gilly *et al.* 1995: 137–8)

It became clear that the rhetoric of Marxist–Leninism did not ring true to the Indians of *la selva* (the jungle) and so the search for 'the words with which to say it' began in earnest.

It was around this time that Marcos wrote one of his first few published poems; it is a piece that perhaps reflects the frustration he felt in trying to communicate his sincere belief in the necessity for revolution, and the fact that he should have chosen the poetic form should by no means be considered accidental. We might also approach his constant search for examples as further proof of a teacher still unsure as to whom it is he addresses. Appropriately enough it is entitled

Problems

This thing that is one's country is somewhat difficult to explain
But more difficult still is to understand what it is to love one's country.
For example
they taught us that to love one's country is, for example,
to salute the flag
to rise upon hearing the National Anthem
To get as drunk as we please when the national soccer team loses
To get as drunk as we please when the national soccer team wins
and a few etceteras that don't change much from one presidency to the next …

And, for example,
they didn't teach us that to love one's country can be
for example,
to whistle like one who's becoming evermore distant, but
behind that mountain there is also a part of our country where nobody sees us
and where we open our hearts
(because one always opens one's heart when no one sees them)
And we tell this country,
for example,
everything we hate about it
and everything we love about it
and how it is always better to say it,
for example,
with gunshots and smiling.

And, for example,
they taught us that to love one's country is,
for example,
to wear a big sombrero,
to know the names of the Boy Heroes of Chapultepec,

to shout 'Viva-arriba Mexico!',
even though Mexico is down and dead,
and other etceteras that change little from one Presidency to the next

And, for example,
they did not teach us that
to love one's country
could be,
for example,
to be as quiet as one who dies,
but no,
for beneath this earth there is also a country
where no one hears us
and where we open our hearts
(because one always opens one's heart when no one is listening)
and we tell our country,
the short and hard history
of those who went on dying to love her,
and who are no longer here to give us their reasons why,
but who give them all the same without being here,
those who taught us
that one can love one's country,
for example,
with gunshots and smiling.
                (Documentos y Comunicados del EZLN 1995: 198–200)

Lunas escondidas – hidden moons

Any difficulties the Zapatistas may have had in explaining their notion of revolution to the Indians were of course only compounded by the seemingly simple barrier of language. Speaking only Spanish, it was unavoidable that the original Indian Zapatistas would have to act as translators on behalf of their urban educated non-Indian companions. Keen to spread *la palabra politica* (the political word), the grounds of an engagement were nearly always centred around the question of history. However, as these initial conversations became increasingly marked by misunderstanding and incomprehension, it became clear that the indigenous held a different and, to the non-Indian, a curious conception of time. As Marcos recalls, 'you weren't always sure about which era they were speaking, when they spoke they could be talking about a story that happened that very week, or that happened five hundred years earlier or even when the world began' (Gilly *et al.* 1995: 133).

Initially, the *mestizo* Zapatistas paid scant attention to the importance of such cultural differences; their outlook was fixed. From their perspective, that of educated urban guerrillas, they saw themselves as the vanguard, and the Indians were simply 'the exploited people – those that had to be organised and shown the path' (Le Bot 1997: 146–7). The universalism of their Marxist analysis and reading of history precluded any meaningful differentiation between sectors in society, and the notion of culture held little purchase outwith the realm of the disdained elite bourgeoisie. To their mind, 'it was the same to talk to a proletariat, a peasant, an employee or a student. All would understand the word of the revolution' (Le Bot 1997: 147–8). So when the Indians told them they did not, it was a profound blow. Marcos explains:

> It's very difficult when you have a theoretical scheme that explains the whole of a society and then you arrive in that society and you realise that your scheme explains nothing. It's difficult to accept; to recognise that you have dedicated all of your life to a project, and that this project is fundamentally warped. It can't even explain the reality into which you are trying to integrate yourself. It was something truly serious.
>
> (Interview in Le Bot 1997: 149–50)

It was at this point, then, that the *mestizo* Zapatistas realised that their problems were not simply ones of translation. They became aware that the Indian language had its own referents, its own cultural markers, which were different, and that if they hoped to have any further or successful contact with the indigenous communities these were differences that had to be understood.

These initial difficult conversations thus started what Marcos calls, 'a process of cultural contamination, in the sense of seeing the world, one that obliged us to reconsider our politics and the way in which we viewed our own historical process and the historical process of the nation' (Gilly *et al.* 1995: 138). It was during this period, as Marcos would later admit, that the non-Indian Zapatistas learnt to listen. What previously had been purely an object of passing curiosity now became an issue of central importance. As they sat round the fire at night, the Indians' stories of Sombreron, of Votan, of Ik'al, of the Black Lord, the stories of the talking boxes and of Ix'paquinte, became not simply a form of entertainment but also the primary means through which the *mestizos* became aware of the cultural richness and otherness of the Indians of the south-east of Mexico (Gilly *et al.* 1995: 134).[6] And so, when they enquired further, and asked where they had learnt these stories, they were told that they in turn had been told them by *los viejos* (the community elders).

They learnt that *los viejos* were in themselves a central source of legitimacy within the communities, and that, in fact, the Indians who were at that time their companions in the jungle camp were only there on account of the approval of the elders. Still unsettled by the seeming confusion of temporalities that littered the indigenous histories, the *mestizos* found it difficult to understand the legitimacy and respect with which such stories and the elders who told them were held. Slowly, however, they came to recognise that outside of the schoolroom and the university this was how history worked.

That in light of the levels of illiteracy within the communities, it had become necessary to choose someone whose task it would be to memorise the history of that community, someone who could act as it were like a 'walking book' (Gilly *et al.* 1995: 134).

It was this experience of history, and the constant invocation of inherited oral history, that provided the basis upon which the language of Zapatismo was constructed. By listening to the Indians' own experience and history of exploitation, of humiliation and of racism, the Zapatistas found the keystones upon which to build a new politics. The local history revealed just how partial non-Indian claims to a national history were, and to a large extent the Zapatistas learnt first hand what it meant to be erased from the history books. Placed in this context we would do well to ponder on the political consequences of an academic knowledge that claims a comprehensiveness and transparency that does not exist. For scholars of international relations in particular we could do worse than accept a poem by Marcos appropriately entitled

A gift and a lesson in politics

A little piece of the moon ...
though really it's not one at all,
but two:
A piece from the dark side,
and one from the bright.
And what must be understood
is that the little piece of the moon
that shines
shines because there is a dark side too.
The dark side of the moon
makes possible the bright.

Us too.
When we are the dark side,
(and we must take turns)
it doesn't mean we are less,
only that it's time
to be the dark side,
so that everyone can see the moon
(to tell the truth,
when it comes down to it, the dark side
is more important,
because it shines in other skies,
and because to see it
you have to learn to fly
very high).

And so it is,
only a few
are willing to suffer so
others won't,
and die
so others live.
And this is so,
given that boots and moon and et cetera
are there.

(Le Bot 1997: 154)

El viejo Antonio – old man Antonio

As these founding Zapatistas experienced a transformation of their role, from one of teachers to one of pupils, one Indian village elder in particular took on the mantle of cultural compass for Marcos especially. His name was *el viejo Antonio* (old man Antonio) and it was he who in large part gave legitimacy to the Zapatistas' early and tentative presence in the Indian communities. He was, in the words of Marcos, the one 'who explained us; who we were and who we should be' (Le Bot 1997: 154). As Marcos would later admit, it was the time spent with *el viejo Antonio* that had the most profound influence on the unconscious transformation of the quasi-Marxist guerrilla army into an Indian rebel army. He was for the Zapatistas a vital bridge, and for Marcos in particular a mirror from within which to reconsider and recreate the nature of the revolutionary struggle to which he had chosen to dedicate his life.

Typically *el viejo Antonio* would appear in a quiet moment when Marcos or his companions had cause to visit his community. Without greeting, he would sit alongside Marcos and begin to roll one of his home-made tobacco cigars whilst Marcos himself would take the opportunity to repack and relight his own pipe. After these moments of individual preparation, and after both had savoured their first draws of smoke, it was nearly always incumbent upon Marcos to break the now heavy silence that hung amidst them and their respective fumes. Most often Marcos would begin with a question and, after a dignified pause, *el viejo Antonio* would characteristically and enigmatically respond with a story.

They were stories of gods who sacrificed themselves to make the sun and the moon, of why carbon is black and yet nonetheless produces light, of lions and mirrors, of night and stars, of colours, of clouds and rain, of questions, of trees, stones, ants and water, and of rainbows (collected and retold by Marcos 1997a; 1998b; 1998c). Each story was in its own right a parable, and although Marcos probably never did receive a straight answer to his questions, he came to consider *el viejo Antonio* his teacher, perhaps even his mentor. And the most important lesson he learnt was patience.

With only a short-wave radio as their principal means to receive news from the outside world, the guerrillas often felt isolated and out of step with the wider changes that were taking place in the international arena. As Radio Havana, Voice of the United States and Radio France Internationale informed them, the Soviet Union was collapsing, peace deals and elections were taking place in Central America, and Reaganism was becoming the ideology of preference among the developed and lesser developed nation states. In fact, their decision to come to the mountains of the south-east of Mexico to foment revolution at times looked increasingly anachronistic. It was during these moments of tempered despair and doubt, however, that *el viejo Antonio*'s parables directed Marcos back to the environment around him. Rather than looking outwards for signs of confirmation, *el viejo Antonio* taught him to look within. As Marcos has said,

> you come from the city accustomed to managing time with relative autonomy. You can extend the day with a light well into the night, to read, to study, to do many activities after dark. But not in the mountain. The mountain says to you from here on in, it's the turn of another world, and we enter effectively another world, other animals, other sounds, another time, other air and another form of being with people, that includes the indigenous that were with us. In the night you are made truly more timid, more introspective, more close, as if looking for a handle on something that has always been prohibited; a night in the mountain.
>
> (Gilly *et al.* 1995: 135)

For Marcos it was during this period that a lasting species of transformation took place among the Zapatistas:

> The idea of a more just world, everything that was socialism in broad brushstrokes, but redirected, enriched with humanitarian elements, ethics, morals, more than simply indigenous. Suddenly the revolution transformed itself into something essentially moral. Ethical. More than the redistribution of the wealth or the expropriation of the means of production, the revolution began to be the possibility for a human being to have a space for dignity. Dignity started to be a word with much strength. It wasn't our contribution, it didn't come from the urban element, this was the contribution of the [Indian] communities. In such a way that the revolution would be the guarantee for dignity, so that it might be respected.
>
> (Le Bot 1997: 145–6)

In more intimate terms, Marcos has written:

> There is in the world a mirror.
> It allows us to know who we are,
> who we were and who we can be.

The first image is not always so agreeable,
the second explains why,
and with the third we show our promise.

The problem is in knowing how to find the mirror.
It's not so easy.
But the really dangerous part
is to dare oneself to look inside.
A little distance from oneself,
assisted by a smile, will help things.

(Marcos 1998a: 24)

El lento despertar – the slow awakening

Whilst Chiapas itself has been home to Mayan Indian groups for over a thousand years, the indigenous with whom Marcos and the Zapatistas made their initial contact were in fact relative newcomers to the Lacandon jungle zone. Beginning in the 1940s, small numbers of Indians, mainly from the highland areas of Chiapas, were encouraged by the federal government to colonise the uncultivated land in the southern parts of the state, close to the border with Guatemala. Although the numbers of communities originally established were few, their creation laid the foundations for a later and substantially larger period of migration that some, in conscious invocation of its biblical connotations, have described as an exodus (Levya-Solano 1993: 23–8; Hernandez-Castillo 1998: 408–11). By 1980 the migrant population had risen to around 100,000 from an estimated 10,000 in 1960; by 1998 it had reached 150,000 and was still rising at an exponential rate (de Vos 1998: 335).

Apart from the sheer magnitude of numbers that such an upheaval and resettlement involved, the factor that gave the Lacandon jungle its distinctive cultural identity was that within this body of migrants existed differences in language, ethnicity, religion and political affiliation that, when combined, resulted in what has been called a 'unique space of social construction' (Aubry 1994: 9; that this was especially the case for Indian women see Hernandez-Castillo 1994: 67–70). In light of these already well-established influences, such as the church, both Protestant evangelical and Catholic liberation theologist, as well as the long active Maoist-inspired political unions of the communities, the indigenous 'culture' that the Zapatistas came to encounter was one both resistant to easy definition and recalcitrant to external political control (see Higgins 2004). Placed in this context it is perhaps not surprising, then, that when the indigenous eventually came to embrace the Zapatista politics of clandestine subversion they did so under conditions of severe economic hardship, and only after the exhaustion of various legal attempts at political expression (see Harvey 1998).

The true extent of the 'Indianisation' of the Zapatista National Liberation Army was, however, only finally formalised after the communities themselves had decided to go to war. With the creation of the Clandestine Revolutionary Indigenous Committee (CCRI) in 1993, the Zapatista general command became completely Indian, and the organisational structure at last reflected the earlier ideological change that had taken place amongst its non-Indian members (Le Bot 1997: 195–6). Consisting of representatives of the four main ethnic groups (Tzeltal, Chol, Tzotzil and Tojolabal) from the three central regions of Zapatista influence in the state (the north, the highlands and the jungle), the CCRI became the central means of co-ordination and dissemination necessary in the preparation for the planned rebel offensive ('An Interview with the CCRI-CG' in *Zapatistas!* 1994: 131–9). It was around this time also that Marcos was appointed chief military commander for the rebel forces.

Nobody was really sure how the 1994 New Year's Day rebellion would go; it had the potential to be a disaster, a horrific bloodbath. As it was, the rebel force of some 6,000 successfully occupied seven of Chiapas's main towns with little bloodshed. In the days that followed, however, and once the Mexican military had recovered from the surprise, many hundreds of lives, Zapatista, military and civilian, were lost. The government was not slow to employ Swiss- and US-manufactured planes and helicopters to bomb the rebel positions, although their superior firepower was to be quickly tempered, not so much by the guerrilla tactics of the Zapatistas themselves, as by the national and international media attention that they had unleashed with their dramatic declaration of war in San Cristobal some days earlier. By 12 January, the government had declared a ceasefire and the possibility for a peaceful resolution to the conflict seemed hopeful.

La lucha sigue – the fight continues

At the time of writing, it has been ten years since those first days of violent insurrection in Chiapas and still blood is shed in the defence of *Zapatismo*. The Mexican federal government has been accused of attempting to 'administer' the war rather than sincerely seek its resolution.[7] Its strategy, both domestic and international, has combined the showmanship of rhetorical and gestural politics, common to much of late-twentieth-century statecraft, with the more classical tactics of counter-subversion already tried and tested in the mountain villages of their Central American neighbours (see Higgins 2001). It is a battle fought on two fronts. Locally in Chiapas, the Indian communities have found themselves surrounded by a military force estimated to be anywhere between 60,000 and 80,000 strong.[8] Whilst their constant patrolling and increasingly regular incursions leave the communities intimidated and tense, it has been the training and arming of 'unofficial' paramilitary groups throughout the region that has given rise to a refugee population of some 16,000, and most horrifically resulted in the

December 1997 massacre of forty-five people, mainly women and children, in the community of Acteal (see Aubry and Inda 1998: 1–4; *Proceso* No. 1104 (28 December 1997) and No. 1105 (4 January 1998); Duran de Huerta and Boldrini 1998; Fray Bartolome de Las Casas Centre for Human Rights 1998).

In contrast to this painful realism of low-intensity warfare under which large parts of Chiapas continue to suffer today, the other aspect of the governmental response has been directed towards the more nebulous frontier of public and international opinion. It has been in this connected realm where the politics of representation and discourse has been most fiercely contested that we must locate and understand the governmental obsession with the unmasking of Marcos. For ever since the first declaration of the Lacandon jungle was proclaimed on New Year's Day 1994, it has fallen upon Marcos as both product and expression of the Zapatista struggle to communicate just why it is the indigenous chose to fight and why it is they continue to fight to this day.

After so many secretive years of survival in the mountains, the sudden arrival of journalists, photographers and camera crews in the Lacandon communities has, instead of making the struggle seem more real, often made the world of national and international politics appear increasingly *sur*-real. At times Marcos has drawn the analogy of his and the Zapatistas' apparition into this new world with that of Lewis Carroll's Alice when she too stepped through a looking glass (e.g. Marcos 1998a: 205–9). At other times he has compared his actions and that of his companions with those heroic moments of madness immortalised in Cervantes' tale of the exploits of Don Quixote de la Mancha and his loyal footman Sancho Panza. For Marcos the saddest part of Don Quixote was always the moment when he was returned to a life of normality, the moment when he would say of himself, 'I was mad, and now I am sane'. It has been Marcos's belief that the Zapatistas have to continue battling in the madness until the very last (Duran de Huerta 1994: 21–2). To this end Marcos has created his own Sancho Panza in the literary character of a tough little beetle, known as *Don Durito* (see the examples collected in Marcos 1998a).

All this might appear too much, too playful, too lightweight in contrast to the daily plight of Indian life in Chiapas were it not for the fact that such stories, such literary allusions and poems have at their core one key message. For the Mexican governmental administration so determined to follow the schematic rules of neoliberal reform, a government whose only recourse is to call upon the cold and at times savage rationalism of economic analysis in sterile defence of their contested legitimacy, the Zapatista message is difficult to counter. Not directed to the head, because the Zapatistas believe they have little to add to existing analyses of Mexico's continued economic crisis, their message aims for 'the heart, the part most often forgotten' (Le Bot 1997: 356). It is not that they simply hope to elicit sympathy, for as Marcos says, we are not saying that we want to create a sentimental discourse, one that's a-political, or a-theoretical, or anti-theoretical, but what we want is to bring theory down to the level of the human being, to what is lived, to share with the people the experiences that make it possible to continue living.

(Le Bot 1997: 356)

As Marcos himself declared at the opening ceremony of the first Zapatista jungle encounter for Humanity Against Neoliberalism in 1996:

Behind our black mask,
behind our armed voice,
behind our unnameable name,
behind what you see of us,
behind this we are you.
behind this, we are the same simple and ordinary men and women who are repeated in all races, painted in all colours, speak in all languages and live in all places.

Behind this, we are the same forgotten men and women,
the same excluded, the same untolerated,
the same persecuted, the same as you.

Behind this, we are you.

(*Zapatista Encuentro* 1998: 24)

It is precisely this appeal to the 'human', a human-ness not articulated in any theory, ideology or doctrine, but one that is only reflected within the literature and speeches of Zapatismo and made intimate through the jungle 'encounters' that have attracted thousands to Chiapas since the conflict first began, that makes the Zapatistas unique (see Higgins and Duran de Huerta 1999: especially p. 275). It has led some to term the struggle the 'first postmodern revolution of the twenty-first century',[9] and whilst remaining sensitive to the hyperbolic appropriation such a claim entails, might there not also be some truth here? Precisely at a time when IR attempts to articulate an ethical and political stance from the theoretical complexity and challenge of poststructuralism (Campbell 1998), might not the cultural humanism of the Zapatista struggle assist us in our quest to engage theory with lived practice? After all, as we move away from the restrictive analyses surrounding a now contested sovereign subject, might we not agree that a new cultural humanism need not rest upon idealism? Perhaps we can now recognise that the kind of subversive humanism promoted by one of poststructuralism's founding fathers, Gaston Bachelard, a humanism that 'rests on a conception of man decentered, transcended by something beyond his control, yet paradoxically neither denied nor destroyed by this transcendent "other", but rather nourished and sustained by it' (in McAllester Jones 1991: 4), is after all possible?

Although the Zapatistas do not claim to have all the answers, maybe in their struggle and the words of Subcomandante Marcos there is hope yet. As Marcos himself puts it, when talking of those fallen Indian fighters, 'making bridges they lived, making themselves bridges they died' (Marcos 1998d: 135).

Post-script for the twenty-first century – Zapatismo goes global

It was in 1997 that Marcos first penned his polemic 'The Fourth World War has Begun' (Marcos 1997b). Published in *Le Monde Diplomatique*, the piece characteristically poked fun at the staid academic analyses of the period, preferring instead to offer readers a hotch-potch of symbols with which to cut and paste. Readers were meant to use the symbols to try and make sense of the world. The point was that neoliberalism does not make sense.

The non-sense of neoliberalism, as opposed to the common sense of neoliberalism, has increasingly been highlighted at meetings of international institutions by that plethora of social movements, non-governmental organisations and members of civil society most often referred to as the anti-globalisation movement. Whilst it would be accurate to say that Zapatismo has had an influence and often a presence at many of these anti-globalisation protests, particularly in Italy where the *Ya Basta!* group is most active, it would also be a mistake to limit the ambitions of Zapatismo to this movement alone.

Recently a group of young film-makers took up Marcos's thesis and made a documentary film called the 'Fourth World War' (Big Noise Tactical n.d.). Tracing a path from Mexico to Argentina, South Africa, Palestine, Korea, 'the North' from Seattle to Genoa, and then to the 'War on Terror' in New York, they eventually concluded in Iraq. It is an epic production, especially for a group of self-taught film-makers from New York, that premiered at the International Documentary Film Festival in Amsterdam, 2003. It is a film that makes links that go beyond the anti-globalisation movement and suggests that what seemed like a contentious piece of agit-prop in 1997 may well look more like tragically fulfilled rebel prophesy in 2003.

Marcos himself returned to the question of global issues in a recent communiqué on the war in Iraq, and rather than speculating further on Zapatismo's international influence, it would seem appropriate, especially in a book entitled *Critical Theories, International Relations and 'the Anti-Globalisation Movement'*, to let *el sup* articulate the rebel movement's international stance directly.

> The foundational act of war of the new century was not the collapse of the twin towers, but nor was it the fall, graceless and unspectacular, of the statue of [Saddam] Hussein. The 21st century began with the globalised

'NO TO THE WAR' which gave humanity back its essence and held it together in a cause. As never before in the history of humanity, the planet was shaken by this 'NO.'

From intellectuals of all stature, to unlettered residents of the forgotten corners of the earth, the 'NO' became a bridge which united communities, towns, villas, cities, provinces, countries, continents. In manifestos and demonstrations, the 'NO' sought the vindication of reason in the face of force.

All resistances, in the history of humanity, have appeared ineffective, not just on the eve, but also well into the night of the attack, but time is, paradoxically, on their sides if it is conceived of in that way.

Many statues can fall, but if the decisiveness of generations is maintained and encouraged, the triumph of resistance is possible. It will not have a precise date, nor will there be tiresome parades, but the foreseeable decline of an apparatus – which turns its own machinery into its project for a new order – will end up being complete. ...

That is why a little respect is needed for the other who is resisting someplace else in his otherly self, as well as a lot of humility in order to remember that much can still be learned from that otherly self, and wisdom to not copy, but produce, a theory and a practice which does not include arrogance in its principles, but which recognises its horizons and the tools that serve for those horizons.

A world where many resistances fit. Not an international of the resistance, but a multihued flag, a melody with many tunes. If it seems dissonant, that is just because the calendar of below is still arranging the score, where every note will find its place, its resonance and, above all, its link with the other notes.

History is far from over. In the future, harmonious coexistence will be possible, not because of wars which attempt to dominate the other, but because of the 'no' which gave human beings – as it did before, in prehistory – a common cause and, along with it, hope: that of humanity's survival, against neoliberalism.

(Marcos 2003)

Notes

1 An earlier version of this article was published in *Alternatives: Social Transformation and Humane Governance*, Vol. 25, No. 3. Copyright © 2000 by Lynne Rienner Publishers. Used with permission of the publisher. Unless otherwise stated, all translations are the author's own.

2 Carlos Tello Diaz tells the story of the Fuerzas de Liberación Nacional (FLN) and its transformation into the EZLN. Marcos refers to Diaz as a historian who has studied history with el CISEN. For academic responses that support such an accusation, see *Proceso* No. 977 (24 July 1995).

3 This situation on the ground is rapidly changing owing to the construction of a new road in the conflict zone. Early warnings of the implications of this 'development programme' were first raised by Neil Harvey (1999).

4 The story told here is principally based upon Marcos's own version of events, as they have been recorded in interviews (in Duran de Huerta 1994; Le Bot 1997; and with Carmen Castillo and Tessa Brissac in Gilly *et al.* 1995: 131–42).

5 Literally, *mestizo* refers to someone who is mixed Spanish/Indian. Indigenous peoples are 100 per cent Indian and in Chiapas they call whites *ladinos* (latins) or, if they are darker, *mestizos*. However, the terms are used fairly interchangeably in Chiapas to indicate someone who is not Indian. *Mestizos* are not considered close to the Indian population, usually because the Spanish/Indian sexual relation happened hundreds of years ago and because of the gulf separating Indian and mainstream Mexican cultures.

6 In this regard also see Gary Gossen's somewhat overly structural approach to a nevertheless interesting question, 'Who is the Comandante of Subcomandante Marcos?' in Gosner and Ouweneel (1996: 107–20).

7 This expression belongs to Carlos Montemayor whose analysis of the Mexican government strategy is incisive; see his regular contributions to *Proceso*, especially No. 1113 (1 March 1998) and No. 1126 (31 May 1998) as well as his useful monograph (Montemayor 1997).

8 Jesus Ramirez Cuevas (1998: 8–10) claims that in the late 1990s there was a soldier for each family in the jungle region.

9 First quoted in the *New York Times*, January 1994. For a more thorough examination of this claim see Higgins (2004) (http://www.utexas.edu/utpress/books/higund.html).

6 Contesting the Free Trade Area of the Americas

Invoking a Bolivarian geopolitical imagination to construct an alternative regional project and identity

Marianne H. Marchand[1]

Introduction

From almost the moment the American states became independent in the late eighteenth and early nineteenth centuries two distinct geopolitical imaginations about inter-American relations and a Western Hemispheric identity emerged. These two geopolitical imaginations are most clearly articulated in the Monroe doctrine and Simón Bolívar's ideas about pan-Latin, or more accurately Hispano-, Americanism. These two geopolitical imaginations have influenced regionalism projects in the Western Hemisphere since the 1820s. From its inception, the Monroe doctrine has represented a regional hegemonic project, while Bolívar's dream has represented counter-hegemonic efforts.

In terms of the political economy of regionalism and regionalisation the developments in the Western Hemisphere are interesting if not unique. The hemisphere has been characterised since the 1860s by the systematic development of an inter-American system through the establishment of institutions such as the Pan American Health Union etc. (Connell-Smith 1971). One could even argue that the Americas have provided a laboratory for the articulation and development of the specific characteristics of US hegemony and also set the stage for counter-hegemony. As is often argued (Gilpin 1987), US hegemony can be distinguished from the British version in that the United States created a multilateral system on which it relied for the exercise of its hegemony. In the nineteenth century, US policy-makers did the same in the Americas to support and exercise its hegemony in the region.

This chapter argues that Monrovian and Bolivarian geopolitical imaginations are reflected in current (opposing) regionalism projects. The Monrovian idea of pan-Americanism is reflected in the project of the Free Trade Area for the Americas (FTAA), first introduced by former president Bill Clinton. The Bolivarian internationalist dream provides the inspiration for an alternative regionalism project, entitled Alternative for the Americas, which is being developed by non-governmental organisations (NGOs) and social movements throughout the hemisphere. These groups have organised themselves in the Hemispheric Social Alliance (HSA) which meets at regular intervals, for instance during FTAA ministerial meetings and at the annual World Social Forum meeting in Porto Alegre. In addition, as is now common practice, members of the alliance stay in close contact through e-mail and via the Internet. Thus the HSA reflects continued contestation and, in my view, the articulation of a counter-hegemony.

Although these two opposing regionalism projects are informed by Monrovian and Bolivarian geopolitical imaginations, the subsequent analysis will show that these ideas have been (re)interpreted and appropriated since they were first articulated. This chapter sets out to provide a postcolonial reading of the original Monroe doctrine, pronounced in 1823, and Bolívar's ideas as expressed in his writings, in particular his Jamaican letter and their subsequent interpretations and appropriations.

Postcolonial theory focuses on how knowledge and power underpin imperial authority (Ashcroft *et al.* 1995: 1). Yet, as Michel Foucault has suggested, every system of dominance creates its own resistance (Foucault 1980). This involves the 'appropriation of imperial culture' and knowledge in counter-colonial projects of resistance (Ashcroft *et al.* 1995: 1). As such, postcolonial theory deals with the encounter between empire and indigenous practices and colonised peoples. A postcolonial reading involves the challenging of imperial knowledge and power by recovering (silenced) subaltern voices (Spivak 1995) and focusing on issues of representation/'othering' and resistance (Said 1995), and of hybridity and difference (Bhabha 1995). In the present analysis, most of these dimensions will appear.

Central to a postcolonial reading is the uncovering of patterns of domination which silence certain voices by not giving them the status of subjects (Spivak 1995). In the context of Latin America, indigenous peoples have long been in this position. In so far as their existence and humanity was recognised, only colonisers or local elites represented their needs. The most indicative act of representation and 'othering' was the seventeenth-century announcement by the Catholic Church that indigenous people were animals and did not have a soul. This decision by the Catholic Church effectively took away the indigenous peoples' subjectivity and the possibility of gaining a voice.

Within existing patterns of domination it is important to identify what kind of resistance is being articulated and how cultural difference and hybridity is being constructed discursively (Foucault 1980; Bhabha 1995). In other words, how much space do hegemonic structures allow for marginalised and oppositional voices to be heard? Postcolonial (and poststructuralist) theory suggests that resistance can only be constructed in relation to patterns of domination, i.e. having the status of subjects and adopting some of the dominant categories for the counter-hegemonic project.

According to Homi Bhabha, 'cultural difference is a process of significa-tion through which statements *of* culture or *on* culture differentiate, discriminate and authorize the production of fields of force, reference, applicability, and capacity' (1995: 206). As such, it is important to know who is constructing cultural difference, how and why. Speaking of colonial experiences, Bhabha suggests that the encounter between cultures creates hybridity.

These insights of postcolonial theory inform the present analysis. In particular, the articulation of the Monroe doctrine and its continuing influence in current regionalist projects contrasts with Bolívar's ideas and their present articulations. How these encounters evolve, how resistance is being articulated, how 'othering' and representation is taking place, how hybridity and identities are constructed, are important questions postcolonial theory allows us to ask.

This chapter is divided into two sections. The first focuses on the original Monroe doctrine and Simón Bolívar's ideas about Hispano-Americanism as well as their contingent identities. The second section will address the current alternative regionalism projects and how they invoke Monrovian and Bolivarian geopolitical imaginations.

Monroe vs. Bolívar

The focus of this section is on the ideas of James Monroe and Simón Bolívar. These two political figures were picked because they have played a central role in intra-hemispheric relations. As one of the first presidents of the United States, James Monroe left an important mark on US foreign policy during the period of decolonisation for most of its southern neighbours. Simón Bolívar led a major independence movement throughout the Southern Hemisphere, in particular the territory encompassing Venezuela, Colombia, Panama, Ecuador and Bolivia. He wrote down many of his ideas and visions and these writings, in the form of letters and papers, have been widely disseminated. They also have been influential in articulating alternative conceptions of intra-hemispheric relations. Although Bolívar left an extensive body of writings, two letters in particular are interesting and revealing concerning his regional designs. These are his Jamaican letter of 1815 (*Carta de Jamaica*) and the Convocation for the Pan-American Congress of 1824 (Bolívar 1815, 1824). In these two writings Bolívar identifies Spain and the United States as the 'other'; hence his idea to strengthen ties with Great Britain, which was not only the most powerful European state but also the enemy of both Spain and the United States (Liscano 1998). In other words, Bolívar is following the Machiavellian logic of siding with the enemies of one's enemies.

The background for the pronouncement of the Monroe doctrine was the US War of Independence and the subsequent US desire to isolate itself from interference by European powers. The US foreign policy of isolationism developed relatively quickly after the country gained its independence in 1776. Statesmen like Thomas Jefferson and Henry Clay had already clearly indicated that in order for this isolationist policy to succeed a Western Hemisphere, separate from 'Europe', needed to be created.

When Monroe pronounced his doctrine on 2 December 1823 it was directed at keeping European powers *out* and *not* at increasing and improving inter-American relations or building an inter-American system. This objective is illustrated by the following passages from the Monroe doctrine:

> [...] the occasion has been judged proper for asserting, as a principle in which the rights and interests of the United States are involved, that the American continents, by the free and independent condition which they have assumed and maintain, are henceforth not to be considered as subjects for future colonization by any European powers. ...
>
> We owe it, therefore, to candor and to the amicable relations existing between the United States and those powers [by which is meant allied European powers] to declare that we should consider any attempt on their part to extend their system to any portion of this hemisphere as dangerous to our peace and safety.
>
> (Monroe 1823)

The Monroe doctrine reflects a particular geopolitical imagination about the Western Hemisphere. The construction of the Western Hemisphere is based on the concept of the 'New World', a term originally coined by the Europeans. This New World is contrasted with the 'Old World' or Europe, which is portrayed as the 'other'. At the same time, however, the Monroe doctrine speaks of America in the singular, referring to the United States, as well as of the American continents, in other words the Americas. In the Doctrine it is not clear what differentiates America/the United States from its southern brethren, but at this point the similarities among American states are being stressed and contrasted with Europe as the 'other'.

The American or 'New World' identity that is being constructed is based on its relatively novel political system. The creation and development of republican institutions is contrasted with the old monarchies across the Atlantic. According to the Doctrine, the Western Hemisphere is characterised by its republican institutions which are by definition democratic – despite the obvious presence of dictatorial regimes in Hispanic America. European monarchies in turn are associated with authoritarianism:

> It is impossible that the allied powers should extend their political system to any portion of either continent [the Americas] without endangering our peace and happiness; nor can anyone believe that our southern brethren, if left to themselves, would adopt it on their own accord. It is equally impossible, therefore, that we should behold such an interposition in any form with indifference. If we look to the comparative strength and resources of Spain and those new Governments, and their distance from each other, it must be obvious

that she can never subdue them. It is still the true policy of the United States to leave the parties to themselves, in hope that other powers will pursue the same course.

(Monroe 1823)

Although the Monroe doctrine does not really try to juxtapose a 'North American/United States' identity onto a Hispanic or 'South American' identity, there are some early indications that US policy-makers are aware of differences. One obvious indication is the use of the plural terms 'continents' and 'Americas'. Another indication is the extension of US national security to the rest of the hemisphere: an invasion by European powers in the south is being interpreted as an infringement of the security of the United States and the latter, therefore, takes it upon itself to counter such interference and 'protect' its southern brethren. Interestingly, of course, this policy is being articulated without the explicit consent of the Hispano-American regimes. As such it could be interpreted as an expression of superiority or benign paternalism. In the further development of the inter-American system, Latin America is increasingly 'othered' in US foreign policy discourse, a process which involves the construction of a feminised and racialised inferior 'other'.

John J. Johnson's study of the use of caricatures in US newspapers since the early nineteenth century reveals an 'othering' of Latin American countries in either feminine or racial terms. For instance, during the nineteenth century Latin America was often portrayed as a young woman who was the object of 'wooing' by the United States and Great Britain alike. When some Caribbean and Central American countries were characterised by domestic strife around the turn of the century, it was Uncle Sam who intervened to put the house back in order. In this imaginary, these countries were displayed as rowdy little black boys, in need of some form of castigation such as spanking. Whether it was portrayed as a 'desirable young white woman' or as a 'rowdy little black boy', it was clear that Latin American countries had to do some growing up before being seen as fully fledged adult states (Johnson 1993; see also Hunt 1987).

In contrast to the Monroe doctrine, Bolívar articulated his own ideas about the direction of the Western Hemisphere and its attendant identity. In so doing, he developed a counter-hegemonic project by appropriating elements of 'imperial [US] knowledge' and invoking hybridity, in particular a *mestizo*, or mixed Spanish/Indian, identity. What emerged was a discursive struggle over inter-Americanism and pan-Americanism whereby Bolívar formulated a pan(Hispano)-Americanism or internationalism in Latin America. In short, he wanted a grouping of Spanish-speaking or Hispanic American countries which were to be allied to Great Britain in order to offset US hegemonic designs in the region.

Bolívar's Jamaican letter reveals that for him, the question of similarity and shared identity with the United States, based on republican political institutions, is very complex and far from self-evident. In the excerpts of his letter cited below, he outlines his thinking:

> We are a young people. We inhabit a world apart, separated by broad seas. We are young in the ways of almost all the arts and sciences, although, in a certain manner, we are old in the ways of civilised society. ... But we scarcely retain a vestige of what once was; we are, moreover, neither Indian nor European, but a species midway between the legitimate proprietors of this country and the Spanish usurpers. In short, though Americans by birth we derive our rights from Europe, and we have to assert these rights against the rights of the natives, and at the same time we must defend ourselves against the invaders.
>
> (Bolívar 1815, my translation)

This excerpt is quite revealing. Bolívar clearly claims a *mestizo* identity for (Latin) America. Also, he disagrees with Monroe about which political institutions are best fitted for the Americas. While Monroe is convinced that the entire Western Hemisphere should have republican institutions, Bolívar thinks that the recently decolonised states are not yet ready for that. He argues that the state of being colonised prevents people experiencing and experimenting with the management of public affairs:

> We have been harassed by a conduct which has not only deprived us of our rights but has kept us in a sort of permanent infancy with regard to public affairs. If we could at least have managed our domestic affairs and our internal administration we could have acquainted ourselves with the processes and mechanics of public affairs. We should also have enjoyed a personal consideration, thereby commanding a certain unconscious respect from the people, which is so necessary to preserve amidst revolutions. That is why I say we have even been deprived of an active tyranny, since we have not been permitted to exercise its functions.
>
> (Bolívar 1815, my translation)

Because recently decolonised states have been deprived of the opportunity to run a country, let alone experiment with different political systems, Bolívar arges for a paternalist government. In his own words:

> Although I seek perfection for the government of my country, I cannot persuade myself that the New World can, at the moment, be organised as a great republic. Since it is impossible, I dare not desire it; yet much less do I desire to have all America a monarchy because this plan is not only impracticable but also impossible. Wrongs now existing could not be righted, and our emancipation would be fruitless. The American

states need the care of paternal governments to heal the sores and wounds of despotism and war.

(Bolívar 1815, my translation)

The metaphor employed by Bolívar is that of a not yet full-grown adult. In other words, the *mestizo* nations of America need to experiment with political institutions and to grow up before they are ready for representative (republican) government. And while republican institutions are rejected at this moment, so is the monarchy. The latter is associated with despotism and abusive rule. Based on his analysis of the identity and state of mind of American states, it is clear that Bolívar views a paternalistic government as best suited for the region especially when it implies that the state will perform a certain kind of 'caring' role. Bolívar summarises his choice as follows: 'Among the popular and representative systems, I do not favour the federal system. It is over-perfect, and it demands political virtues and talents far superior to our own' (Bolívar 1815, my translation).

Interestingly, Bolívar is postulating the notion of hybridity, in the form of a *mestizo* identity, but at the same time he is internalising a racial hierarchy, according to which *mestizo* people are not (yet) ready for a republican system of government.

What we can observe, in other words, is two rather distinct regional projects, geopolitical imaginations and attendant identities. In particular, Bolívar's geopolitical imagination challenges the US-generated hegemonic myth of what unites the American continent(s). This myth insists that what unites the Americas is: (a) separation from Europe (a negative factor); (b) shared historical experiences: being European colonies and having to struggle for independence; (c) geographical proximity; (d) common political ideals and institutions: a government of popular representation, democracy, a republic and liberty (Connell-Smith 1971). Bolívar clearly undermines this myth, in particular by elaborating the different historical trajectories of American states and the divergent needs of these states in terms of political institutions. Moreover, Bolívar is aware of US hegemonic designs in the region and does not hesitate to establish alliances with European powers to offset such designs. In other words, even Latin American relations with Europe do not follow the same path as those of the United States.

Invoking Monrovian and Bolivarian geopolitical imaginations

The two contrasting geopolitical imaginations, first articulated by James Monroe and Simón Bolívar, are reflected in two current regionalism projects. These are the US-sponsored FTAA and the Alternatives for the Americas, as developed by the HSA. The FTAA clearly reflects a neoliberal agenda and is part of the US hegemonic project in the region. As such it is interesting that the Monroe doctrine is not explicitly mentioned or invoked. However, for the US government, the FTAA reflects an effort to counterbalance regional developments in Asia and especially Europe. Although the FTAA is being defended as an instance of 'open regionalism' it is clearly designed to foster the competitiveness of US companies.

The FTAA is also a reflection of the Monrovian-inspired inter-American system (IAS). In order to garner support and build a broad base, the help of the Organization of American States (OAS) and the Inter-American Development Bank (IADB) has been called upon. Also, the framers of the FTAA charter are to draw upon the experiences and expertise of the Economic Commission for Latin America and the Caribbean (ECLAC) as well as the Pan-American Health Union.

Overall, we can say that there is a serious discrepancy between the social, political and environmental goals of the FTAA – as stated for instance in the declaration produced by heads of state at a summit to discuss the overall direction of hemispheric relations, in Miami, 1994 – and the actual organisation of the working groups and draft documents. In the Miami Declaration and subsequent declarations in Santiago (Chile, 1998) and Quebec (Canada, 2001) the objectives are very broad. The Miami Declaration defines the following four: 'To preserve and strengthen' democracy and good government; 'promote prosperity through economic integration and free trade'; 'eradicate poverty and discrimination' in the hemisphere; and 'guarantee sustainable development' and conservation of the environment (First Summit of the Americas 1994). Under the first item, two other principles are included which have received significant attention: the promotion of good government and the eradication of corruption; and the fight against organised crime, drugs and arms trafficking, and terrorism.

The four principles of the Miami Declaration reflect a comprehensive agenda for integration and co-operation in the Americas. However, there is a significant discrepancy between these principles and the actual points around which the FTAA negotiations are centred. This is because economic integration and free trade have been identified as the principal objective to be reached by 2005. As a result, all attention has been directed at developing a free trade agreement which complies with World Trade Organization (WTO) rules as well as existing hemispheric trade agreements, and which is compatible with environmental policies as well as workers' rights. Moreover, such an agreement is also supposed to provide special support for the smallest economies (Red Mexicana de Acción Frente al Libre Comercio (RMALC) 2002).

Both the principles of the Miami Declaration and the actual FTAA project reflect a modern-day Monrovian geopolitical imagination in which possible discrepancies are ignored. Although not stated explicitly in the declaration, the efforts at creating a 'partnership for development and prosperity'[2] are aimed at strengthening intra-hemispheric relations and providing a counterpoint to regionalism projects in Asia and Europe. This is not so much about keeping other powers out, as about being able to compete effectively in an increasingly globalised world (cf. Bøås *et al.* 1999). Whereas the declaration identifies various 'others', including organised crime, illegal drug and arms trafficking as well as terrorism, the section on economic integration and free trade perceives only those responsible for imposing impediments to free trade and market access as the 'other'.

Although intra-hemispheric relations and free trade are clearly the primary objective, these are situated in the context of the wider world economy. The shared identity of the Americas is reflected in the stated principles of democracy, free trade and sustainable development (First Summit of the Americas 1994) which are supposed to be the cornerstones of a modern-day IAS. Although such principles are broad-based, the United States still defines the political and economic agenda and sets the priorities for the IAS.

The two elements that distinguish this modern-day Monrovian geopolitical imagination from its nineteenth-century precursor are the inclusion of Canada and the Caribbean in the IAS and the explicit acknowledgement of difference:

> We recognize that economic integration and the creation of a free trade area will be complex endeavors, particularly in view of the wide differences in the levels of development and the size of economies existing in our Hemisphere. We will remain cognizant of these differences as we work toward economic integration in the Hemisphere. We look forward to our own resources, ingenuity, and individual capacities as well as to the international community to help us achieve our goals.
>
> (First Summit of the Americas 1994)

The call to use local resources, ingenuity and individual capacities to foster development does not necessarily mean that one can choose a development trajectory outside the parameters set by the declaration and the attendant Plan for Action. This is reiterated in the Miami Declaration (First Summit of the Americas 1994): 'Our continued economic progress depends on sound economic policies, sustainable development, and dynamic private sectors. A key to prosperity is trade without barriers, without subsidies, without unfair trading practices, and with an increasing stream of productive investments.' In other words, attempts to steer a different course, as exemplified by the government of Hugo Chavez in Venezuela, are being forcefully opposed.

The intra-hemispheric open regionalism project has stirred up significant opposition from civil society groups. Much of this organising predates the emergence of the anti-globalisation or critical globalisation movement during the WTO meeting in Seattle. It is with the negotiations around the North American Free Trade Agreement (NAFTA) that a three-country, transnational opposition movement emerged. At the time this transnational opposition movement consisted of NGOs, social movements and civil society groups representing a range of interests, including workers' rights, women's rights, the environment, human rights and democracy. Organising around NAFTA provided an important experience in collaborating with Canadian and US-based organisations. Moreover, it provided the first concerted effort to formulate a consistent and broad-based response to dominant neoliberal economic policies. These efforts coincided with other intra-hemispheric transnational struggles around issues of the environment, democracy and human rights, indigenous rights and women's rights. By 1994, such efforts received another impulse through the Zapatista uprising in Chiapas (Mexico). With their two *encuentros* (meetings) in Mexico and Spain, the Zapatistas were able to provide face-to-face fora for civil society groups. This task has now been taken over by the annual Social Forum meetings in Porto Alegre, bringing together not only groups and individuals from throughout the hemisphere, but also like-minded groups from around the world. The experiences gained from this transnational organising have helped to galvanise relatively quickly an alliance of groups and organisations from throughout the hemisphere to counter the state-led FTAA project.

As early as the first meeting of heads of state in Miami in 1994, various civil society groups voiced their opposition to the comprehensive hemispheric agenda, and in particular the plans for economic integration. At the ministerial meeting in Belo Horizonte, Brazil, in 1997, civil society organisations made the first concerted attempt to formulate an alternative plan for hemispheric integration. A year later, at the second summit in Santiago, Chile, an alternative People's Summit was held. It was during this meeting that final steps were taken to create the Hemispheric Social Alliance (HSA) which was founded in 1999 (RMALC 2002). Using the framework of the HSA, civil society organisations started to formulate a counter-regionalism project entitled 'Alternatives for the Americas'. Needless to say, modern technology and means of communication (in particular the Internet) have been important in the organisation and co-ordination of this counter-regionalism project.

Opponents of the FTAA have defined it as 'an integration project which will consolidate US hegemony through political, economic and military dominance' (Reunión de Redes de la Campaña contra el ALCA 2002: 1, my translation). In the document *Convocation for Days of Continental Resistance against the FTAA* ,the issues which are being opposed are: neoliberalism, debt, militarism and the dominance of the United States in the region (Reunión de Redes de la Campaña contra el ALCA 2002: 1, my translation). Both the US and Canadian economies are seen as the biggest threats for the smaller Latin American economies.

The Declaration of the Second People's Summit of the Americas (Quebec, 2001) draws clear lines of demarcation between the state-led FTAA plans and the HSA's alternative regionalism project. In the Quebec Declaration this is articulated as follows:

> We reject this project of liberalised trade and investment, deregulation and privatisation. This neo-liberal project is racist and sexist and

destructive of the environment. We propose to build new ways of continental integration based on democracy, human rights, equality, solidarity, pluralism and respect for the environment.

(Alianza Social Continental (ASC) 2001)

The alternative regionalism project suggested by the HSA is clearly inspired by the ideas of Simón Bolívar. Graciela Rodriguez of the Brazilian Network for People's Integration articulates this explicitly:

I had the feeling when I left Costa Rica of being back in the era of Simón Bolívar, caught up in the old dream of integrating the people of the Americas ... but now constituted differently. This time it is led by social organizations through movements of farmers, campesinos, workers, community activists, women, academics and environmentalists. Together they make up civil society throughout the hemisphere, in an alliance.

(HSA 1999)

However, in order to make a claim to Bolívar's ideas, they have to be appropriated, reinterpreted and rearticulated. The 'other' for the HSA is US-based and supported global and regional capital: 'The FTAA project is a charter of investors' rights and freedoms, sanctions the primacy of capital over labour, transforms life and the world into merchandise' (ASC 2001). In other words, the 'other' is still US related, but has been transformed from the state to a diffuse coalition of economic actors. The 'other' is also referred to as economic and legal corporate power and can be found (by extension) throughout the Western Hemisphere. In opposition to this corporate 'other' the HSA represents an alternative 'us', consisting of a rainbow coalition of 'unions, popular and environmental organisations, women's groups, human rights organisations, international solidarity groups, indigenous, peasant and student associations and church groups' (ASC 2001). Again, the identity of 'us' has been transformed from the state to a diffuse alliance of non-state actors. These transformations are the result as well as an integral part of the changing global and regional political economy, which provides the context in which non-state actors undertake their activities.

The rearticulation of Bolívar's geopolitical imagination involves not only a reconstruction of the other, but also a reinterpretation of political goals. In the texts produced by the HSA, Bolívar is mentioned when discussing issues of justice and democracy. This interpretation of his ideas is a far cry from his own statements about the *mestizo* identity of Latin Americans and a paternalistic regime being the most appropriate form of government. Now, it is quite the opposite. Corporate-led globalisation/regionalisation is seen as profoundly undemocratic, because it 'negates human rights, sabotages democracy and undermines state sovereignty' (ASC 2001). To counter this neoliberal project, the HSA offers an alternative in the form of a plan for 'continental integration based on democracy, human rights, equality, solidarity, pluralism and respect for the environment' (ASC 2001).

The HSA regionalism proposal is comprehensive and multidimensional. In contrast the FTAA project prioritises economic integration and free trade over issues such as human rights, workers' rights, fighting poverty, eliminating discrimination and sustainable development. Although these issues are mentioned in the Miami Declaration of 1994, they are not seen as inextricably related, to the extent that they need to be addressed in a comprehensive plan. Instead the different objectives are hierarchically ordered, with preference given to economic interests. Although the Miami Declaration does not ignore the links among its stated goals, it suggests that most of the objectives can be accomplished through prioritising free trade and economic integration (First Summit of the Americas 1994).

The HSA *Alternatives for the Americas* plan identifies explicitly the links among its objectives and tries to find a balance among them. In so doing it not only presents an alternative development trajectory, but also claims to be more democratic in its decision-making process as well as more inclusive than the state-led FTAA project. Although this oppositional stance is justified by invoking a Bolivarian geopolitical imagination of justice and democracy for the Americas, such a reference requires a significant rearticulation of his ideas. Rather than engaging in a comprehensive reinterpretation, the HSA ignores Bolívar's ideas about republicanism and instead invokes his image as South America's liberator from colonialism:

> The aspiration to build a more egalitarian and respectful society throughout the hemisphere transcends national boundaries and has a long historical tradition in the Americas. It goes back at least as far as the struggles to create free and independent countries in the American hemisphere. Almost two centuries ago ... Simón Bolívar led the movement to liberate a large part of South America from colonialism.
>
> (HSA 2002: 4)

To some extent, the use of this image collides with the fact that the HSA is a coalition of civil society organisations from throughout the Western Hemisphere, not just South America. For the liberator reference to work, two distinct geopolitical imaginations of the Americas are being constructed. One is the 'colonising' America of corporate and legal power, interested in pursuing a neoliberal agenda of regionalisation, and elitist and undemocratic in its decision-making process. The other is the 'alternative' America, consisting of a rainbow coalition of civil society groups, pluralist in character, pursuing participatory democracy and a regionalism project based on sustainable, inclusive development. Interestingly, in an ironic turn of events, the 'colonisers', as representatives of hegemonic regional power, are being equated with the 'Old World', while the 'alternative alliance' is strengthening its ties with

European civil society groups that are part of the critical globalisation movement, and representing itself as the 'New World'.

The most notable example of growing ties with European groups is perhaps the strong European presence at the annual World Social Forum meetings in Porto Alegre. Members of ATTAC, which originated in a French campaign on international financial issues, play a particularly key role in the forum (see ATTAC International 1999). The Transnational Institute (TNI n.d.) based in Amsterdam also has strong links with the Forum and with Red Mexicana de Acción Frente al Libre Comercio in Mexico, one of the founding members of the HSA. Further, Peter Bakvis of the International Confederation of Free Trade Unions (ICFTU 2004) collaborated on the Alternatives for the Americas document and is one of the co-ordinators for the HSA team working on labour. These and many other examples of collaboration point to a growing alliance between the HSA and European civil society in opposition to US hegemony; they also demonstrate the ways in which the alternative identity for the Americas is being constructed in complex, internationalised and internationalist ways.

Conclusion

This chapter has presented a different perspective on the politics of resistance and globalisation. It set out to provide a postcolonial reading of two different regionalism projects for the Americas. Both cases, either explicitly or implicitly, invoke certain historical geopolitical imaginations about the Americas to make their claims. The dominant FTAA project, which recently has run into serious problems, represents a Monrovian geopolitical imagination about the IAS and intra-hemispheric relations. The alternative project, proposed by the HSA, invokes Simón Bolívar's ideas to justify its objectives. It is interesting that, in an age of globalisation, framers of different (transnational) regionalism projects need to reach back to the 'local' past to find a justification. The images used are full of historical baggage and, in particular, that of Bolívar resonates with large sections of the population. What this reading suggests is not only that such geopolitical imaginations are occurring, but also that they are very important in the formulation and channelling of political projects. Without such references to historical ideas and myths, much of the justification for these projects disappears. The geopolitical imaginations also provide the source for identity construction and 'othering', while at the same time limiting the options and direction for (historically) embedding such political projects.

In some ways it can be argued that there has been no significant change in the Monrovian-inspired regionalism project. It still entails a US-dominated hegemonic project and aims at keeping external powers, in this case European and Asian competition, out. Two major differences are, however, that the focus has shifted from security concerns to a predominantly economic agenda and that the FTAA project is supported by political and economic elites in the United States as well as in Latin American countries. In other words, the FTAA is not just a state-led project but tends to involve non-state actors, primarily representatives of the business community.

In contrast, the Bolivarian geopolitical imagination has undergone significant rearticulation. Bolívar has always been associated with the underdog or the marginalised. This first came through in his role as liberator from the colonial power Spain. Subsequently he claimed a voice for Latin American countries and space for Hispano-internationalism in the Western Hemisphere. Interestingly, he is also invoked to justify claims for justice and democracy. This use of his image is more problematic, as he was no defender of democracy. Yet, that part of his ideas seems to have been silenced and reinterpreted. The elements of his ideas which are most used include indirect references to his Hispano-internationalism and his views on Spanish colonialism. It is perhaps no coincidence that in creating alliances, Bolívar himself also sought allies in Europe to oppose US hegemony. Two centuries later, *l'histoire se répète*.

Notes

1 I wish to thank Abel Gómez Gutiérrez for his assistance in preparing this chapter.
2 The full title of the Miami Declaration of Principles is: 'Partnership for Development and Prosperity: Democracy, Free Trade and Sustainable Development in the Americas'.

7   Globalisation and the 'politics of identity'

IR theory through the looking glass of women's reproductive rights activism

Bice Maiguashca

Introduction

Over the past few years, the field of International Relations (IR) has been abuzz with talk of 'globalisation', 'de-territorialisation' and 'identity'. The picture being painted by some IR theorists is one of a world being compressed into a single space by the forces of global capitalism, the flow of new technology, the movement of vast numbers of people and the cultural swirl of cosmopolitan ideas. The general argument seems to be that, within this context, a new form of politics is emerging which can no longer be subsumed under old statist frameworks. What I will call the 'politics of identity' is generally equated with transnational social movements such as women's movements, ecological movements, ethnic and religious movements and gay/lesbian movements (significantly, 'the anti-globalisation movement' is not usually interpreted as an exemplar of this kind of politics). Identity-based movements are seen not only as generating new, non-territorial political identities, but also as representing a distinct type of politics which revolves around cultural and lifestyle issues rather than the class and material interests understood to be at the root of older, workers' movements and more recent 'anti-globalisation' activism.

This chapter aims to evaluate critically the way identity and, more particularly, the politics of identity have been conceptualised thus far in IR. More specifically, it seeks to assess the claims being made on behalf of this type of politics in light of one strand of 'the anti-globalisation movement', that is, the women's reproductive rights movement. The central argument put forward here is that there are two prevalent conceptions of the politics of identity in IR. The first highlights the cohesive nature of identity and characterises the politics of identity in terms of what I shall refer to as a 'politics of solidarity'. The second emphasises the divisive nature of identity and, as a result, conceptualises the politics of identity as a 'politics of difference'. My claim will be that while these two perspectives constitute serious efforts to address the question of identity and its relation to politics, they remain limited by their fundamentally theoretical approach to the subject matter. Indeed, drawing on my substantive research into the particular political practices of a specific social movement, I argue that the notion of the politics of identity understood as a politics *about identity* obscures more than it reveals. Political theories using this notion are liable to misrepresent both the movements they equate with the politics of identity and those supposedly transcendent of it.

This argument is developed in four parts. In the first two parts of the chapter I review the works of a number of critical scholars in IR who implicitly or explicitly evoke the notion of the politics of identity. In the first part, I address two scholars, Jan Aart Scholte and Andrew Linklater, who tend to conceptualise this politics in terms of what could be called a 'politics of solidarity'. In the second part, I turn to the work of R. B. J. Walker and William Connolly who prefer to see the politics of identity as an expression of the 'politics of difference'. In each case I assess their claims in light of three questions: how they conceptualise identity and more particularly collective identity, the context in which they locate identity construction and the political significance that they attribute to the politics of identity. In the third part of the chapter I critically revisit these claims in light of the way identity is constructed and mobilised within the international women's reproductive rights movement. In the conclusion, I suggest an alternative starting point for theorising identity and its relationship to the political.

Globalisation and the 'politics of solidarity'

Both Scholte and Linklater situate the politics of identity in the context of globalisation, which they see as changing the social, political and economic landscape of international relations. The problem, however, is that both thinkers conflate the politics of identity with social movements and then describe these movements as the collective expression of *cultural* identities. In doing this, they tend to reach for a 'levels of analysis' approach which locates the construction of identity at the local, national or global level. Furthermore, by seeing the politics of identity as a newly emergent and distinct form of politics which has erupted in the wake of globalisation, they implicitly suggest that these movements are in some ways fundamentally different from previous forms of conflict; culture is presented as the new terrain of politics with difference and identity being the main issues at stake. Thus, as we shall see, they present the politics of identity as a politics over and for identity *tout court*.

Scholte and the politics of 'collective identities'

Scholte's central argument is that globalisation presents a fundamental challenge to the concept and practice of state sovereignty and, thereby, to the state system as conceived by realists (Scholte 1996; 2000b). Global production, finance, communications and threats such as environmental degradation, he argues, have all increasingly undermined the state's ability to exercise control over what happens within its own territory. Along with this decline in state sovereignty, globalisation has engendered the formation of alternative political identities which reflect new patterns of self–other identification, and, thereby, new forms of what he terms 'identity politics' (Scholte 1996: 39; 2000b: 86, 107).

Despite making some very interesting and relevant points regarding the need to restructure IR theory so that it can take into account these new trends, there are a number of difficulties with Scholte's approach. The first concerns his concept of globalisation and its usefulness as a starting point to examine the question of political identity. In his account, globalisation is a nameless, faceless force that moves ineluctably forward leaving a trail of 'identity politics' in its wake. It is the mother of all things, fostering homogeneity and heterogeneity, supra-territoriality and 'new localisms', ethnic revivalism and cultural convergence, planetary dangers and potential emancipation. In this sweeping current, the only agents that come into view are social movements. But even these actors are portrayed more as the *effects* of globalisation than as active participants. As he states:

> Globalisation has facilitated an upsurge of so called 'identity politics' that has since the 1960's eroded the position of the state-nation as the preeminent structure of community and promoted the rise of multiple alternative frameworks of solidarity. In the process, constructions of collective identities have tended to become more multidimensional, fluid and uncertain.
>
> (Scholte 2000b: 182)

In this picture, 'identity politics', identity construction and new forms of community are all seen as a response to and function of this sweeping trend of globalisation.

A second problem concerns Scholte's tendency to reify collective identities and to treat them as though they have an ontological status independent of human agency. Collective identities become the 'signifiers' of certain social movements and, in fact, Scholte refers to 'identity politics', collective identities and social movements interchangeably (2000b: 172–8). But surely, as he himself says so clearly, collective identities are socially constructed and change in the context of the *politics* that gives birth to them. Moreover, as he also admits, social movements and collective identities cannot be conflated since many social movements give rise to multiple identities.

A third difficulty arises with his conceptualisation of 'local' versus 'global' identities. In terms of the politics of locality or 'new localisms', for instance, he refers to indigenous peoples' movements, such as the Chiapas movement in Mexico, which, according to Scholte, arose in large part as a response to the intrusions of globalisation. To the extent that the North American Free Trade Agreement (NAFTA) and the political decisions of the Mexican government can be seen as the manifestations of the globalisation process, Scholte is right. But his implicit characterisation of this movement as an effort 'to search for enclaves of familiarity and intimacy at a time when globalising technologies have exposed the self to an infinity of locations, persons, things and ideas all at once' seems less on the mark (Scholte 1996: 55). In this view, the mobilisation of territorial identities is seen as an attempt to root oneself personally and culturally within a community. While this may be partly true, indigenous peoples' movements also, fundamentally, seek to resist specific power relations that threaten to annihilate them, battling material inequalities, domination and physical as well as cultural genocide (see Maiguashca 1994).

Turning to global identities, according to Scholte, women's movements and gay and lesbian movements form part of a supra-territorial politics where 'more and more persons have situated important aspects of their identity in global (and to some extent instead of) three-dimensional space' (Scholte 1996: 53). But how do identities of a global kind differ from identities of a local kind? Moreover, why is gender politics seen as producing collective identities at the global level while the similarly internationalised indigenous peoples' movement is seen as a politics of 'new localism'?

In short, although Scholte's critique of prevailing conceptualisations of identity in IR is well taken, his own efforts to offer an alternative perspective are limited by his highly speculative approach and lack of substantive research into the movements to which he refers. Thus, while Scholte does bring social movements into view – no mean feat in IR – by labelling these movements as *identity* politics and by skimming over the specific power relations that have engendered them he downplays the political nature of these movements while highlighting their cultural orientation (Scholte 2000b: 159). To this extent, Scholte unintentionally offers up IR fare as usual; that is, identity is implicitly associated with culture and culture with the non-political.

Linklater and the 'politics of recognition'

For Linklater the central problem for critical international relationists is as follows: '[t]he critical project in International Relations needs to understand the interconnections between different levels of exclusion *but it should focus the greater part of its attention on the sovereign state as a problematic form of political community*' (Linklater 1994: 129, emphasis added). The state, he claims, is problematic, and has been so since its inception, because it works as a system of inclusion and exclusion. It separates the citizen, the insider, from the non-citizen or alien, the outsider, and in this way erects barriers between human beings living within different national communities. It also allows for the marginalisation of the 'internal other': that is, minority cultural groups who live within the state boundaries, but who are excluded from full participation in that political community.

Given his formulation of the problem, it is evident that Linklater chooses to privilege three sources of identity: the first is based on cultural difference, the second on national affiliations and the third on our universal sense of belonging to a common humanity. The key question to be addressed is how to reconcile our universalistic loyalties with what he refers to as our 'strong emotional attachments to specific communities' (Linklater 1998: 2). In other words, the central task for IR theory is to find a way of acknowledging these competing identities and to articulate alternative socio-political arrangements that can simultaneously defend and nurture both the universal and particular dimensions of our identity.

The solution, according to Linklater, lies with the development of a post-Westphalian citizenship that can give expression to all three levels of our identity (Linklater 1998: 2). While our allegiances to specific communities can be protected by the granting of rights to minority (read cultural) groups, the enactment of our universal obligations and identity can be ensured by the granting of rights to aliens or non-citizens. Snuggling in between the local and the global, our national identities can find safe haven in the form of state citizenship. Thus, Linklater presents us with three identities protected by a three-tier, spatially organised concept of differentiated citizenship.

Now while Linklater's efforts to defend cultural differences are compelling and worth taking seriously, his characterisation of what he calls the 'politics of recognition' raises a number of questions. Although Linklater at no point actually specifies what he means by the concept of identity, he treats identity as an expression of our collective social bonds, as a representation of the collective experience of a particular group of people (Linklater 1996a: 96; 1998: 180–1). Furthermore, he goes on to characterise it fundamentally in *cultural* and *universal* terms. In this context, indigenous peoples' movements and women's movements – both referred to as exemplars of the 'politics of recognition' – are seen as struggles for the protection of cultural difference.

But why does Linklater constrict his vision of exclusionary practices to only those which can be formulated in cultural or statist terms? In my view the reason has to do with three assumptions that Linklater makes about the nature of exclusionary politics and their relationship to identity. First, like Scholte, he believes that exclusionary practices arise primarily as a response to the existence of *differences*. This concern with taming conflicts around difference is expressed when he explains that 'the politics of recognition demands new expressions of sensitivity to difference and new possibilities for expanding the range of permissible disagreements within political communities' (Linklater 1998: 187). Second, Linklater assumes that cultural differences pose the greatest challenge to a post-Westphalian world order. The problem, however, is that by elevating cultural exclusion over other forms, Linklater is actually making a rather controversial claim about what forms of domination are most important in global politics. After all, why should struggles over cultural identity be privileged over others and why should 'critical' IR scholars pay more attention to this form of exclusion? Finally, by separating cultural marginalisation out from other exclusionary practices he does not seem to recognise the complex ways in which power relations around gender, class, race and sexuality intersect and generate their own insider/outsider dynamics as well as a plethora of diverse marginalised identities.

Despite a number of important differences, it is my contention that Scholte's and Linklater's work offers a similar framing of the politics of identity which can be characterised as the 'politics of solidarity'. In terms of how they conceptualise identity, it seems clear that both see it as referring to a cultural, social or psychological sense of self and as being embedded in and forming part of our individual or collective subjectivity. In this way, identity is both naturalised and conferred an ontological status. So while women's movements are seen to engender 'gender identities', ethnic movements give rise to 'cultural identities' and gay movements to 'sexual identities'. This essentialist view of personal identity is complemented by two other tacit assumptions about the nature of our collective identities. First, it is assumed that collective identities are born out of common experiences (Scholte 2000b: 175). In this view, experience is treated as immediately accessible to us and a direct link is drawn between how we experience our lives, who we are and how we see ourselves. The second assumption tacitly at work is the idea that identity operates according to a unitary or cohesive principle. So, while Linklater sees post-Westphalian citizenship as a way to bind people together at the subnational, national and supranational levels, Scholte sees it as a cohesive force uniting a constituency of marginalised peoples.

Turning to the context in which identities are constructed, both see the politics of identity as a response to and function of globalisation. The claim is that identities have become dislodged from their territorial moorings and must be rethought outside the spatial parameters of the nation state. It is this de-territorialisation of identity that allows them to depict the politics of identity as a *distinct, new* form of politics. This is in implicit contrast to the form of politics represented by 'older' movements, which mobilised around class and agitated for equality and redistribution – a form of politics that some also see as revived in recent years by 'the anti-globalisation movement'. The solidarity of the movements with which these authors are concerned is seen as based on demands for cultural recognition and for the extension of legal rights. In short, for both authors, the politics of identity is, as the nomenclature suggests, a struggle over and in the name of identity.

Globalisation and the 'politics of difference'

In contrast to this picture of the politics of identity as a politics of solidarity, Connolly and Walker present us with an alternative conception of identity and the politics that emerges from it. As we shall see, despite different starting points, both share an understanding of the contingent, *political* nature of identity construction and a common concern with the potential limits of what I shall term the 'politics of difference'.

Connolly and the 'politics of the other'

According to Connolly, identity refers to what he terms the 'fictive we': that is, it has to do with questions concerning who we are. On the one hand, it represents our own sense of self, or what Connolly calls our 'dense self': that is, the self from which choosing, wanting and consenting proceed (Connolly 1991a: 64, 158). On the other hand, it also represents those labels that others ascribe to us and publicly recognise. In this sense, then, identity is the end result of a socially constructed process of identification that asserts or resists the social and political significance of a variety of personal dispositions and traits. Given this, identity must be understood as historically contingent and inherently relational in form rather than as the bearer of a fundamental intrinsic truth. This view does not imply that identity is unimportant to our lives, but rather that 'no identity reflects being as such: no identity is the true identity because every identity is particular, constructed and relational' (Connolly 1991a: 46). Furthermore, according to Connolly, identity is always constituted and mediated through the establishment of difference. As he states, 'an identity is established in relation to a series of differences that have become socially recognised. ... Identity requires difference in order to be, and it converts difference into otherness in order to secure its own self-certainty' (Connolly 1991a: 64). Thus, it is not the establishment of identities per se that creates the Other, but our need and propensity to stamp truth onto these identities.

And this for Connolly is the main problem. By translating difference into hierarchies of truth, we turn difference into Other, and Other into evil. This tendency for identities to congeal into 'hard doctrines of truth and falsity, self and otherness, good and evil, rational and irrational, common sense and absurdity', in turn, poses an ethical and political challenge: that is, how do we find '*ways* to cultivate care for identity and difference in a world already permeated by ethical proclivities and predispositions to identity' (Connolly 1991a: 10, emphasis in original)?

Connolly's answer to this challenge is three-fold. First, he proposes that we understand identity as the product of contingency and ambiguity. In other words, identity must be continually disturbed and politicised so that the differences between us as well as tensions within ourselves can find a space. As he states, 'The one who construes her identity to be laced with contingencies ... is in a better position to question and resist the drive to convert difference into otherness to be defeated, converted or marginalized' (Connolly 1991a: 180).

This proposal for what Connolly refers to as a 'counter-ontology' for understanding identity is accompanied, second, by a normative argument regarding the need for us to cultivate an 'ethic of care for life' which draws on our recognition of our interdependence on each other and which therefore embodies an ethic of agonistic respect for difference. As he states, 'The capacity for ethicality exceeds the bounds of identity, once the ethical bond is seen to encompass the agonism of difference' (Connolly 1991a: 167).

Lastly, in addition to these ontological and normative claims, Connolly calls for an alternative politics – a non-territorial, democratic politics. It is clear that, for him, this politics involves a variety of social movements revolving around human rights, ecological issues and peace. As he states:

> What the time demands, today and tomorrow, is the formation by non-state activists of regional combinations organized across and against state boundaries, focusing on particular global problems and the practices though which specific states and constellations of states produce and perpetuate them.
>
> (Connolly 1991a: 218)

While he admits that the political orientation of these movements cannot be predetermined because identity can be articulated in different ways according to contingent factors, he nonetheless puts them forward as representing a challenge to statist politics and as offering an articulation of alternative possibilities.

For Connolly, therefore, the politics of identity can be either enabling or constraining, liberating or dangerous, depending on the spirit in which it is enacted. Those movements which are guided by a sense of irony and of their own contingency and which are animated by loyalties other than those to the state may potentially contribute to the pluralisation of democratic politics. Those, on the other hand, which seek to defend their identities as truth, as self-certain, threaten to perpetuate a 'politics of resentment' (Connolly 1991a: 192, 211).

Despite Connolly's efforts to tackle the question of identity head on, a number of puzzles remain. For Connolly, identity is portrayed as a site of strife between two types of labelling: that is, our self-descriptions and the labels assigned to us by others (Connolly 1991a: 163, 175). Now this understanding of identity raises a number of questions: what kind of subject is capable of participating in this identification process? Why do we privilege certain traits and dispositions over others when forming our identities? And what kind of politics does it produce?

In terms of the first question, it is clear that any understanding of identity as something that is at least partially chosen, rather than entirely conferred on us, requires a conception of the subject as conscious, capable of reason and as self-reflective. Yet, no such subject is elaborated on in Connolly's work. Instead, the logic of identity and difference is given a life of its own which seems to bypass the subject altogether. We are told that identity spells difference and difference, the Other. Our intentions and motives when constructing, mobilising and defending identities are subsumed under the generalising and totalising dynamic of identity/difference. In this sense then, both identity and difference become givens (albeit socially constructed ones) in a predetermined equation which pits the two against each other.

Turning to the question of why certain traits become the subject of identity and not others, Connolly argues that it is primarily a contingent matter (Connolly 1991a: 92, 171, 174). Now, at the level of personal identity, it is possible to see what Connolly means by this. After all, we are all shaped by a variety of forces which are not only historically and socially constructed, but which are also subject to our own idiosyncratic interpretations. When one considers the construction of collective political identities, however, then it is harder to accept Connolly's characterisation of identities as entirely contingent. From the perspective of social movements, at least, the politicisation of particular traits and dispositions needs to be seen as a collective response to perceived power relations and as a collective effort to resist them. In other words, the process of identity formation in the context of social movements requires us to make choices about what we stand for and against and, as such, is by its very nature a politicised activity. Thus, while contingency plays a part in the construction of specific identities in particular circumstances, it cannot fully explain the origins or function of political identity.

Moreover, if these alleged forms of the politics of identity are not actually about identity or difference per se, but rather about resisting certain power relations that are deemed to be unjust, then how and why should they follow Connolly's recommendation and cultivate an 'agonistic respect for difference'? After all, our political identities are only meaningful to us if they reflect a commitment we have made, a disposition or trait we wish to defend or a worldview that we choose to fight for. Thus, while we certainly do not need to elevate our identities to the status of Truth, we need to hold onto them as 'our truths' at a particular time. Indeed, why should we seek to tolerate the truths of those we perceive to be unjust and oppressive? Connolly is not able to help us here. Finally, his emphasis on the differential nature of identity begs the question of why and how it is we are able to unite together in collective struggles. For if our identities are as contingent and oppositional as he suggests then it seems hard to imagine how a sense of solidarity can be maintained within any collective social effort, unless, of course, one allows for the possibility that these social movements exceed the quest for identity and are oriented towards alternative political possibilities that do not in fact centralise the question of identity per se.

Walker and the politics of social movements

An unrelenting critic of mainstream IR theory and highly impatient with even the not-so traditional approaches, Walker has focused much of his theoretical work on exposing the ways in which politics and the political have been marginalised in a discipline ostensibly dedicated to their study (Walker 1988; 1994; 1999; 2000). Within this context, much of his criticism has been levelled at the way in which questions of human identity and what he refers to as political subjectivity have been reduced to simplistic answers about the state and its corollary, sovereign citizenship.

Contrary to this reification of the political, Walker argues for an alternative conception of politics and political identity that learns from the political practices of 'critical' social movements (1988; 1994). He goes on to suggest that social movements can be seen as representing two types of politics: a 'politics of connection' and a 'politics of movement' (1988: 55–80; 1994: 699). In terms of the former, social movements make three types of connections. First, in trying to respond to specific problems, movements are forced to broaden their understandings of the processes that affect particular struggles. Second, they are able to discover connections between processes that are conventionally understood to be separate, such as changes in the division of labour, unemployment, mass advertising, welfare policies, racism, and so on. Third, they learn to interpret ways in which people's everyday lives are inserted into seemingly remote structures and how these structures are registered and integrated into language and emotion (Walker 1988: 63). In sum, as Walker suggests, 'whatever it might come to mean to establish a politics of connection, it is unlikely to look like the politics of inclusions and exclusions … expressed by the modern territorial state' (1994: 699).

In terms of the 'politics of movement', Walker steers away from the idea that just because they make connections, social movements today represent a 'counter-hegemonic bloc' with a singular political identity. Indeed, he hesitates to attribute any universal aspirations to these movements. In this way, Walker insists on acknowledging the contingent, fluid nature of social movement politics and the way this belies any attempt to see them as a direct reflection of overall structural changes or a singular logic of action and identity. Rather, social movements manifest political identities that are fractured and dispersed among a multiplicity of sites. Thus, contrary to IR theory's liberal ontology, which presumes that we are self-representing, self-identical subjects, political agents today actually engage in a plethora of political practices which yield diverse, contested and contingent identities.

Although I agree with Walker's suggestion that movements can be seen as a 'politics of connection', I would argue that he tends to undervalue the nature and degree of the connections being made. First, many movements claim to be responding to and struggling against the same structural forces, that is the globalisation of capitalism, the extension of the state into civil society and the elevation of neoliberalism as the dominant global framework within which we seek to organise ourselves socially, politically and economically. Second, at the institutional level, many of these movements have sought to build local, national, regional and global networks with each other. In other words, they have forged alliances, albeit fluid ones. Third, movements have sought to analyse critically the connections between the political, economic and cultural dimensions of their struggles. In this context, as we shall see, the construction of political identity is a more complex, nuanced affair than allowed for by either the universal/particular or structural/contingent dichotomy.

Turning to Walker's conceptualisation of a 'politics of movement' I find there is less on offer. While the argument that social movements are marked as much by fragmentation and flux as by cohesion and stability may be true, it is not enough simply to assert this. The interesting question concerns why and how our political identities are fragmented and why and how we still manage to come together to fight for our visions of a political future. While Walker is not suggesting that we do not engage in common fights, his efforts to counter any universalising interpretation of movements may play into the hands of those IR thinkers who wish to ignore social movements precisely because they are dispersed and seemingly weak. If Walker is right and social movements can play a role in rethinking and reshaping world politics, then these movements must be credited with enough coherence, focus and insight to make them worth taking seriously. In other words, they must be seen as having enough longevity and stability to enable them to have a critical, historical perspective. The views of a transient or nomad may amuse, mesmerise or even be insightful, but they are an unlikely source of rooted, historical interpretations of the world.

In sum, more than Scholte or Linklater or even Connolly, Walker recognises that any meaningful discussion of political identity must begin with a study of the political practices that give rise to it. Moreover, he rightly reminds us that these political practices cannot be contained within the matrix of the sovereign state and that to be curious about political identity means looking beyond conventional IR categories that hide social movements from view.

Unfortunately, however, Walker does not take us further than this starting point. While suggesting that identity is fluid, multiple, not necessarily territorial and the response to contingent forces as much as structural ones, he gives no guidance as to where we go from here. Walker certainly betrays his suspicions of universalist approaches such as Linklater's, but if our political identities have no universal resonance then how do we go about mapping the connections between our infinite differences and, more importantly, why bother? Indeed, one is left with the sense that the politics of social movements is too ephemeral, too elusive, too fluid to conceptualise; it is here, there and everywhere, or as Walker more poetically puts it, '[l]ike the rivers that cannot be stepped into twice, social *movements* cannot be pinned down, cannot keep their power in place' (Walker 1994: 677, emphasis in original).

At present then IR provides us with two competing narratives about the politics of identity. According to the first, identity is seen as an intrinsic part of our subjectivity and being and as grounded in our experiences. Operating as a cohesive force, it serves to bind different people together around a common cause or struggle. The second story, in contrast, decouples identity from the subject and prefers to see it as a socially and politically constructed feature of our social interactions. Our identities, therefore, are not seen as grounded in our personal or collective experiences, but as emerging within the context of discursive, contingent relations. As such they are seen as both plural and relational and as constituted around a differential principle.

These two renditions of the politics of identity, however, do share some common ground. Both camps tend to see this form of politics as new and distinct from earlier forms of class politics and do not relate it to the kind of politics represented by 'the anti-globalisation movement'. Whether conceptualised as a 'politics of difference' (or 'alterity') or as a 'politics of solidarity' (or 'recognition'), it is understood primarily as a struggle *about* and *for* 'identity'. Furthermore, there seems to be agreement all round that the main embodiments of this new form of politics are social movements and, in particular, women's, gay, ecological and ethnic movements. Finally, both these conceptions of the politics of identity tell us more about the theoretical preferences of the scholars themselves than they do about the social movements in question. For, I would argue, it is only after one has done empirical research into the concrete political practices of movements that it is possible to appreciate both the insights and limitations of these two perspectives.

Pinning down the politics of identity in 'the anti-globalisation movement': the case of women's reproductive rights activism

Interestingly, although 'the anti-globalisation movement' itself has not been characterised as a form of the politics of identity in the IR literature, many of the movements that make it up – including indigenous peoples' movements, ecological movements, gay and lesbian movements and women's movements – fit the profile. In this third part of the chapter I explore one such movement, that is the international women's reproductive rights movement, which dates back to the mid-1970s and which has, in the last three years, sought to integrate its struggle with that of 'the anti-globalisation movement'. Given the very broad scope of women's reproductive rights activism and the limitations of space, my discussion focuses on the Women's Global Network for Reproductive Rights (WGNRR), one key network of women's organisations. After briefly identifying some of the main goals and practices of this network, I go on to explore what the notion of 'collective identity' might mean in this context and in what ways it has been constructed and deployed. To this end, I draw out the range of different and even competing identities that are being contested within this movement, identify the different sites of struggle that generate these particular identities and illustrate how these differing political identities are mobilised within 'strategic coalitions'.

In form, the WGNRR is a network of diverse, autonomous groups and individuals in every continent who are linked together by a shared concern for women's reproductive rights and health.[1] These groups include feminist and women's organisations, medical organisations, documentation centres and trade unions. In an effort to create solidarity at the international level, every three years the WGNRR holds a Members Meeting where they convene to discuss their strategies and their political platform. Moreover, in order to sustain alliances with other similar networks many of these same groups attend the International Women's Health Meetings (IWHM) also held every three years. Thus, the WGNRR forms part of a broader women's reproductive rights movement that, in turn, forms a key strand of an even wider women's health movement.

What holds these very diverse 'members' together is the common belief that any struggle for women's reproductive rights is both a political struggle – rather than a technical or management issue – and a feminist struggle to the extent that it is waged for and by women. Despite varying opinions on how best to achieve change, there is a general consensus on the three main goals of the movement. The first is to offer a critique of the dominant neoliberal economic agenda and its attendant population and development discourses/practices. As Martha Rosenberg states in her report on the World Social Forum of January 2002, 'it is crucial to fight the neoliberal concentration of capital, since it will be impossible to resolve issues of gender outside the framework of a fair redistribution of wealth' (Rosenberg 2002: 1). The second is to resist and struggle against these practices at the local, national and international level and the third is to articulate an alternative vision of development that revolves around the needs of people rather than those of rich states or corporations (Keysers 1993: 49).

One of the most important moments for the international women's health movement came in 1994 with the UN Conference on Population and Development (ICPD) held in Cairo. In an effort to build a broad coalition of women's organisations that could intervene effectively in the UN proceedings, the 'Women's Alliance '94' was created. This ad hoc coalition committed itself to a three-pronged strategy which included the drafting of a Women's Declaration on Population Policies that could serve as a reference document and political tool in the negotiations, the organisation of a women's meeting in Rio just before the ICPD in order to consolidate a common platform, and a critique of the draft UN Plan of Action.

Here I shall only examine the first element of the strategy, that is the drafting and support of the Women's Declaration. The Women's Declaration was initiated and drafted by a number of women's organisations gaining approximately 2,400 signatories from 105 countries by 1993 (Sen *et al.* 1994: 53). Despite this broad support, some thought that the document was too conservative and that it did not adequately critique mainstream population discourses as sexist, imperialist and racist. Of this faction some decided to support it anyway as a strategic move that would allow them to participate in a broader coalition of women's organisations at Cairo. Two such groups were **GABRIELA**, a national coalition of Philippine organisations, and the

WGNRR. Still others, such as FINRRAGE (Feminist International Network of Resistance to Reproductive and Genetic Engineering) opted to reject the Declaration *in toto* (FINRRAGE 1993: 28).

In this way, the Women's Declaration represented a contingent alliance of diverse women's organisations who recognised its limitations but who also acknowledged its *strategic* value. The statement made by GABRIELA, published in the WGNRR Newsletter, makes this tension explicit when it states that the women of GABRIELA

> reaffirm support for the Women's Voice '94 but only in the context that it is to be used for the UN Conference on Population and Development. ... We recognise that the documents and processes that arise out of struggle within the framework of large patriarchal international bodies are often flawed and particularly susceptible to co-optation. We have faith however that feminists who choose these tactics are aware of this danger and will take all measures necessary to remain critical and to protect themselves and the feminist movement from adverse effects of this form of struggle.
>
> (GABRIELA 1993: 8)

In the end, the Women's Alliance '94 was successful in influencing both the proceedings and Action Plan of the Cairo Conference. While each women's organisation was free to do its own independent work and lobbying, in strategic moments the 'political front' took over as the dominant negotiating force. The outcome of the conference was a new Programme of Action which recognised women's empowerment, gender equality and reproductive rights as essential elements to the process of development. Rather than attributing their success to either a 'politics of diversity' or a 'politics of solidarity', the women's health movement chose to recognise the mutually constitutive and mutually re-enforcing relationship between both these forms of politics. As the position paper of the International Women's Health Coalition (IWHC) states:

> As the women's movement we are both strong (moving, challenging) and weak (compared to the immense anti-women forces). Therefore we have to work on the basis of unity (which is not sameness) and solidarity (differences as a source of strength) inside and outside and at community and international levels simultaneously, keeping in mind the need for constant movement-building (through trust and transparency) from the local level up. ... We will have political impact: our power tools are diversity and subversion.
>
> (IWHC and CEPIA 1994: 33)

If we pursue the notion of the politics of identity and explore its relevance for the WGNRR, two questions need to be addressed. The first is what specific identities are being mobilised within the women's reproductive rights movement and what points of conflict are emerging around this process of self-labelling? The second related question concerns the context in which these identities are both formed and change.

Turning to the first, it is evident that a panoply of identities is being constructed and contested within the movement and, more specifically, within the WGNRR. A sample reveals conflicting identities revolving around the question of liberal vs. socialist, feminist vs. non-feminist, Southern women vs. Northern women, heterosexual vs. homosexual, white vs. black, and so on. Despite this diversity, it is equally important to acknowledge that a 'common identity' has been constructed and mobilised at certain moments. According to Loes Keysers, this sense of solidarity was expressed very explicitly at the IWHM held in Manila in 1990 when a woman representative, funded by the Ford Foundation to film the proceedings, was kicked out of the room because it was felt that she did not belong to the movement and that she did not share its common goals (interview, The Hague, August 1999).[2] As we have seen, this 'common identity' was once again mobilised at the Cairo Conference where differences were set aside in order to forge a political front. In this way, diversity became the foundation of a negotiated consensus that contributed to its success in this particular forum, and to the strengthening of the movement as a whole.

In terms of the second question, there seem to be at least three sites of struggle that could be seen as shaping identity formation. The first area of contestation is in the realm of discourses. For many of the WGNRR activists, discourse is seen as a site of power in which identities are fixed and alternative identities foreclosed. Describing the hegemonic function that discourses play, Keysers states:

> Communication has increasingly become a tool of power since the turn of the century. A profound transformation of the system of social control took place from violence and bribery to persuasive means. The advent of mass communications industries gave rise to a system of 'scientific and systematic engineering of consent'. It was known that these soft strategies ultimately created far less resistance than violence or the use of economic or political clout.
>
> (Keysers 1993: 8)

Well aware that the discourses used by some groups within the movement were alienating others, the WGNRR came together in Madras in 1993 to open up a dialogue about its own use of terminology. The final report of this meeting suggests a very nuanced and self-reflexive discussion over the pros and cons of using terms such as 'reproductive rights' (WGNRR 1993).

A second area of contestation concerns the material conditions in which women find themselves. In other words, the divide between 'Northern' and 'Southern' women within the movement is not only a matter of skin colour, cultural traditions or language differences; it is also a matter of economic justice and material life chances. So while in the North, sexism and homophobia are seen as the main issues, in the South the struggle has focused more on the negative effects of structural adjustment policies and the need to redistribute material resources and power from the North to the South and from men to women. It is in this context that some women in the South have refused to adopt the label 'feminist' as they associate this political identity with rich Western women.

A third factor shaping identity construction is the role of *spatial relations*. One important space for women's organisations has been the NGO fora which run parallel to the conferences and which also provide a 'safe haven' for their deliberations. At the Beijing Conference in 1995, for example, there was much annoyance at the fact that women's representatives were housed far from each other and that the NGO fora were some distance away from the official proceedings, making it hard for women activists to create a sense of solidarity and organise common actions. Another sense in which space has been important concerns its symbolic dimension. In 1993 it was decided that the fourth IWHM was to be held in Kampala, Uganda, even though there was much apprehension about this move given that the organising committee was being funded by the World Health Organization and, therefore, was seen as representing the population establishment's agenda. Despite much controversy, however, the location for the conference was not vetoed because there was a consensus that it was time to bring the movement into a 'Third World' space (interview with Loes Keysers, The Hague, August 1999). A third way in which space is important has to do with the way in which women living within the same 'territory' experience life very differently as a result of the particular space they live in. For example, some American black women have argued that their experience of 'urban space' is very different from that of their white sisters and that it is only by organising themselves separately (in groups such as the Sistersong Women of Colour Reproductive Health Collective) that they can foster a sense of shared identity and express their common needs (Sistersong 2004).

In sum, identity formation within the women's reproductive rights movement must be situated within the discursive, material and spatial relations that define this particular struggle of resistance. Furthermore, it must be understood as a two-pronged struggle that seeks to contest those gendered discourses that objectify women and to oppose the material and institutional inequalities that define most women's lives. In this sense, then, it represents not only a politics of identity, but also a politics of redistribution. Finally, as we have seen, any degree of solidarity that has been achieved within the movement has been carefully constructed and maintained on the basis of negotiating differences. Identity within this precarious political context cannot be taken for granted and has to be seen as contingent and strategic.

So to what extent do our two stories of the politics of identity help us to conceptualise this movement? Starting with the 'politics of solidarity' perspective, Scholte's and Linklater's vision of the politics of identity is corroborated to the extent that the WGNRR does represent a relatively coherent social movement mobilised around de-territorialised (if not de-spatialised) identities. Moreover, organisationally, it comprises a 'supra-territorial' network of organisations which follows Linklater's three-layered pattern of local, national and supranational linkages. These strengths notwithstanding, the limitations of this perspective are considerable. Talking, as Scholte does, of 'gender identities' – or any other category of identities for that matter – serves to simplify and reify the complex set of diverse and conflicting allegiances at work in any women's movement. Moreover, while the notion of 'gender identities' may be helpful to highlight particular forms of power relations, one cannot assume that these power relations automatically yield political identities. Nor indeed can one infer, as Scholte and Linklater seem to, that common experiences necessarily give rise to common identities. While the women of the WGNRR can be said to share at some level a common experience of oppression, as we have seen, they have generated a range of political identities that only at times have coalesced into a 'collective identity'. In other words, the 'politics of solidarity' perspective tells us a very one-sided story about why the politics of identity, in the form of certain social movements, has emerged and what they are actually about. By conceptualising them in terms of the politics of identity, movements are reduced to a quest for cultural recognition and, thereby, the varied and complex power relations that they are struggling to resist are overlooked.

Turning to our second perspective, both Connolly's and Walker's insistence on seeing identity as constructed rather than pre-given, and multiple rather than singular, does have some purchase on the way the women's reproductive rights movement has developed. It certainly draws our attention to the diversity of political identities within the movement, and, thereby, allows us to appreciate better the achievement of the Women's Alliance '94. Moreover, by highlighting the discursive realm, they encourage us to explore the way in which identities are the product of dialogical practices.

Nonetheless, this perspective also has a number of blind spots. First, it tells us little about the nature of the human subject involved in constructing these identities. Indeed, identities seem to have a life of their own animated by the difference principle and independent of any coherent author. To this extent, we lose any sense of personal or collective agency. And yet, the WGNRR is a highly self-reflexive movement which has developed an historical memory and which is oriented to particular normative and political goals. Thus, while their political identities may well be contingent, the normative and political vision that binds them together is not. A second difficulty concerns the emphasis placed by those in this camp on the differential basis of identity. If in fact identity inevitably works only to differentiate us from others then how do we explain the longevity of and solidarity within movements? After all, while the Women's Alliance '94 does represent a strategic coalition based on short-term goals, it is clear that such a coalition could not have succeeded and would have had no meaning outside of a long-term collective struggle for women's rights. Finally, this perspective does little to illuminate the origins of these movements. Certainly for Connolly the main source of the politics of identity is the challenge of living with difference. And yet, the politics of the WGNRR is not about difference per se, but rather about resisting particular power relations that perpetuate not only the social marginalisation of women but also their material deprivation.

Conclusion: reflections for future IR theorising

If neither of these conceptualisations of the politics of identity tells us the full story, then how should we think about identity and politics in IR? Indeed, what does identity mean anyway? In this conclusion I would like to suggest three requirements for future theorising in IR about identity in general and about social movement organising in particular.

The first requirement is methodological and concerns the need to do some empirical research into the origins and nature of social movements. In other words, if we want to conceptualise political identity then we need to examine the concrete political practices that give rise to it. While I am not suggesting that social movements are the only kind of political practices that produce political identities I am saying that if we choose to equate the politics of identity with social movements, as some IR scholars do, then we need to explore these movements in more substantive terms.

A second requirement for future IR theorising is that if we want to talk about the politics of identity we need to define in far more explicit terms what we actually mean by identity. Now, while I agree with Scholte when he states that identity has to do with our 'sense of self', along with Connolly, I would also argue that our sense of who we are only becomes clear in the context of differentiating ourselves *from* some and identifying ourselves *with* others. Thus, for me identity implies a conscious, selective process of self-identification. In this context, political identity needs to be understood as the outgrowth of a process of identification which asserts solidarity with one collective and antagonism towards, or resistance against, another. It is born out of conflict and contestation and is therefore less about who we are, in an ontological sense, than about what we are for. As Nira Yuval-Davis states, referring to the political identity of the women's health movement, 'the boundaries of this coalition should not be set in terms of who we are, but in terms of what we want to achieve' (Yuval-Davis 1997: 126).

If identity concerns the labels we give ourselves at certain times and in certain contexts, then I would go on to argue that we must conceptualise it as multivalent and relational in nature rather than singular or fixed. Identity allows us to place ourselves in relation to the social world we live in and, given that we inhabit many 'social contexts' simultaneously, our identities may well be multiple and, at times, even contradictory.

Turning to the third requirement for theorising politics of identity, we need to explore, in a more substantive and integrated way, the various sites where identity is constructed. From the example presented here I have identified at least three areas that need to be examined, namely the discursive, the material and the spatial realm. Recognising the discursive dimension of identity formation means accepting that language is not a neutral medium and that how we talk about issues is essential to how we think about them and act on them. By taking account of the material dimension of identity, one is forced to acknowledge how the material conditions in which we live affect how we experience our lives and, thereby, who we think we are and what we aspire to. Last but not least, we must remember that our political identity is also shaped in important ways by our physical environment as well as by the spatial metaphors that we use discursively to map where we 'stand'. Although all three sites are important for identity construction, the two perspectives examined here only offer us a partial glimpse of them. While the 'politics of difference' approach does help us to see the discursive construction of identity, it tends to hide from view the material and spatial dimension of identity construction. Conversely, while the 'politics of solidarity' perspective focuses much of its attention on the spatial context of identity formation, that is the de-territorialisation of identity, it has little to say about the material and discursive dimensions of identity construction.

With these three requirements in place, I end this chapter by proposing that we drop the notion of the politics of identity altogether and focus instead on deconstructing three underlying dichotomies that underwrite this paradigm regardless of its particular articulation: the dichotomy between cultural politics and class politics; the dichotomy between solidarity and difference; and the dichotomy between structural and contingency-based explanations of identity.

In terms of the first, the politics of identity, on the whole, has been understood as a politics about and for cultural recognition and, therefore, as different from class-based politics. But as even a cursory examination of women's reproductive rights activism tells us, and as feminist philosopher Nancy Fraser reminds us, social movements around gender, sexuality and race must always be understood as struggles over both cultural recognition and material redistribution (Fraser 1997). In other words, labelling movements as 'identity politics' makes it too easy for us to forget that women's movements, along with all of the other movements comprising 'the anti-globalisation movement', are waging a struggle against particular relations of oppression that are reproduced simultaneously in the economic and socio-cultural realm and that are reinforced by the state.

A second dichotomy that has implicitly, if not explicitly, marked discussions over the politics of identity is whether it is best represented as a politics of solidarity or as a politics of difference. Again, however, as we have seen, this either/or dichotomy does not help us. Solidarity is built through a process of negotiating – rather than resolving – differences and, at times, accepting that effective resistance requires the temporary setting aside of these differences in order to forge a shared political identity. Seen in this way, the articulation of political identity becomes a *means* of constructing and sustaining a sense of commonality and purpose.

The last advantage of moving away from the notion of the politics of identity is that we are no longer encouraged to misconstrue this form of politics as a struggle over and about identity per se. Indeed, by locating identity within the context of shifting political practices and by seeing it as the social product of a collective effort to resist power relations, we can avoid the trap of having to explain it in either structural/essentialist or contingent/relational terms. Instead, an empirical examination of one strand of 'the anti-globalisation movement' allows us to see how political identities are constructed around both structural and contingent forces which, in turn, can be discursive, material or spatial in nature.

Notes

1 The network dates back to 1977 and currently has 1,730 members and subscribers in 157 countries (WGNRR 2004).
2 Loes Keysers is a founding member of the WGNRR, women's health activist and Lecturer in Population and Development at the Institute for Social Studies in The Hague. I conducted a series of interviews with her in August 1999.

Part III
Politics/strategy/violence

8 Resistance and *compromiso* at the global frontlines

Gender wars at the US–Mexico border

Irasema Coronado and Kathleen Staudt

Case No. 1 January 23rd. *Alma Chavira Farel.* Young girl strangled and beaten, raped both anally and vaginally, bruise on the chin and a black eye. Was wearing a white sweater with design and short blue pants. Occurred in Campestre Virreyes.

January 25th. *Angelina Luna Villabos.* Age 16 … White, pregnant and robust form. She was strangled with the cable of a stolen television.

March 14th. *Jessica Lizalde León.* Radio DJ murdered by gunshots.

April 21st. *Luz de la O García.* Died as a result of being beaten on the streets of G. Prieto and Altamirano.

May 5th. *Identity unknown.* Age 35. Five months pregnant, dark complexion, dark hair, short pants, barefoot. Raped and strangled. Attacker unknown.

May 8th. *Elizabeth Ramos.* Age 26. Killed by boyfriend with a firearm.

May 13th. *Identity unknown.* Age 25 … White skin, light colored hair, wearing jeans and cloth shoes. Raped and stabbed. Attacker unknown.[1]

Introduction

We write from the Ciudad Juárez–El Paso region, a large metropolitan area of 2 million people that spans the international boundary between the United States and Mexico. Ciudad Juárez, Mexico's fifth largest city, has been at the frontlines of globalisation for decades. Mexican and public policies have facilitated the establishment here of mostly US-owned export-processing factories, known as *maquiladoras*, by encouraging capital investment, lowering tariffs and making available a pool of cheap, mostly female, labour. Ciudad Juárez is now home to hundreds of *maquiladoras* that, at their high point in 2000, employed a quarter of a million workers, the majority female (Staudt and Coronado 2002).

Since the early 1990s, over 300 girls and women have been murdered here and many hundreds have disappeared. Most of the victims are Mexican teenagers and young women, although others are from the United States, Honduras and the Netherlands (Washington Valdez 2002; Benítez *et al.* 1999; González 2002; Staudt and Coronado 2002: ch. 6). A third of the victims were mutilated before death, in horrendous and gruesome ways, their bodies left to decay in the outlying desert. The death tally keeps rising, although absolute numbers are contentious and continually revised by the Mexican authorities. In February 2003, four more victims were found within a week, including several teenage girls and a 6-year-old child. The judicial authorities have done little to investigate the murders of these girls and women, most of them poor, and their families lack the political clout and economic means to secure justice. Activist organisations and networks on both sides of the international border are struggling to confront this violence, the globalised political–economic system in which it is produced and the inadequacies of a Mexican state and judicial system which has little interest in solving the murders and which lacks respect for the victims' families.

We propose that these murders need to be understood in the context of pervasive violence and gendered conflict at the border. The concept of 'gender wars' is useful here. Gender wars occur at three levels: (1) overt, brutal violence against women; (2) normalised, everyday violence involved in the struggle for survival for women and their families, with *maquiladora* workers earning the Mexican minimum wage of $30 a week; and (3) conflict between women activists (and a few men) and the disinterested, male-dominated state.

How are these gender wars linked to globalisation? At the most basic level, the porous character of the border is significant. Globalisation is often associated with the eradication of borders, the capacity of social problems to transcend particular territories and the consequent inability of states to respond to these problems on their own. Certainly, gender wars in Ciudad Juárez are not contained by the international border but rather amplified by it. Many of these killings could well have been carried out by people who are border-crossers and this militates against their prosecution. More fundamentally, the border has helped to create a context in which the female labour pool has been sexualised and viewed as disposable. From the days of prohibition, when border cities like Ciudad Juárez became centres for bars and nightclubs catering to North Americans and prostitution became rampant, to the establishment of Ciudad Juárez as a free trade zone, the economy in the region has burgeoned on the backs of women. Women's labour is crucial to the *maquiladora* industries but the women themselves are seen as low status and not fully respectable. Indeed, negative stereotypes of young *maquila* women have become embedded in the minds of police and policy-makers to such an extent that they encourage inaction in addressing the crimes of murder and mutilation. Finally, the globalisation of the masculinised state is key to the women's predicament. The Mexican state will not prosecute the murders if this is likely to jeopardise the *maquiladora* system on which its economy depends; conversely the United States and corporate owners claim no responsibility for this 'Mexican problem'. This situation forces activists attempting to apply political pressure into creative and complex transborder political strategies in response.

In this chapter, we focus on one particular activist organisation, the binational 'Coalition Against Violence Toward Women and Families at the

US–Mexico Border', hereinafter called the Coalition. We are both participants in this organisation, with Irasema acting as co-chair since 2002. The Coalition, with its central focus on violence against women, would not generally be considered part of the 'anti-globalisation movement' that is the subject of this book. Why? Theorists and activists rarely link the issue of violence against women to globalisation processes. It is our view that this is a major limitation of established discourses on resistance to globalisation. The concept of gender wars elaborated above shows how violence against women in the region is intrinsically linked to the global *maquiladora* system, the seemingly 'disposable' workers it creates, and also to transnationalised political hierarchies and strategies that evacuate responsibility and allow impunity. Further, the Coalition explicitly sees itself, and is seen by other groups, as an integral part of the broader resistance to globalisation in the border region and beyond. It was born after a labour-organised solidarity meeting in Ciudad Juárez in 2001 in which violence against women emerged as a major issue for women workers. A subsequent labour-organised meeting in November 2002 drew activists and commitments to the Coalition from as far afield as Canada and the Caribbean. Activists in the Coalition have links, past and present, to anti-violence programmes, grassroots community and feminist organisations, non-governmental organisations (NGOs), labour unions and the Coalition for Justice in the *Maquiladoras*.

In what follows, we develop the argument that the struggle around violence against women, as represented by the Coalition, must be acknowledged as central to resistance to globalisation. We do this in two stages. In the first part, we expose the limitations of dominant discourses on resistance to globalisation from a grounded feminist perspective. In the second part we correct the imbalances and silences of those discourses by giving a detailed empirical account of Coalition aims, strategies and outcomes. In addition, in the third part of the chapter, we argue for the need to interrogate the relationship between resistance and academic knowledge, reflecting from our position as both activists and feminist academics. As part of our elaboration of a grounded feminist perspective, we introduce and affirm the concept of *compromiso*, which compels us in our study of globalisation and resistance to move beyond the collection of data and to work with others to connect theory with practice in the struggle for justice. We reflect on the implications of *compromiso* for academic work. How do we balance our commitments as activists and scholars? What responsibility do we have to students and to the groups in which we are involved when teaching about resistance?

Gendering discourses of resistance to globalisation

In recent years, academic and activist accounts of 'resistance to globalisation' have grown by leaps and bounds. These accounts cover a range of ideological agendas and actions, from reactionary religious revivalism (Barber 2001) to protest coalitions at world meetings of trade moguls (Smith

2002), and from efforts to reform the WTO or instil social accountability principles (selections in Broad 2002) to adaptations of Marxist political economy by academic critics updating their language and strategies for these global times (Mittelman 2000). But where are women and gender in this literature? A grim déjà vu sinks in at this point. Women and gender are not central to most analyses, sometimes appearing editorially, or in a token chapter, or in lists of 'interest groups' that have problems with global neoliberal economics (Staudt *et al.* 2001). The relationship between women and resistance to globalisation is central only to avowedly feminist texts (see, among many, Peterson and Runyan 1999; Meyer and Prügl 1999; Kelly *et al.* 2001). The marginalisation or absence of this dimension of resistance indicates some very significant problems with non-feminist accounts of resistance to globalisation.

In our view, most accounts converge on a representation of resistance that paints just a partial view of reality. Activists are depicted as 'summit jumpers' who travel to distant global cities, usually in developed country locations, from Prague to Sydney, and who use direct action against symbols of globalisation associated with international financial institutions and transnational corporations. Alternatively, the role of organised labour may be stressed, whether in terms of union resistance to transnational corporations in the workplace or in terms of a more fundamental revolutionary role. All resistance literature from the North privileges English as its lingua franca and it may also rely heavily on theoretical language that abstracts from the reality of people's lives. Each of these dimensions of accounts of resistance produces gendered exclusions.

To begin with, the habit of locating resistance in abstract, capital city, high-level, global realms functions to detach protest from local contexts and everyday worlds. It privileges the activism of white, Western middle-class youth who can afford to protest at distant conferences. It encourages the anti-globalisation activist to fly to Prague or Sydney, rather than coming to the border and queuing in lines to cross the international border bridge. Further, the representation of resistance as oriented towards the operations of abstracted economic processes and international financial institutions says little or nothing about patriarchy and the systemic, multifaceted subordination of women. It hardly speaks of the problem of sexual aggression or violence against women, and of the need for women to resist the violence they may face in public and private worlds. The prioritising of engagement with international institutions encourages the neglect of other institutional sites at the national and local levels, which may be more pressing in terms of countering violence. Activists in Ciudad Juárez seek to strengthen Mexican democracy, reform the state judiciary and combat corruption. They are compelled to seek assistance from, as well as to challenge, flawed and complicit political and police authorities.

Academic analyses focusing on work and organised labour also need to broaden their focus. Trade unions such as the AFL–CIO increasingly use discourses of transnational solidarity rather than nationalist protection in their bid to position themselves as central to resistance to globalisation (Sweeney 2002). Academic literature on resistance needs to catch up with labour union organising on this point: as Jackie Smith states in her analysis of the 1999 'Battle of Seattle', 'social movement scholars may need to rethink their assumptions about relationships between the social movement sector and organised labour' (2002: 223). In the literature on labour, women have received some attention in analyses of global assembly-line production and the informal sector, including within Mexico (Hemispheric Social Alliance 2002; Sklair 1994; Fernández-Kelly 1983; Staudt 1998). Yet to 'gender' resistance fully, we also need to move beyond a narrow focus on labour in terms of paid work and attend to unpaid or informal work along with violence in the home and on the streets. *Maquiladora* workers in Ciudad Juárez and other border communities also worry about affordable and safe housing, access to water, transportation, and access to education for their children.

The notion of resistance as a revolutionary challenge to the globalisation of capitalism raises even deeper questions. How does this speak to those compelled to enter the 'belly of the [global] beast' by seeking employment in export-processing factories? It is notable that the families of the murdered women and activists organising on their behalf have not called for a boycott of *maquiladora* work and some have raised funds for their struggles by engaging in micro-enterprise. In Ciudad Juárez, poor families have to pool their resources in order to survive. It is common for several family members to share a small dwelling, contribute to the household economy in a variety of ways, exchange baby sitting and, even after working a nine-hour day, work in a second job which can range from making *tamales* and *empañadas* to selling cosmetics. At the same time, these families are demanding services such as garbage collection, water delivery and other basic urban services. A revolutionary perspective would be likely to dismiss or misinterpret such actions as encouraging petty capitalism and continued integration into the 'global assembly line'. Resistance to globalisation needs to be conceptualised in ways that allow for strategies of survival and subversion as well as direct confrontation. The feminist distinction between 'practical' and 'strategic' interests may be useful here (Moser 1993; Molyneux 1985). But from our perspective, analysing and acting within the Coalition, any dichotomy between everyday survival and systemic challenge is ultimately unsustainable.

With regard to the privileging of direct action in discourses on resistance to globalisation, we wonder why the sometimes stridently male protest actions – confrontational and even violent – get such attention, both in academic writing and in the media. This mode of action may be problematic, especially for women challenging male violence and mutilation murders. As we show later, organising in Ciudad Juárez involves a strong emphasis on symbolic drama, with religious overtones, that seeks to challenge rather than sustain the norm of violence. It also aims to gain broader public support than may be possible for more confrontational modes of direct action.

Finally, we would also highlight the limitations of an exclusive focus on the English language in discourses of resistance to globalisation. This moves beyond a general feminist concern with seeking to include space for gender analysis and women's activism within the discourse on resistance to globalisation. It reflects more specifically a Third World or postcolonial feminist concern with racialised and geopolitical hierarchies and the ways they intersect with gender and class (Mohanty *et al.* 1991; Alexander and Mohanty 1997; Saunders 2002). English is often the dominant language for Internet use, prominent in the kinds of resistances to globalisation emphasised above; and it also dominates other forms of activism and analyses of them. This generates obvious exclusions. In Ciudad Juárez, CNN reporters and journalists from prominent dailies seek out English speakers. The person who is engaged in conversation with the reporter clearly has an advantage in presenting their side of the story and in making other connections. Spanish speakers are at an obvious disadvantage, both in accessing information and in presenting themselves as sources of information. Further, at least with respect to Spanish, translation into English neutralises, sterilises or depersonalises complex, radical or emotional language. It is often dry (*seca*), technical, narrow and bland. For example, in English the word 'education' means formal education; in Spanish *educación* can mean one's manners and social graces. In Spanish the word *lucha* can mean struggle and fight in English, but it evokes a very strong emotion when used in the case of social justice.

Critiques of exclusions generated by language must attend not only to the problem of English as a hegemonic language but also to the problem of obtuse and abstract theorising about resistance. Gender, for a start, does not translate well as a concept into other languages (Jahan 1995). Comprehensive theories, including some developed by feminists, are often written at very abstract, conceptual levels, rather than drawing on knowledge that emerges from the muddy and complex realities of desperate needs. Marnia Lazreg has questioned abstract theories that fail to 'comprehend [women's] lived reality' (2002: 128). The lived reality of poverty and violence must be central to any discourse on globalisation and resistance that is to be inclusive and hold out potential for real change.

The theory and practice of resistance to globalisation that we elaborate in the rest of the chapter is eclectic in its use of feminist theoretical resources, drawing on elements ranging from liberal to socialist, and from radical to postcolonial. Moreover, it is pragmatic to the extent that it is grounded in the everyday lived realities of women's lives. Finally, it is informed by our *compromiso*, the literal translation of which means 'commitment' or 'engagement'. In Spanish, however, the term implies a far deeper obligation towards a cause than both these English words convey. In certain cases, a *compromiso* implies a sense of indebtedness for services rendered. For example, when working in poor *colonias* to interview victims of crime or their family members, researchers can express a sense of *compromiso* with the people providing the data, a commitment which transcends friendship to ensure that the research in some way benefits or addresses the cause. We work closely with people, greet with *abrazos* (hugs), and care about each other.

Compromiso obviously involves socialisation for the academic that is very different from the positivist training provided in 'scientific' research, which privileges objective, quantitative approaches. We live and work at the border, often called the 'Third World' given its poverty and associated characteristics (Sharp 1998; Staudt 1998). Perhaps academics in more privileged territory can easily afford to maintain distance and neutrality from what they are studying in ways that we cannot. The political demands of the border context are too pressing, particularly given the epidemic of violence against women. Like Paulo Freire (2000), we do not wish to pretend neutrality on violence. We are against violence towards women, not in between. We move from analysis to action immediately, not waiting for the usual processes of peer review, journal publication and validation through which academic knowledge is constructed. In the starkest terms, we ask: how many more women would die with the wait? Names and faces are connected to our data, rather than abstract numbers. We think of the names of female victims, attached to carnations given to visitors at *Día de los Muertos* (Day of the Dead) altars in El Paso and Ciudad Juárez. We think of Anna Chavira Farel, Jessica Lizalde León, Angelina Luna Villalobos – and the many others whose names are unknown.

Compromiso demands that the researchers bring together their empirical work and political involvement. Thus in the next part of the chapter, we offer an account of the Coalition, outlining its strategies and achievements not as abstract academic questions but rather as pressing political concerns in which we ourselves have a personal investment. This empirical account of the Coalition's diverse strategies also functions as an important corrective to the absences recorded above in the discourses on resistance to globalisation. The Coalition – its participants, strategies and struggles – needs to be incorporated if that discourse is to be inclusive and relevant to women's lives on the border.

Analysing Coalition resistances

The Coalition Against Violence Toward Women and Families at the US–Mexico Border draws together individuals and organisations from many walks of life. It is a loosely knit, non-hierarchical network, *not* itself an officially registered, formally structured tax-exempt organisation (known in the United States as a 501c3). Core Coalition activists come from formal NGOs and from academia, labour unions (as mentioned at the start of the chapter, the Coalition emerged from union meetings) anti-violence centres, faith-based groups and others. Several of the NGOs bring resources garnered from US, Canadian and European sources: from private citizens, state organisations and corporations. Within the Coalition network, individuals and groups can act autonomously and pursue different priorities. Some focus on work with the victims and their families, particularly in terms of fundraising for anti-violence services ('practical' interests). Others emphasise systemic policy change and the need to challenge the authorities ('strategic' interests). The shared goal of all participants is to draw public attention to the murders, demand judicial responses and to broaden the range of voices being heard.

The Coalition operates in a complex political setting. On the one hand, it has to confront unresponsive political authorities on both sides of the border. Both Mexico and the United States are ostensibly federal democracies. In Mexico, the Partido Revolucionario Institucional (PRI) lost its seventy-one-year grip on the executive branch of government in the 2000 elections. Multiple parties are now represented in the legislative branch of government, at national, state and local levels, contrasting with the two-party system. However, Mexico still has a 'clientelist' system wherein powerful people and those with access to them (and occasionally their pocketbooks) exert inordinate influence. Political parties historically have co-opted NGOs (or *asociaciones civiles*) in order to secure votes; alternatively, NGOs may be threatened and intimidated by the police or hired hugs. Legal experts declare that the 'rule of law' does not exist in Mexico, and the judiciary lacks independence (Domingo 1999; Human Rights Watch 1999; Taylor 1997; Giugale *et al.* 2001: 136). Thus political activists in Mexico face great difficulties in accessing power. Local governments and agencies are not much more responsive, given that the system there is characterised by an 'elite pluralism' in which access to positions of influence is restricted.

On the other hand, Coalition activists must deal very sensitively with the victims' families who are at the heart of their work. The families are disempowered in several ways. Victims tend to come from poor working-class families who lack resources. As a consequence, just attempting to earn a living consumes most of family members' time and they rarely have the opportunity or the inclination to participate in political activity. Only after they have been contacted do some get involved. Most feel intimidated in their dealings with governmental agencies, as exemplified by the common complaint '*no tengo las palabras para expresarme bien*' ('I do not have the words to express myself well'). This sense of inarticulacy and powerlessness is exacerbated by the fact that agencies and the international media privilege the English language. It is further aggravated by the fact that many of the families feel too ashamed to speak publicly about their situation given the sexualised nature of the murders and the subsequent stigmatisation of the victims. Thus the Coalition has a heavy responsibility: it has to speak forcefully on behalf of silenced families, while remaining sensitive to the problems of representing those less powerful than themselves.

In this context, what strategies are pursued by the Coalition? In what follows, we describe four distinct but interrelated strategies: lobbying politicians in an effort to bring about legislative change; working with cross-border and international agencies with the aim of influencing their practice; building solidarity with organised labour; and holding demonstrations and making other symbolic interventions designed to highlight the murders and to influence public opinion. Almost all of these strategies are pursued bi-nationally, involving complex layers of cross-border co-operation.

First, in terms of lobbying politicians, the Coalition has met frequently with Texas State Senator Eliot Shapleigh, one of the few politicians who proactively supports anti-violence actions and who has been willing to let us use his name to push for bi-national co-operation. Further, Senator Shapleigh, with Representative Norma Chavez, introduced a joint resolution for the Texas legislature on the investigations, with hearings held in early April 2003 in both House and Senate committees. These were audio-taped, video-taped and made available online. The Coalition was invited to testify in front of Representatives and Senators, and Coalition-supplied black-crossed pink pins were placed on politicians' lapels to indicate their support. The measure passed.

In addition to working with Shapleigh, Coalition members have targeted the wives of politicians and other influential figures, in an effort to create a sense of solidarity amongst women in the region and to influence male decision-makers indirectly. For example, Coalition members dressed in mourning at luncheons hosted by the Twin Plant Wives Association and the Republican Women's Club. Twin-plant wives, who reside in El Paso, are married to the managers and corporate executives of the largely US-owned assembly plants in Ciudad Juárez. The murders have been discussed and wage inequalities critiqued at these events. The First Lady of Texas, Anita Perry, was willing to be 'pinned' with the symbolic black cross on pink and participated in brainstorming sessions on strategy.

Furthermore, in early 2003, the Coalition spoke with city and county political representatives in Ciudad Juárez in order to get a resolution passed condemning the violence and a proclamation issued for International Women's Day. The resolution that was passed had a narrow focus, calling for a bi-national task force and the pooling of cross-border police resources and information, amongst other things. The proclamation that was issued was more general, aimed at educating the general public about systemic gender inequalities and gender violence in everyday life.

The efforts of Coalition members to get the attention of national, political figures and departments have been rather less successful. The Coalition has sent numerous letters to President Bush, the Departments of Justice and State, and the FBI. Months pass before responses are received. Most define the issue as a narrow judicial matter that Mexico must resolve on its own, unless the government asks officially for the assistance of the United States. However, in October 2003, Congresswoman Hilda Solis, a Democrat from Los Angeles, led a Congressional delegation to visit both sides of the border and has since introduced a bill on the topic into Congress, with the support of the Hispanic and Women's Caucuses.

Turning to the second strategy, that is working with agencies on both sides of the border, the Coalition has called for a bi-national task force to foster cooperation over investigating the crimes. In particular, it has demanded greater FBI involvement. This is despite the fact that for some in the Coalition it is problematic to look to police and investigative agencies for solutions. Through the good graces of Senator Shapleigh's office, Coalition members were put into contact with FBI officials. Since then, a bi-national task force on the crimes has been created and the FBI has responded to a Mexican government invitation to become involved, albeit in a limited training rather than investigative role.

Another example of this focus on cross-border agencies can be seen in the collaboration of the Coalition with the non-governmental Transborder Consortium on Gender and Health at the US–Mexico Border. In an effort to modify a report issued by the government-appointed US–Mexico Border Health Commission, which made no reference to violence against women, the Transborder Consortium proposed a series of amendments which are now being considered by the official Commission (still unresolved at the time of writing).

It is worth noting that the Coalition has also worked with international agencies such as the United Nations. The UN 47th Commission on the Status of Women invited two Coalition members to New York City to participate in its session in March 2003. This provided another channel through which pressure could be put on the Mexican authorities, although human rights commissions tend to report abuses rather than enforce solutions. Travelling to New York also enabled the Coalition to develop networks with sympathisers in distant locales.

The third strategy involves the Coalition continuing to build links with cross-border labour organising. In a sequel to the meeting that gave birth to the Coalition, a labour anti-violence conference was held in Ciudad Juárez on 22 November 2002. Although the mayor of El Paso refused to attend and the Municipal President of Ciudad Juárez left immediately after his short speech, solidarity within the labour movement was reinforced, with leaders of unions such as the *telefonistas* offering to support Coalition campaigns with strike action.

Fourth, there have also been numerous dramatic and heavily symbolic actions, ranging from demonstrations to theatrical performances, which are aimed at influencing public opinion more generally. Every year, on International Women's Day on 8 March, large-scale demonstrations are held. On International Women's Day in 2002, for example, hundreds of people held rallies on each side of the border, then blocked border traffic by converging near the large wooden crucifix-like cross in downtown Ciudad Juárez, onto which nails for each victim have been hammered. Some protestors dressed in dramatic and symbolic colours and the quasi-religious symbolic signs of the deaths were everywhere: black crosses on pink backgrounds. Day of the Dead celebrations on both sides of the border have also been a focus for mourning and protest, with student activists displaying altars covered with candles, artefacts and memories of the deceased. In April 2002, students in the Feminist Majority Leadership Alliance of the University of Texas at El Paso sponsored a silent mourning, holding large black crosses on pink placards, in a well-traversed part of campus. Many newspapers snapped photos of the 150 mourners, including one dressed in full costume as the 'grim reaper'. In Ciudad Juárez, short, shocking 'guerrilla' theatre performances have gained attention on the streets. Lourdes Portillo's award-winning documentary film, *Senorita Extraviada*, which focuses on the murders and especially the victims' families, has been shown many times by activists, both for public education and for fundraising. The film has dramatically increased public awareness of the murders. Interviews with city councillors in El Paso reveal that Portillo's film has created feelings of empathy and solidarity with the victims and their families. Further, Eve Ensler's play, *The Vagina Monologues*, has been performed several times in the border region, and Ensler herself visited Ciudad Juárez for 'V-Day', 7 February 2003, for a full day of cultural events and meetings with state officials. In 2004, V-Day worldwide focused on the murders of girls and women in Ciudad Juárez. Ensler once again visited the border and marched across it with celebrities from Mexico and the United States, and approximately 7,000 activists and concerned people, in solidarity with the victims' families and NGOs (see V-Day n.d. for further information on V-Day).

Recently, the Coalition has been working to extend its strategies in new directions: identifying 'model' legislation in other states for potential adoption in the region; attending Congressional hearings; building new national and bi-national coalitions; contesting the economic pressures on Mexico. It can be seen that the Coalition is neither timid nor purist in the strategies that it pursues but rather pragmatic, imaginative and adaptable, changing strategies to suit particular contexts in pursuit of the overall goal of an end to violence against women in the region. All Coalition work remains informed by awareness of globalised political and economic structures that produce 'cheap' labour at $30 a week and images of disposable young women. Yet, as we have seen, resistances at the border face many challenges and the murders continue.

Compromiso in academic activism

We are political scientists, working in academia. As such, we were trained to take an objective, neutral stand towards the subject of our research. However, our involvement with the Coalition as researchers has required us to cross the line into activism – an activism compelled by the urgency and horror of the violence against women in our back yard. We suggested in the first part of the chapter that adopting the concept of *compromiso* compels us to use our insights and skills for political purposes. Thus what follows in this last section of the chapter are our individual, personal reflections about our roles as both activists and academics. What is at stake in taking *compromiso* seriously? What kinds of questions and dilemmas does *compromiso* raise?

Irasema

Professional concerns

The fact that I am an untenured assistant professor scares me at times because traditional views of academia dictate that one should write theoretical or empirical, number-crunching pieces, publish in prestigious journals, and advance the creation of objective knowledge. Will my colleagues value my work when I am going up for tenure? What worth will my newspaper articles or contributions to various community newsletters be given by tenure committees? Also, what will my university say about my activism, especially in a relatively small community where the university has a very high profile in television and the print media? Am I becoming better known for my activism than for my academic work? This balance is also a major concern because I consider myself an academic first and an activist second.

Should I be spending more time on researching and writing rather than raising awareness about the mutilated and murdered women of Ciudad Juárez? After all, even crossing the border takes time: up to one hour for each crossing, increasing to up to three hours with the security alerts since 11 September. At least I can justify attending meetings and rallies because they are also places and opportunities to gather data. Participant observation as a methodology is valid and legitimised in the social sciences, and first-hand experiences and actual contact with people give greater insight into the issue and its surrounding dynamics.

Another professional concern has to do with the use of university resources. I have spent some of my own money on airfares, telephone calls, photocopies, faxes and donations to women's organisations in Ciudad Juárez. I exercise great care in not using any university resources for these purposes in order to minimise any appearance of impropriety. I do not use the university email or telephone or copy machine for my activism, though I feel torn at times when the activism is a legitimate part of my research.

I have a final concern here to do with teaching. It is possible that some of my students may feel that I am likely to reward those who attend rallies or choose violence against women as an area of research. Of course, it is enriching to hear in class discussion from those who have been able to attend rallies and meetings or those who have got more involved in the Coalition. I also sense that such students gain respect from other students. However, I do not reward them in any way. I am acutely aware that many students have many responsibilities and time constraints that preclude them from becoming involved in community actions.

Activist concerns

I sometimes wonder if the families have read, or even know about, my published work in newspapers, newsletters and academic books about the murdered women of Ciudad Juárez. If they have read it, I wonder what they think about it. Is it an accurate portrayal? Even more worrisome to me, am I benefiting from their pain (*lucran con mi dolor*)? Is my work respectful of them and their feelings?

In terms of my relationships with other activists, I strive to avoid taking sides. Many women's organisations have emerged in Ciudad Juárez that support and promote this cause. It is a source of consternation to me that the organisations have different modus operandi, different levels of government recognition and make alliances with different political parties and factions, all of which serve to divide women and their efforts. There have recently been allegations that one organisation has misused funds and this causes me discomfort because many women on the US side have donated money to the struggle at my behest. What kind of explanations do I give to people who ask me if 'their' money was misused?

It is also difficult working as a Mexican activist critical of the Mexican government. Many people in the United States have a stereotyped, negative image of Mexico and much of my work thus tries to present Mexico in a positive light to them. However, it is irresponsible to pretend that the legal and political systems in the country are working well. With the election of President Vicente Fox, the first opposition party member to win an election in over seventy years, many North Americans thought that a wave of democracy would sweep the country and corruption would be stamped out. This has certainly not been the case and Mexican institutions have a long way to go in that regard. It saddens me to hear the stories that family members tell of their experiences with the local police, the attorney general's office, the Ministry of Justice, and the like. The fact that the representatives of these institutions are not well trained, well funded or politically motivated to solve the crimes of the mutilated and murdered women indicates a systemic problem. How can these institutions be strengthened and fortified to legitimately fulfil their missions?

Kathy

My issues are slightly different from Irasema's, given the semi-security of tenure I gained two decades ago. Having entered academia in the late 1970s, I expected to face gender discrimination, so my record represents that of an overachiever with plentiful refereed publications to ensure that tenure denial would be legally actionable. Of course, most of those publications were 'buried' in highly specialised journals in political science and development during a time when the audience for this analysis was miniscule. Even with job 'security', I am acutely aware of risks that I take in crossing political and institutional lines.

My work and life at the border for a quarter of a century make me identify myself as a *fronteriza*, the quintessential border crosser (Anzaldúa 1987). However, my name marks me as an 'Anglo' and I am acutely aware of my privilege as an Anglo and as an academic. This functions to position me at the top of the hierarchy of voice and knowledge claims at the border, where 80 per cent of residents claim Mexican heritage. My preferred leadership style in the community is that of a 'behind-the-scenes-enabler' but I am often pushed into more prominent roles at rallies or in front of television cameras. This makes me uncomfortable, and I tell people so, because I cannot speak for the majority Mexican-heritage residents.

I feel a deep obligation to use my talents and skills for social justice, and, for me, walking the walk, not just talking the talk, has always been important. My classrooms are very much about civic engagement, critical thinking and dialogue, and student empowerment. I believe academia should play a much stronger role in facilitating student leadership and practical political skills. How many students graduate knowing how to organise meetings, get rally permits, engage in strategic planning, write press releases or policy papers? Indeed, how many faculty members know and practise these skills?

Some of my activism takes place in formal political institutions, where I am often disgusted at the hypocrisy and attention-seeking behaviour of some politicians and officials and at the compromises I have to make (in the English sense of the term). I feel like screaming inside sometimes at their outrageous and ignorant remarks, but I have learned to keep a straight, even pleasant, face. If they vote to support the resolution that I am fighting for, that is what counts for me. When they do not support what I struggle for, or when new elections change the cast of characters, I must counter the weary fatigue that sets in about starting over and/or cultivating new relationships and coalitions. Sometimes the fatigue is overwhelming.

I share with Irasema a certain wariness of journalists. We have been misquoted, and in one case 'burned' by an overzealous, out-of-town reporter who quoted us to a local official when we had thought we had given the information in confidence. However, we have been very happy to work with other journalists who seek to publicise the issue abroad and in other parts of Mexico and the United States and who are prepared to share information with us that they have gleaned from interviews with Mexican officials and victims' families (Guillermoprieto 2003).

I fear for some of these journalists, as well as others who are vocal about these issues. In Mexico, reprisals can come in a variety of forms. Reporters can lose their jobs; academics may not be promoted; police stop, harass and beat lawyers. I am sometimes anxious for my own safety, wondering if politicians and public officials have read my work. Are myself and Irasema on a Mexican government list of political subversives? Are we are being watched in some manner? I still have a child at home. My face is on television, criticising the police (however diplomatically). We know other activists whose family members have been threatened. All this is in the back of our minds, but does not really affect how we work. While our *compromiso* may put us in danger, it also gives us the strength to continue.

Conclusion

We began this chapter by describing the numerous gender wars at the US–Mexico border, detailing the globalised power relations that render poor women's lives nasty, brutish and short. We then went on to describe the work of the Coalition Against Violence Toward Women and Families, focusing on the diverse strategies it has deployed to resist and transform those power relations. We have suggested that, although localised in the border region and dealing with the issue of violence against women, such activism should also be seen as resisting globalisation. Is such organising of less worth than sporadic trips to the meetings of international financial institutions like the WTO? We think not, yet such organising around violence issues is virtually invisible in discourses of resistance to globalisation, whether academic or activist.

The Coalition is succeeding in building new political relationships, developing intricate knowledge of political institutions, and spreading ever-expanding ripples of awareness throughout the region, Mexico and the United States, and the world. Power relations at the border are changing, if ever so slightly. However, we must be aware that patriarchy continually causes division and competition between activists, which serves only to reinforce the power of male-dominated governments and the inequalities within the global economy. It behoves activists and academics to recognise the danger of such divisions and to work in solidarity to build peace in the region, to respond to women's concerns, and to open up space for silenced voices.

Note

1 These details about murdered women are taken from a list kept by Ester Chávez Cano of Casa Amiga since 1993, as cited in a PowerPoint presentation by Amigos de las Mujeres de Juárez entitled *Ni Una Mas*. The details excerpted here are only the first seven cited, with all murders appearing to have occurred within a single five-month period, presumably in 1993. There have been many, many more victims since. The PowerPoint document, and further information, can be obtained from Amigos de las Mujeres de Juárez, PO Box 2449, Mesilla Park, NM 88047, USA, e-mail: amigosdemujeres@yahoo.com (see also Amigos de las Mujeres de Juárez 2004).

9 Organic intellectuals and counter-hegemonic politics in the age of globalisation
The case of ATTAC

Vicki Birchfield and Annette Freyberg-Inan

Introduction

Another world is possible[1] is the unofficial motto and hopeful mantra of the social movement ATTAC, which was launched in France in 1998 and has now expanded to include associations in forty countries as well as a transnational network that plays a key role in the World Social Forum. ATTAC's extraordinary capacity for recruitment and mobilisation is a political phenomenon of tremendous significance for the broader anti-globalisation movement – or to use the terminology preferred by ATTAC members, for the 'alternative globalisation' or 'globalisation-critical' movement. Students of this movement have been working to identify the rallying force for its diverse membership, ranging from public intellectuals, teachers and ecumenical leaders to small farmers, environmentalists and advocates for the homeless and unemployed. What unites them is a critique of neoliberal globalisation, understood as an ideology and set of policy programmes that prioritise greater freedom and protection for financial markets and multinational corporations and reduce the autonomy and prerogatives of communities and citizens. The distinctiveness of ATTAC's ideational contestation of neoliberalism lies in its construction as 'critique turned towards action', which encompasses both identity and distributional struggles, is based upon solidarity between the developed and developing worlds, and insists on the primacy of agency at the local, grassroots level.

As its motto implies, ATTAC's mission as a movement of social transformation is to offer real alternatives to the present global political economic order. What are these alternatives and what are the strategies employed to attain them? How can ATTAC be ideologically open, politically pluralistic and globally inclusive as well as coherent and effective? Where do we locate ATTAC on the broader theoretical map of social movements and anti-globalisation politics? To answer these questions, this chapter analyses the normative agenda, organisational structure and political practices of ATTAC at the national and international levels. Guided by a Gramscian theoretical framework, we also assess the extent to which ATTAC is emerging as a counter-hegemonic force in world politics. We begin by laying out the salience of Gramscian concepts and their usefulness for interpreting the rise and role of ATTAC. Next, we describe the origins of the movement and examine its organisational structures in two of the largest national associations, ATTAC France and ATTAC Germany. In subsequent sections we consider the ideological values and normative agendas of ATTAC and discuss the transnational dimensions of its counter-hegemonic organising. We end with an analysis of ATTAC's collective 'self-understanding' and purpose as a movement of popular education, highlighting its congruence with a Gramscian model of counter-hegemonic politics that grants a crucial role to the 'organic intellectual'.

Towards a Gramscian model of counter-hegemonic politics

Antonio Gramsci is a significant figure in the critical theoretical tradition and the post-positivist effort to forge a theory and practice of social change. His rich body of thought provides a non-totalising yet encompassing and profound way of thinking about power at both macro-structural and micro-individual levels. While acknowledging that Gramsci's complex and fragmentary ideas resist easy definition, we identify four concepts that appear key to his work and to an analysis of ATTAC: hegemony, counter-hegemony, the historic bloc and the intellectual. In this section, we sketch out the meaning Gramsci attributed to each of these core concepts and show how their interconnections constitute what we believe to be a useful model of democratic theory and praxis for the global epoch.

Imprisoned by Mussolini during the last ten years of his short life, Gramsci's political writings are compiled in his prison notebooks and primarily devoted to an attempt to understand the failure of revolution in the West and the rise of fascism in Italy (Gramsci 1971). His search for understanding led him to discern a new form of power or domination – one that extended from the state to civil society and relied on a combination of force and consent. He used the term 'hegemony' to refer to this form of power and its embodiment in myriad political, cultural and social practices. Thus, Gramsci turned his attention to the complex of institutions that stood between the state and economy to analyse the way in which consent was organised, i.e. through political parties, schools, churches, etc. For Gramsci, civil society was the terrain upon which power relations or 'relations of force' came to be established in capitalist societies, and thus it was also within civil society that opposition (counter-hegemony) could be constructed.

If the concept of hegemony can be understood, at least partially, as the means by which the state or 'ruling class' secures its leadership through some combination of consent and coercion, then counter-hegemony designates the strategies for working for change within the present hegemonic system (i.e. the capitalist mode of production and bourgeois polity).

Gramsci argued that counter-hegemonic forces should call into question the forms of power (both ideational and material) that perpetuate marginalisation by slowly building foundations for an alternative system of state–society relations, a process he described as a 'war of position' (Gramsci 1971: 229–39, 242–3). As a Marxist, Gramsci believed that leadership of this counter-hegemonic struggle lay with the proletariat, but it is important to underscore that his vision called for alliances to be built that brought in all of the 'subordinate classes' including peasants and other social groups such as small merchants.

This theoretical view of power, understood in terms of hegemony and counter-hegemony as a struggle for societal control, is connected to a model of political action through the concept of 'historic blocs'. Gramsci understood historic blocs as the stable, institutionalised relationships between socio-economic structure and the superstructural realm of ideology, ideas and politics. Such blocs, according to Gramsci, are contingent on the existence of a hegemonic social class that dominates society. As he wrote: '[s]tructures and superstructures form an "historical bloc". That is to say the complex, contradictory and discordant ensemble of the superstructures is the reflection of the ensemble of the social relations of production' (Gramsci 1971: 366).[2]

Thus, we might argue that the extent to which neoliberal globalisation is hegemonic derives from the combination of the structural and material power of capital and the expanding ideology and institutionalisation of market fundamentalism. But as the growing 'alternative globalisation' forces place pressure on states and international financial institutions such as the International Monetary Fund (IMF) and World Bank, it is clear the neoliberal historic bloc is at least becoming destabilised at the ideological level. While Gramsci certainly saw individual actors and groups as constrained by political and economic conditions, he dismissed materialist reductionism and depicted historic blocs as more than mere alliances of class interests. He also sought to show that dominant structures are not monolithic and that an understanding of mass conformity and adherence to the status quo must be sought in both the base and superstructure – the social institutions and consciousness of human actors. This led Gramsci to emphasise the role of intellectuals and education both in establishing consent and in contesting dominant power relations by demystifying prevailing norms, social roles and institutional practices.

As many scholars have pointed out, Gramsci's complex theory of the role of intellectuals spans the entire prison notebooks, and we agree with Marcia Landy that, 'for Gramsci, the study of intellectuals and their production is synonymous with the study of political power' (1986: 53). The radical and inclusive nature of a Gramscian model of counter-hegemonic politics flows from this emphasis, and from his unconventional conception of non-elitist intellectualism, in which he sees all individuals as intellectuals/philosophers in the sense that everyone has a fundamental conception of the world that is shaped by and may shape prevailing hegemonies. Not overly romantic or naive, however, Gramsci was acutely aware of the often contradictory and fragmentary nature of such conceptions as held by the masses. This then led him to develop the idea of 'organic intellectuals', as opposed to 'traditional intellectuals'. The former possess a critical consciousness and a desire to question and change existing social conditions, while the latter disseminate knowledge that legitimises the status quo (see discussions in Showstack Sassoon 1986: 137–68; Holub 1992: 151–90). Gramsci's conceptual schema actually defies a simplistic, rigidly dualistic categorisation, given his insistence that every social group contains both types of intellectuals. However, he employed the notion of 'organic intellectuals' more often than not to identify the organisers of, and advocates for, systemic change. It is in this spirit that we invoke the concept in the title of this chapter and in our characterisation of ATTAC as a critical education movement, discussed in a subsequent section.

Envisioning a closing of the gap between the leaders and the led, Gramsci identified the need for an expansion in numbers of organic intellectuals (especially among workers and peasants) who could begin to break down ways of thinking that legitimated existing forms of social and political control. In an important passage where he discusses the need for a reflexive understanding between the popular and intellectual elements of a counter-hegemonic struggle, Gramsci invoked the radically democratic notion that the popular element must come 'to know' and the intellectual element must come 'to feel' for true transformation to occur:

> If the relationship between intellectuals and people-nation, between the leaders and the led, the rulers and the ruled, is provided by an organic cohesion in which feeling-passion becomes understanding and thence knowledge (not mechanically but in a way that is alive), then and only then is the relationship one of representation. Only then can there take place an exchange of individual elements between rulers and ruled, leaders and led and can the shared life be realised which alone is a social force – with the creation of the 'historical bloc'.
>
> (Gramsci 1971: 418)

This passage effectively conveys how Gramsci's core concepts cannot be fully understood in isolation but rather are interconnected in what we believe emerges as a model of democratic politics running throughout his body of work. Dante Germino (1990), in a superb study of Gramsci as an 'architect of a new politics', argues that the persistent theme in Gramsci's *oeuvre* is a non-hierarchical politics of inclusion. This is encapsulated in Gramsci's words above, which evoke the necessity of dissolving the boundaries between the rulers and the ruled. In terms of the centrality of intellectuals for actual praxis, Gramsci again reminds us that: 'A human mass does not "distinguish" itself, does not become independent in its own right, without, in the widest sense, organising itself; and there is no organisation without intellectuals' (Gramsci 1971: 334). Thus, a Gramscian framework as applied to the politics of globalisation compels us to consider the degree to which neoliberal globalisation has been construed by 'traditional intellectuals' and political leaders as inexorable, and the way in which counter-hegemonic forces – understood as organic intellectuals with a varied political and social base – contest this conception both ideologically and politically. ATTAC professes to do just that; its membership includes many prominent public intellectuals and it sees itself as an educational movement above all else. Considering each of Gramsci's concepts as they relate to ATTAC allows us to assess the movement's credibility and potential as a key force in an emerging historic bloc, capable of engendering social transformation at the nexus of local and global politics.

A caveat should be issued, however, regarding the extrapolation of Gramsci's theory of politics from the exigencies of fascist Italy and the capitalist crisis of the era before the Second World War to our present concern with globalisation. While it is true that Gramsci paid little attention to political organising at the global level, it is significant that his starting point was a critique of capitalism as a social order that knows no national boundaries, and that he emphasised the marginalisation (both economically and socio-culturally) of southern Italy from the more prosperous north. Although there is certainly no blueprint of political strategy in Gramsci that we can apply directly to the contemporary context, there are interesting parallels that can help elucidate the tensions faced by ATTAC national associations as they attempt to act in solidarity at the regional or global levels and to organise locally against undemocratic global forces.

Furthermore, since the seminal work of Robert Cox appeared (1983; 1986; 1987), drawing upon the ideas of Gramsci to build a theory of world order and historical change, a growing and diverse set of Gramscian and neo-Gramscian contributions have been made to the critical international relations and international political economy literatures (Gill 1993; 1995; 2000; Golding 1992; Maiguashca 1994; Murphy 1998; Rupert 1995; 1998; Ryner 2002). Yet we suggest that there has not yet been a systematic application of Gramsci's model of politics to new developments in world politics and particularly to global social movements. Although we recognise that there are contested interpretations of Gramsci's writings, and debates about their limitations (Blaney 1994) and ambiguities (Anderson 1976; Germain and Kenny 1998), it seems to us that our loose sketch of a Gramscian model of politics, as opposed to the adoption of a rigid mode of analysis or ideological position, is consistent with the radical and emancipatory thrust of Gramsci's life and work. His key notions of hegemony, counter-hegemony, historic blocs and the role of intellectuals, and the interconnections between them, offer a powerful model of politics within which the actions and visions of the alternative globalisation movement and ATTAC's role therein can be fruitfully interpreted.

The crisis of global capitalism and the emergence of ATTAC

The emergence of ATTAC must be understood as resulting from profound crises in the economic, social and ideological context. Two events served as triggers for the birth of ATTAC and the transformation of a critical discourse involving a small group of intellectuals into an organised and active social movement in France and beyond.

First, the Asian financial crisis of 1997 sparked a reaction among French intellectuals culminating in a widely discussed editorial by Ignacio Ramonet in *Le Monde Diplomatique*, published in December 1997. As the East Asian economies began to crash owing to rampant capital flight and the ensuing collapse of their currencies, Ramonet used the crisis as an opportunity to underscore the consequences of deregulated global financial markets and the volatility and systemic risks generated by short-term, speculative capital flows. Calling for a 'disarming of the power of financial markets', Ramonet concluded his essay by highlighting the inherent insta-bility and inequity generated by unregulated global capitalism and proposing the implementation of a 'Tobin' tax on currency speculations and financial market transactions to impose some degree of control over financial markets (1997: 1).

Originally, the acronym ATTAC was derived from the French for 'Action for a Tobin Tax for the Aid of Citizens'; later the organisation would be offi-cially renamed the 'Association for the Taxation of Financial Transactions for the Aid of Citizens'. The idea of a Tobin tax comes from a proposition made by the Nobel Prize winning economist James Tobin in 1972 to place a levy of 0.1 per cent to 0.5 per cent on foreign exchange transactions, in order to discourage private speculation in money markets which can undermine national monetary policies. Additionally, the tax was intended to stabilise global markets and create a fund for developing countries (see Boukhari 1999). The plea for a Tobin tax was a clever discursive move on the part of Ramonet as it allowed for a critique of unrestrained capitalism while at the same time proposing a strategy for change – one that emphasised the inter-connection of societies in the developed and developing worlds.

It is important to recall that France had undergone the most massive multisectoral strikes since May 1968 just two years before, and that globali-sation was widely seen as contributing to the bleakness of the domestic economic situation. Indeed, it was invoked by the Chirac/Juppé government as necessitating austerity and cutbacks in public services and social security benefits. Criticism of the *pensée unique* or singularity of thinking about the economy, and of capitulation to the 'Washington Consensus' and neoliber-alism, was widespread. According to opinion polls, as much as 71 per cent of the French population supported the idea of an international solidarity tax (Sondages CSA cited in Ancelovici 2002: 429). Thus, Ramonet's critique resonated with many in French society and produced an outpouring of thousands of letters of support, professing solidarity and endorsement of the Tobin tax. The letters of support precipitated a meeting in March 1998, bringing together intellectuals, trade unions, civic groups, representatives from political publications and others to discuss the general political and moral principles shaping their views of globalisation and to seek agreement on strategies and goals to pursue.

The three main points agreed on at this first meeting were the following: (1) the need to confront the hegemony of neoliberalism and propose credible alternatives; (2) the necessity of curbing increasing economic insecurity and inequality through the implementation of a Tobin tax; and (3) an urgent call to transcend traditional cleavages in French society and reinvigorate participatory politics locally and globally in order to counter the ill effects of financial globalisation (ATTAC 2000: 11). This meeting was followed up three months later and the association was formally established on 3 June 1998 with the first general assembly electing a board of directors and a president, Bernard Cassen, Managing Director of *Le Monde Diplomatique*, and adopting an official platform. Coinciding with discussions and preparations for the meeting, but actually preceding the formal launching of ATTAC, the second trigger event occurred, which revolved around the negotiations for the Multilateral Agreement on Investments (MAI) taking place at the headquarters of the Organisation for Economic Co-operation and Development (OECD) in Paris.

A coalition of seventy different associations in France and many prominent individuals such as Susan George and François Dufour, who later became vice-presidents of ATTAC, had actively opposed the MAI and lobbied the French government to pull out of the negotiations. The MAI was (and still is) an effort to produce a comprehensive framework for the liberalisation of international investment and, according to its opponents, would severely limit the ability of national governments to regulate certain public sectors and aid domestic culture industries. On 10 February 1998, the unions of the French film industry issued the following statement: 'The MAI is leading us to a real change of civilization. We are going from the right of peoples to self-determination to the right of investors to dispose of peoples' (cited in Ancelovici 2002: 436). Such caustic criticisms and intense political pressure, coupled with increasing internal disputes among OECD members themselves, led the French officially to pull out of the negotiations (for details of the MAI negotiations see Korbin 1998: 97–109). Upon announcing withdrawal, the French government released the *Lalumière Report*, in which it argued that opposition to the MAI

> marks a step in international economic negotiations. For the first time we are witnessing the emergence of a 'global civil society' represented by non-governmental organizations [NGOs], which are often active in several countries and communicate across borders. This is no doubt an irreversible change.
>
> (cited in Laxter 2001:1)

As for the position adopted in the report, Susan George, a founding member of ATTAC France, commented in her published debate with Martin Wolf, Associate Editor and Chief Economics Commentator of *The Financial Times*, that the Jospin government actually incorporated most of the arguments she and other opponents had made against the MAI (George and Wolf 2002: 160). Such tangible influence provided considerable motivation for the more comprehensive action that would come to define the essence of the ATTAC movement.

Thus it is in the context of these two events, the Asian financial crisis and the collapse of the MAI in 1998, that an intellectual critique of neoliberalism crystallised into deliberate, sustained contestation in the form of a social movement. Many French NGOs and intellectuals, including the late Pierre Bourdieu, had long agitated against the increased powers of the World Trade Organization (WTO), the neoliberal direction of European Union (EU) integration and growing foreign ownership of French companies, pension funds and the stock market. However, it was not until the establishment of ATTAC that coherent links were mapped between all of these developments and an effort made to unite theory and practice.

Thus, the emergence of ATTAC seems theoretically congruent with a Gramscian framework in that it can be seen as a response to the ideational and material forces of the latest phase of global capitalist instability. Linking the structural crisis of global capitalism to the local realities of everyday life of ordinary citizens and wage-earners is an important step in establishing the connections between the material power of capital and its ideological influence on the state as well as actors in civil society. Hegemony is only preserved when material forces are coupled with ideological power. Once the *pensée unique*, or singularity of thinking, was exposed as a legitimising façade for maintaining the structural power of capital and the speculative and unjust nature of the current regime of accumulation, the groundwork was in place for the construction of a counter-power that needed institutional expression. Next we will examine how the critique of neoliberalism was transformed into a concrete organisational structure. We will draw specifically on the examples of the association in France, where the movement was born, and in Germany, where it has also been extremely successful.

ATTAC's counter-hegemonic organising

First and foremost, ATTAC associations see themselves as part of a movement for critical, popular education. All ATTAC publicity material, whether on websites or in print publications, describes the association as an educational movement and a counter-establishment social force, as opposed to a conventional NGO or issue-based social movement. Christophe Ventura, Secretary for International Affairs at ATTAC France, has emphasised the distinction between NGOs and ATTAC as a popular movement, the key difference being that in ATTAC there is 'no hierarchical order and no top-down decision-making about common actions' (interview conducted by Vicki Birchfield, ATTAC office, Paris, June 2002). Such a position appears consistent with a Gramscian theory of democratic politics and counter-hegemonic strategy in its commitment to breaking down the separation between the rulers and the ruled.

In terms of its composition, in France there are 30,000 ATTAC members, of whom all but 556 are individual members. The 556 represent legal entities such as media publications, small business organisations, other associations or NGOs, and trade unions. Individual members form a truly diverse cross-section of society, with about one-third representing teachers, students and intellectuals and the remainder coming from occupational groups ranging from lawyers and civil servants, to farmers, white-collar professionals, workers and the unemployed. Public intellectuals are very much an active part of the leadership within ATTAC France and were instrumental in its creation. Founding members include the previously mentioned editor-in-chief of *Le Monde Diplomatique*, Ramonet, scholars such as George and the late Bourdieu, author Viviane Forrester, who wrote a widely read book on economic fatalism (*L'Horreur Économique*, 1996), and singer Manu Chao, among others.

As for its leadership and administrative structure, ATTAC France has an elected board of directors, currently composed of a president, Jacques Nikonoff, elected in November 2002; two honorary presidents, Cassen and Ramonet; two vice-presidents, George and Dufour; plus a secretary-general, a treasurer and eight other individual members. There is also an administrative council drawn from the otherwise symbolic college of the founding members which includes eleven individuals and thirty-eight *personnes morales* – legal entities such as unions and civic organisations (interview with Ventura, conducted by Birchfield, ATTAC office, Paris, 2 March 2002).

ATTAC Germany, founded in 2000, today consists of around 100 regional chapters with over 11,000 individual members and over 100 member organisations. As in France, some of those member organisations are high profile, such as the vast transport and service sector labour union ver.di and the BUND (Association for the Protection of Environment and Nature). They are also highly diverse, ranging from organisations for Third World debt relief and sustainable development to Linksruck, an organisation of revolutionary socialists. Aside from the regional chapters, ATTAC Germany includes working groups on all its main themes, ranging from the regulation of financial markets, through tax evasion, the WTO and world trade, social welfare systems and the world of work, to education. An 'action group' is responsible for organising publicity-raising activities nationwide and also supports the regional groups in local initiatives of this nature. A 'women's network' studies the impact of globalisation on women and monitors gender relations within the organisation itself. ATTAC Germany purposely excludes political party organisations from membership. Local party organisations may, however, become supporters without membership privileges, and party youth organisations are excepted from the ban.

Echoing this unease about political parties and established elites, the French association also insists that 'ATTAC is not, nor will it ever become a political party' (*Lignes d'ATTAC* 2001a: 4). It endorses no candidates and supports no political party and instead claims that its ideas, analyses and propositions are entering public debates and campaigns as 'candidates in their own right' (2001a: 4). Although clearly committed to maintaining its autonomy from official political actors and institutions, the association nevertheless includes among its active members an increasing number of elected officials (see Ancelovici 2002: 441–2). At the General Assembly meeting prior to the 2002 elections in France, the following statement was released which illustrates ATTAC's preoccupation with this issue:

> Political parties are situated on the side of power – whether holding power or wishing to, including the most radical among them. ATTAC serves as a counter-power. We wish to construct a counter-force in society where citizens have space for freedom and real influence. It is within this complicated dialectic of power and counter-power that we must define our relationship with political parties.
>
> (*Lignes d'ATTAC* 2001b: 8)

Like many NGOs or other civic associations, ATTAC France, as well as its sister associations in Germany and elsewhere in Europe, is a dues-paying organisation, and it is from membership dues that it derives 71.5 per cent of its funding. Additional support comes from public subsidies and donations (Ancelovici 2002: 443). Encouraging the robustness of its decentralised, grassroots structure, ATTAC France redistributes 25 per cent and ATTAC Germany 35 per cent of its dues back to the local chapters.

What is most significant about ATTAC's overall organisational form is the inclusiveness of the decision-making procedure. Although some key figures and intellectuals undoubtedly spearhead campaigns, vocalise critiques and forge major positions of ATTAC, particularly in France, there seems to be a real connection with the rank and file members and an appreciation of the fact that they represent the lifeblood of the movement. This is an important general fact to keep in mind, notwithstanding some cross-national variation: despite the development of a 'National Conference of Local Committees' to co-ordinate local efforts to contribute to the agenda and objectives of the national association, and notwithstanding claims that local groups have gained increasing independence in how they implement 'central guidelines for action' (Ruggiero 2002: 203), there is no question that the overall direction of ATTAC France flows from Paris. Here is where one notices a difference between the ATTAC network in France and other national associations, particularly that in Germany, where any potential directive power of the national office is contested with great confidence by the grassroots level. This difference is perhaps not very surprising given the historically greater centralisation of French political society, but may nonetheless be significant when it comes to identifying the decisive influences on the organisational set-up of a supranational ATTAC network. Before considering the supranational level or organisation in detail, however, we turn next to the normative and political agenda of the ATTAC movement.

Ideology, values and political agenda

The platform adopted by the General Assembly of ATTAC France on 3 June 1998 begins by stating that financial globalisation exacerbates economic insecurity and social inequality, bypassing democratic institutions and sovereign states and reducing people's choices (see ATTAC 2000; also ATTAC France 1998). It refers to financial globalisation as guided only by speculative logic and the private interests of multinational corporations and financial market actors. The platform lays out a critique of the economic fatalism and claims of inevitability that are often associated with the present transformation in the global economy and argues that only vigilant pressure on governments can halt the process. It specifically mentions the hegemony of US-inspired neoliberalism and criticises the EU for being a hand-maiden to the crusade even though it would jeopardise the public welfare and the audio-visual and agricultural sectors throughout Europe. There is a reference to the growing gap between the global North and South and a call for the implementation of the Tobin tax. Action is supported for encouraging greater resistance, giving more room to manoeuvre to states and citizens and, most importantly, for restoring the centrality of politics in steering collective fates. In the conclusion, the proposal for a formal association is made, including a call for common action at the European and international levels. In addition to the rhetorical device of invoking the need 'to reclaim our future', the platform specifies the following more concrete objectives: (1) to hinder international speculation; (2) to tax financial capital transactions; (3) to sanction tax havens; (4) to inhibit the globalisation of pension funds; and, more generally, (5) to oppose the abandonment of state sovereignty to investors and markets.[3]

Like its neighbour organisation in France, ATTAC Germany focuses on the regulation of financial markets and the Tobin tax, among many other issues (ATTAC Germany 2002). However, in spite of significant pressures to expand the agenda to reflect members' awareness of the interconnections between policy domains, it is the official policy of the movement not to attempt to develop a position on every issue on the domestic or transnational political agenda. As is also stressed at the international level of organisation, ATTAC's central principle is one of ideological pluralism. Oliver Moldenhauer, member of the national co-ordination circle of ATTAC Germany and responsible at the national office for Internet, Finances and the WTO action group, explains: 'Whether Christian or atheist, socialist or supporter of a regulated market economy – we concentrate on the demands on which we agree – without being thereby forced to develop a common utopia' (our translation, Moldenhauer 2002: 16).

The general political orientation of ATTAC Germany, which emerges from the plurality of its members' concerns and activities, is basically identical to that of ATTAC France. There are slight differences in emphasis, but not in nature, between the agendas of the two organisations, and the same is true for ATTAC associations more generally. Noteworthy is the recent inclusion of a strong emphasis on pacifism, encouraging topical alliances with similarly minded groups, as in the wave of demonstrations against the war on Iraq. Furthermore, at the time of writing, ATTAC Germany includes a special focus on battling the social policy reforms advocated by the Schroeder government. In this case as in may others, the movement shows sensitivity to the connections between domestic policy reform and the evolution of the international political economy, as well as flexibility in mobilising in 'real time' to affect the course of policy at all levels of governance. In ATTAC associations across Europe, there is a strong emphasis on opposition to the WTO-sponsored GATS (General Agreement on Trade in Services), which aims to deregulate and privatise previously public sector services such as education, health care, cultural services and water management and poses dangers particularly for the provision of and democratic control over basic services at the community level.

Referring to the need to distinguish ATTAC's ideas from nationalism and traditional protectionism, Ramonet in an interview with the *European Voice* urged EU leaders to have the courage to forge a social Europe to stem the tide of far-right populism, and expressed his concern that '[s]ocial issues have been marginalised in today's EU; the politicians just seem to be there to serve the free-market global economy' (Cross 2002: 11). He suggested that many of those who are now turning to right-wing, nationalist politics were once traditional left-wing voters who feel that 'globalisation has left them by the wayside' (2002: 11). The struggle between these two broad responses to globalisation is not limited to Europe where nationalism has a long historical tradition. Mark Rupert (2000) has shown how progressive and right-wing anti-globalisation groups in the United States offer contending reconstructions of popular 'common sense' and visions of world order. Although we believe that ATTAC as an international movement[4] clearly represents what Rupert calls the 'cosmopolitan and democratically-oriented left' (2000: 15), vigilance must be applied in disassociating its opposition to globalisation from that of nationalists and at every turn clarifying how its normative base and political agenda differ from those of other so-called anti-globalisation groups. Susan George speaks for many in the movement when she says:

> I bristle when we are referred to as 'anti-globalisationist'. We are internationalist, in solidarity with the peoples of the South and committed

to a better life for everyone, but fully conscious that this won't happen as long as the economic doctrine and methods engendered by neoliberalism prevail.

(George 2002: 161)

George is also concerned with countering any association with Le Pen or other ultra-nationalist groups by underscoring that ATTAC actively supports the rights of immigrants (including voting rights) and that there is neither an affinity nor any interaction between ATTAC and far-right groups. Revealing the pragmatic, as opposed to revolutionary, stance of the movement, George also affirms that its members are not posing as the 'Fifth International' but that it is rather through politics and the state that their initiatives must pass (2002: 169).

Although class-based politics and discourse are not a prominent feature of the movement, there is a desire to curry favour among workers and an overlap between the political agenda of ATTAC and that of trade unions. In fact, the president of one of the biggest trade unions in France, Pierre Tartakowsky, holds a position as ATTAC France's secretary-general. George says that ATTAC is like 'May '68 in slow motion' (2002: 125). However, she is quick to add that while militant students are certainly on board, the critical connection with workers is not fully realised and without it the movement cannot succeed. At the same time, there is an explicitly stated position, in France as well as in Germany, of not becoming defined by big interest groups in society. The evident dilemma here reveals the complexity of trying to define summarily ATTAC's ideological agenda and orientation.

Another challenge lies in the very fact that the ATTAC label is an umbrella for a plurality of different groups, interests and identities. One example illustrates this point. Whereas the tenor of ATTAC's critical discourse is generally non-Marxist, it could also be pointed out that at least two of the organisational members of ATTAC France, Droits Devant and Obsérvatoire de la Mondialisation, rely on a heavily anti-capitalist discourse and openly state their conviction that capitalism is not 'reformable'. In Germany as well, some Marxists are on board. However, vastly more striking than such an apparent contradiction is the existence of a clearly identifiable, apparently stable and obviously highly motivating consensus among extremely diverse groups and individuals. Despite ideological tensions such as the above, there is a strong and growing solidarity around the idea that economics cannot and should not trump politics, that neoliberalism by its very nature curtails democratic deliberation and that profit maximisation cannot be the only organising principle of society at the local, national or transnational levels. Such a vision appears consistent with, on the one hand, with Gramsci's rejection of a rigid or classical Marxism and, on the other, with his vigorous critique of capitalism and his recognition of the need for broader political alliances. It is precisely Gramsci's own rejection of the orthodoxy of the Third International that conveys his openness to the idea of ideological pluralism, even though he firmly believed that the working class had to be at the centre of the alliance against established structures of power. Whether interpreted as radical or reformist, the basic objective of ATTAC is:

> to challenge the domination of finance in a world where everything progressively becomes a commodity, where everything is sold and bought; ... to challenge the organization of economic, human, social and political relations; ... [and] finally to place ... [itself] in an eminently political field with the will to transform the world by means of democratic and civic mobilizations.
>
> (ATTAC 2000: 22)

Herein lies what distinguishes ATTAC from the multitude of other movements and NGOs dealing with similar issues and what enables it to connect with, perhaps even serve as the fulcrum of, the larger alternative globalisation movement. There is, in other words, a worldwide ATTAC consensus that could support the emergence of coherent global opposition. This is a promising observation indeed. The establishment of an effective global organisation that could embody this normative and political consensus, while also holding fast to the commitment seen in national ATTAC groups to the organisational principles of transparency and grassroots participation, is an enormous challenge. However, as we will see in the following section, the first steps towards meeting this challenge have already been taken.

Internationalisation of the ATTAC movement

Only six months after the establishment of ATTAC France, and at the initiative of its founding members, the international movement was launched and a platform adopted on 11–12 December 1998 in Paris. Representatives from Africa, Asia, Europe and Latin America were present as well as numerous social networks and NGOs. Three broad objectives were identified: (1) to launch an international movement for the democratic control of financial markets and institutions; (2) to enlarge and consolidate the political struggle against neoliberalism and its consequences; (3) to develop more effective means of communication and to provide information and counter-expertise about the international economic situation (ensuring access for networks and movements that are not connected to the Internet).[5]

Subsequently, the ATTAC movement internationalised rapidly – as mentioned in our Introduction, there are now forty associations in different countries around the world. The international level of organisation has also grown in importance. As early as June 1999, the first official international conference was held in Paris under the title 'The Dictatorship of Markets: Another World is Possible'. The next major event took place at the WTO meeting in November 1999 in Seattle, when ATTAC delegations mobilised and joined the protests under the slogan 'The World is not a Commodity'. Simultaneous protests were held by ATTAC groups across Europe, with an estimated 20,000 marching through the streets of Paris, for example. ATTAC's international campaign against the WTO has since included a call for a moratorium on negotiations in the areas of agriculture, services and intellectual property; a challenge to the legitimacy of the WTO's dispute resolution panels; and proposals to incorporate principles from the UN Declaration on Human Rights as well as the standards of other international bodies and agreements (George 2001: 93–5).

At the global level, the counter-summit is the key organisational form for ATTAC; it began with the idea of mounting an alternative to the annual World Economic Forum, usually held in Davos, Switzerland. According to one of the ATTAC organisers:

> The aim is not to get involved in the agenda of this forum, but to take advantage of its presence and its repercussions in the media to sound another note, giving voice to the social resistance movements and to critical intellectuals, while seeking alternatives to neoliberalism and the new modalities of accumulation.
>
> (Houtart and Polet 2001: 78)

The first such meeting took place in 1999 in Davos and brought together social movements from five different continents in a dialogue initiated and facilitated by ATTAC in association with the Coordinating Centre against the MAI, the World Forum for Alternatives and a Latin American branch of SAPRIN – the Structural Adjustment Participatory Review International Network. In 2001, a conference was held both in Davos and in Porto Alegre, Brazil, to emphasise the contrast between the 'planet of superrich and Porto Alegre, the planet of the poor, marginalized, and concerned' (Ruggiero 2002: 54).

What has become known as the World Social Forum has, at the time of writing, met for four years running, in what seems to be a relatively institutionalised process. Unofficial declarations are made at the conclusion of each meeting by participant groups and plans are laid for upcoming mobilisations for future meetings of the global elite, but otherwise the forum seems to be primarily a space for debate, networking and sharing knowledge and local experiences. Given its enormous and growing popularity, as well as the alternative globalisation movement's continuing commitment to decentralised organisation and grassroots participation, we are currently witnessing a rapid proliferation of local, national and regional social fora. These aim to fulfil the same basic functions of information exchange and mobilisation at lower levels and are emerging as part of a flexible, multilayered structure of global organisation.

With regards to the regional level of action of ATTAC in Europe, there appears to be increasing transnational co-ordination among groups to mobilise protesters to converge on Brussels and other EU summit locales as well as on the European locations of important meetings of the protagonists of neoliberal globalisation. Other than these demonstrations and the yearly European Social Forum, there is no specific, ongoing collaboration, nor is there an ATTAC Europe. However, as Christophe Aguiton of ATTAC France suggests, 'we can observe the embryonic but real beginnings of a coordination of struggles ... with European Marches, but also workers' struggles such as those at Renault Vilvorde and in trade union demonstrations like those organized by the European Trade Union Confederation' (cited in Houtart and Polet 2001: 94–5).

These co-ordinated efforts at the regional and global levels illustrate ATTAC's recognition that protectionist responses based on local, material interests will not advance the movement's underlying goal of contesting the very logic of neoliberalism. They reveal insight into the dynamics set in motion by the dominance of the 'corporate agenda' of neoliberal globalisation. These dynamics have been aptly portrayed by Jeremy Brecher and Tim Costello as a 'downward spiral' in which countries rich and poor are caught up in a 'race to the bottom'. This can only be effectively countered by a global 'Lilliput strategy' of 'globalisation-from-below', based on the recognition of the shared threat and the enlightened solidarity of the threatened (Brecher and Costello 1998).[6]

The fact that a more permanent transnational organisational structure has yet to emerge (there is no international headquarters, for example) is a reflection of ATTAC's commitment to local autonomy and cultural diversity, and its recognition that unanimity on anything other than the need for a full frontal attack on neoliberal ideology is not possible. Yet, rather astonishingly, given the sheer numbers of individuals from literally all over the planet and the enormous organisational effort involved, the movement has achieved mass mobilisations against the undemocratic nature of global economic negotiations at the national, regional and global levels, particularly through the World Social Forum process. Further, there is evidence that transnational co-ordination and exchange of ideas can occur within the movement also outside the context of the forum. For example, there are two communications and press release lists on ATTAC International's website, which are shared by all ATTAC groups. Finally, the recent action of ATTAC Japan, delivering 3,000 signatures petitioning French President Chirac to grant José Bové a pardon and release from prison,[7] provides just one interesting example of the ways in which the network is able to transnationalise what might be considered domestic political issues.

Stephen Gill, in an essay on the Seattle protests, drew an analogy to Gramsci's 'Modern Prince' (the Communist Party), suggesting that the protests and social movements we are witnessing today may well be the twenty-first-century equivalent. He argues that a 'new "postmodern Prince" may prove to be the most effective political form for giving coherence to an open-ended, plural, inclusive and flexible form of politics and thus create alternatives to neoliberal globalisation' (2000: 140). Given the diversity of identities and interests represented by ATTAC, combined with its unifying agenda of contesting the ideological hegemony of neoliberal globalisation, Gill's characterisation appears felicitous for depicting the nature of ATTAC as a key force in the constitution of an emerging transnational historic bloc.

Collective organic intellectuals? ATTAC as a critical education movement

As the previous empirical analysis has revealed, Gramsci's concepts offer a powerful interpretive construct for understanding the ideological and political appeal of ATTAC and its spectacular success in bringing a multiplicity of interests into its alliance. We conclude by considering ATTAC's role as an educational movement and assessing its congruence with the notion of 'organic intellectuals', whose involvement Gramsci specified as a precondition for a counter-hegemonic politics.

At the ideational level, ATTAC's self-perception as an educational movement is realised through numerous methods. These range from pamphleteering campaigns, aimed at informing citizens of the major policy implications of the increasing liberalisation of trade and financial markets, to the popular ATTAC-sponsored *universités d'été* (summer academies or workshops), held to enable activists, intellectuals and ordinary citizens to engage in dialogue about these issues and their impact on daily life. In Germany, working groups develop and spread expertise on an impressive range of issues and the network maintains a highly topical publication series. In contrast, in France there is a scientific council – headed by George, a trained social scientist – responsible for publishing books, articles and tracts of general, critical education on the global economy. Institutionally speaking, the emphasis on education is reflected in both countries in the local ATTAC associations, which adopt campaigns that suit the local concerns and needs but which also contribute to the formulation of ATTAC strategies at the national and global levels. The plethora of grassroots chapters seems indicative of a need to expand awareness of and support for alternative worldviews through the cultivation of organic intellectuals.

While the preceding observations tell us about priorities at the local and national levels, where does the role of intellectuals and education come into play in the context of ATTAC's professed solidarity between the global North and South? If ATTAC cannot successfully offer alternatives that transcend 'social democratic' solutions in their various national settings that only protect and privilege the North, the hope of consolidating a historic bloc through which a global counter-hegemony can be achieved is slight. So far, however, ATTAC's focus on critical education and the presentation of alternative views on the global economy, its flexible alliance and mobilisation strategy, and its instrumental role in the World Social Forum seem to have served as appropriate methods for moving towards such consolidation.

ATTAC seems to be engaged in the types of educational strategies that are necessary for radical transformation. Gramsci noted that traditional intellectuals in Italy, whether active in literature, the cultural arts or philosophy and politics, never identified with or related to the conditions of the common people. This is why, he asserts, Italy never fully realised the type of revolution and unification that was the experience in France, for example. Although his ideas relate specifically to the Italian case, what is undoubtedly relevant for our own times and circumstances is this emphasis on the central role to be played by education and organic intellectuals in eroding the separation between those who rule and those who are ruled. As ATTAC contains elements of organic intellectualism tied to marginalised segments of the world both globally and locally, we interpret the movement's activities as reflective of such a radical and fundamental strategy for progressive change. However, in the face of critiques such as that of Naomi Klein (2003), who charged that 'participatory democracy is usurped at the World Social Forum by big men and swooning crowds', it is important that ATTAC continues to strive to put its emancipatory principles into practice as successfully at the global level as it does at the national level. In the same spirit as Gramsci urged the erosion of the separation between the leaders and the led, ATTAC must embody the crucial role of what could be called the 'collective organic intellectual'.

This will include overcoming the conception of the developed world as furnishing 'teachers' for developing South 'learners'. This dichotomy must be replaced with an educational principle in which learning between 'teacher' and 'pupil' is, in Gramsci's words, 'active and reciprocal':

> Every relationship of 'hegemony' is necessarily an educational relationship and occurs not only within a nation, between the various forces of which the nation is composed, but in the international and world-wide field, between complexes of national and continental civilizations.
>
> (Gramsci 1971: 350)

As Teivo Teivainen insightfully suggests, practices in the South, such as the Port Alegre participatory budget policy, offer lessons and concrete practices to the developed world that can 'help break the Eurocentric and neocolonial structures of knowledge production that are dominant in our world' (2002: 621–32). As ATTAC sees its paramount mission to be one of education and consciousness raising, its success will be determined by how well it can actively facilitate and engage itself in precisely this kind of global learning to promote a more just world for all.

Conclusion

Gramsci's equal emphasis on political will and the need for organising is a prominent theme of his prison notebooks and he placed great faith in the ability of the 'Modern Prince' to unite people of the subaltern classes. His deeper insights about the need to end the distinction between leaders and the led resonate with the commitment to participatory democracy found in ATTAC and the alternative globalisation movement – whether this commitment is expressed through conventional or unconventional politics. Furthermore, many of Gramsci's polemics against the false dichotomies of politics/economics, base/superstrucuture and the way in which such divisions serve as a source of control over subordinated classes are also important features of the ideology and values of the ATTAC movement, as we have illustrated through a careful examination of the values and campaigns of national associations and at the supranational level.

While NGOs and transnational activism in general have proliferated in the past two decades, ATTAC seems to represent something qualitatively different both in terms of content and in terms of form. The movement enjoys rapidly rising popularity in diverse locations and sectors of populations. It swiftly expanded its agenda to turn from a single-issue interest group focused on the Tobin tax into a broad-based, transnational social movement that encompasses a range of unified positions, from critiques of the WTO to opposition to the war in Iraq. Owing primarily to its particular dynamism, ATTAC seems at present even better poised to operate as a counterweight to global capital than labour unions, which are still struggling against time to organise effectively on a transnational scale. If the growth of organic intellectuals is fostered by the movement and more and more individuals come to understand globalisation as a phenomenon rightfully subjected to democratic deliberation and control, steered to the mutual benefit of North and South, then ATTAC will have accomplished its mission. In so doing, ATTAC constitutes a key part of the counter-hegemonic social force in world politics upon which a transition towards a more humane and equitable new world order depends.

Notes

1 ATTAC's first international conference, held in Paris in June 1999, was organised under this title, and the popular slogan continues to be invoked in ATTAC's public education campaigns. Founding member Susan George used the motto as the title of an article published in *The Nation* (George 2002), explaining it as a direct response to and rejection of the Thatcher era's 'TINA': 'There is no alternative'.

2 In Robert Cox's (1986) application of this concept at the international level, historic blocs are constituted by the social relations of production and specific forms of state and world order, with Pax Americana serving as a prime example. Mark Rupert further adds that 'the construction of an historic bloc is a precondition for the exercise of hegemony … and entails a reconstruction for state–society relations through organically related processes of political, economic and cultural change' (1995: 29). The Bretton Woods system, for example, was hegemonic in the sense that it reflected a balance of material and ideological power aided and abetted by the classic compromise between labour and capital.

3 The platform is reprinted in ATTAC (2000) and posted on the ATTAC France website (ATTAC France 1998), but this summary is based on our own translations from documents obtained from the Paris office.

4 Hereafter when we refer to ATTAC per se we are not speaking about any particular national association but rather the movement as a whole.

5 This summary was developed from documents obtained from the Paris office. The international platform can also be viewed as an internal window on the ATTAC International website. Go to http://www.attac.org/indexen/index.html and click on 'referring to the platform' in the left-hand margin (ATTAC International 1999).

6 The reference to Brecher and Costello is more than just cosmetic here. Not only have their writings been highly influential within the movement, but ATTAC as described in this paper emerges as something of a poster child of their agenda for resistance.

7 Information obtained through participation in ATTAC France e-mail list, attacfr@attac.org, received on 1 May 2003.

10 'We are heartbroken and furious!'

Violence and the (anti-)globalisation movement(s)[1]

Sian Sullivan

> the militant is the one who best expresses the life of the multitude: the agent
> of biopolitical production and resistance against Empire.
>
> (Hardt and Negri 2000: 411)

2003 – A summer of protest

EU summit, Thessaloniki, June

*I am at the European Union (EU) 'counter-summit' in Thessaloniki. Prior to
the main protests on 21 June, the last day of the summit, I spend several hours
in Thessaloniki's Aristotle University campus, where squatting militant
activists are taking advantage of the legal asylum granted on university
premises. Here, in a philosophy department strewn with somewhat nihilistic
graffiti ('peace, love and petrol bombs', 'from pigs to bacon', 'middle class
war', 'fuck the world, destroy everything' (see, e.g. Figure 10.1), glass bottles
are being transformed into molotovs, gas masks are being tried on, and 'anti-
globalisation' protesters are calmly anticipating one of 'the biggest riots
Thessaloniki has ever seen'. I feel overwhelmed by a lack of humour, a swag-
gering machismo, a palpable hatred of the police – matched by an intention to
do physical injury – and a welter of self-harm scars on the flesh of several
protesters. This is hardcore. I leave the campus before the protest is due to
begin, feeling confused and alienated by this calculated preparedness for
violence and an obvious antipathy to intellectual reflection, as well as
concerned for my friends there.*

*In the evening I walk back through the streets of Thessaloniki, which for
more than two days remain thick with acrid teargas. Several businesses have
been gutted and are blackened with the soot from petrol bombs. Pools of
blood are noticeable on the tarmac. An image that stays with me is of an old
Greek man in a small corner café patiently brushing away broken glass
from the steel window-trays that normally would be filled with syrupy sweet
pastries.*

Figure 10.1 'Viva nihilism!' Graffiti on the walls of the Philosophy Department at
Thessaloniki's Aristotle University during the EU 'counter-summit',
June 2003
Source: Sian Sullivan, personal archive

DSEi, London, September

*The arms dealers are back in town! DSEi – Defence Systems and Equipment
International – is again holding its government-subsidised trade fair in
London. This is where arms producers from around the world meet to display
the latest weapons technology: where global businessmen deal in death. It is
10 September, the 'spiky' direct action day for which people have been invited
to protest DSEi using whatever means they choose, the guiding principle
being no violence to life. I have joined London-based activist samba band
'Rhythms of Resistance' (see Rhythms of Resistance 2003), partly so that I
am part of an active affinity group, but also because I connect with their
apparent experiential approach to political praxis: an anti-capitalist orientation that combines humour, celebration, costume, community, music and
dancing in drawing attention to a range of interconnected issues. Rhythms
meet early at the squat where our compadres from Sheffield Samba Band are
staying, and we agree that our aim is to join others in drawing attention to
the arms fair and to our dissent by causing as much disruption as possible.
We launch ourselves into the streets and soon are running from police,*

climbing over fences taller than me (not easy in a long green tutu), and eventually stopping traffic on the several-laned A13 north of the Excel Exhibition Centre. The police begin to form a linked cordon across the road. All I want is to get to the other side, but a policeman grabs me as I run. I'm not going anywhere, but he slams me into the concrete barrier that's in the middle of the road, bends me over it with my arms behind my back, and then shoves me so hard into the road that I land face down on the tarmac, bashing and twisting my elbow in the process (it's more than two months before I can stretch my arm without pain). At this point I really think I'm about to be attacked further, but thankfully he melts back into what is now a wall of policemen. I do not even catch his number.

It is the next day, 11 September, the anniversary of that moment when global politics crystallised as a politics of violence, terror and war. Bizarrely, the UK government has chosen this day to entertain the world's arms dealers in a gala dinner at the opulent Lancaster Gate Hotel. Police barricades have been set up to protect those inside from the protesters gathering outside. I arrive with the samba band and join the crowd. I think of the women and children killed and still being killed in Iraq and feel anger rising within me. Facing the two rows of uniformed policemen protecting those who profit from war, conflict, violence and death, I also feel fear. As I hit the agogo[2] that I'm playing I sense the physicality of this act become a release and focus for the grief and rage that I feel. I wonder if this physicality is so very different from smashing a McDonalds' window or throwing a molotov? Something 'clicks' and I think I begin to understand why these practices become part of people's repertoire of protest ...

Introduction

This chapter is intended as an exploratory comment on the militancy emerging in (anti-)globalisation political practice and in the policing of such practice. As someone who finds themselves crossing boundaries between, and contesting the categories of, the organic and traditional intellectual (see Gramsci 1971; Barker and Cox 2003) – engaging in the practice of activism as well as the theorising of activist practice – the piece has emerged from my own process of sense-making regarding violence in the '(anti-)globalisation movement(s)'.[3] It flows from my experiences of irruptive protest situations, as well as from my perceptions of the contextual and experiential factors that draw people towards, and make possible, the physicality of violence in these situations.

In reaching towards analysis and interpretation, my aims are three-fold: first, to explore a view that consciously militant tactics – namely, violence to property and preparedness for confrontation with police – are gaining legitimacy amongst protesters in (anti-)globalisation politics; second, to attempt a nuanced and contextual analysis of *why* this is the case, beyond a simplistic and moralistic framing of whether such tactics are strategically 'good' or 'bad' for 'the movements'; and, third, to offer some views regarding the subversive and transformative potential, or otherwise, of violent praxis in opening up possibilities for post-capitalist and post-representational subjectivities and social relations. What I suggest in this chapter is that any analysis of violence within the '(anti-)globalisation movement(s)' be framed in terms of both the global context of structural violence in which we live and the individual affective circumstances that shape our subjectivities, desire and agency. More specifically, I fore-ground the roles of depression and rage as two potent emotional sources that animate the politics and tactics of the '(anti-)globalisation move-ment(s)'.

My 'data' derive from 'observant participation' in relevant contexts; discourse analysis, focusing on unpublished and independently published texts that together indicate themes and ideas influencing contemporary activist praxis; and reflection on my own subjective and embodied experi-ence/s. Theoretically, I draw on a poststructuralist analytics that owes much to my reading of Foucault (e.g. 2001 [1965]; 1998 [1976]), Agamben (1994; 1998) and Hardt and Negri (2000) in considering subjective locations and experiences of the sovereignty effected by the biopower of global contexts. In particular, I note the psychological and physical docility effected by the panopticon society of censored subjectivities of late modernity: a docility that is *required* and enforced by modernity's current greedy incarnation in the sovereignty of global corporatism and US unilateralism. It seems to me that Foucault, in combination with contemporary anti-psychiatry philosophers Deleuze and Guattari (1988 [1980]; also see Fanon 1967 [1963]; Laing 1967), 'post-anarchist' political theorists such as Newman (e.g. 2000; 2001; 2003), and a feminist and anthropological legitimation of ontological differences and plural subjectivities, offer much by way of elucidating a corresponding *hunger* for acts and discourses of bio/psycho-political disobedience and dissent in (anti-)globalisation politics.

Discourses/practices of destruction: violence and the (anti-)globalisation movement(s)

Violence as a tactic of protest is as old as contested authority. But if it is possible to talk of the emergence of a *new* global social movement that is challenging the current status quo of inequalities, then I think it also is possible to perceive a globalisation of proactively militant discourse and practice. By this I refer to a transnationally understood and practised suite of tactics involving both symbolic violence to property and preparedness for direct confrontation with police and *not* to attacks on human life. With the property damage and the violent clashes that have occurred between police and 'anti-globalisation' activists at significant protest events in the post-industrial North in recent years (Wood 2004), violence is now expected in these contexts.[4] One author, for example, refers to 'the habitual violence at anti-globalisation rallies' (Toje 2002: 3). Policing strategies and the corporate media both reflect *and create* these expectations and actualities (see Notes from Nowhere 2003: 307). Techniques for crowd control comprise a major and growing focus for military and police, as well as an economic boom industry for the manufacturers of a whole new wave of crowd control weaponry (discussed further in Sullivan 2004b; 2004c).

The financial costs of policing protest events, as well as the costs of damage to property and of lost business, provide a conventional measure of the significance of confrontational practices in these contexts. But a look at the published and unpublished expressions of intent made by protesters confirms a transnational strategic militancy in contemporary (anti-)globalisation protest politics (emphasis added for all quotes):

> *We want to destroy government and rich peoples' privileges.* We want to get rid of the control that police, government and bosses have over our everyday lives.
>
> > (Anarchist Youth Network: Britain and Ireland 2003)

> *[L]et's fight so hard,* and live so hard, that others inside the cages of mainstream life can see us and are inspired to join us in *our complete rejection of the old world* and all its bullshit.
>
> > (CrimethInc. Workers' Collective 2001: 165)

> One of the world's biggest ever trade fairs for guns, bombs, military planes & ships, small arms, mines and tanks is scheduled to take place in London from 9–12 September 2003. ... *You are invited to help destroy this market of death.*
>
> > (Destroy DSEi 2003)

> [W]e, as insurrectionists must wage war on terror: the terror of the state, the terror of hierarchy, the terror of war and most importantly the terror of civilization.
>
> > (Wildfire 2003)

Taken together, these statements comprise a coherent, combative and open discourse of destruction that makes a discursive challenge to the state's assumed and masked monopoly over the legitimacy of using violence to further aims. It clearly positions activists of many flavours – anarcho-primitivists, insurrectionists, CrimethInc. dropout culturists, to name a few represented by the sources of the texts – as separated by a qualitative abyss from the 'pathological passivity' (Roszak 1971 [1968]: 22; Churchill *et al.* 1998) of reformist agendas, i.e. positions that, while critical of the status quo, seek to influence existing institutions and structures rather than imagine some sort of disaffiliation from them. In the last few years, this discourse has been accompanied by two key practices in militant (anti-)globalisation protest politics in the post-industrial North, encompassing the 'black bloc'[5] tactic of violence to the physical symbols of corporate capitalism and the Tute Bianchi/Disobedienti/WOMBLES[6] tactic of padding-up in order to engage in 'confrontational defence' – 'non-violent warfare' – in articulating with police lines.

An argument common both within and without 'the movement(s)' is that violence perpetuated (against property and police) by advocates of a militant anti-capitalism is a fringe element that discredits and delegitimises 'the movement' as a whole (Cross 2003: 11). Media and popular attention focuses particularly on the apparently mysterious and shadowy 'black bloc' – demonised and misrepresented as the dark underbelly of alienated anti-capitalist youth (e.g. in Watson 2003). While appealing to the voyeuristic tendencies of the media and thereby at least drawing attention to the incident of protest – that is, 'no fights, no coverage' (Broughton 2003) – violence is framed as distracting focus from issues that activists are protesting against and for, and as a strategy that is divisive for 'the movement(s)' as a whole (e.g. Yechury 2003: 3). For others, there is little difference between violence at a protest and riots at a football match, the violent act in both contexts being low on instrumental strategy and high on cathartic release and momentary self-indulgence.

Given the pluralistic and multifaceted social context of the (anti-)globalisation movements – with their rhetorical emphasis on 'unity in diversity' – all of these critical views have legitimacy. Their dismissal of militant practices, however, masks several dimensions pertinent for a nuanced analysis of both the occurrence of violence *within* protest events and the relationship of violence in these contexts to the wider socio-political milieux in which they take place.

One only has to open a newspaper or watch the news to come face to face with the fact that we inhabit a global economic and political system that is built on, pervaded with and powered by gut-wrenching levels of physical and psychological violence. Bourgois, following Galtung (1969), asserts that the contemporary world (dis)order is infused with *structural violence* such that

> the political-economic organization of society ... imposes conditions of physical and emotional distress ... rooted, at the macro-level, in structures such as unequal [i.e. unfair] international terms of trade and ... expressed locally in exploitative labour markets, marketing arrangements and the monopolization of services.
>
> (Bourgois 2001: 7)

At the same time, and as New York columnist Thomas Friedman wrote prior to the Gulf war in 1991, it is becoming increasingly difficult to ignore the hidden fist of the (United States) military that has been behind the hidden hand of the 'free' market (in Cookson n.d.; Higgott 2003); or the accompanying and increasingly militarised suppression of dissent and protest worldwide (Sullivan 2004c). Analytically, these constitute *political violence* (Bourgois 2001: 7): administered in the name of the political ideology of neoliberalism (what Graeber (2002: 62) refers to as 'market Stalinism'), in combination with an aggressive American unilateralism (PNAC 1997; Donnelly 2000; White House 2002; Higgott 2003; Rilling 2003).

Newman (2000) points out that for Marx the state's oppressive apparatus reflected economic exploitation and the desires of the empowered capitalist class, while for late nineteenth-century anarchist writers such as Bakunin and Kropotkin, the state itself *originates* in and has a sustained logic of violence (also Perlman 1983). Today, it is tempting to see structural violence emerging from a strong collusion of both state and capitalist interests, e.g. in today's social democratic adherence to the ideology of public–private partnerships, in combination with state-supported arms industries and the apparent use of military might to defend and expand economic interests. If this line of thought has validity, then it is impossible not to connect it with Mussolini's understanding of fascism as 'corporatism' – 'the merger of state, military and corporate power' (Pilger 2004: 20) or to envisage an emerging contemporary form of global corporatism that favours the United States as the world's largest capitalist economy and military power, and in which the state, to varying degrees, becomes an appendage of a combined and ongoing transnational and imperialist policing.

Böhm and Sørensen (2003: 2) conceive this 'globality' of violence as '*warganization*'. This is the bio-political total war (Foucault 1998 [1976]; Deleuze and Guattari 1988 [1980]) 'embedded in the very organisation of Empire'; indeed, *required* by the continual, multidimensional expansion of Empire's biopower (Hardt and Negri 2000). It signals the end of war as a bounded event – 'where war is conceived as a limited enterprise in which you engage and disengage' – and thereby also signals the end of a utopian imaginary of peace as a state of not war (Böhm and Sørensen 2003: 10). In these circumstances, *war* – war on terror, war on drugs, war on individual and civil liberties effected by the constructed paranoia of current surveillance culture and the securitisation of everyday life – becomes *the* 'organizing principle that is constantly at play everywhere' (Böhm and Sørensen 2003: 9). Ironically it is ' "sold" to us as a war for "freedom" ' (Böhm 2002: 329), or for peace – an irony embodied in the caustic slogan, seen frequently on anti-war demonstrations, that 'fighting for peace is like fucking for virginity'.

Thus 'the enemy is everywhere and everybody: … "total war" is in fact a civil war in the sense that it is a war from *within* the social, *against* the social' (Böhm 2002: 329, emphasis in original).[7] Indeed, this total war is distributed more minutely throughout society in that it also is located throughout our selves and psyches: giving currency to the analysis by South African activist Steven Biko that 'the most potent weapon in the hands of the oppressor is the mind of the oppressed' (Biko 1989 [1978]). It is the 'symbolic violence' (Bourdieu 1998; 2001) absorbed by both individuals and collectives that maintains hegemonic domination through the internalisation and legitimation of the categories that make the social order appear self-evident: 'producing the unwitting consent of the dominated' (Bourgois 2001: 8; also Laing 1967; Foucault 1998 [1976]). And it is thereby ever present as the internal effort – the fight – required in any waking up to our contingent power and individual freedom (Fromm 2001) that makes possible an active consciousness and overcoming of the 'regulated "interiorization" ' exacted by the corporate state (Newman 2000: 5, after Nietzsche).

An increasingly and globally connected consciousness of the central and multiplicitous roles of violence to the creation and maintenance of global inequalities also is of emerging and defining significance in contemporary (anti-)globalisation politics. This is powerfully indicated by the existence and interpenetration of both an 'anti-capitalist' movement that is global in reach and a global peace/anti-war movement that showed its presence in the streets on 15 February 2003 (e.g. Koch 2004). It is animating ongoing direct action politics as well as street protests worldwide. This understanding – that global patterns of inequality and injustice are established and perpetuated by systemically coercive and violent relationships in the realm of the social and the subjective, and therefore that political violence is not limited to the frontline of military conflict – is articulated clearly in activist statements such as: capitalism is 'a social system that condemns the vast majority of people to stunted and unfulfilled lives despite our best efforts' (Jazz 2001: 87 in Graeber 2002: 4), and: 'We could never match the violence of society. The bottom line is, we live in a society where you have to fuck people over to achieve security for yourself' ('Joe' in Thompson 2003).

In the following section I consider some ways in which relationships between this multiplicitous and multifaceted political violence and activist bio-political agency might be conceptualised and interpreted.

Finding frontlines: activism in search of agency

I know one bitingly articulate activist whose existential pain was so extreme that he would slash his own arms and torso to pieces. One cut required more than 80 stitches. At activist gatherings and mobilisation meetings I have seen the scars of physical self-laceration on more people than I care to remember. Others retreat into the temporary psychic cotton wool of drugs – from alcohol to ketamine. And who in the activist communities does not know of someone who has attempted or succeeded in suicide? All these are tools for pain management. *We are heartbroken and furious!* I mean, how many of us, and to what degree, do we have to be hurting before the reality of where we're at collectively begins to sink in?

(Interview with 'Sam', activist, personal notes 23 November 2003)

> There is no divine order, other than to love the life you live and to spread joy. But if that is the case, then I must be a fundamental human.
>
> (Rupture 2004: 3)

The story so far is one where political violence in the service of global corporatism and American unilateralism permeates social, psychological and economic relationships. Where bodily and subjective docility are required by these colonising structures, and extended via the disciplining governmentality of universalist discourses, 'civil society' and representational 'democracy' (see Tormey 2004). Where, short of suicide, it is impossible to extract oneself from these violating global contexts.

How do people cope and retain hope under the weight of these contexts? How do individuals come to struggle; to attempt to effect change by exerting agency? And how might 'anti-globalisation' politics really be radical – in the sense of opening up and constituting spaces for 'the' post-capitalist, post-represented human?

Internalising rage: denial, depression, desire

> I'm trying to say what I think brotherhood really is. It begins – it begins in shared pain.
>
> (Le Guin 1974: 54)

The psychoanalytic and psychotherapy literature is rich with observations and analyses of the ways in which humans and animals cope with extended suffering and trauma. A pattern is of desensitisation to the repeated experience of, or exposure to, violence such that traumatic experience becomes normalised and thereby denied (see Miller 2001 [1979]: 100; Pinkola Estes 1993: 244–6; Jensen 2000; and references therein).[8] This process appears enhanced when people become 'used to not being able to intervene in shocking events' because of 'formidable punishments for breaking silence, for fleeing the cage, for pointing out wrongs, for demanding change' (Pinkola Estes 1993: 246). By this reckoning, violence – *violation* – is normalised via the denial or silencing of felt experiences of violation, as well as the internalising of the rage that such experiences can engender. This constitutes a *depression*/repression of affective experience, and a corresponding suppression of an ability to act according to desires to transform situations, even if the possibility for transformation presents itself. As such it permits the internalised 'symbolic violence' by which, as noted above, a hegemonic and violating status quo is legitimated through 'our' own consent (Bourdieu 1998; 2001).[9] Further, because emotions are felt – experienced – bodily, i.e. are embodied (Csordas 1994), alienation from emotional responses to trauma can extend into alienation from 'the' body (Totton 2002), translating into bodily as well as psychological self-harm practices. Self-mutilation or cutting, the use of drugs that afford escape from pain, eating disorders and suicide: all these are increasing, are certainly present in activist communities (i.e. as indicated by the statement with which this subsection opens) and are interpreted by many as sacrificial practices offering pain, blood and control for release from existential pain (Wolf 1992; Milia 2000; Wurtzel 1999 [1994]).[10]

This rise of depression is interpreted here as signalling psychological and affective distress at the forms of social–political and economic organisation in which individuals are embedded. It is accompanied by the suppression of this distress via extensive medication and the removal of such 'disordered' people from society (Foucault 2001 [1965]; Smail 1984; Baron 2003; Sontag 2003: 5). From an anti-psychiatry perspective, depression and the subjectivities and practices that flow from this state of being emerge from a necessary dissociation or splitting from subjective experiences of trauma (e.g. Laing 1967; Smail 1984). Thus, '[d]epression consists of a denial of one's own emotional reactions ... in the service of an absolutely essential adaptation' to traumatising contexts (Miller 2001 [1979]: 46). In this reading depression might be more a barometer of *social* (ill-)health, than a mental illness that inhabits unfortunate individuals (i.e. as conventionally analysed and treated). Further, as a phenomenon of socio-economic and socio-political denial and disengagement, accompanied by subjectivities of negation and the attacking of self, depression represents a reducing of the socio-political layers that construct modernity's 'normal' and manageable citizens (Agamben 1994; 1998). Depression, and the subjectivities and practices with which this state of being is associated, thereby *coherently constructs the affective and physical body as the experienced locale of socio-political relationships* – the biopower of *Empire* (Hardt and Negri 2000).

My experience is that depression and self-harm practices are talked about somewhat more candidly among activists engaging in 'anti-globalisation' political praxis than in other everyday contexts (which is not to say that these phenomena are not present in other contexts). At the 2003 UK Earth First! summer gathering, for example,a workshop on mental health issues in the activist communities was so popular that a second session was rescheduled. It was as if once a space had been created where these experiences could be shared the floodgates opened, enabling voice after voice to speak of the pain, fear and anger felt at the multiplicitous violence of modern society, and a yearning for release from these contexts. For some, depression embodied a long-term and recurrent sense of alienation at modernity's fragmenting and devaluing of relationship. For others, depression and symptoms of post-trauma distress had arisen in response to the experience of police violence in protest situations, such as at the infamous G8 meeting in Genoa in July 2001 (see Indymedia 2002); sometimes as a sense of guilt if friends had been attacked while chance circumstances had led one away from a potentially dangerous situation. Still others talked of their alienating experiences at the hands of the formal psychiatric system. Indeed, a recent study suggests that participation in activism increases a sense of well-being and mitigates symptoms of depression (University of Sussex 2002; Drury 2003), confirming that activists might be both choosing appropriate channels for the self-treatment of depression and accurately addressing contextual causes of distress.

It seems to me that this nexus of interrelationships sheds light on the unfolding of a confrontational bio-politics in contemporary (anti-)globalisation protest. As Wurtzel (1999 [1994]: 299) argues, 'one of the striking elements of this depression breakout is the extent to which it has gotten such a strong hold on so many young people. ... Affecting those who [should] have so much to look forward to and to hope for', as well as the generation(s) that are most clearly identified with current militant practice in (anti-)globalisation politics. In this aspect depression represents an individual withdrawal from desiring the future, since it signals a loss of hope, of optimism, in the possibilities that the future holds. But by stripping away conventional engagement with the political-economic status quo – which, as Jensen (2000: 108) puts it, requires adhering to the commandment that 'Thou shalt pretend that nothing is wrong' – the subjectivities of depression also create spaces for the experience and articulation of new *desires*. From here, the 'politics of possibility' (Sullivan forthcoming) of the (anti-)globalisation movement(s) – of the World Social Forum's slogan 'another world is possible' and its reframing as 'other worlds are possible' by activists of a conscientiously pluralist orientation – can be interpreted as a radical reinsertion of a politics of *desire* regarding the future. This indeed is 'a new offensive in the arena of dreams, of rights, of liberty, for the conquest of the future' (Cuevas 2000: 3). And imagining – desiring – something different is the first step towards dissent, defiance and disobedience regarding the status quo.

Externalising rage: anger, activism, agency and affinity

> When actions are performed
> Without unnecessary speech,
> People say, 'We did it!'
>
>   (Lao Tsu 1972)

A common perception of militant activism is that it is a childish and reactionary *acting out* of anger driven by adolescent angst and a displacing of Oedipal rage onto 'papa state'. As Miller argues (Miller 2001 [1979]: 121) '[p]olitical action can be fed by the unconscious rage of children ... [and] partially discharged in fighting "enemies", without having to give up the idealization of one's own parents'. It gives rise to comments such as: '[s]mashing things comes off as a little kid whining in the streets about how much he doesn't like his little situation' (Frank 2003); or, 'you did a great job of acting like children on a tantrum while erroding [*sic*] the credibility of the peace rally' (Shot By You 2003).[11]

Perhaps some physically confrontational protestors indeed are attracted by the very potential of violence to the moments of protest that are part of anti-capitalist/(anti-)globalisation politics. Violence in this reckoning would be an end in itself, although importantly the brutality of a context of *everyday violence* (e.g. football riots, pub brawls, domestic violence, etc.) is shifted into the *political violence* of the protest (Bourgois 2001).[12] *Activism* as opposed to *reactivism*, however, is a targeted and strategic expression of the emotion of anger, as well as an ethical assertion of *the right to be angry*, given contextual circumstances that are thought and felt to be wrong. Thus '[t]he point about the Black Bloc is that people simply want the autonomy to be able to express their anger as they see fit' (Anon. 2004: 7).

It is not difficult, therefore, to perceive the targeted violent act in the context of protest as generating an immediate and individual experiential satisfaction, in part through effecting direct concrete results in exterior public space (see Fanon 1967 [1963]). These actions transform the lack of agency many experience given a global political economy that constrains options for spontaneity and self-determination and which generates the permanently unfulfilled desire of consumer capital. But when such physical acts also are part of a strategy of 'smashing' coherently selected targets, it is not appropriate to frame them as violence as an end in itself, since they embody a conscious subversion of the *symbolic violence* that otherwise fosters collusion in disempowering contexts. Militants themselves are quick to distinguish their actions from those of incoherent, unstrategic riotous activity. In fact, it seems to me that there is not a great deal of difference between these actions and the carefully planned sabotage of deliberate 'monkey-wrenching' acts (Abbey 1991 [1973]; Do or Die 2003) occurring outside the circumstances of major street protests. Consider, for example, the statement made by veteran UK Trident Ploughshares activist Ulla Roder, arrested in March 2003 for causing criminal damage to a Tornado ground attack aircraft in protest at the attack on Iraq:

I looked at the seat in the cockpit in the streamlined white Tornado warplane, which I had just entered. In my mind I had the picture of a young pilot, boy, son, father; the many years of fear for the people of Iraq; for their survival; for a new world war – nuclear war; fear of losing the little bit of freedom we people have left in this world, to a state which has officially declared that it wants 'Full Spectrum Dominance' on earth as well as in space and which has shown all willingness and cynicism to use whatever means of power to gain this. All this made me lift the red and black bolt-cutters in my hand. Crash! I shouted out aloud in the hangar. There was no-one to hear, but it helped. 'We don't want your war, Bush and Blair!' This for all the dead civilians in Iraq and all the children still suffering at poor hospitals, caused by 12 years of sanctions against civilians. Crash! The control panel was out of commission.

(Roder 2003)

Here we find coherence of intent as well as beautiful, angry passion. It is unlikely that many people will appreciate or accept the parallels between the sober, directed sabotage of an older woman such as Ulla, and the smashing tactics of '(anti-)globalisation' protesters, black bloc or otherwise. But these parallels exist in both intent ('mindful destruction' of things that cause, or represent causes of, violence to life (Anon. 2004)), and felt experience (anger and need for release). Even the clear difference in activist style between accountability and clandestinity[13] appears to be breaking down, if Ulla's non-appearance at two recent court hearings is anything to go by (Roder 2003).

Another example of strategic militancy in 'the movements' can be found in the tactics of the Italian Tute Bianchi (now Disobedienti) who go into police lines, prepared not to attack but to invite a defensive confrontation (as indicated by their mock salute of a fist with the little finger raised, waved at the police to mean 'Come on, break it!' (Anon. 2001: 3)). This is a conscious strategy to draw out the tendency towards violence of the police, thereby making explicit the violence that is systemic to contemporary capitalism: exposing the fallacy and fantasy – the contradictions – of the Hobbesian 'social contract' (e.g. WOMBLES 2003a). As such, it constitutes an instrumental bio-politics (Foucault 1998 [1976]): a means of physically confronting the repression of the state and its support for corporatism as the primary means of structuring society. Foucault (among others) articulates body (and psyche) as the locale(s) of power's micro-physics which, as argued above, can be self-attacked in multiple ways as a further expression of this micro-physics. In this bio-political tactic of protests, the body is reconstituted individually and collectively as the appropriate (and only possible) locale of rebellion.

Participation in the organising and practice of actions that transgress the boundaries of 'good bourgeois behaviour', especially when accompanied by a clear cosmology that conveys the broader meaning of such actions, also has socio-psychological significance in terms of reinforcing internal social and psychosomatic coherence (or *habitus*) (also in Cross 2003, after Bourdieu 1990 [1980]). This is in part by ritualising the experience of repression in these contexts (Mueller 2004a). The sharing of such extreme experiences is integral to the building of solidarity. As Barker and Cox note,

> [f]or many activists ... it is a turning-point to be at the receiving end of police aggression and to discover that an institution they have been brought up to see as underwriting their safety and the moral order is in fact prone to violence against 'ordinary people' ... pursuing what they understand to be eminently moral (and often altruistic) pursuits.
>
> (Barker and Cox 2003: 8)

And again,

> [b]eing attacked by heavily armed riot police is terrifying. It has happened to me many times now and I think you never get over the fear.

But I have come to feel more and more like fighting back and I have come to understand more the value of the Black Block.

(WOMBLES 2003a)

Perhaps the most politically powerful aspect of protest actions, however, is not the actions themselves, but the social and psychological dimensions that infuse organisation and experience(s) of them. Take, for example, the forming of groups of affinity: small, extra-institutional socio-political groupings arising from direct relationships, trust, shared interests and actions, reciprocity and an emphasis on consensus and inclusive processes of decision making. These attempt a shift to group emergence from shared values as opposed to conventional identities (such as sex, race, religion, etc.) or geographical location (e.g. WOMBLES 2003b: 10). This emphasis on direct relationships in the context of affinity groups can be considered, and is consciously framed as, an insurrectionary act and process in itself. It arises from an understanding that capitalism means that 'most of our encounters have already been defined in terms of predetermined roles and relationships in which we have no say' (Willful Disobedience n.d.), and that it functions in part by fragmenting social relations – favouring competition over co-operation and requiring objectification (e.g. people = human resources, 'nature' = natural resources) rather than communion.

Of course, the dynamics of any group or organisation can be conservative and constraining, and activist communities are no exception to this. For example, the internal structuring of what Marcellus (2003: 3) describes as a 'pretentious and authoritarian elitism' among those prepared to commit violent acts can itself take on a conservative and exclusionary tendency, such that participation becomes 'more about just identifying oneself with a … group' than about libertarian and strategic/creative political action. Or the pressure to be 'radical' and to eschew any form of populism again can propagate an exclusionary elitism (see Anon. 2001: 4). But in ideal terms, the presence of dynamic organisational practices emphasising autonomy and affinity in themselves constitute the means to mitigate against a potential sedimenting – or 'molarising', to use Deleuze and Guattari's term (1988 [1980]) – into the restrictive and regulated structures characterising legally constituted social groupings. Such practices include: the fluid, dynamic and temporary nature of affinity groups formed for the purposes of specific actions; the access activists have to emerging trans-local cultures of resistance and disobedience – located virtually (via the Internet e-lists, discussion groups, etc.) and physically (at meetings, parties, actions, etc.) – that recursively open and shape activist values and tactics; and the conscious adherence to anarchist and network principles of organisation that recognise the value of horizontal networks as well as temporary hierarchies.

To summarise, a gulf of difference distinguishes activist agency involving violence to property and preparedness for confrontation with police from an unconsciously reactive, infantile acting out of anger. The former are manifestations of broader and recursive cultures of practice, organisation and discourse. They represent the weaving of a social fabric based on mutual aid, affinity, reciprocity, direct relationship and solidarity that in itself constitutes a psycho-cultural break with the accepted warp and weft of a modern sociality (i.e. of de Sade, Darwin, Hobbes and Freud) that assumes individualism, competition and tendencies towards violence as the dominant drives for humanity. While the experiential power of the 'rite of passage' of irruptive situations and the contri-bution of such 'peak experiences' (Maslow 1973) to individual and collective identities cannot be underestimated (Mueller 2004b), the social practices with which they are accompanied arguably are at least as politically challenging as the moments of protest constituting a direct action bio-politics.

But …

> When you are acted upon violently, you learn to act violently back.
> > (CrimethInc. Workers' Collective 2001: 36)

> If this movement progresses in terms of escalating violence alone then we will lose, because they have guns and we do not.
> > (Anon. 2004: 19)

The above analysis locates me outside a strictly pacifist activist discourse and practice, or at least, in support of a position of 'deep' questioning of a reactionary violence/non-violence dichotomy in protest politics. Indeed, I actively affirm the transformational and communicative value of 'sitting in the fire' of anger and conflict (Mindell 1995).

But please read the small print. Debord (1983) famously wrote that alien-ation cannot be combated 'by means of alienated forms of struggle'. Indeed, if (anti-)globalisation politics is about moving *beyond* the oppositional cate-gories that support the status quo – about proleptically imagining other possibilities for being/becoming, and about a process of creating and doing the new as well as contesting the old – then violence surely has a compro-mised place within 'the movement(s)'. It is a response that is defined by, and thereby increases, the reactionary violence of the state in its support of *Empire*, and that can slip easily into a reactive opposition that strengthens rather than outgrows the strong (Newman 2000: 3). It reinforces the power that is, by definition, present in opposition to its resistance, while also making the opposition more and more like its enemy, amounting to 'a terribly ugly mirror image' (Böhm and Sørensen 2003: 13). This is the familiar equation that violence + violence = more violence. Thus, just as the structural and political violence of neoliberalism sediments into interper-sonal violence in everyday domains (Bourgois 2001: 29) – constituting what Bourdieu (1998) refers to as the 'law of the conservation of violence' – violence in the context of protests also easily shifts between the 'meaningful' political act and the boring violence of the everyday (also see Marcellus

2003). By resonating with the particular masculinities of a conventional, humourless and Leninist left perspective that emphasises the violent necessity of the revolutionary moment,[14] a politics that otherwise is framed as anti-establishment and subversive becomes conventional rather than radical: overly bound by past imaginings of what is possible. On this point, a strengthening of particular 'hegemonic masculinities', i.e. that valorise physical strength, machismo (in relation to other men as well as to women) and emotional passivity (discussed in Cross 2003: 14–15; also Viejo 2003), perhaps also generates its own momentum and problematic – one which is akin to that represented by the machismo of a male-dominated, body-armoured riot police. Given reports of sexual harassment made by women at the anarchist encampment at Thessaloniki's Aristotle University in June 2003, for example, it indeed is tempting to see an emerging dynamic in militant factions whereby 'worthy' political violence is transmuted and normalised 'back' into the banal and disempowering violence of everyday sexism.[15]

Thus, it is hard for me not to stay with the conclusion that a conscious orientation towards violent praxis acts to buttress inequalities, as well as being 'profoundly disabling', both physically and psychologically (Bourgois 2001: 12). Given the context of structural and symbolic violence characteristic of late capitalism, of the distributed biopower of *Empire* (Hardt and Negri 2000) and of US military imperialism, however, it also is hard to avoid the corresponding conclusion that the period of social change in which we find ourselves will be associated with escalating levels of violence, in (anti-)globalisation protests as elsewhere.

And now? Becoming uncivil society

> It starts when you care to act, when you do it again after they say no, when you say '**We**' and know who you mean, and each day you mean one more.
>
> (WOMBLES 2003c: 39, emphasis in original)

Following Foucault, Agamben and Hardt and Negri, the sovereignty of the global manifests and is sustained as biopower. This 'not only regulates human interactions but also seeks directly to rule over human *nature*' (Hardt and Negri 2000: xv, emphasis added). Given this omnipresence – the pervasive structural violence that permeates the global in which 'we' all are located, together with the accompanying tyrannies of universalising liberal civil society discourses – is it possible for individuals to come to agentic struggle that might subvert, transgress and *unravel* these structures?

Perhaps this problematic can be framed differently as engendering a multiplicitous *opportunity* for empowerment, since it also implies that the frontlines of struggle, indeed, are everywhere – investing all thought, action and sense of self with political meaning and potential (Sullivan 2003). As Hardt and Negri (2000: 21) suggest, the omnipresence of Empire's biopower is precisely the medium in which 'a completely different ethical and ontological axis' becomes articulated, becoming a social revolution of subjectivities.

But where and how might this 'ontological basis of antagonism' (Hardt and Negri 2000: 21) emerge? Is it possible to experience, articulate and share understandings of structures and practices that are 'dehumanising' in their violence without being interpreted as promoting a constructed, hegemonic humanist and universalising rationalism that discounts difference? And can this alternative come into being without constructing a corresponding liberal tyranny of the safe and 'nice'?

What I have attempted to articulate in this chapter is that it is unsurprising that violence is emerging in (anti-)globalisation politics as a conscious transformation of the felt experience of rage in relation to the glue of structural violence that makes possible the biopower of *Empire*. I have suggested further that the related experiences of depression and rage are affective articulations with alienating and violating contexts that in (anti-)globalisation politics become animated by the desire for new praxes of being human. In this analysis, the stripped down subjectivities of a contemporary upwelling of affective depression comprise political locales of latent desire: echoes of Agamben's philosophy of 'bare life' (1994; 1998) as comprising spaces emptied of citizenship from where 'new' philosophies and praxes of what it means to become human might emerge. I have also indicated that militant practices can be both empowering and radical, and constraining and conservative, and that it is only with the explicit locating of such practices within the discourses, situations and subjectivities in which they emerge that intent and effect can be elaborated and interpreted.

Of course, struggle also implies and requires tactics. Just as for Negri (2002) the 'multitude' is 'a whole of singularities' that cannot be collapsed into a homogenous mass of people, the material discussed in this chapter also suggests that the political tactics of the multitude do not comprise competing alternatives to each other: instead they are complementarities that in themselves affirm the pluralism sought by the rhetoric of the movements. The difference and singularities embodied by tactics are themselves politically heretical given the fundamentalism associated with global power and universalist agendas (Baudrillard 2003: 4). In other words, no one has a monopoly on tactics. But actions will be stronger in total if their experience is communicated and debated amongst individuals and collectives, such that the corresponding openings – and reclaimings – of social, physical and subjective spaces are able more fruitfully to jostle, overlap and recreate each other.

As made clear in the accounts with which this chapter opens, I locate myself as someone who desires and participates in struggle for change. For myself, I am inspired by a brilliant image by graffiti artist Banksy, of a masked protester with arm raised to throw violently – not a molotov, but a bunch of flowers (see Figure 10.2). This captures both the engaged anger and the seriously subversive and celebratory creativity comprising the hallmarks of a global politics of defiance that has its feet planted firmly in the twenty-first century. My desire is for a processual, *interstitial*, Dionysian radical politics that exploits, explodes and subverts the instability of correspondences between signifier and signified, inside and outside, the messiness of experience and the reified categories of modernity. And in doing so attempts a continual transcendence – a going beyond – that acknowledges the destruction inherent in creativity, but that is not a call for nihilism as an end in itself.

In this reading, militancy in (anti-)globalisation politics is a proactive politics of the lived rather than the managed human. The supraterritorial soil in which it is fertilised is the painful legacy 'we' have been bequeathed: of the Holocaust and Hiroshima; of Chernobyl, Bhopal and the *Exxon Valdez*; of Thalidomide, BSE and the technocratic penetration of genes and atoms; of advanced democracies promoting the trade of arms and the precursors of WMDs to repressive regimes worldwide; of endless privatisation and commodification – from nature, to states of mind, to knowledge; of the

Figure 10.2 Attacking with flowers instead of molotovs
Source: Sian Sullivan, personal archive

construction of a 25 feet (8 metres) high concrete wall to separate communities even as the memory of the Berlin Wall is still warm. Is it surprising that 'we' distrust and even despise modernity's fabricated ideologies of self-interested economic rational man, of 'there-is-no-alternative' political realism and of faith in civilisation and technocratic solutions? Or that we fill our subjective spaces with the identities and practices of activist, nomad, anarchist, pagan, outlaw, raver, 'wild woman', sambista, poet, WOMBLE, clown, shaman, hactivist, heretic – modernity's 'freaks' – everywhere? I feel not. But then, of course, I could just be depressed …

Notes

1 A longer version of this piece is available at Sullivan (2004a), which builds on and substantially reworks an earlier piece (Sullivan 2004b).

2 Hand-held bells hit with a wooden drumstick.

3 The term 'anti-globalisation' is problematic for several reasons. For example, 'the movement' draws on and is made possible by the same processes and technologies that have made contemporary globalisation phenomena possible (e.g. Sullivan forthcoming). This, together with the movement's support for 'the effacement of borders and the free movement of people, possessions and ideas', suggests that we could talk more accurately of the 'globalisation movement' (Graeber 2002: 63), hence my bracketing of 'anti'. Mueller (2002; 2004a) describes 'the movement' more accurately as the 'globalisation-critical movement', while Chesters (2003) refers to the 'alternative globalization movement'. Further, an emphasising of 'the movement' as merely reactionary, or 'anti' (e.g. Williamson 2003), masks and diminishes what protagonists actually may be campaigning and motivating for, such that much corporate media and other analysis becomes dislocated from the discourses and practices emerging within, and constructing, 'the movements'. I pluralise movements to reflect the realities of diversity and difference among the collectives that are contesting the status quo worldwide, and the equally diverse and situated imaginings and practices for socio-political change that they embody (as captured in the title of Kingsnorth's (2003) recent book *One No, Many Yeses*). This also is intended as a conscious rhetorical and conceptual shift away from modernity's constant drive towards the singular, towards the root or deep structure of things (Deleuze and Guattari 1988 [1980]: 3–25).

4 I am not forgetting that those in the 'Global South' who are contesting the insidious effects of neoliberalism on their lives and livelihoods have had to endure much higher levels of violence for much longer, and it is not unusual for protests to culminate in the death of protesters at the hands of police (e.g. Bretton Woods Update 2003). It is in part due to outrage and empathy regarding these incidents and trends that people in the post-industrial North are contesting and critiquing current globalisation processes, particularly the securitisation of the inequities and injustices required by global state–corporate capitalism.

5 Although generally perceived as 'anarchists', in continental Europe, where a strong centrally organised left tradition remains a political *tour de force*, a black bloc on a protest might incorporate militant members of worker-oriented parties as well as anti-imperialist nationalists (e.g. Anon. 2004). Thus,

> [a] Black Bloc is a collection of anarchists and anarchist affinity groups that organize together for a particular protest action. The flavor of the Black

Bloc changes from action to action, but the main goals are to provide solidarity in the face of a repressive police state and to convey an anarchist critique of whatever is being protested that day. ... Black is worn as the colour that symbolises anarchism [i.e. governance without leaders], to indicate solidarity and to provide anonymity.

(Infoshop 2003)

6 White Overalls Movement for Building Libertarian Effective Struggles (for more information, see WOMBLES 2004).

7 Witness, for example, the increasing incidence of requests by states that citizens report 'suspicious behaviour' observed in fellow citizens: from Irish Health Minister Michael Martin proposing to set up a telephone hotline so that people can inform on those breaking the country's new smoking law (West 2004); to plane-spotters at Fairford military base (from where B52 bombers took off to bomb Iraq in 2003) being provided with relevant phone numbers for the reporting of 'anything of a security nature' during the war on Iraq (T. Lee 2003).

8 This suggests that there indeed is *qualitative pattern* to experiences and ways of accommodating (and perpetrating) patterns of trauma and violence. This is not the same as saying that every person experiences events and processes in exactly/absolutely/quantitatively the same way. Further, perpetrators as well as victims are created by brutalising contexts and discourses. A well-known social psychology prison experiment illustrates, for example, that a social situation sanctioning a discourse of dehumanisation (in this case of prisoners) is all that is required to shift the behaviour of 'ordinary people' into that of vindictive perpetrators of physical and psychological violence, even where they have no apparent previous history of such behaviours (Zimbardo 2004: 21–50).

9 Denial also might be seen in the detachment of spiritually oriented positions that fetishise retreat and withdrawal into interior reflective and perhaps personally transformative spaces as the primary means to engage with exterior transformation. As argued in Willful Disobedience (n.d.; also Mindell 1995), these make the problematic and incoherent assumption that by addressing first-order alienations (between subject and object, nature and culture), the violations effected by second-order alienations (e.g. private property, the division of labour, and alienated power) will be simply transcended or slip away. My personal stance is that becoming conversant with ordinary spiritual/mystical experiences of 'ekstasy' is a seriously subversive political practice that extends ontological consciousness, claims mind–body–spirit spaces not sanctioned by modernity's fetishising of rational consciousness, and which can become tools in extending experiences of the possible in searching for and constituting 'the' post-capitalist and post-representational human (Sullivan 2001; 2004d). But, if asserting agency requires articulation between interior and exterior spaces, then such flight from the organised particulate body will itself not be enough to effect socio-political change. Assuming a 'spiritual rank' (Mindell 1995: 62–3) or high ground that delegitimises the potential for transformative action through engagement with contexts, thereby becomes as helpful as its mirror attitude – that of denying the role/s of individual and collective spirituality in aiding an envisioning and engendering of societal alternatives open to multiplicitous human experience.

10 While not a new 'disease', depression or 'melancholy' as a category of 'illness' *has* increased dramatically in post-industrial society. In the early 1990s the results of a long-term, international and multigenerational study indicated that people born after 1955 were '*three times* as likely as their grandparents' generation to suffer from depression'. Similar findings emerged for countries as disparate as Italy, Germany, Taiwan, Lebanon, Canada, France, Puerto Rico and New Zealand, suggesting that this trend is global in reach (figures reported in Wurtzel

1999 [1994]: 298–9, emphasis in original). Also indicative of this trend are the rocketing numbers of prescriptions made for anti-depressant drugs in recent years, causing some commentators to describe this as a 'legal drug culture' (New York Times 1992, quoted in Wurtzel 1999 [1994]; 298; also Boseley 2003; Laurence 2003). Figures for suicides articulated as responses to the marginalising effects of neoliberal policy also are rocketing worldwide (e.g. Sharma 2003: 2). This phenomenon was brought into sharp relief by the public suicide of Lee Kyung Hae, leader of the Korean Federation of Advanced Farmers Association, at the Fifth Ministerial meeting of the World Trade Organization in September 2003 (Carlson 2003).

11 Given the perennial conflict between socialist hierarchical and anarchist positions towards socio-political change – or between the 'verticals' and 'horizontals' as these orientations are coming to be known in the current UK context – it is pertinent to note that this accusation of infantilism was precisely what Lenin (1993 [1920]) used to discredit an emerging anarcho-syndicalism in the early part of the last century. He, of course, favoured Bolshevik discipline, organised revolutionary force and administrative centralisation. Nietzsche too dismissed the militant practice associated with nineteenth-century anarchism as a reactive politics of *ressentiment* – as 'the spiteful politics of the weak and pitiful, the morality of the slave' and the 'vengeful *will to power* of the powerless over the powerful' (Newman 2000: 1–2, emphasis in original).

12 It certainly is not unknown for such contextual relocations of violence from the everyday to the political to occur. As a Salvadoran guerrilla fighter expressed to Bourgois (1982: 24–5), for example,

> [w]e used to be *machista*. We used to put away a lotta drink and cut each other up. But then the Organization [the FMLN – Farabundo Martí Liberation Front] showed us the way, and we've channeled that violence for the benefit of the people.

13 This is the difference between accepting that the legal system provides an appropriate space for the justification of one's actions, versus carrying out actions while masked and with every intention of avoiding arrest and trial by a justice system perceived to be supporting the structures being contested.

14 Italian Marxist Antonio Negri in the 1980s, for example, writes that

> [p]roletarian violence, in so far as it is a positive allusion to communism, is an essential element of the dynamic of communism. To suppress the violence of this process can only deliver it – tied hand and foot – to capital. Violence is a first, immediate, and vigorous affirmation of the necessity of communism. It does not provide the solution, but is fundamental.
>
> (1984: 173 in Callinicos 2001: 4)

15 This is *not* the same as saying that discourses and practices of bio-political violence are somehow an exclusively male domain. Indeed, numerous references regarding different times and spaces indicate that this is not the case (e.g. Klausmann *et al.* 1997; Ruins 2003; LeBrun n.d.).

11 Seattle and the struggle for a global democratic ethos

Roland Bleiker[1]

Introduction

'It was just like May 1968', said José Bové, sheep-farmer and French anti-globalisation hero, about the events in Seattle of December 1999 (Bové cited in Schoch 2000: 5). Four days of massive street protests against the World Trade Organization (WTO) turned the city into a battle ground – literally and metaphorically. Bové joined some 700 non-governmental organisations (NGOs) and an estimated 40,000 demonstrators, including steelworkers, environmentalists, AIDS activists, farmers, anti-capitalists, anarchists, students and concerned local citizens. What began as a peaceful protest march ended in a violent confrontation with the Seattle police. The authorities called in the National Guard and declared a state of emergency. Global television networks were delivering hourly updates on the situation, turning the protests into a major media event.

For some, the 'Battle for Seattle' was a 'turning point' (Levi and Olson 2000: 325), an event that symbolised the world's discontent with the spread of globalisation, with policies that promoted free trade and corporate greed over the interests of average people and the environment. Others stress that Seattle 'was the first time that the political presence of a range of new actors was taken seriously' (Kaldor 2000: 106; for other commentary on Seattle see e.g. Shiva 1999; Woodley 2000; Bello 2000; St Clair 2002; Halliday 2000a; Scholte 2000a; Gill 2000). Similar interventions and protests, some non-violent, others less so, followed in the subsequent months: thousands of demonstrators interfered with gatherings of the World Economic Forum in Melbourne and Davos, or with meetings of the International Monetary Fund (IMF) and the World Bank in Washington and Prague. Indeed, major popular protests against international political and economic institutions soon became a common feature of key political meetings, from Quebec summit discussions on the Free Trade Agreement of the Americas (April 2001) to the European Union gathering in Gothenburg (June 2001) and the G8 summit in Genoa (July 2001). Perhaps the biggest simultaneous demonstrations took place on 15 February 2003, when millions of people took to the streets in cities worldwide to demonstrate against the then looming war in Iraq.

This global wave of popular dissent expresses more than mere discontent with the effects of globalisation. The fact that countless people around the globe see street protests as the only means to voice their opinions symbolises a much more systemic and alarming crisis of legitimacy, one that has to do with the lack of democratic accountability of the major state and multilateral institutions that shape global politics. In some sense the events of Seattle highlight what Joan Bondurant (1967: x) already identified decades ago as a key weakness of liberal thought: that is, 'the failure to provide techniques of action for those critical occasions when the machinery of democratic government no longer functions to resolve large-scale, overt conflict'.

The purpose of this chapter is to re-examine anti-globalisation protests through a broadly conceived critical theoretical framework. I am focusing in particular on street protests, rather than the broader anti-globalisation movement. The latter includes a range of other engagements, such as lobbying, media work or the promotion of alternative political fora and communities. But street protests are perhaps the most symbolic, and certainly the most visible aspects of the anti-globalisation movement. They also symbolise one of the quintessential features of a postmodern politics: spontaneous, local and transnational resistance against the imposition of a universalised grand narrative (White 1991: 10–12). But for many the respective dissident activities are highly problematic because they may jeopardise political order and stability. Not so argues this chapter.

Anti-globalisation protests can be seen as a crucial element in the establishment of a global democratic ethos. To sustain this argument, the chapter draws upon the work of several innovative international political theorists who have sought to demonstrate that an ethical approach to politics must be based not on a fixed set of rules, but on a fundamentally open attitude. David Campbell, for instance, speaks of an 'affirmative antitotalitarian manner' and a corresponding 'undedicable and infinite character of justice' (Campbell 1999: 50–1). Michael Shapiro, likewise, stresses the need to conceptualise ethics in a way that does not correspond to an 'institutionalised normativety and foundational conceptuality' (Shapiro 1999: 77). William Connolly is perhaps the theorist who most extensively discusses how such open attitudes can contribute to the establishment of a post-national form of democracy. He advocates an 'ethos of critical engagement': a form of politics that can never be reduced to pre-existing norms and moral codes (Connolly 1995: 129). To draw upon theorists such as Connolly, Shapiro and Campbell is to make a conscious shift from politics to ethics – a shift that entails acknowledging and exploring the normative and inherently contested and contestable dimensions of global politics. Perhaps the word 'ethos' is more appropriate than ethics, for it captures the need to promote a political orientation that is 'vivified more by a spirit or sensibility than by any set of rules of conduct' (White 2000: 116). Seen from such a perspective, an ethical approach to global politics should be based not only on specific laws and institutions, but also on an ongoing questioning process that calls these established constellations to account. Without such challenges, existing political norms and practices simply serve to legitimise specific interests and power relations. Connolly goes so far as to suggest that there are moments when 'it takes a militant, experimental, and persistent political movement to open up a line of flight from culturally induced suffering' (2002: 129). The task of this chapter is to scrutinise the extent to which anti-globalisation protests can play a positive role in such an effort to locate lines of flight towards a more democratic and accountable form of global politics.

Globalisation, speed and the crisis of legitimacy

Before probing the links between protest and a democratic ethos a brief enquiry into the nature of globalisation is necessary. Given the existence of a vast literature on the subject (e.g. Held *et al.* 1999; Kiely 2000; Mittelman 1996; Pieterse 2000; Scholte 2000b), such an endeavour can only illuminate a few select aspects. A more limited reading is thus in order – one that draws attention to the crisis of legitimacy that has given rise to anti-globalisation protests. Of particular relevance here is the increasingly porous nature of state sovereignty. Paul Virilio (1977: 131) noted a quarter of a century ago that the contraction of distances had become a strategic reality. He is one of several innovative thinkers who have illuminated this phenomenon. We are, he says, witnessing a revolution in global relations, comparable to the funda-mental impact of changing mass transportation in the nineteenth century and means of telecommunication in the twentieth. We are undergoing a sea change in social dynamics. This change, Virilio argues, revolves around the emergence and regulation of speed.

Speed signifies the relationship between various phenomena, notably space and time. Space has become annihilated, Virilio claims, and time has taken over as the criterion around which global dynamics revolve. The instantaneous character of communication and mass media has annihilated duration and locality. The 'now' of the emission is privileged to the detri-ment of the 'here', the space where things take place. What matter is no longer the three spatial dimensions of height, depth and width, but above all a fourth one, time (Virilio 1995: 21–34). Virilio argues that the globe is no longer primarily divided spatially into North and South, but rather tempo-rally into different forms of speed. The 'haves' are those who live in the hyper-real shrunken world of instant communication, cyberdynamics and electronic money transactions; the 'have-nots', more disadvantaged than ever, live in the real space of local villages, cut off from the temporal forces that drive politics and economics (Marongiu 1995: xi). Expressed in other words, inequality increasingly defies the state-based spatial dimensions of political life. On the one hand, one can frolic in the virtual world of speed and enjoy its privileges from virtually anywhere on the planet. A person with access to a computer, modem and phone line in, say, rural Lesotho or Tibet can be as much a part of global dynamics as a corporate executive in New York's World Trade Center. On the other hand, one can be situated in the middle of the world's metropolitan cores, say, in Los Angeles, Paris or Tokyo, and miss out entirely on the revolution of speed.

It is not surprising, then, that voices of concern have become more vocal. We hear of a nation state that is no longer able to uphold its sovereignty and the spheres of justice and civility that the corresponding boundaries were supposed to protect. We witness a decline in state responsibility for social affairs, which has been either relegated to the non-governmental sector or simply left to market dynamics. But the latter, of course, operate along principles other than those necessary for the establishment of social justice. Decades after decolonisation was introduced in most parts of the world, the gap between rich and poor has widened substantially. A report by the United Nations Development Programme, for instance, informs us that the assets of the world's three richest people amount to more than the combined GNP of all least developed countries on the planet (UNDP 1999). Disempowerment and disentitlement have become key features of globalisation. We hear of a neoliberal world order that is increasingly run by a few powerful multilateral institutions and multinational corporations – big, unaccountable structures, whose strategic leitmotifs and decision-making processes reflect the imperatives of short-term material objectives rather than principles such as the protection of people and the survival of an increasingly stretched global ecosystem.

The existence and exact significance of these and many other aspects of globalisation can be debated at length. There are other accounts of globalisation, of course, which view economic and social processes from more positive and altogether different angles. Far less disputable is the fact that the phenomena described above are among a range of issues, diverse and subjectively perceived as they may be, that worry a great number of people around the globe. Consider the participants in the Seattle protests: they arrived from many parts of the world and represented a multitude of different interests, from labour to the environment. Their voices ranged from radical anarchists who sought to abolish the WTO to more moderate reformers who argued for a world economic system that is fairer and more democratic.

The main common target of the diversely motivated protest actions in Seattle, Prague and other cities is the three key institutions of the liberal world economy: the World Bank, the IMF and the WTO. Some protesters lament the lack of democratic accountability that characterises these influential organisations. Kelly Quirk, head of the Rainforest Action Network, worries that 'the WTO has the right to completely rescind any law passed by the citizenry to protect the environment, health and labour rights' (cited in Rowell 1999). Other critics focus more generally on the neoliberal agenda that is promoted by all the key economic institutions. They stress that the ensuing global free trade regime is sacrificing the poor and the environment in favour of the short-term dictates of profit-seeking capital. Vandana Shiva, for instance, is convinced that the WTO is enforcing 'anti-people, anti-nature decisions to enable corporations to steal the world's harvests through secretive, undemocratic structures and processes' (1999: 2). Many agree, even the less radical critics, pointing towards a variety of WTO decisions that have favoured commercial interests over, for instance, the protection of dolphins and turtles. Or they emphasise that the so-called non-tariff trade barriers, which the WTO seeks to eliminate, are actually 'hard-won environmental and food safety protections' (Knapp 1999). Others draw attention to the many gendered effects of IMF interventions in the developing world. Women often bear the brunt of, for example, reduced expenditures on social services, which are a common element of the privatisation and fiscal austerity policies that accompany structural adjustment programmes (O'Brien *et al.* 2000: 35–41). Others again stress that structural adjustment programmes not only leave few policy options for nation states, but also fail to address the root of the problem – seen as the enduring crisis of productivity of capital in industrialised countries (Ygarteche 2000; for a more general overview of the various grievances expressed by global activists, see Starr 2000).

It is not the purpose of this chapter to discuss and evaluate these and many other criticisms that have been directed against the WTO, the IMF and the World Bank. Rather, the point is simply to draw attention to an increasing crisis of legitimacy – one that relates not just to economic policy, but to the domain of national and global politics in general.

The effects of speed, and processes of globalisation in general, have made the challenge of representation even more problematic and political than it already is. In a world dominated by temporal rather than spatial dynamics, the prevailing democratic institutions of the nation state are no longer able to provide spaces for political participation and legitimisation. And many of the institutions that shape global relations, from international organisations to multinational companies, are neither transparent nor accountable to a democratic constituency. To draw attention to this problematic feature of globalisation is not to deny that states continue to play a key role in domestic and global politics (Bernauer 2000). But nation states are no longer the only player in a world where financial, productive, cultural and informational dynamics have come to disobey, transgress and challenge the deeply entrenched principle of sovereignty. Moreover, globalisation is gradually eroding not only the privileged position of the state but also, and perhaps more importantly, the discourses that have come to justify this privileged standpoint. Jürgen Habermas (1998: 120), when analysing the role of global markets, refers to a legitimacy crisis of the nation state.

One could go a step further and draw attention to a more fundamental political crisis related to the advent of speed: while politics has become increasingly globalised, the corresponding ethical discourses are still very much intertwined with old state-centric attitudes. Didier Bigo and Elspeth

Guild, for instance, look at how the widespread and often violent suppression of anti-globalisation protests is an expression of a deeper-seated tension – an asymmetrical power relationship so to speak – between the forces of transnational governance and the possibilities for holding these increasingly problematic practices of domination to account:

> while we witness, at an unprecedented speed, the transnationalisation of governance at a global level, everything is undertaken to prevent the emergence of a transnational realm of contestation that could create a public space of the same dimension as that of governance.
>
> (Bigo and Guild 2002)

The very existence of this political tension is at the origin of Connolly's attempt to theorise the possibilities of applying democracy to a post-national realm. The challenge then consists of extending democratic accountability to the struggle over the direction of global politics and the various political, social and economic dynamics associated with it. Such a move is, of course, far from unproblematic. Democracy, as we know it, is closely intertwined with the institutions and territorial boundaries of the nation state. How to extend its application into the transnational realm is far from clear, although the desirability of such a move is underlined by the growing literature on cosmopolitan democracy (Falk 1995; Habermas 1998; Held 1995; 2002). Connolly stresses that virtually all aspects of life today transgress the boundaries of sovereign states, from the flow of capital and labour to criminal organisations and media networks. 'Only democratic citizens', he stresses, 'remain locked behind the bars of the state' (Connolly 1995: 157). He also admits that 'it is probably impossible even to imagine a form of democratic politics today that breaks entirely with [the model of territorial imaginary]' (1995: 136). But Connolly has hope too, and his hope is located in viewing democracy not merely in institutional terms, but also, and perhaps even primarily, as a cultural disposition, as a certain ethos. Anti-globalisation protests can be seen as constituting an important element in the conception and implementation of this ethos.

Dissident agency in the world of globalisation

In order to understand and theorise the links between transnational protests and a post-national democratic ethos it is necessary to view globalisation in more nuanced ways than usual. Contrary to the positions advocated by or implied in the Seattle protests, globalisation does not necessarily, or at least not only, lead to a centralisation of power and a corresponding loss of democratic participation and political accountability. While these phenomena are undoubtedly occurring – and pose increasingly difficult ethical and political challenges to the world community – they are not the only aspects of globalisation. A focus on speed allows us to recognise the contradictory forces of globalisation, the manner in which its whirl-winds push and pull politics, from the local to the global, in a variety of directions.

Globalisation has not annihilated possibilities for dissent – quite to the contrary. There are at least two domains in which speed has magnified the possibilities for interfering with the conduct of global politics. This interference is, of course, different from traditional forms of institutionalised democratic participation. It is linked to two more broadly based and interrelated challenges to the foundations of transnational politics.

First, speed provides activists with a range of new tools to organise and co-ordinate their actions. Many of the protesters that went to Seattle, Melbourne and Prague, for instance, were brought together by e-mail correspondences and a variety of websites that organised resistance against neoliberal forms of globalisation. The increased ability to exchange information across large differences has had a tremendous influence on the mobilisation of dissent within civil society. Social movements and NGOs that had hitherto existed in isolation can now easily communicate with each other. They can share data and insights about similar concerns and organise common actions in ways that was not possible before (O'Brien *et al.* 2000: 7). A study on citizen activism against the Multilateral Agreement on Investment (MAI), for instance, suggests that the Internet played a vital role in the relative success of the movement, in so far as it facilitated communication among activists, permitted publication of related information and helped to put pressure on politicians and policy-makers in member states (Deibert 2000). Cyber-based protest organisation has become more extensive and sophisticated as activists have learned from previous experiences. The protests in Quebec City, for instance, gave rise to numerous websites that continue to exchange information and co-ordinate actions.[2] Not surprisingly, this move into cyberspace takes place on both sides of the struggle, with international organisations like the World Bank engaging in online conferences (Riley 2001). Yet some commentators have stressed that these innovations in communications technologies favour groups that are organised as networks. International organisations and government departments, by contrast, tend to be less effective users of these technologies, for they have hierarchical structures that revolve around the control of information flows (Varney and Martin 2000).

Second, and perhaps even more importantly, speed has fundamentally changed the spatial dynamics of dissident practices. Protest actions, such as street demonstrations or acts of civil disobedience, used to take place in a mostly local context. They engaged the spatial dynamics that were operative in the interactive relationship between ruler and ruled. The contraction of space, however, has altered the very foundations of these socio-political dynamics. An act of protest, as it took place in Seattle, now interacts in a much wider and more complex array of political spaces. Images of a protest march may flicker over television screens worldwide only hours after people have taken to the street. As a result, a local act of resistance can acquire almost immediately a much larger, cross-territorial dimension.

Any protest action that draws sufficient media attention has the potential to engender a political process that transcends its immediate spatial environment. It competes for the attention of global television audiences and thus interferes with the struggle over values that ultimately shapes the world we live in. 'A world united by Benetton slogans, Nike sweatshops and McDonald's jobs might not be anyone's utopian global village', says Naomi Klein (2001: 357), 'but its fibre-optic cables and shared cultural references are nonetheless laying the foundations for the first truly international people's movement'. But the recent wave of global protests is hardly the first international movement of its kind. Nor is it as unproblematic as Klein suggests. For some the revolution of speed is too random to allow for critical interference and, indeed, for human agency. Jean Baudrillard, for instance, believes that the distinctions between reality and virtuality, political practice and simulation are blurred to the extent that they are no longer recognisable. Our media culture, he says, has annihilated reality in stages, such that in the end its simulating image 'bears no relation to any reality whatever: it is its own pure simulacrum' (Baudrillard 1983: 11). Television, the unproblematic transmission of the hyper-real, has conditioned our mind such that we have lost the ability to penetrate beneath the manifest levels of surface (Baudrillard 1985: 126–34).

Patterns of global protest do not confirm the pessimistic views that Baudrillard and others espouse. The blurring of reality and virtuality has not annihilated dissent. The fact that televised images are hyper-real does not necessarily diminish their influence. Independently of how instantaneous, distorted and simulated images of a protest action may be, they still influence our perceptions of issues, and thus also our political responses to them. To accept the logic of speed, then, is not to render political influence obsolete, but to acknowledge multiple and overlapping spatial and temporal spheres within which political practices are constantly being shaped and reshaped.

Judged from such a vantage point, the actions in Seattle and other cities are not quite as ineffective as they appear at first sight. Even without engendering immediate institutional transformations, traces of these protest events continue to influence the struggle over global values – and thus over the direction of politics. The repeated presence of protest actions around the world guarantees that a number of key issues, from environmental protection to minimal labour standards, remain discussed in the public sphere. Indeed, even before Seattle, Robert O'Brien and his collaborators concluded that the interaction between social movements and multilateral economic institutions had transformed the nature of global economic relations. The authors label this transformation 'complex multilateralism' in order to recognise that actors other than states now can and do express the public interest and shape key political issues (O'Brien *et al.* 2000: 206). The ensuing dynamics testify to the emergence of a new kind of global politics – one in which key political struggles occur beyond the control of the national state. Consider, for instance, how global networks of communication have enabled indigenous peoples in the United States, Canada, Australia and New Zealand to engage in forms of activism that ensured them an audience beyond their immediate surroundings. For Connolly, this transnational dynamic confirms that speed has multiple dimensions: not only an encroaching and disabling one, but also one that 'supports the possibility of democratic pluralization' (2002: 179).

Anti-globalisation protests represent a particular crucial component of this pluralisation process, for they constantly problematise foundational norms, the 'final markers' that Connolly (1995: 154) sees as obstacles for a transnational democratic ethos. Perhaps one can even see these manifestations of protest as a key instance of the very struggle for and on behalf of alterity that Campbell (1999: 50) identifies as an essential element in an adequate ethical approach to global politics.

Who speaks for whom? The problem of representation

If anti-globalisation protests are indeed part of a democratic struggle to safeguard difference and alterity then a number of difficult ethical questions must be posed and addressed. How can alterity be represented? And by whom? The issue is not obvious, particularly since questions of representations are not discussed widely in the context of anti-globalisation protests. Look at how a participant in the Prague demonstrations formulates the movement's purpose in a particularly broad-based manner: 'To advance citizens' control [over globalisation]' (de Filippis and Losson 2000: 1).

As soon as one looks at the protests in more detail, questions of representation become central. As mentioned at various points in this chapter, the people that participated in the protest actions in Prague and other cities represented a great variety of different and at times conflicting interests and constituencies, from steelworkers to feminists and environmentalists. They range from radical anarchists to moderate reformers. 'There was a cacophony of voices and issues', say Margaret Levi and David Olson (2000: 325) about Seattle. And once these voices were picked up by global television networks, they became intertwined with an infinitely more diverse and random array of voices and images, all flickering and babbling away without much form or direction. Media representations follow their own logic – different from the logic of the events they seek to capture – blending information and entertainment in often highly problematic ways. This is one of the reasons why Virilio believes that 'the paradoxical logic of the video-frame privileges the accident, the surprise, over the durable substance of the message' (1998: 140). It also privileges a specific key target audience: the television viewers of the Western world, those with the spending power to sustain the networks' advertisement rates and corporate profits (Boltanski

1999). It is hardly surprising, then, that not all forms of protest receive the same level of media attention. There is a significant difference between coverage of activism in developed and developing countries.

For decades, sustained popular protests against the key multilateral economic institutions have taken place in many parts of the Third World. Countless IMF-sponsored structural adjustment programmes have triggered sustained protest reactions by the local populace. These protests have increased in recent years. One can find many examples for the year 2000 alone: 20 million Indian workers went on strike to oppose IMF and World Bank policies; some 5,000 students, environmentalists and displaced people overwhelmed police lines protecting an Asian Development Bank meeting in Chiang Mai; small anti-IMF protests in Argentina were dispersed by the police, but precipitated a mass protest of 80,000 people; tens of thousands of Korean workers and students repeatedly took to the streets to protest against IMF-mandated austerity measures. The list could go on, and would also include protests in Bolivia, Ecuador, Paraguay, Mexico, Brazil, Colombia, Costa Rica, Honduras, Haiti, South Africa, Nigeria, Kenya, Malawi and Zambia, to name just a few countries, and only for protest during the year 2000 (see e.g. Woodroffe and Ellis-Jones 2000; Bond 2000).

Widespread and massive though these protests were, they received relatively little coverage in the global print and television media. Most warranted barely a line, or none at all, in the *New York Times, Le Monde* or the *Frankfurter Allgemeine Zeitung* and rarely made the BBC or CNN World News. The Battle for Seattle, by contrast, was located at the heart of the industrialised world, and thus immediately turned into a global media spectacle. A single molotov cocktail in Seattle, Washington or Quebec is worth far more media capital than an entire protest march in Cochabamba, Lagos or Port-au-Prince. Conversely, 20 million Indian workers on strike or 80,000 Argentineans descending into the streets generate far less global attention than two-dozen protesters in Davos, Melbourne or Gothenburg. Southern social movements clearly operate not only in a different local environment, but also according to very different rules of power (see Wignaraja 1993). But what does this say about the dynamic of protest? About the struggle for voice and representation?

One of the main criticisms against the protests in Prague and Seattle was that the protesters were predominantly from the West and thus represented a very particular, often white and middle-class perspective. Here too, one could go on debating the provenance and motivations of the protestors. They certainly were not all rich and not all Westerners. But in most protest actions, the Third World was clearly underrepresented. Significant political implications result. Some go as far as arguing that the new wave of global activism runs the risk of reproducing the very same neoliberal practices of exclusion it so strongly opposes (Scholte 2000a: 119). It is questionable, for instance, to what extent the calls for higher labour and environmental standards, which was a central demand of most protest actions, is actually shared in the Third World. Many developing countries face the challenge to promote basic economic growth and may not be able to afford the same environmental standards that are now established in the developed world. Indeed, some representatives of the Third World in Seattle argued that the US government was able to use the protest as a convenient pretext to break off discussions on trade issues, for a successful WTO negotiation round could have brought certain benefits to the developing world and undermined the traditional support base of the Democratic Party (Kaldor 2000: 112).

Such quarrels over the meaning and direction of protest actions illustrate how the struggle over legitimate representation is one of the most pivotal political challenges faced by anti-globalisation activists. Greater sensitivity to processes of inclusion and exclusion is essential for the establishment of a transnational culture of democracy. But even in an ideal scenario, some problems of representation cannot be solved. Even the most carefully planned and sensitively executed protest action will be based on a structure of exclusion: it will privilege some voices and perspectives over others. But anti-globalisation protests, incomplete as their own representational politics inevitably are, can still make an important contribution to promoting the level of accountability and political transparency necessary for such a global democratic ethos. The key here lies in viewing representation not as a formal and institutionalised mechanism, but as a far more disorderly and ongoing process. Indeed, the very lack of central control over its agenda makes anti-globalisation protests a key instance of a political force that fosters, in Connolly's terms, 'a recurrent problematization of final markers' (1995: 154). Of course, the activists in Seattle can only speak for themselves, and they inevitably do so in incomplete and distorted ways. But this does not mean that they cannot engage political problems and challenge, say, issues related to economic policy or North–South relations. In fact, the process of convincing others across political, cultural and linguistic divides is the very subject of politics. By questioning political, social and economic privileges, and by disturbing the stable foundations upon which these privileges rest, protest actions may contribute to a democratisation of global politics, even if they cannot always perfectly represent all people affected by unequal globalisation processes.

The importance of form: violent versus non-violent protests

Form is as important as content in the promotion of a post-national democratic ethos. Indeed, the centrality that the form of protest plays is underlined by the events in Seattle, Washington, Prague, Melbourne, Quebec, Gothenburg, Davos and Genoa. Without doing injustice to the uniqueness and complexities of each event, it is fair to say that most of them proceeded in a comparable way: the overwhelming majority of protesters engaged in a variety of peaceful and non-violent forms of protest, while a small minority committed acts of violence.[3] At times, as in Seattle, molotov cocktails and battles with riot police led to looting and the destruction of property. Media attention often focused on such isolated violent incidents, leading to a relatively uneven representation of the overall protests. As a result, a few violent episodes largely overshadowed both the substance of the protests and the presence of an overwhelmingly non-violent majority of dissidents.

The inclusion of violence in anti-globalisation protests poses a number of key questions for both collective agency and the promotion of a global democratic ethos in general. What is the exact nature and impact of violence? To what extent can violence be justified as an act of dissent? Is violence an effective way of promoting social change? How can peaceful activists who engage in non-violent protests or civil disobedience co-exist with those who advocate violence as a revolutionary strategy? Do they belong to the same protest actions? Do their different engagements reinforce or hinder each other?

To engage with these difficult questions it is necessary to enter terrains that are both analytical and normative. Consider one of the organisers of the Prague protests, a young Czech chemistry student. In principle she is against the use of violence, but believes that 'at times it is nevertheless legitimate'. When talking about the actions in Prague, she insist on drawing a distinction between different forms of violence: 'Violence committed by demonstrators against objects; violence committed by the police against demonstrators, and, worst of all, violence committed by institutions like the IMF and the World Bank that rob millions of people of their livelihood' (Alice Dvorska, cited in Stehli 2000). She is not alone in drawing such a distinction. 'They are worried about a few windows being smashed', said a Philippino participant in the Seattle protests. 'They should come and see the violence being done to our communities in the name of liberalisation of trade' (Vidal 1999: 3).

The debate between violent and non-violent forms of protest is, of course, not new. Frantz Fanon (1985) famously argued that violence is inevitable if existing structures of power – as those of colonialism – are being challenged and overthrown (see also Sorel 1972 [1908]). It is an integral part of social change. Others disagree. They advocate non-violent forms of dissent, basing their positions on a long tradition of thought and activism that stretches back to the words and deeds of Henry David Thoreau (1966 [1848]), Leo Tolstoy (1967), Mohandas Gandhi (1958; 1984[1938]), Clarence Marsh Case (1923) and Martin Luther King (1986 [1958]), to name just a few key figures. They consciously employ non-violent forms of protest when the official channels for political action, such as elections, referenda, petitions or lobbying, do not exist or are considered inadequate for the resolution of the conflict in question. Non-violent action thus seeks to empower those who do not have access to conventional forms of political influence. While such actions usually occur only in desperate circumstances, they are not necessarily a manifestation of powerlessness, as Jonathan Freedland (1999) suggested with respect to the events in Seattle.

Non-violent dissent can also be seen as an effective resistance strategy in itself. Indeed, the choice of non-violent over violent protest should be considered not only a moral, but also a strategic decision. Richard Gregg, in a classic study on the subject, suggests that non-violence works by way of producing a change of mental attitude in the mind of those against whom the action is directed. Non-violent action thus works not unlike military strategies, for it seeks 'to demoralise the opponent, to break his will, to destroy his confidence, enthusiasm and hope' (Gregg 1934: 89; see also Sharp 1973). But instead of using violence to counter violence, which would only drain the resisters' energy and reassure the attacker about the adequacy of the chosen method of repression, non-violence is considered to be a more effective form of political intervention. More recent studies have found mixed evidence about the ability of non-violent action to change the position of its opponents. Instead, they stress that non-violence can engender social change by influencing third parties (Weber 1993).

This is where the debate over the politics of protest actions becomes explicitly strategic and tactical. The issues at stake are well illustrated by how activists differ about the point at which an action does and perhaps should become violent. Some non-violent activists reserve the right to employ violent means for reasons of self-defence. They argue that they have a moral right to self-protection, perhaps even to physical responses, if attacked by the police.[4] Others disagree. They advocate a more principled adherence to non-violence, and this for ethical and, above all, for strategic and tactical reasons. The classical example here is Gandhi, who urged his fellow activists to adhere to strict principles of non-violence. He called off a protest march as soon as the slightest acts of violence were committed by activists. For him this was necessary because the power of non-violence is located in its manipulative potential, in its ability to convert the opponent or third parties. Non-violence, then, is seen as a psychological weapon, an intervention that causes emotional and moral perturbations, which in turn trigger processes of social change. It seeks a conversation with the consciousness of the opponent and the public at large. Violent acts of protest generally fail to reach this objective, Gandhi argued. Principled non-violence, by contrast, can be an exceptionally effective means. Recall the moment when Gandhian activists were beaten by the police without attempting any form of retaliation. It remains one of the most striking and powerful images of the resistance movement against Britain's colonial occupation of India. Striking because these images capture an ethical and political commitment that can hardly be matched. Powerful because they manage to initiate forces of transformation that violent acts never can: they evoke pity which, in turn, can either convert the opponent or generate public pressure that can lead to a process of accommodation (for discussions on this issue, see Gandhi 1958; 1984 [1938]; Bondurant 1967; Brown 1977; Iyer 1973). Amartya Sen (2001: 7, 11) advances a similar position by arguing that anti-globalisation protest would be far more effective if it were to employ not violence, but humour as a strategy of dissent and transformation.[5]

Speed has greatly increased the importance of the relationship between violent and non-violent means of protest. In an age of global media networks, the target of a protest action is, as mentioned, of a temporal, rather than spatial nature. The protesters in Seattle did not aim their actions on the actual participants of the WTO meeting – or at least not only, and not directly. The target audience were global television viewers, the public at large, the direction of global consciousness. Shifts in this last may, in turn, put pressure on national governments and thus alter the negotiation dynamics at meetings like those in Seattle. Virilio would say that 'the strategic value of the non-place of speed has definitively supplanted that of place' (1998: 46). And he would add that the key lies in the image projected by a protest action, rather than its actual physical presence in, say, the streets of Seattle (Virilio 1998: 5). Speed also increases the scholarly need to understand the global interaction of domination and resistance not only in causal and analytical terms, but also as part of a normative challenge. This is why debates about the respective merits of violence and non-violence should be seen as part of a larger engagement with the ethical dimensions of global politics.

The verdict of Seattle on the relationship between violence, non-violence and speed is mixed. On the one hand, violence attracts far more media attention than non-violence does. In a world where entertainment and information are intrinsically linked, a molotov cocktail or a street fight between protesters and police offers far more spectacular and attractive 'news' material than does a peaceful protest march. On the other hand, this media attention is gained at a certain price. Recall that the main purpose of the protest, and of the ensuing media spectacle, was to draw attention to the underside of globalisation and to win the hearts and minds of global television audiences. This is where the dissident event could leave its most enduring impact on the policy debates that surround globalisation. The fact that the events in Seattle turned violent, however, gave critics an easy target: the protesters could now be dismissed as disgruntled youths or demonised as dangerous anarchist radicals who are not in tune with the needs and wishes of the general populace (Viner 2000: 23). This is why some commentators were able to speak dismissively of a 'counter-culture carnival' (Bishop 1999), of the 'globetrotting anti-globalisation mob' (Johnson 2000), of 'hippies and yippies' with their 'bedraggled beards and their mobile phones hooked up to the internet' (Johnson 1999). It is also unlikely that violence leading to the destruction of property can win over the sympathy of the public, especially in the United States where, as one commentator puts it, 'private property is God' (Rowell 1999: 3). These issues are central not only to the political foundations of global activism, but also to its tactical and strategic efficiency. Little does it matter, at least from a strategic perspective, that the police forces often played a key role in precipitating violent encounters. Consider a series of rather shocking public inquires into the violence that plagued the G8 meeting in Genoa in 2001. According to extensive interviews and research conducted by the state prosecutor's office, the police often used violence without any form of provocation. Falsification of evidence was as widespread as generic policy brutality against protestors who behaved in a strictly non-violent manner (Schlamp 2002: 76–8; see also Bayon and Masse 2002).

The fact that many instances of dissident violence are provoked by police actions does not make violence a less problematic element in the promotion of social change and transnational democracy. Indeed, the terrorist attacks of 11 September 2001 have further highlighted the crucial relationship between violence and dissent. Consider the World Economic Forum of February 2002, which was held in New York rather than Davos. The significant presence of protesters both in New York and at the alternative World Social Forum in Porto Alegre revealed that opposition to free-market-oriented globalisation remains strong. But the strategic dimensions of dissent have changed fundamentally. It would have been a major public relations disaster for protesters to embark on a violent street fight with members of the New York police, who are considered among the heroes of 9–11. Many protest groups that stress strict adherence to non-violence thus stayed away from New York. And those that went to Porto Alegre faced the challenge of articulating some sort of common manifesto, one that seeks to articulate, as one commentator puts it, 'a methodology of protest that distinguishes them from terrorists, bloody revolutionaries and bomb-throwing malcontents' (Harding 2002: 7).

Conclusion

This chapter has sought to demonstrate why and how anti-globalisation protests can be seen as representing a crucial element in the promotion of a global democratic ethos. To appreciate the ensuing potential it is necessary to recognise that globalisation does not necessarily, or at least not only, lead to a centralisation of power and a corresponding loss of democratic participation and political accountability. Taking the anti-WTO protest actions in Seattle as a case in point, the chapter has argued that globalisation has also increased the potential to engage in acts of dissent that can subvert the very processes of control and homogenisation. In doing so, the chapter counters images of a hyper-real world, of an increasingly shallow and media-dominated globe in which nothing can penetrate beneath the surface. Political dissent, according to this doomsday scenario, becomes all but impossible, for there is nothing left to dissent from. For twenty-four hours a day there is only a blur of information and entertainment. We are caught in a world that resembles J. G. Ballard's Eden-Olympia: a financially thriving but highly unequal high-tech information society, seemingly run by a few successful elites, but in reality spinning out of control and spiralling into an ever deeper moral void, fed by the very need for progress and economic expansion (Ballard 2000).

While engendering a series of problematic processes, globalisation has also increased the possibility to engage in dissent. Before the advent of speed, for instance, a protest event was a mostly local issue. But the presence of global media networks has fundamentally changed the dynamics and terrains of dissent. Political activism no longer takes place solely in the streets of Prague, Seoul or Asunción. The Battle for Seattle, for instance, was above all a media spectacle, a battle for the hearts and minds of global television audiences. Political activism, wherever it occurs and whatever form it takes, has become intrinsically linked with the non-spatial logic of speed. It has turned into a significant transnational phenomenon.

With the exploration of new terrains of dissent, global activists also face a series of political dilemmas. This chapter has addressed two of them: the tension between violent and non-violent means of resistance, and the issue of unequal representation, the question of who can speak for whom. Rather than suggesting that these issues can be understood and solved by applying a pre-existing body of universal norms and principles, the chapter has drawn attention to the open-ended and contingent nature of the puzzles in question. Protest actions against the key multilateral institutions of the world economy will continue, and so will debates about the nature and direction of globalisation. Keeping these debates alive, and seeking to include as many voices, perspectives and constituencies as possible, is a first step towards something that may one day resemble globalisation with a human face. But making global politics more humane, more transparent and more democratic is no easy task. Principles of transparency and democracy have historically been confined to the territorial boundaries of the sovereign nation state.

An extension of democratic principles into the more ambiguous international realm is as essential as it is difficult. Such a move requires extending understandings of democracy, contested and contestable as they are, beyond models and institutions into a procedural realm – a move that is well accepted, or at least intensely discussed, among political theorists (Dryzek 2000). Connolly points in the right direction when arguing for a democratic ethos. The key to such cultural democratisation, he believes, 'is that it embodies a productive ambiguity at its very centre, always resisting attempts to allow one side or the other to achieve final victory' (Connolly 1995: 154–5). Some aspects of democratic participation can never be institutionalised. Any political system, no matter how just and refined, rests on a structure of exclusion. It has to separate right from wrong, good from evil, moral from immoral. This separation is both inevitable and desirable. But to remain legitimate the respective political foundations need to be submitted to periodic scrutiny. They require constant readjustments in order to remain adequate and fair.

Anti-globalisation protests, problematic as they may be at times, can make a key contribution to this struggle for fairness and transparency.

Indeed, the significance of these dissident engagements is located precisely in the fact that they cannot be controlled by a central regulatory force or an institutional framework. By constantly challenging institutionalised relations of power, protest actions engender the very idea of productive ambiguity that may well be essential for the long-term survival of democracy.

Notes

1 This chapter started off as an attempt to expand on my 2002 article 'Activism after Seattle: Dilemmas of the Anti-Globalisation Movement', *Pacifica Review: Peace, Security and Global Change* (Australia) 14 (3): 191–207. In the end, though, little remains of the original piece, for Catherine Eschle and Bice Maiguashca's intellectual engagement and editorial probing pushed me in directions I would otherwise have left unexplored. Particular thanks to them and to others who commented on previous drafts, most notably Didier Bigo, Jean-Louis Durand, Bronwyn Evans-Kent, Tony Lang, Brian Martin, Karl-Erik Paasonen as well as audiences at the Institute d'Études Politiques in Paris and the Institute of Social Studies in The Hague.
2 See, for instance, the 'Stop the FTAA Web-site' (http://www.stopftaa.org/), the site of the 'Centre for Media Alternatives of Quebec' (http://www.quebec.indy-media.org) or the Z-Net site on Quebec (http://www.zmag.org/a20quebec.htm).
3 Speaking of Prague, one commentator (Viner 2000: 7) notes that even the wildest interpretations estimated the number of violent activists at no more than 1–2 per cent of the 15,000 protesters.
4 For this interpretation, I have relied on the insight of Karl-Erik Paasonen, who has conducted extensive interviews with protesters debating the issue of violence and non-violence while planning the protest against the Commonwealth Heads of Government Meeting in Brisbane in 2002.
5 The classical example of humour as an effective strategy of dissent and social change remains Rabelais' sixteenth-century text (1966). For an analysis of its social and political impact see Bakhtin (1968).

Conclusion

Catherine Eschle and Bice Maiguascha

This book has brought together critical theorising in IR and 'the anti-globalisation movement'. Our aims have been, first, to provide empirical mappings of the movement and, second, to interrogate these mappings in the light of a number of different critical theories. We have sought to explore what these different perspectives offer to our understandings and analysis of this movement and, conversely, what the study of this movement has to tell us about critical theorising. The chapters have ranged widely in their discussions. This Conclusion aims to compare and contrast the insights offered by the chapters, to analyse the ways in which their theoretical and empirical accounts speak to each other and where they conflict. In what follows, we organise our discussion in terms of the three parts of the book. Each part has dealt with a different set of interlinked themes: power/resistance/movement; discourse/identity/culture; and politics/strategy/violence. We strive to show how the chapters in each part address the themes of that part and to draw out the specific contributions of their perspectives and case studies. Further, we seek to identify questions that still need to be answered and thus to sketch out a research agenda for future critical theorising on 'the anti-globalisation movement'.

Power/resistance/movement

We begin by exploring what our chapters in the first part of the book have to say about the notion of 'the anti-globalisation movement' before discussing them in terms of resistance and then power.

In Chapter 1, Eschle strongly defends the notion that a movement, as such, does exist. She is clear that a form of collective agency is being generated, notwithstanding the fact that she is wary of labelling the movement an actor per se (which may bring with it assumptions about pre-formed interests and a single will), and that she is keen to acknowledge the vast spectrum of resistances it encompasses. For her, a movement is by definition a heterogeneous social force that is diverse in form and ideological orientation. What holds it together is the process of collectively constructing an identity through which participants establish relationships with each other and differentiate themselves from others. Following on from this, Eschle argues that the 'objective' existence of this movement is contingent in large part upon the self-identification of activists with the movement. In Chapter 2, Rupert shares Eschle's conviction that diverse resistances can and should be characterised as a social movement, one he chooses to label 'the global justice movement'. He also points to the subjective dimension involved in the constitution of this movement by conceptualising it as an 'imagined community'.

A rather different picture is painted in Chapter 3 by Gruffydd Jones, who is certainly open to the possibility and desirability of an 'anti-globalisation movement' but is much more sceptical about its current existence on a transnational scale. For her, the movement form is premised on the emergence of a collective political consciousness that can give rise to co-ordinated practices aimed at social transformation. Her study indicates that, judged in these terms, 'the anti-globalisation movement' simply does not exist in Mozambique. For Gruffydd Jones, any proclamations about the nature and significance of 'the anti-globalisation movement' must be tempered by an objective appraisal of the conditions of possibility for the emergence of such a movement.

All three authors look in very different places to find their evidence for the existence of the movement. Rupert's focus is on anti-neoliberal and anti-war activism within 'the belly of the beast', that is to say within the hegemonic US state. Eschle draws instead upon activist discourses generated by transnational networks and posted on the Internet. These are both locations and actors widely associated with 'the anti-globalisation movement'. Gruffydd Jones again performs an important service here by shifting our gaze to a less familiar terrain for critical theorising on the movement, taking us to Mozambique and to the struggles of everyday life. A similar move is made by some of the chapters in other parts of the book. For example, for Coronado and Staudt and for Maiguashca, women's struggles around gender violence and reproductive rights in various parts of the world are central to their understandings of 'the anti-globalisation movement', while Pettman's focus on Asia directs us to yet another under-studied location for 'anti-globalisation' resistance.

As we argued in the Introduction, the notion of 'resistance' and its relation to 'movement' is complex and contested. One way of thinking about this relation is implied by Rupert, and other authors in the book, who use 'resisting' as a verb to indicate an oppositional and potentially transformative action undertaken by individuals or movements. Another way is suggested by Eschle's passing reference to 'the proliferation of resistances' composing 'the anti-globalisation movement' (p. 19). This is to use resistance as a noun, as an empirical entity or process that makes up a movement. Gruffydd Jones also uses resistance as a noun, but in a way that implies a crucial analytical and political distinction between 'resistance' and 'social movement'. Examining journalists' struggles against corruption and the coping strategies of the impoverished underclass in Mozambique, she argues that these resistances 'can in fact be seen as the antithesis of an "anti-globalisation movement" ' (p. 69). For Gruffydd Jones, participation in a movement presupposes a certain normality, stability and security, as well as a level of political consciousness and collective organisation that are simply lacking in Mozambique. So resistances here are positioned as less politically developed than movements. Further, we should be careful not to assume that resistances will automatically develop into movements. Indeed, her argument is that they quite frequently do not.

Exploring the structures and relations of power that both enable and constrain the emergence of movements, for Gruffydd Jones, implies analysing globalisation understood as 'a specific period in the world-historical development of capitalism' (p. 53). More specifically, she focuses on processes of enforced adjustment in the interests of global capital that are managed by local state and capitalist elites and that manifest themselves in Mozambique in terms of systematic forms of violence in everyday lives. Rupert too contextualises his analysis of the movement in terms of recent developments in global capitalism, this time drawing on neo-Gramscian arguments to emphasise the key role of the US state and particularly the recent shift in its policies from consensually based hegemony to a more overtly coercive and violent brand of imperialism. Taken together, these authors draw attention to the need for both geographical specificity and historical awareness in analyses of capitalism and globalisation. Beginning her analysis from activist conceptualisations of structures and relations of power, Eschle points out that many activists understand *economic* globalisation more specifically in terms of neoliberal policies and corporate power, and that the ongoing effort in some movement strands to equate 'anti-globalisation' with 'anti-capitalism' can be founded on rather reductive analytical frameworks that are heavily contested. Attempting to move away from what she sees as economic reductionism, Eschle supports an 'intersectional' understanding of globalisation *in general* as 'multiple global structures and relations of power, which intersect to manifest themselves in complex, context-specific and contingent ways' (p. 30). Such structures and relations of power include, for example, the globalised gendered, racialised and geopolitical hierarchies highlighted in the analyses of Coronado and Staudt, Higgins and Marchand later in the book.

In addition to pointing to multiple structures and relations of power, our authors also draw attention to several mechanisms or techniques of power that are being mobilised against and by the movement. We want to highlight three of these. First, there is what we would call 'material power'. Rupert and Gruffydd Jones, for example, foreground material techniques of power in their discussions of militarised violence and financial extraction and accumulation. The second is what we would call 'ideological power'. This is strongly emphasised by Rupert, who argues that the consensus generated around neoliberal ideology has functioned to mask the degree of coercion and violence involved in sustaining a capitalist world order. It is precisely the unravelling of this ideological consensus that has increased US reliance on more material, brute techniques of power. In addition, a role for ideological techniques is hinted at by Gruffydd Jones when she speaks of the depoliticising effects of religion on the Mozambican poor. Third, Eschle's analysis points to what could be called 'discursive power', with her emphasis on the capacity of academic discourses to construct social movements, and, by extension, the world that we study. The chapters in the second part of the book all also emphasise the constitutive role of discourse.

Notwithstanding these insights, there are many questions that remain to be asked about power, resistance and movement. Given our argument that power operates through material, ideological and discursive means and techniques, it seems to us that more work needs to be done on the relationship between them and on how they mutually reinforce each other with regard to 'the anti-globalisation movement'. Rather than assuming a priori that one technique is more dominant than another in shaping the movement and in terms of movement strategy, we need instead to do more empirical research on the relative importance of each in specific contexts of power and resistance. To take Gruffydd Jones's analysis, for example, it would be interesting to explore further the interrelationship between religious ideology and material power in the form of colonial invasion, war and globalised capitalism, in order to enrich further our understanding of the limits to struggle in Mozambique. It would also be interesting to examine what ideological and discursive techniques of power have been mobilised against Mozambican journalists in order to delegitimise their campaigns against corruption. Similarly, given that the chapters indicate that globalisation can be seen as implicating different structures and relations of power, we would argue that more work needs to be done on how capitalist, gendered, racialised and geopolitical hierarchies mutually reinforce and contradict each other in the construction of 'the anti-globalisation movement' in different contexts.

We suggest that there is an additional problem here, in that a critical theorising on the movement often has a tendency to extrapolate its nature and significance directly from an analysis of structures and relations of power. This is a reflection of a larger problem with critical theorising in IR, particularly Marxist versions, that tends to focus its efforts on mapping power relations rather than theorising resistances to it. We suggest that globalised power in and of itself does not give rise to resistance; rather resistance is more specifically a response to relations of *domination and oppression*. In our view, domination and oppression cannot be understood only as an objectively discernible condition, but also as subjectively experienced and perceived. The meaning that we give to the power relations we experience, the extent to which we define them as oppressive, matters in terms of whether or not and how we choose to contest them. Gruffydd Jones hints at this in her emphasis on political consciousness. This implies for her not only an awareness of oppression but also a recognition of the possibility and desirability of collective struggle, and this consciousness has to be in place before a movement can emerge. Whereas Gruffydd Jones emphasises the need to study the objective material conditions that make such a political consciousness possible, we would suggest the need for other lines of enquiry. What, for example, of the role of contingency in shaping political action? And what about the possibility that political consciousness is negotiated in and through movement mobilisation and is not a prior condition of it?

Another question we would like to raise here concerns the categorisation of ways of thinking about resistance that we outlined above. We suggested that the chapters revealed three ways of thinking about resistance: as an oppositional action undertaken by individuals or movements; as an entity or process that is a constituent part of a movement; and as an entity or process which is analytically separable from, and more politically underdeveloped than, a movement. We want to suggest now that there is a fourth way of conceptualising resistance, one which animates both this book and critical theorising more generally, but which remains largely implicit and undertheorised, and that is resistance as a form of politics. There are many ways of understanding politics and, for us, 'the politics of resistance' is the particular type that should be the focus of critical theory. In our view, it implies conscious, intentional action, which is to say that it cannot be understood as entirely irrational or as a direct product of structures, but rather as involving mediating processes of critical reflection. In addition, the politics of resistance implies the identification of relations of oppression and domination and a critique of those relations; and also, importantly, the articulation and pursuit of alternatives to the status quo. Thus ,for us, the politics of resistance is not simply oppositional, but involves a reconstructive moment. This can be cached out in various ways, including in terms of emancipation, transformation, revolution, counter-hegemony and the 'new politics' sought by many poststructuralists. On our understanding, the politics of resistance is a larger category than that of social movements; indeed, social movements are one, collectively organised manifestation of this politics.

Thus, taking the politics of resistance seriously requires, in our view, that critical scholars undertake more substantive, empirical research into social movements. In the current conjuncture, 'the anti-globalisation movement' is one key site for such enquiry, as our chapters attest. However, several empirical questions remain about the character and composition of this movement. First, how might the movement be manifested in parts of Africa and Asia that we have not discussed in this book and also in the Middle East? For us, a particularly pressing lacuna in current scholarship is the challenge that Islamist resistances may or may not offer to globalisation processes. Second, further investigation is required into the ways in which structures and relations of power operate within 'the anti-globalisation movement'. As Eschle warns us, the marginalisation of certain ideologies and actors undermines the potential of the movement to be a site and source of radical democracy. Finally, critical theorists need to examine in more detail the concrete practices and strategies of the movement, a point to which we shall return in the third section of this Conclusion. But we turn now to the second set of themes, as discussed in the second part of our book.

Discourse/identity/culture

We shall begin here with what the chapters in Part II tell us about the forms and function of discourse in the construction of 'the anti-globalisation movement'. Each chapter in this part explores a different form of discourse. In Chapter 4, Pettman uses the label to refer to an 'analytical framework' (p. 77) or a way of making sense of the world that indicates an interconnected set of values, ideas and practices. More specifically, his chapter seeks to uncover the hidden power relations generated by the discourses associated with globalisation (understood here in terms of 'the modernist project') which universalise a very particular Western understanding of who we are as human beings and how we can live together. Pettman then highlights the 'anti-globalisation' potential of the 'politico-cultural discourses' surrounding Japanese understandings of heritage and the 'politico-spiritual discourse' of Buddhist economics. In Chapter 5, Higgins appears to agree with Pettman that discourses can be understood in terms of foundational worldviews, with his exploration of the distinctiveness of Indian ways of thinking and speaking in Chiapas, Mexico. Higgins also points to an alternative, narrower definition of discourse as written and spoken texts, with his more specific focus on the ways in which the Indian worldview shapes the poetry of Subcomandante Insurgente Marcos and the role that this poetry plays in the Zapatista uprising. In Chapter 6, Marchand has a similar textual focus in her analyses of the speeches and treaties that contribute to competing constructions of regional identities in the context of the Free Trade Area of the Americas. Maiguashca, in Chapter 7, examines both academic writing about movements and activist-produced texts.

In what ways do these different forms of discourse help to construct 'the anti-globalisation movement'? The chapters show us that discourses can constitute an effort to open up relationships between people, both within a movement and between a movement and the wider audience, as well as to close communication down. In his narrative about the Zapatista uprising, Higgins treats both Marcos and 'his words as living bridges between the Indian world of the Mexican south-east and the ever more pervasive world of global politics' (p. 88). In contrast to didactic political discourses based on assertions of truth, Marcos's poetry disrupts monopolistic claims to knowledge and defamiliarises the world around us, painting alternative pictures of human potentiality. The poetry form mobilises evocative metaphors, images and allegories which inspire and open up our creative and moral imaginations and establish new relations of empathy and solidarity. As well as functioning as a 'living bridge' between peoples, Higgins reminds us that discourses can reflect and reproduce hierarchical power relations and close down the possibility of mutual understanding. The Marxist–Leninist discourse of Marcos and his cohorts, grounded in urban, educated, modernised Mexico and loaded with universalist and teleological assumptions, made little sense to the Indians of the Lacandon jungle and thwarted efforts at collective organisation. It is only as Marcos was transformed from teacher to pupil that a discourse was constructed of shared understandings and shared dreams. Drawing on a very different, more overtly strategic discourse in terms of political speeches and treaties, Marchand also shows how connections and differences are established, in this case in terms of the construction of competing regional identities. Furthermore, by highlighting the racialised and gendered nature of Simon Bolívar's discourses of Latin American unification, Marchand, like Higgins, reminds us that discourses do not just contest structures and relations of power but also reify and reproduce them.

For several of our authors, discourse operates in and through culture. Higgins refers to 'Indian culture' in ways that show that he understands the term 'culture' to mean the shared traditions, values, habits and ways of life of a particular community. Furthermore, his notion of 'cultural humanism' points to the possibility of constructing 'living bridges' of empathy across these communities. In addition, his analysis suggests that culture should be understood in more philosophical terms as the basis of ways of being and knowing. For example, the Chiapan Indians have built a distinctive conceptualisation of who they are, what their place is in the world and in the cosmos, and how knowledge about that cosmos can be generated and shared. It is this ontological and epistemological dimension of culture that is perhaps the key element of their differentiation from *ladino* and *mestizo* Mexico, and from the modernised world. Pettman seems to us to share some of this understanding of how culture operates. He draws attention to continuities in the distinctive cultural practices of the Japanese state and to the individualistic ontology and rationalist epistemology specific to 'modernist' Western culture. Moreover, Pettman's use of the category of 'politico-cultural discourse' to explain the way in which cultural forms are articulated and universalised reminds us that culture is not somehow a realm separate from politics, as often conceived in IR, but rather that it is embedded within and reproduces power relations and frames the ways in which we organise our social, economic and political lives.

For all of these authors, culture is clearly implicated in the construction of identities. Two main sites of identity are discussed. Higgins and Maiguashca focus primarily on the self-construction of identity by social movement activists, while Marchand's and Pettman's work highlights the ways in which larger regional identities, in terms of 'Latin America', 'Asia' and 'the West', are created, contested and exported. These very different kinds of identity are shown, however, to share common features. They are all rooted in cultural practices that have developed within a particular community. But importantly, they are not culturally pre-given or fixed, but are rather socially and politically constructed. More specifically, all these chapters emphasise the discursive nature of identity-formation. For example, Marchand highlights the influence of the Monroe doctrine and Bolívar's key writings on the generation of two contemporary, competing geopolitical imaginations, while Higgins shows how a sense of identification with the Zapatistas is created through Marcos's poetry. Maiguashca argues that identity construction must not be reduced to its discursive dimension, but must also be seen as shaped and constrained by the 'material conditions' and 'spatial relations' in which activists operate. She gives the example of identity construction within reproductive rights activism, pointing to the significance of North–South divisions in undermining 'feminist' identifications and of spatial separation in international conferences in weakening solidarities (p. 131-2). Our authors also suggest that identity construction is to a large extent context specific and relational. For example, we note that the Chiapan Indians use the notion of the *mestizo* to refer to the non-Indian, while Bolívar and his contemporary followers use it to refer to a hybrid identity that embraces both Indian and Spanish heritage. The chapters go on to remind us, however, that identity must not be seen as structurally and contextually determined. It is also the product of conscious, selective and strategic interventions by activists. One example here is provided by Marchand's analysis of the ways in which contemporary activists have taken up Bolívar's discourse. While they have appropriated the anti-imperial and republican elements of this discourse, they have discarded its more paternalistic elements.

Thus, our contributors offer several insights into both the general process of identity construction and the particular ways in which identity is mobilised in concrete instances of 'anti-globalisation' movement politics. However, we are still left with questions about the nature of identity-formation in 'the anti-globalisation movement' as such, that is, as a transnational social movement. If, as Eschle asserts in Chapter 1, movements are by definition at least in part a continual process of negotiation and contestation over collective identity, then the study of movement identity becomes a crucial way of enquiring into whether or not a movement exists and how it might be sustained. Eschle begins her own enquiry into this question with regards to 'the anti-globalisation movement' by examining identity claims made on the websites of international networks widely seen as key members. Higgins finds a different way into this question with his discussion of the manner in which the Zapatistas speak from their local context to an international audience, thus strategically positioning themselves at the heart of a wider 'anti-globalisation movement'. These are interesting starting points for enquiry into the construction of collective identity in 'the anti-globalisation movement', but we clearly need more sustained research into how such local and international identities interpolate and what kinds of solidarities and conflicts are thus produced.

What is more, it is our view that the notion of identity per se and its relation to culture needs to be unpacked more carefully. One helpful way of thinking about this in the context of studying movements in IR might be to distinguish between 'cultural identity' and 'political identity'. It seems to us that cultural and political identities serve different functions and operate in different contexts. Maiguascha focuses in Chapter 7 on the construction of political identity in particular, understood as a process of 'differentiating ourselves *from* some and identifying ourselves *with* others. ... It ... is therefore less about who we are ... than about what we are for' (p. 134). Cultural identity, in contrast, could be seen as an expression of kinship and sameness. Drawing on the unquestioned, familiar terrain of 'habitus', it functions as the shared narrative backdrop which gives meaning to our everyday lives and which we all need to take for granted in order to act. Unlike political identity, then, the assertion of cultural identity, while often implicitly requiring the establishment of differences, does not imply the assertion of resistance. This is not to say, however, that such cultural identities cannot in certain circumstances become politicised and, therefore, become political identities. What needs to explored in both theoretical and empirical terms is when, why and how cultural identities become politicised. In what ways are cultural symbols used to reinforce political identities and what are the strengths and dangers of politicising culture in this way?

Finally, we would argue that much more work needs to be done by critical theorists in IR on discourse in terms of both a substantive area of enquiry and a methodological approach to the investigation of movements. More specifically, there is a need to address at least three questions. First, what kinds of discourse should scholars of movements be examining? In terms of texts, we think that poetry is a potentially exciting area of further research. And what about moving beyond written texts to examine visual imagery and representations? Second, the notion of discourse itself needs more elaboration among movement scholars. What does it include and not include? What is its relationship to material contexts, ideologies and belief systems? In our view, critical theorists interested in exploring movements need to be more attentive to broader debates about the nature of discourse and methods of studying it. Third, more empirical work is needed on the implications of language and its relation to movement discourses. As Higgins notes in his analysis of the Zapatistas, and as confirmed by Coronado and Staudt in their discussion in the next part of women's organising against violence, language differences can be a significant barrier to communication, mobilisation and inclusion. This is because people cannot make sense of each other's words; more than that, it is because languages bring with them fundamental assumptions about the world that are not easily translatable. Furthermore, some languages are positioned as more powerful than others and thus function to dominate and silence. In the context of movement mobilisation, linguistic differences are clearly political and require more attention as such.

Politics/strategy/violence

The question of the nature of 'politics' more generally has been raised at several points in this book. The chapters in the third part make the form of politics represented by 'the anti-globalisation movement' central to their analyses. In Chapter 9, Birchfield and Freyberg-Inan draw explicitly on a Gramscian conception of politics to frame their analysis of ATTAC and to interpret its significance. This means that they evaluate ATTAC in terms of its counter-hegemonic potential, that is its role in helping to construct a new historic bloc and to bring about the wholesale transformation of the capitalist system. One of the key protagonists in the Gramscian vision of counter-hegemony is the 'organic intellectual' whose role is to demystify social relations. For Birchfield and Freyberg-Inan, ATTAC performs this role, mainly through its efforts at popular education and consciousness-raising. We suggest that this understanding of the relationship between knowledge and political organising is predicated on two assumptions. The first is that knowledge is acquired cognitively. This reason-based conception of knowledge is made explicit when Birchfield and Freyberg-Inan, quoting Gramsci, state:

> If the relationship between intellectuals and people-nation, between the leaders and the led, the rulers and the ruled, is provided by an organic cohesion in which feeling-passion becomes understanding and thence knowledge ... then and only then is the relationship one of representation.
>
> (p. 157)

The second is that only through acquiring and disseminating knowledge about the world is collective action possible. Thus truth precedes counter-hegemonic politics. We suggest that a similar understanding of the relationship between knowledge and politics is articulated by Gruffydd Jones in her emphasis on political consciousness, as discussed earlier.

In Chapter 8 on the anti-violence Coalition in Ciudad Juárez, Coronado and Staudt also echo Gruffydd Jones, this time in terms of their emphasis on the coping strategies of the marginalised and disempowered. Unlike Gruffydd Jones, however, they reject the distinction between individualised, unorchestrated resistance, on the one hand, and transformative social movements, on the other. Instead, both coping strategies and organised collective action are declared to be political. Furthermore, the conception of politics at work here is a far less mediated one than that articulated both by Gruffydd Jones and by Birchfield and Freyberg-Inan. Indeed, Coronado and Staudt are explicit about their discomfort with being positioned as 'organic intellectuals' within the movement and their preference for allowing women to speak for themselves. Here we find little interest in popular education as such; consciousness-raising should not be aimed at the people experiencing oppression and violence, but rather at political and media elites. In addition, although their account demonstrates a feminist concern with the politics of everyday life – emphasising the ways in which power operates and is resisted in homes, sexual relations and intimate life – it also centralises state institutions as the key site of political action for the Coalition.

Sullivan's account in Chapter 10 of 'anti-globalisation' protests in Thessaloniki and London gives us a quite different conception of politics. She describes these protests as a reaction to the structural violence of our current world order and as the targeted expression of the resulting rage felt by activists. For her, they represent a 'politics of *desire*' (p. 184), emphasis in original) that is future oriented and that is premised on imagination, creativity, emotional energy, ethical aspiration as well as rational calculation. Sullivan cites Cuevas to describe this politics as a 'new offensive in the arena of dreams, of rights, of liberty, for the conquest of the future' (p. 184), which implies that it is not just reactive but also proactive. Unlike Birchfield and Freyberg-Inan or Coronado and Staudt, whose central concern is with collective action and the construction of movement politics, Sullivan is more interested in the construction of non-managed subjects, their emotional and psychological responses and their embodied, lived experiences.

Bleiker, in Chapter 11, shares Sullivan's interest in making sense of protest actions and street demonstrations, this time at Seattle. Starting from an analysis of the systemic crisis of legitimacy within which protests arise, Bleiker is concerned with conceptualising them in terms of an 'ethos of critical engagement' and, citing Connolly, 'as lines of flight towards a more democratic and accountable form of global politics' (p. 196-7). He suggests that his approach involves a move beyond politics to ethics. In contrast to the mainstream liberal view of ethics as a set of universal laws of right action discernible through reason, most of the chapters here understand ethics in terms of acting for the greater good, fighting domination and seeking to create a better world. For Bleiker, ethics also involves an open orientation or disposition which seeks to problematise foundations and defend difference. Bleiker implies, though, that the distinction between ethics and politics is hard to sustain, which is why he turns instead to the notion of an ethos of critical engagement as an attitude that should inform political action. He further suggests, in opposition to Sullivan, that activist rage and violence are not compatible with this ethos.

Despite such disagreements, we propose that all of the conceptions of politics in this part of the book exemplify what we describe above as the 'politics of resistance'. We defined this in terms of conscious intentional action, a critique of relations of oppression and a reconstructive moment, involving the articulation of alternative possibilities. In addition to sharing this understanding of politics, our contributors all offer interesting ways of further elaborating on it. In the first place, they highlight the ethical orientation of this form of politics: that is, the fact that it is enacted on behalf of others and is oriented to the realisation of a normative project. In the second place, a number of the authors, including Birchfield and Freyberg-Inan and Bleiker, underline the democratic aspirations and potential of this form of politics. In their view, because of its central focus on questions of globalised domination and exclusion, 'the anti-globalisation movement' has a responsibility to interrogate critically its own political practices in these terms and to organise in a way that is egalitarian, inclusive and accountable. In the third place, these authors draw our attention to the role of emotions as a crucial constitutive force shaping the politics of resistance. Coronado, Staudt and Sullivan are perhaps the most explicit about the role of affective relations in animating this kind of politics and develop insightful analyses of the ways in which shared feelings of empathy, pain, anger and fear can provide the terrain on which resistance erupts and solidarity is built. For these authors, then, the politics of resistance is a matter of the heart as well as the head.

In addition, a number of our authors point to the strategic dimension of the politics of resistance by offering interesting empirical analyses of the different strategies pursued by 'the anti-globalisation movement'. Birchfield and Freyberg-Inan's analysis of ATTAC suggests that perhaps its most distinctive feature is the way in which it organises in order to facilitate a diversity of strategies. ATTAC is composed of local, national and international networks which act with relative autonomy from each other. What is more, it is a founder of the annual World Social Forum, the central purpose of which is to create a space for the articulation of diverse alternatives to the neoliberal world order. This is a very different kind of counter-hegemonic project from the one identified by Gramsci, then, as it has diversity rather than unity of purpose at its very core. Coronado and Staudt point to several distinctive strategies deployed by the Coalition in Ciudad Juárez. Like ATTAC, the Coalition is centrally concerned with cross-border organising and alliance building. Further, Coronado and Staudt emphasise its efforts to exert influence over state institutions by directly lobbying politicians and, more indirectly, by networking with male politicians' wives. This last move suggests that Coalition members seek to gain access to elites through gender-based alliances. Perhaps most interestingly for our purposes, the Coalition moves beyond institutionally oriented strategies with its participation in symbolic actions. Theatrical performances, film and vigils are used in several ways: to inform, engage and move a wider public; to bear witness to victims of violence as a way of re-humanising police statistics and supporting victims' families; to build solidarity amongst women in the region; and, finally, to generate further pressure upon elites.

Both Sullivan and Bleiker focus on the violence involved in some strategies deployed by 'the anti-globalisation movement'. Sullivan identifies several ways in which violence is used: sabotage; damage to property seen as symbolic of capitalist exploitation and violence; and aggressive or defensive confrontation with police in order to draw out the violence at the heart of the state. She rejects out of hand analyses of such violent strategies which reduce them to the acting out of irrational or childish frustrations, insisting that most of them are coherently thought through and carefully targeted.

Moreover, she suggests that these strategies must also be understood in ethical and ontological terms as a response to structural violence in the world and to the violated subjectivities, emotional turbulence and damaged bodies that this produces. They are a necessary part of 'a proactive politics of the lived rather than the managed human' (p. 191). Bleiker reaches rather different conclusions about the use of violence. He argues that '[f]orm is as important as content' in movement struggles; that is, that movement organising should embody the world it seeks to create (p. 205). He goes on to emphasise the efficacy of non-violent action, suggesting that it 'seeks a conversation with the consciousness of the opponent and the public at large' that is capable of generating social transformation in a way in which violent strategies are not (p. 207).

These are thought-provoking interventions by both Bleiker and Sullivan on the topic of violence in movement strategies, but some key questions remain about the nature of their disagreement. More precisely, it seems to us that Bleiker and Sullivan share a concern with both the ethical and strategic dimension of movement violence but that they are working with very different conceptualisations of ethics and strategy. Sullivan starts from the position of a participant in 'militant' activism, seeking primarily to understand its origins, imperatives and possibilities. In so doing, she emphasises its strategic character in terms of how it is reasoned and targeted and its ethical character in terms of its potential for human and social transformation. Bleiker writes as an outsider to movement violence, seeking to evaluate its strategic nature in terms of efficacy and its ethical character in terms of the extent to which it sustains an ethos of critical engagement. Our interest here is not to confirm the approach of either Sullivan or Bleiker but rather to point to the significance of their underlying disagreement about the nature of strategy and ethics; to indicate the importance of disentangling their assumptions even further; and to suggest that interesting insights could be yielded by bringing their different approaches into dialogue.

We have an additional point to make about strategy more generally. We suggest that the empirical study of movement strategy is important not only in itself but also because it can offer a basis for the theorisation of politics. In other words, instead of building such theories purely from abstract principles, we need also to draw on substantive research into concrete movement strategies. Our case studies provide some pointers as to how this might be done. In Coronado and Staudt's chapter, the Coalition's emphasis on lobbying state elites, either directly or indirectly, arguably indicates an understanding of politics as primarily located within state institutions. Sullivan's analysis of the protest strategy of defensive confrontation with police points to a very different understanding of the state as controlling and disciplining political participation, ultimately through violence. Thus political possibility can only flourish on other terrains. We are not suggesting here that these scholars have no conceptions of politics in place when studying movement strategy; after all, it is a basic assumption of critical theorising that there is no such thing as theory-free empirical research. However, we are suggesting that critical theorists more generally need to reflect on and even rethink their theoretical conceptions of politics in the light of empirical research into movement strategies of the kind that these authors have undertaken.

Having made some suggestions for further lines of enquiry into violence, strategy and politics, we have one final point to make on the latter. We have argued above that all of our authors see 'the anti-globalisation movement' as in some sense a politics of resistance and that this form of politics includes, amongst other things, a reconstructive moment. By this we mean that it brings with it a struggle for alternatives to the current social order, which can be conceptualised in various ways. For example, Birchfield and Freyberg-Inan and Rupert assess the potential of the movement in terms of whether or not it can contribute to the construction of counter-hegemony; Gruffydd Jones emphasises the obstacles to what she calls 'transformatory practice' (p. 70); Sullivan desires a politics of subversion and transgression in order to open up the possibility of 'a social revolution of subjectivities' (p. 190); while Bleiker aspires to the creation of a 'global democratic ethos' (p. 196). These are intriguing glimpses into the political potentiality of 'the anti-globalisation movement'. However, we think that this reconstructive moment needs further fleshing out, in both theoretical and empirical terms. At least three lines of theoretical enquiry could be pursued. First, more work could be done on grounding these conceptions of the reconstructive moment more explicitly in existing critical theory traditions. Second, the relationship between the reconstructive moment and the prior critical analysis of power needs more attention. As we argued above, it seems to us that calls for a transformative politics assume a relation of oppression and domination that needs to be transformed. However, we need to know more about what different critical theory traditions have to say about the nature of oppression and domination and how this shapes their aspirations for change. Third, critical theorists need to reflect more systematically on the normative and political criteria by which they judge the reconstructive visions of movements to be progressive, regressive or neither. In addition, more empirical work has to be undertaken on these reconstructive visions. We have only just begun such work in this book and need to know more about the specific normative and political goals of 'anti-globalisation' activists. What are the commonalities and tensions between their different visions? This kind of empirical work on movement self-understandings should help critical theorists reflect upon their own normative aspirations and ethical criteria. After all, the reflexive interrogation of political practices and possibilities is what critical theory in IR is supposed to be about.

Theory/practice

We began the book by emphasising our twin concerns with both critical theorising and the practices of 'the anti-globalisation movement'. We would like to end by reflecting briefly on the theory–practice relationship. The engagements with 'the anti-globalisation movement' in this book strongly confirm the basic critical theory claim that academic study is both shaped by and constitutive of the world around us. They also point to, but do not fully develop, the claim that our own knowledge production is political: it is bound up with, reflects or contests relations of power. As Eschle argued in Chapter 1, the study of social movements in general, and the identification and interrogation of 'the anti-globalisation movement' in particular, has political consequences. This entails a rejection of the idea that we can evaluate the practices and self-understandings of movement activists from a neutral, non-political position and requires us to be more explicit about our political and normative investments in the movement we seek to study. Coronado and Staudt's discussion of *compromiso* (p. 144) offers us one way of engaging with this imperative. *Compromiso* brings with it a strong sense of responsibility to the activists in a movement and a commitment to orientate research so that it makes a positive contribution to the movement struggle. For us, this necessitates an acknowledgement of the power that academics wield when we represent and interpret movements. Which voices do we privilege when we write our stories? How do we translate and interpret these voices without misrepresenting them? How do we share our research conclusions with movement activists? Coronado and Staudt remind us that *compromiso* also brings with it intellectual and personal challenges. In our globalised, professionalised universities, the space for conducting such politicised scholarship is increasingly under threat and we need to engage in our own politics of resistance to defend it.

We do not want to close, however, by emphasising the struggles of critical theorists within academia. Rather, we want to stress, as we have throughout the book, the political significance of the struggles of 'the anti-globalisation movement'. This is not simply because we see the movement as enacting important political potentialities in a globalised world. It is also because movement activists are producers of knowledge about that world and should be seen as equal partners in the critical theory project, broadly defined as 'the self-clarification of the struggles and wishes of the age' (Marx 1975 [1843]: 209). Higgins has told us how the political vision and practice of Subcomandante Marcos was transformed when he renounced his teacher role in order to learn from the Lacandon Indians. Likewise we would suggest that critical scholars in IR need to become pupils of 'the anti-globalisation movement' if we are to contribute in more valuable ways to the creation of other possible worlds.

Bibliography

Abbey, E. (1991 [1973]) *The Monkey Wrench Gang*, London: Robin Clarke.

Afshar, H. and Barrientos, S. (1999) *Women, Globalization and Fragmentation in the Developing World*, Basingstoke: Macmillan.

Agamben, G. (1994) 'We Refugees', trans. Michael Rocke, Online. Available HTTP: <http://ww.egs.edu/faculty/agamben/agamben-we-refugees.htm> (accessed 25 March 2004).

—— (1998) *Homo Sacer: Sovereign Power and Bare Life*, trans. Daniel Heller-Roazen, Palo Alto, CA: Stanford University Press.

Agence France Presse (2003) 'Millions Give Dramatic Rebuff to US War Plans', 16 February.

Ahmad, A. (1992) *In Theory: Classes, Nations, Literatures*, London: Verso.

—— (2000) 'A Century of Revolutions', *Frontline*, 17 (2). Online. Available HTTP: <http://www.flonnet.com/fl1702/17021230.htm> (accessed 24 April 2004).

—— (2002) *On Communalism and Globalization: Offensives of the Far Right*, New Delhi: Three Essays.

Alexander, M. J. and Mohanty, C.T. (eds) (1997) *Feminist Genealogies, Colonial Legacies, Democratic Futures*, New York: Routledge.

Alianza Social Continental (ASC) (2001) *Declaration of the Second People's Summit of the Americas, Québec: No to the FTAA! Another Americas is Possible!* Online. Available HTTP: <http://www.asc-hsa.org/cumbre/declarationeng.html> (accessed 27 August 2002).

Alvarez, I. (2003) 'Opposition Grows in Britain to Iraq War', Agence France Presse, 23 January.

Alvarez, S. E. (1999) 'Advocating Feminism: The Latin American Feminist NGO "Boom" ', *International Feminist Journal of Politics*, 1 (2): 181–209.

Amigos de las Mujeres de Juárez (2004) Amigos de las Mujeres de Juárez home page. Online. Available HTTP: <http://www.amigosdemujeres.org/> (accessed 5 May 2004).

Anarchist Youth Network: Britain and Ireland (2003) *Whose Streets? Our Streets! An Introduction to Anarchy*, London: Anarchist Youth Network: Britain and Ireland.

Ancelovici, M. (2002) 'Organizing against Globalization: The Case of ATTAC in France', *Politics and Society*, 30 (3): 427–63.

Anderson, B. (1991) *Imagined Communities*, 2nd edition, London: Verso.

Anderson, P. (1976) 'The Antinomies of Antonio Gramsci', *New Left Review*, 100: 5–80.

—— (2002) 'Force and Consent', *New Left Review*, 17: 5–30.

Anderson, P. and Mertes, T. (2002) 'Pacific Panopticon: Interview with Walden Bello', *New Left Review*, 16: 68–85.

Anon. (2001) 'Who are the White Overalls? And Why are They Slandered by People who Call Themselves "Anarchists"?' Online. Available HTTP: <http://www.nadir.org/nadir/initiativ/agp/free/genova/busload.htm> (accessed 20 January 2004).

—— (2004) 'Anti-Capitalist Resistance in Genoa: A Personal Reflection', in J. Carter and D. Morland (eds) *Anti-Capitalist Britain*, Gretton, Cheltenham: New Clarion Press.

Anzaldúa, G. (1987) *Borderlands/La Frontera: The New Mestiza*, San Francisco: Spinsters/Aunt Lute Press.

Armstrong, D. (2002) 'Dick Cheney's Song of America', *Harper's Magazine*, October: 76–84.

Armstrong, K. (2000) *Buddha*, London: Phoenix.

Ashcroft, B., Griffiths, G. and Tiffin, H. (eds) (1995) *The Post-Colonial Studies Reader*, London: Routledge.

ATTAC (2000) *Tout sur ATTAC*, Paris: Mille et Une Nuits.

ATTAC France (1998) 'Statuts de l'Association'. Online. Available HTTP: <http://www.france.attac.org/a604> (accessed 22 April 2004).

ATTAC Germany (2002) 'Attac-Erklärung'. Online. Available HTTP: <http://www.attac.de/erklaerung/erklaerung.php> (accessed 19 April 2004).

ATTAC International (1999) 'Platform of the International Movement ATTAC'. Online. Available HTTP: <http://attac.org/indexen/index.html> (click on 'Referring to the Platform' in the left-hand margin) (accessed 19 April 2004).

Aubry, A. (1994) *La Historia de Chiapas Identifica a los Zapatistas*, Doc. 043-VI, San Cristobal de las Casas, Mexico: INAREMAC.

Aubry, A. and Inda, A. (1998) 'La Paramilitarizacion en el Nuevo Paisaje Social de las Guerras Campesinas', *La Jornada* supplement *del Campo* (25 February 1998), 64: 1–4.

Austin, K. (1994) *Invisible Crimes: US Private Intervention in the War in Mozambique*, Washington, DC: Africa Policy Information Center.

Baker, G. and Fidler, S. (2003) 'America's Democratic Imperialists', *Financial Times*, 6 March.

Baker, L. (2002a) 'Activists vow Europe-wide Protests against Iraq War', *Reuters*, 7 November.

—— (2002b) 'Half a Million March in Antiwar Rally in Italy', *Reuters*, 9 November.

Bakhtin, M. (1968) *Rabelais and His World*, trans. H. Iswolsky, Cambridge, MA: MIT Press.

Ballard, J.G. (2000) *Super-Cannes*, London: Flamingo.

Balogun, O. (1997) *Adjusted Lives: Stories of Structural Adjustments*, Trenton, NJ: Africa World Press.

Banksy (n.d.) Banksy home page Online. Available at: HTTP:<http://www.banksy.co.uk> (accessed 12 August 2003).

Barber, B. (2001) *Jihad v. McWorld*, New York: Ballantine Books.

Barker, C. (2001) 'Socialism', in E. Bircham and J. Charlton (eds) *Anti-Capitalism: A Guide to the Movement*, 2nd edition, London: Bookmarks.

Barker, C. and Cox, L. (2003) ' "What Have the Romans Ever Done for Us?" Academic and Activist Forms of Theorising'. Online. Available HTTP: <http://www.iol.ie/~mazzoldi/toolsforchange/afpp/afpp8.html> (accessed 20 January 2004).

Baron, D. (2003) 'Another Humanity is Possible: Towards a Performative Pedagogy of Self-Determination', Seminar given in the Department of Sociology, University of Warwick (27 February).

Barry, T. and Lobe, J. (2002a) 'US Foreign Policy: Attention, Right Face, Forward March', *Foreign Policy in Focus Policy Report*. Online. Available HTTP: <http://www.foreignpolicy-infocus.org/papers/02right/index.html> (accessed 12 October 2002).

—— (2002b) 'The Men who Stole the Show', *Foreign Policy in Focus Special Report*. Online. Available HTTP: <http://www.foreignpolicy-infocus.org/papers/02men/index.html> (accessed 5 November 2002).

Batchelor, S. (1990) 'Buddhist Economics Reconsidered', in A. Badiner (ed.) *Dharma Gaia: A Harvest of Essays in Buddhism and Ecology*, Berkeley, CA: Parallax Press, 178–82.

Baudrillard, J. (1983) 'The Precession of Simulacra', in *Simulations*, trans. P. Foss, P. Patton and P. Beitchman, New York: Semiotext(e), 1–79.

—— (1985) 'The Ecstasy of Communication', trans. J. Johnston in H. Foster (ed.) *Postmodern Culture*, London: Pluto Press, 126–34.

—— (2003) 'The Violence of the Global', trans. F. Debrix, *Theory, Technology and Culture*, 26 (1–2): Article 129. Online. Available HTTP: <http://www.ctheory.net/text_file.asp?pick=385 > (accessed 21 May 2003).

Bayon, N. and Masse, J.-P. (2002) 'Petits Impressions Génoises: Chroniques Quotidiennes d'une Mobilisation Anti-Mondialisation', *Cultures et Conflits: Sociologie Politique de l'International*, 46. Online. Available HTTP: <http://conflits.revues.org/article.php3?id_article=608> (accessed 20 April 2004).

Beaulieu, E. and Di Giovanni, J. (2003) 'The March at the 3rd Intercontinental Youth Camp', *Newsletter* (February), 6 (1). Online. Available HTTP: <http://www.ffq.qc.ca/marche2000/en/bulletin/02–2003.html> (accessed 30 June 2003).

Becker, E. (2003) 'US Unilateralism Worries Trade Officials', *New York Times*, 17 March.

Bello, W. (2000) 'From Melbourne to Prague: The Struggle for a Deglobalized World'. Online. Available HTTP: <http://zmag.org/melbourne_to_prague.htm> (accessed 2 January 2005).

—— (2002a) 'East Asia's Future: Strategic Economic Cooperation or Marginalisation', Speech delivered at the University of Nagoya (7–8 February). Online. Available HTTP: <http://www.focusweb.org/publications/2002/east-asias-future.html> (accessed 9 March 2004).

—— (2002b) *Prospects for Good Governance: The View from the South*, Report prepared for the Bundestag, Federal Republic of Germany, Focus on the Global South, Bangkok.

Bello, W. and Bullard, N. (2001) 'The Global Conjuncture: Characteristics and Challenges', Speech delivered at the National Convention against Globalization, New Delhi (21–23 March). Online. Available HTTP: <http:www.nadir.org/nadir/initiativ/agp/free/bello/globalconjuncture.htm> (accessed 9 March 2004).

Benítez, R. et al. (1999) *El Silencio que la Voz de Todas Quiebra: Mujeres y Victimas de Ciudad Juárez*, Chihuahua: Azar.

Benjamin, M. (2003) 'Response to David Cortright', *The Nation*, 21 April.

Bennis, P. and Cavanagh, J. (2003) 'Response to David Cortright', *The Nation*, 21 April.

Bernauer, T. (2000) *Staaten im Weltmarkt: Zur Handlunsfähigkeit von Staaten trotz wirtschaflticher Globalisierung*, Opladen: Leske und Budrich.

Bhabha, H. K. (1995) 'Cultural Diversity and Cultural Differences', in B. Ashcroft, G. Griffiths and H. Tiffin (eds) *The Post-Colonial Studies Reader*, London: Routledge, 206–9.

Big Noise Tactical (n.d.) Big Noise Tactical home page. Online. Available HTTP: <http://www.bignoisefilms.com/home.htm> (accessed 14 April 2004).

Bigo, D. and Guild, E. (2002) 'De Tampere à Seville, Vers une Ultra Gouvernementalisation de la Domination Transnationale?', *Cultures et Conflits: Sociologie Politique de l'International*, 45. Online. Available HTTP: <http://conflits.revues.org/article.php3?id_article=585> (accessed 20 April 2004).

Biko, S. (1989 [1978]) *I Write What I Like: A Selection of Writings*, Oxford: Heinemann International Literature and Textbooks.

Bircham, E. and Charlton, J. (eds) (2001) *Anti-Capitalism: A Guide to the Movement*, 2nd edition, London: Bookmarks.

Bishop, P. (1999) 'Small Cheese Faces Big Mac on Home Ground', *Daily Telegraph*, 30 November.

Blaney, D. L. (1994) 'Gramscian Readings of the Post-Cold War Transition', *Mershon International Studies Review*, 38: 283–4.

Bleiker, R. (2000) *Popular Dissent, Human Agency and Global Politics*, Cambridge: Cambridge University Press.

Blum, W. (1995) *Killing Hope: US Military and CIA Interventions since World War II*, Monroe, ME: Common Courage Press.

Bøås, M., Marchand, M. H. and Shaw, T. (1999) 'The Political Economy of New Regionalisms', *Third World Quarterly*, 20 (5): 897–910.

Böhm, S. G. (2002) 'Movements of Theory and Practice', *ephemera: critical dialogues on organization*, 2 (4): 328–51.

Böhm, S. G. and Sørensen, B. M. (2003) ' "Warganization": Towards a New Political Violence', Pamphlet prepared for a 4 July event at the Nineteenth EGOS Colloquium 'Organization Analysis Informing Social and Global Development', Copenhagen, Denmark.

Bolívar, S. (1815) 'Carta de Jamaica', in C. Mendoza y F. J. Yanes (coll.), *Colección de Documentos Relativos a la Vida Pública del Libertador de Colombia y del Perú, Simón Bolívar, para servir a la Historia de la Independencia de Sudamérica*, Caracas: Devisme Hermanos/G. F. Devisme/Damiron y Dupuy (1826–1833). Online. Available HTTP: <http://www.bolivar.ula.ve/cgi-in/be_alex.exe?Ejemplar=T011900000090/0&Nombrebd=BOLIVAR&ForReg> (accessed 27 August 2002).

——— (1824) 'Convocatoria del Congreso de Panamá', in C. Mendoza y F. J. Yanes (coll.) *Colección de Documentos Relativos a la Vida Pública del Libertador de Colombia y del Perú, Simón Bolívar, para servir a la Historia de la Independencia de Sudamérica*, Caracas: Devisme Hermanos/G.F. Devisme/Damiron y Dupuy (1826–1833). Online. Available HTTP: <http://www.bolivar.ula.ve/cgi-win/be_alex.exe?Ejemplar=T011900000082/0&Nombrebd=BOLIVAR&ForReg> (accessed 27 August 2002).

Boltanski, L. (1999) *Distant Suffering: Morality, Media and Politics*, trans. G. Burchell, Cambridge: Cambridge University Press.

Bond, P. (2000) 'The African Grassroots and the Global Movement'. Online. Available HTTP: <http://www.lbbs.org/CrisesCurEvts/Globalism/african_grassroots.htm> (accessed December 2000).

Bondurant, J. V. (1967) *Conquest of Violence: The Gandhian Philosophy of Conflict*, Berkeley, CA: University of California Press.

Boseley, S. (2003) 'Mood Drug Seroxat Banned for Under-18s', *Guardian*, 11 June.

Boukhari, S., Anbarasan, E. and Kohut, J. (1999) 'James Tobin: Reining in the Markets' (Interview), *UNESCO Courier*. Online. Available HTTP: <http://www.unesco.org/courier/1999_02/uk/dires/txt1.htm> (accessed 24 April 2004).

Bourdieu, P. (1990 [1980]) *The Logic of Practice*, Cambridge: Polity Press.

—— (1998) *Acts of Resistance: Against the New Myths of Our Time*, Cambridge: Polity Press.

—— (2001) *Masculine Domination*, Oxford: Blackwell.

Bourgois, P. (1982) 'What US Foreign Policy Faces in Rural El Salvador: An American caught in a Government Attack that Chiefly Killed Civilians', *Washington Post*, 14 February.

—— (2001) 'The Power of Violence in War and Peace: Post-Cold War Lessons from El Salvador', *Ethnography*, 2 (1): 5–34.

Boyer, P. (2003) 'The New War Machine', *The New Yorker*, 30 June: 55–71.

Brah, A. (2002) 'Global Mobilities, Local Predicaments: Globalization and the Critical Imagination', *Feminist Review*, 70: 30–45.

Brecher, J. and Costello, T. (1998) *Global Village or Global Pillage: Economic Reconstruction From the Bottom Up*, 2nd edition, Cambridge, MA: South End Press.

Brecher, J., Costello, T. and Smith, B. (2002) *Globalization from Below: The Power of Solidarity*, 2nd edition, Cambridge, MA: South End Press.

Brennan, T. (2000) *Exhausting Modernity: Grounds for a New Economy*, London: Routledge.

Bretton Woods Update (2003) 'SAP Protests Still Raging: Latin America Examples', *Bretton Woods Update*, 36: 3.

Broad, R. (ed.) (2002) *Global Backlash: Citizen Initiatives for a Just World Economy*. Lanham, MD: Rowman and Littlefield.

Broughton, P. D. (2003) 'Orderly Anarchists on Fringe of G8 are not Happy Campers', *Daily Telegraph*, 31 May.

Brown, C. (1994) ' "Turtles All the Way Down": Anti-Foundationalism, Critical Theory and International Relations', *Millennium: Journal of International Studies*, 23 (2): 213–36.

Brown, J. (1977) *Gandhi and Civil Disobedience*, Cambridge: Cambridge University Press.

Bubna-Litic, D. (2000) 'Buddhism Returns to the Market Place', in D. Keown (ed.) *Contemporary Buddhist Ethics*, Richmond: Curzon.

Burbach, R. (2001) *Globalization and Postmodern Politics: From Zapatistas to High-Tech Robber Barons*, London: Pluto Press.

Burrows, N. (2002). 'The World March of Women at the World Social Forum in Porto Alegre (Brazil, February 4 2002)'. Online. Available HTTP: <http://www.ffq.qc.ca/marche2000/en/fsm2002b.html> (accessed 15 December 2002).

Call of Social Movements (2002) 'Resistance to Neoliberalism War and Militarism: For Peace and Social Justice'. Online. Available HTTP: <http://www.forumsocialmundial.org.br/dinamic/eng_portoalegrefinal.asp> (accessed 9 December 2002).

Callinicos, A. (2001) 'Toni Negri in Perspective', *International Socialism Journal*, 92. Online. Available HTTP: <http://www.isj1text.ble.org.uk/pubs/isj92/callinicos.htm> (accessed 23 June 2003).

—— (2003a) *An Anti-Capitalist Manifesto,* Cambridge: Polity Press.

—— (2003b) *The New Mandarins of American Power*, Cambridge: Polity Press.

Cammack, D. (1987) 'The "Human Face" of Destabilization: The War in Mozambique', *Review of African Political Economy*, 14 (40): 65–75.

Campbell, D. (1992) *Writing Security: United States' Foreign Policy and the Politics of Identity,* Manchester: Manchester University Press.

—— (1998) 'Why Fight: Humanitarianism, Principles, and Post-structuralism', *Millennium: Journal of International Studies,* 27 (3): 497–521.

—— (1999) 'The Deterritorialization of Responsibility: Levinas, Derrida, and Ethics after the End of Philosophy', in D. Campbell and M. J. Shapiro (eds) *Rethinking Ethics and World Politics*, Minneapolis: University of Minnesota Press, 25-56.

Campbell, K. (2003) 'Antiwar Protesters in a PR Fix', *Christian Science Monitor,* 2 April.

Cardoso, C. (1987) 'A Country Without Coups d'Etat', in K. Danielson (ed.) *Mozambique!*, Stockholm: The Culture House, 10–14.

Carlson, L. (2003) ' "The WTO Kills Farmers", In Memory of Lee Kyung Hae', Online. Available HTTP: <http://www.mindfully.org/WTO/2003/Lee-Kyung-Hae-WTO11sep03.htm> (accessed 24 September 2003).

Carnoy, M. (1984) *The State and Political Theory*, Princeton, NJ: Princeton University Press.

Carr, D. (2003) 'White House Listens when Weekly Speaks', *New York Times*, 11 March.

Carte Blanche (2003) 'Fight for Justice: Carlos Cardoso Murder Trial', 2 February. Online. Available HTTP: <http://www.mnet.co.za/CarteBlanche/Display/Display.asp?Id=2156> (accessed 24 April 2004).

Case, C. M. (1923) *Nonviolent Coercion: A Study in Methods of Social Pressure*, New York: Century.

Castel-Branco, C., Cramer, C. and Hailu, D. (2001) *Privatization and Economic Strategy in Mozambique*, Discussion Paper No. 2001/64, World Institute for Development Economics Research, United Nations University. Online. Available HTTP: <http://www.wider.unu.edu/publications/dps/dp2001-64.pdf> (accessed 24 April 2004).

Chefo, C. (2003) 'Cultura da Pobreza: Um Estudo da Lixeira do Hulene na Cidade de Maputo', Unpublished thesis (Tese de licenciatura), UFICS, Universidade Eduardo Mondlane.

Chesters, G. (2003) 'Shape Shifting: Civil Society, Complexity and Social Movements', *Anarchist Studies*, 11: 42–65.

Chin, C. B. N. and Mittelman, J. H. (2000) 'Conceptualizing Resistance to Globalization', in B. K. Gills (ed.) *Globalization and the Politics of Resistance*, Basingstoke: Palgrave, 29–45.

Chinoy, I. and Kaiser, R. (1999) 'Decades of Contributions to Conservatism', *Washington Post*, 2 May.

Churchill, W., Ryan, M. and Mead, E. (1998) *Pacifism as Pathology: Reflections on the Role of Armed Struggle in North America*, Winnipeg: Arbeiter Ring Publishing.

Ciment, J. (1997) *Angola and Mozambique: Postcolonial Wars in Southern Africa*, New York: Facts on File.

Ciria-Cruz, R. (2003) 'Peace Movement Crossroad', *Pacific News Service,* 10 April.

Cleaver, H. (1998) 'The Zapatistas and the Electronic Fabric of Struggle'. in J. Holloway and E. Pelaez (eds) *Zapatista: Reinventing Revolution in Mexico,* London: Pluto Press, 81–103.

—— (2003) 'Zapatistas in Cyberspace: A Guide to Analysis and Resources'. Online. Available HTTP: <http://www.eco.utexas.edu/faculty/Cleaver/zapsincyber.html> (accessed 12 March 2004).

Cliff, J. and Noormahomed, A. R. (1988) 'South African Destabilization and Health in Mozambique', *Review of African Political Economy,* 15 (42): 76–80.

Cockburn, A., St Clair, J. and Sekula, A. (2000) *Five Days that Shook the World: Seattle and Beyond,* London: Verso.

Cohen, J. (1982) 'Between Crisis Management and Social Movements: The Place of Institutional Reform', *Telos,* 52: 21–40.

Cohen, J. and Arato, A. (1992) *Civil Society and Political Theory,* Cambridge, MA: MIT Press.

Cohen, R. (2003) 'Bush, the Bad Guy', *Washington Post,* 28 January.

Colaço, J. C. (2001) 'Lixeiros da Cidade de Maputo', *Estudos Moçambicanos,* 18: 25–74.

Colás, A. (2002) *International Civil Society: Social Movements in World Politics,* Cambridge: Polity Press.

—— (2003) 'The Power of Representation: Democratic Politics and Global Governance', *Review of International Studies,* 29 (3): 97–118.

Coletivo Contra-a-Corrente (2000) 'We Will Not Go to The World Social Forum! And We Are Not Alone!'. Online. Available HTTP: <http://www.nadir.org/nadir/initiativ/agp/free/wsf/nowsf.htm> (accessed 15 December 2002).

Collier, A. (1994) 'Value, Rationality and the Environment', *Radical Philosophy,* 66: 3–9.

Collins, P. H. (2000) *Black Feminist Thought,* 2nd edition, London: Routledge.

Connell-Smith, G. (1971) *El Sistema Interamericano,* trans. N. Wolf, Mexico: Fondo de Cultura Económica; originally published as *The Inter-American System,* Oxford: University of Oxford Press, 1966.

Connolly, W. E. (1991a) *Identity/Difference: Democratic Negotiations of Political Paradox,* Ithaca, NY: Cornell University Press.

—— (1991b) 'Democracy and Territoriality', *Millennium: Journal of International Studies,* 20 (3): 463–4.

—— (1995) *The Ethos of Pluralization,* Minneapolis: University of Minnesota Press.

—— (2002) *Neuropolitics: Thinking, Culture, Speed,* Minneapolis: University of Minnesota Press.

Cookson, M. (n.d.) 'The Iron Fist Behind Profits', *Socialist Worker.* Online. Available HTTP: <http://www.socialistworker.co.uk/1768/sw176815.htm> (accessed 16 July 2003).

Couto, M. (2002) 'Pobres dos Nossos Ricos', *Savana,* 13 December.

—— (2003) 'Dente Careado em Boca de Leão', *Savana,* 22 January.

Cox, R. (1983) 'Gramsci, Hegemony, and International Relations', *Millennium: Journal of International Studies,* 12 (2): 162–75.

—— (1986) 'Social Forces, States and World Orders: Beyond International Relations Theory', in R. O. Keohane (ed.) *Neorealism and its Critics,* New York: Columbia University Press, 204–54.

—— (1987) *Production, Power and World Order: Social Forces in the Making of History,* New York: Columbia University Press.

—— (1997) 'Democracy in Hard Times: Economic Globalization and the Limits of Democracy', in A. McGrew (ed.) *The Transformation of Democracy? Globalization and Territorial Democracy,* Cambridge: Polity Press.

—— (1999) 'Civil Society at the Turn of the Millennium: Prospects for an Alternative World Order', *Review of International Studies,* 25 (1): 3–28.

Crass, C. (n.d.) 'Beyond the Whiteness – Global Capitalism and White Supremacy: Thoughts on Movement Building and Anti-Racist Organizing'. Online. Available HTTP: <http://www.tao.ca~colours/crass4.html> (accessed 2 December 2001).

CrimethInc. Workers' Collective (2001) *Days of War, Nights of Love: Crimethink for Beginners,* Atlanta: CrimethInc Free Press.

Cross, J. (2003) 'Anthropology and the Anarchists: Culture, Power, and Practice in Militant Anti-Capitalist Protests', *THEOMAI Journal, Society, Nature and Development Studies,* 7. Online. Available HTTP: <http://www.unq.edu.ar/revista-theomai/numero7/artjamiecross7.htm> (accessed 10 July 2003).

Cross, S. (2002) 'ATTAC Founder Offers Strategy to Fight Far-Right' (Interview with Ignacio Ramonet), *European Voice,* 6–11 June: 11.

Csordas, T. J. (1994) *Embodiment and Experience: The Existential Ground of Culture and Self,* Cambridge: Cambridge University Press.

Cuevas, J. R. (1998) 'Un Soldado por Familia', *La Jornada* supplement *Masiosare,* 25 January.

—— (2000) 'The Body as a Weapon for Civil Disobedience', trans. from Spanish by Irlandesa, La Jornada. Online. Available HTTP: <http://www.nadir.org/nadir/initiativ/agp/s26/praga/bianche.htm> (accessed 20 January 2004).

Curtis, M. (2003) *Web of Deceit: Britain's Real Role in the World,* London: Vintage.

Daalder, I. and Lindsay, J. (2003) 'Bush's Priority in Iraq is Not Democracy', *Financial Times,* 11 November.

Danaher, K. and Burbach, R. (eds) (2000) *Globalize This! The Battle Against the World Trade Organization and Corporate Rule,* Monroe, ME: Common Courage Press.

Danaher, K. and Marks, J. (2003) *Insurrection: The Citizen Challenge to Corporate Power,* London: Routledge.

Daniel, C. (2002) 'Hard Man who Sits at the Heart of US Foreign Policy', *Financial Times,* 19 December.

DAWN (Development Alternatives with Women for a New Era) (2002a) 'World Social Forum'. Online. Available HTTP: <http://www.dawn.org.fj/global/globalisation/socialforum.html> (accessed 12 December 2002).

—— (2002b) *Addressing the World Social Forum: A DAWN Supplement.* Online. Available HTTP: <http://www.dawn.org.fj/global/globalisation/socialforum.html> (12 December 2002).

de Bary, W. T., Hay, S., Weiler, R. and Yarrow, A. (1958) *Sources of Indian Tradition,* New York: Columbia University Press.

de Filippis, V. and Losson, C. (2000) 'Prague Submergée par la Rue', *Libération,* 27 September.

de la Grange, B. and Rico, B. (1997) *Marcos: La Genial Impostura,* Mexico: Aguilar.

de Vos, J. (1998) 'El Lacandon: Una Introduccion Historica' in J. P. Viquiera and M. H. Ruiz (eds) *Chiapas: Los Rumbos de Otra Historia,* Mexico: UNAM, 331–61.

Debord, G. (1983) *Society of the Spectacle,* Detroit: Black and Red.

'Declaration of a Group of Intellectuals in Porto Alegre' (2002). Online. Available HTTP: <http://www.forumsocialmundial.org.br/dinamic/eng_declara_grupo_in.asp> (accessed 9 December 2002).

Deibert, R. J. (2000) 'International Plug 'n Play? Citizen Activism, the Internet and Global Public Policy', *International Studies Perspectives,* 1 (3): 255–72.

Deleuze, G. and Guattari, F. (1988 [1980]) *A Thousand Plateaus. Capitalism and Schizophrenia,* Vol. 2, London: Athlone Press.

Della Porta, D., Kriesi, H. and Rucht, D. (eds) (1999) *Social Movements in a Globalizing World,* Basingstoke: Palgrave Macmillan.

Depelchin, J. (1981) 'The Transformations of the Petty-Bourgeoisie and the State in Post-Colonial Zaire', *Review of African Political Economy,* 8 (22): 20–41.

—— (1999) 'Braudel and African History: Dismantling or Reproducing the Colonial/Capital Paradigm?', in W. G. Martin and M. O. West (eds) *Out of One, Many Africas: Reconstructing the Study and Meaning of Africa,* Urbana and Chicago: University of Illinois Press, 157–74.

Der Derian, J. and Shapiro, M. J. (eds) (1989) *International/Intertextual Relations: Postmodern Readings of World Politics,* New York: Lexington Books.

Destroy DSEi (2003) Destroy DSEi home page. Online. Available HTTP: <http://www.destroydsei.org/index.htm> (accessed 18 September 2003).

Devetak, R. (2001) 'Critical Theory', in S. Burchill, R. Devetak, A. Linklater, M. Paterson, C. Reus-Smit and J. True, *Theories of International Relations,* 2nd edition, Basingstoke: Palgrave, 155–80.

Diamond, S. (1995) *Roads to Dominion: Right-Wing Movements and Political Power in the US,* New York: Guilford.

Diani, M. (2000) 'The Concept of Social Movement', in K. Nash (ed.) *Readings in Contemporary Political Sociology,* Oxford: Blackwell, 155–75.

Diaz, C. T. (1995) *La Rebelion de las Canadas,* Mexico: Cal y Arena.

Dixon, C. (n.d.) 'Finding Hope after Seattle: Rethinking Radical Activism and Building a Movement'. Online. Available HTTP: <http:www.zmag.org/dixonseattle.htm> (accessed 1 February 2001).

Do or Die (2003) 'Voices from the Ecological Resistance', *Do or Die* No. 10, Brighton.

Documentos y Comunicados del EZLN, Vol. 2 (1995) Mexico: Era.

Domingo, P. (1999) 'Rule of Law, Citizenship and Access to Justice in Mexico', *Mexican Studies/Estudios Mexicanos,* 15 (1): 151–91.

Donnelly, T. (principal author) (2000) *Rebuilding America's Defenses: Strategy, Forces and Resources For a New Century, a report of The Project for the New American Century.* Online. Available HTTP: <http://www.newamericancentury.org/RebuildingAmericasDefenses.pdf> (accessed 2 April 2003).

Drew, E. (2003) 'The Neocons in Power', *New York Review of Books,* 12 June. Online. Available HTTP: <http://www.nybooks.com/articles16378> (accessed 4 August 2003).

Dreyfuss, R. (2002) 'Tinker, Banker, Neocon, Spy', *The American Prospect,* 18 November. Online. Available HTTP: <http://www.prospect.org/print-friendly/print/v13/21/dreyfuss-r.html> (accessed 4 August 2003).

—— (2003a) 'The Thirty-Year Itch', *Mother Jones,* March 1. Online. Available HTTP: <http://www.motherjones.com/news/feature/2003/10/ma_273_01.html> (accessed 13 March 2003).

—— (2003b) 'Just the Beginning: Is Iraq the Opening Salvo in a War to Remake the World?', *The American Prospect*, 1 April. Online. Available HTTP: <http://www.prospect.org/print-friendly/print/v14/4/dreyfuss-r.html> (accessed 3 May 2003).

Drury, J. (2003) 'What Critical Psychology Can('t) Do for the "Anti-Capitalist Movement"', *Annual Review of Critical Psychology*, 3: 90–113.

Duran de Huerta, M. (1994) *Yo Marcos*, Mexico: Ediciones del Milenio.

Duran de Huerta, M. and Boldrini, M. (1998) *Acteal, Navidad en el Infierno*, Mexico: Times Editores.

Dryzek, J. S. (2000) *Deliberative Democracy and Beyond: Liberals, Critics, Contestations*, Oxford: Oxford University Press.

Eakin, E. (2001) 'On the Lookout for Patriotic Incorrectness', *New York Times*, 24 November.

Egan, C. and Robidoux, M. (2001) 'Women', in E. Bircham and J. Charlton (eds) *Anti-Capitalism: A Guide to the Movement*, London: Bookmarks, 81–91.

Ehrenreich, B. (2003) 'Another World is Possible', *In These Times*, 31 January.

Epstein, B. (2001) 'Anarchism and the Anti-Globalization Movement', *Monthly Review*, 53 (4). Online. Available HTTP: <http://www.monthlyreview.org/0901epstein.htm> (accessed 14 October 2003).

Eschle, C. (2001) *Global Democracy, Social Movements, and Feminism*, Boulder, CO: Westview Press.

—— (2004) 'Feminist Studies of Globalisation: Beyond Gender, Beyond Economism?', *Global Society*, 18 (2): 97–125.

—— (2005) ' "Skeleton Women": Feminism and the Anti-Globalisation Movement', *Signs: Journal of Women in Culture and Society*, 30 (3).

Eschle, C. and Stammers, N. (2004) 'Taking Part: Social Movements, INGOs and Global Change', *Alternatives: Global Local Political*, 29 (3): 335–74.

Esteva, G. and Prakash, M. S. (1998) *Grassroots Post-Modernism: Remaking the Soil of Cultures*, London: Zed Books.

Ética Moçambique (2001) *Estudo Sobre Corrupção – Moçambique 2001*, Maputo: Ética Moçambique/Afrisurvey.

Everest, L. (2004) *Oil, Power and Empire*, Monroe, ME: Common Courage Press.

Falk, R. (1995) *On Humane Governance*, Cambridge, Polity Press.

—— (1999) *Predatory Globalization*, Cambridge: Polity Press.

—— (2002) 'The New Bush Doctrine', *The Nation*, 15 July. Online. Available HTTP: <http://www.thenation.com/issue.mhtml?i=20020715> (accessed 6 March 2003).

Fanon, F. (1967 [1963]) *The Wretched of the Earth*, London: Penguin.

—— (1985) *Les Damnés de la Terre*, Paris: Édition de la Découverte.

Farhi, P. (2003) 'For Broadcast Media, Patriotism Pays', *Washington Post*, 28 March.

Farley, M. and McManus, D. (2002) 'To Some, Real Threat is US', *Los Angeles Times*, 30 October.

Fauvet, P. (2000) 'Obituary: Carlos Cardoso 1951–2000', Agência de Informacão de Moçambique newscast, 23 November.

Fauvet, P. and Mosse, M. (2003) *Carlos Cardoso: Telling the Truth in Mozambique*, Cape Town: Double Storey Books.

Feminist International Network of Resistance to Reproductive and Genetic Engineering (FINRRAGE) (1993) 'A Critical Appraisal of the Women's Declaration on Population Policies', *WGNRR Newsletter*, 42: 28.

Feminist Review (2002) Special Issue on Globalisation, 70.

Fernández-Kelly, M. P. (1983) *For We Are Sold, I and My People: Women and Industry on Mexico's Northern Frontier*, Albany, NY: SUNY Press.

First Summit of the Americas. Declaration of Miami (1994) 'Partnership for Development and Prosperity: Democracy, Free Trade and Sustainable Development'. Online. Available HTTP: <http://www.ftaa-alca.org/Summits/Miami/declara_e.asp> (accessed 30 April 2004).

Fisher, W. F. and Ponniah, T. (eds) (2003) *Another World Is Possible: Popular Alternatives to Globalization at the World Social Forum*, London: Zed Books.

Ford, P. (2002) 'Is America the "Good Guy"? Many Now say "No" ', *Christian Science Monitor*, 11 September.

—— (2003) 'Antiwar Movement Awakens Over Iraq', *Christian Science Monitor*, 18 February.

Foreign Policy in Focus (2004) Foreign Policy in Focus home page. Online. Available HTTP: <http://www.foreignpolicy-infocus.org/> (accessed 12 March 2004).

Forrester, V. (1996) *L'Horreur Économique*, Paris: Fayard.

—— (1999) *The Economic Horror*, Oxford: Blackwell.

Foucault, M. (1980) *Power/Knowledge: Selected Interviews and Other Writings 1972–1977*, ed. C. Gordon, New York: Pantheon.

—— (1991) 'Politics and the Study of Discourse', in G. Burchill, C. Gorden and P. Miller (eds) *The Foucault Effect: Studies in Governmentality*, Chicago: University of Chicago Press, 53–72.

—— (1998 [1976]) *The Will to Knowledge: The History of Sexuality*, Vol. 1, London: Penguin.

—— (2001 [1965]) *Madness and Civilisation*, London: Routledge.

Frank (2003) 'Frank', '2000 Anarchists Go on Rampage in San Francisco'. Online. Available HTTP: <http://indymedia.org/news/2003/01/1562024_comment.php#1567370> (accessed 19 January 2003).

Fraser, N. (1995) 'What's Critical about Critical Theory?', in J. Meehan (ed.) *Feminists Read Habermas: Gendering the Subject of Discourse*, London: Routledge, 21–55.

—— (1997) *Justice Interruptus: Critical Reflections on the Post-Socialist Condition*, London: Routledge.

Fray Bartolome de Las Casas Centre for Human Rights (1998) *Camino a la Masacre*, Mexico: Centro de Derechos Humanos Fray Bartolome de las Casas A. C.

Freedland, J. (1999) 'Powerless People', *Guardian*, 12 February.

Freeman, A. (2003) 'Daggers Out as Davos Turns on US', *Globe and Mail*, 25 January.

Freire, P. (2000) *Pedagogy of Freedom: Ethics, Democracy, and Civic Courage*, Lanham, MD: Rowman and Littlefield.

Friedman, T. (1999) *The Lexis and the Olive Tree*, New York: Farrar, Straus and Giroux.

Fromm, E. (2001) *Fear of Freedom*, London: Routledge.

GABRIELA (1993) 'Resolution by GABRIELA on Women's Voices 94', *WGNRR Newsletter*, 43: 8.

Gaddis, J. (2002) 'A Grand Strategy of Transformation', *Foreign Policy*, 133: 50–7.

Galtung, J. (1969) 'Violence, Peace, and Peace Research', *Journal of Peace Studies*, 6: 167–91.

Gandhi, M. (1958) *Satyagraha*, trans. V. G. Desai, Ahmedabad: Navajivan.

—— (1984 [1938]) *Hind Swaraj or Indian Home Rule*, trans. M. Desai, Ahmedabad: Navajivan.

Garafoli, J. (2003) 'War Foes Hear Gripes, Change Tactics', *San Francisco Chronicle*, 30 March.

Gastrow, P. and Mosse, M. (2002) 'Mozambique: Threats Posed by the Penetration of Criminal Networks', Paper presented at International Security Studies regional seminar, 'Organised Crime, Corruption and Governance in the SADC Region', Pretoria (18–19 April). Online. Available HTTP: <http://www.mol.co.mz/analise/crimes/mosse01.html> (accessed 24 April 2004).

George, J. (1994) *Discourses of Global Politics: A Critical (Re)Introduction to International Relations*, Boulder, CO: Lynne Rienner.

George, S. (2001) *ATTAC: Remettre l'OMC à sa Place*. Paris: Mille et Une Nuits.

—— (2002) 'Another World is Possible', *The Nation*, 9 January.

George, S. and Wolf, M. (2002) *Pour & Contre: La Mondialisation Libérale*, Paris: Grasset & Fasquelle.

Germain, R. and Kenny, M. (1998) 'Engaging Gramsci: International Relations Theory and the New Gramscians', *Review of International Studies*, 24 (1): 3–21.

Germino, D. (1990) *Antonio Gramsci: Architect of a New Politics*, Baton Rouge: Louisiana State University Press.

Gill, S. (1993) *Gramsci, Historical Materialism and International Relations*, Cambridge: Cambridge University Press.

—— (1995) 'Globalization, Market Civilisation, and Disciplinary Neoliberalism', *Millennium: Journal of International Studies*, 24 (3): 399–423.

—— (2000) 'Toward a Postmodern Prince? The Battle in Seattle as a Moment in the New Politics of Globalisation', *Millennium: Journal of International Studies*, 29 (1): 131–41.

—— (2003) *Power and Resistance in the New World Order*, Basingstoke: Palgrave Macmillan.

Gills, B. K. (2000a) 'Introduction', in B. K. Gills (ed.) *Globalization and the Politics of Resistance*, Basingstoke: Palgrave Macmillan, 3–11.

—— (ed.) (2000b) *Globalization and the Politics of Resistance*, Basingstoke: Palgrave Macmillan.

Gilly, A., Ginzburg, C. and Subcomandante Marcos (1995) *Discusion Sobre la Historia*, Mexico: Taurus.

Gilpin, R. (1987) *Political Economy of International Relations*, Princeton, NJ: Princeton University Press.

Giugale, M., Lafourcade, O. and Nguyen, V. (2001) *Mexico: A Comprehensive Agenda for the New Era*, Washington, DC: World Bank.

Glasius, M. and Kaldor, M. (2002) 'The State of Civil Society: Before and After September 11', in M. Glasius, M. Kaldor and H. Anheier (eds) *Global Civil Society 2002*, Oxford: Oxford University Press.

Glasius, M., Kaldor, M. and Anheier, H. (eds) (2002) *Global Civil Society 2002*, Oxford: Oxford University Press.

Globalise Resistance (2001) 'We're Going to Genoa', *Resist: Official Zine of Globalise Resistance*, April: 4.

—— (2002a) 'What Globalise Resistance Stands For'. Online. Available HTTP: <http://www.resist.org/about/standfor.html> (accessed 31 January 2003).

—— (2002b) 'Why Not Join the Resistance?', *Resist: Official Zine of Globalise Resistance*, 7: 8.

—— (2002c) 'Next Stop Florence', *Resist: Official Zine of Globalise Resistance*, 8: 4–5.

Goldberg, M. (2002) 'Mau-mauing the Middle East', *Salon*, 30 September.
—— (2003a) 'New York State of Mind', *Salon*, 16 February.
—— (2003b) 'Rage or Reason', *Salon*, 27 March.
Golding, S. (1992) *Gramsci's Democratic Theory: Contributions to a Post-Liberal Democracy*, Toronto: University of Toronto Press.
González, S. (2002) *Huesos en el Desierto*, Barcelona: Anagrama.
Gosner, K. and Ouweneel, A. (eds) (1996) *Indigenous Revolts in Chiapas and the Andean Highlands*, Amsterdam: CEDLA.
Gossen, G. (1996) 'Who is the Comandante of Subcomandante Marcos?', in K. Gosner and A. Ouweneel (eds) *Indigenous Revolts in Chiapas and the Andean Highlands*, Amsterdam: CEDLA, 107–20.
Government of Mozambique (GOM) (2001) *Action Plan for the Reduction of Absolute Poverty 2001–2005*, Maputo. Online. Available HTTP: <http://poverty.worldbank.org/files/Mozambique_PRSP.pdf> (accessed 24 April 2004).
Gowan, P. (1999) *The Global Gamble: Washington's Faustian Bid for World Dominance*, London: Verso Books.
Graeber, D. (2002) 'The New Anarchists', *New Left Review*, 13: 61–73.
Gramsci, A. (1971) *Selections from the Prison Notebooks of Antonio Gramsci*, trans. and ed. G. Nowell-Smith and Q. Hoare, New York: International Publishers.
Gregg, R. B. (1934) *The Power of Nonviolence*, Philadelphia: J.B. Lippincott.
Grzybowski, C. (2002) 'Is a More Feminine World Possible?'. Online. Available HTTP: <http://www.dawn.org.fj/global/globalisation/socialforum.html> (accessed 12 December 2002).
Guardian (2003) 'BAE Faces Corruption Claims Around World', 14 June.
Guidry, J. A., Kennedy, M. D. and Zald, M. N. (eds) (2000) *Globalizations and Social Movements: Culture, Power, and the Transnational Public Sphere*, Ann Arbor: University of Michigan Press.
Guillermoprieto, A. (2003) 'Letter from Mexico. A Hundred Women. Why has a Decade-Long String of Murders Gone Unsolved?', *New Yorker*, 29 September: 82–93.
Habermas, J. (1998) *Die Postnationale Konstellation: Politische Essays*, Frankfurt: Suhrkamp.
Hacking, I. (1982) 'Language, Truth and Reason', in M. Hollis and S. Lukes (eds) *Rationality and Relativism*, Oxford: Basil Blackwell, 48–66.
Halliday, F. (2000a) 'Getting Real About Seattle', *Millennium: Journal of International Studies*, 29 (1): 123–9.
—— (2000b) 'Culture and International Relations: A New Reductionism?', in M. Ebata and B. Neufeld (eds) *Confronting the Political in International Relations*, Basingstoke: Palgrave, 47–67.
—— (2002) 'The Pertinence of Imperialism', in M. Rupert and H. Smith (eds) *Historical Materialism and Globalization*, London: Routledge, 75–89.
Hamel, P., Lustiger-Thaler, H., Roseneil, S. and Pieterse, J. N. (eds.) (2001) *Globalization and Social Movements*, Basingstoke: Palgrave.
Hanlon, J. (2002) 'Bank Corruption Becomes Site of Struggle in Mozambique', *Review of African Political Economy*, 29 (91): 53–72.
Harding, J. (2002) 'A New Era of Protest', *Financial Times*, 2 February.
Hardt, M. and Negri, A. (2000) *Empire*, Cambridge, MA: Harvard University Press.

Harvey, D. (1996) *Justice, Nature and the Geography of Difference*, Oxford: Blackwell.

Harvey, N. (1998) *The Chiapas Rebellion: The Struggle for Land and Democracy*, Durham, NC, and London: Duke University Press.

—— (1999) 'Balas de Azucar', *La Jornada*, 29 August.

Healy, P. (2001) 'On Campus: Conservatives Denounce Dissent', *Boston Globe*, 13 November.

Held, D. (ed.) (1995) *Democracy and the Global Order: From the Modern State to Cosmopolitan Governance*, Cambridge: Polity Press.

—— (2002) *Theory, Culture and Society*, Special Issue on *Cosmopolis*, 19 (1–2).

Held, D. and McGrew, A. (2002) *Globalization/Anti-Globalization*, Cambridge: Polity Press.

Held, D., McGrew, A., Goldblatt, D. and Perraton, J. (1999) *Global Transformations: Politics, Economics, Culture*, Cambridge: Polity Press.

Hemispheric Social Alliance (HSA) (1999) 'Building a Hemispheric Social Alliance in the Americas. Draft Agenda'. Online. Available HTTP: <http://www.webnet/comfront/cfhems.htm> (accessed 27 April 2004).

—— (2002) 'Alternatives for the Americas'. Online. Downloaded as PDF file from: <http://www.art-us.org/> (accessed 27 April 2004).

Hernandez-Castillo, R. A. (1994) 'Reinventing Tradition: The Women's Law', in *Akwe:kon Journal*, 11 (2): 67–70.

—— (1998) 'De la Sierra a la Selva: Identidades Etnicas y Religiosas en la Frontera Sur', in J. P. Viquiera and M. H. Ruiz (eds) *Chiapas: Los Rumbos de Otra Historia*, Mexico: UNAM, 407–23.

Hersh, S. (2003) 'Lunch with the Chairman', *The New Yorker*, 17 March. Online. Available HTTP: <http://www.newyorker.com/printable/?fact/030317fa_fact> (accessed 23 March 2003).

Higgins, N. (2000) 'The Zapatista Uprising and the Poetics of Cultural Resistance', *Alternatives*, Special Issue on Poetic World Politics, 25 (3): 359–74.

—— (2001) 'Mexico's Stalled Peace Process: Prospects and Challenges', *International Affairs*, 77 (4): 885–903.

—— (2004) *Understanding the Chiapas Rebellion: Modernist Visions and the Invisible Indian*, Austin: University of Texas Press.

Higgins, N. and Duran de Huerta, M. (1999) 'An Interview with Subcomandante Insurgente Marcos, Spokesperson and Military Commander of the Zapatista National Liberation Army (EZLN)', *International Affairs*, 75 (2): 269–79.

Higgott, R. (2003) 'American Unilateralism, Foreign Economic Policy and the "Securitisation" of Globalisation', *CSGR Working Paper*, No. 124/03. Online. Available HTTP: <http://www.warwick.ac.uk/fac/soc/CSGR/abwp12403.html> (accessed 23 September 2003).

Hoffman, M. (1987) 'Critical Theory and the Inter-Paradigm Debate', *Millennium: Journal of International Studies*, 16 (2): 231–49.

Holub, R. (1992) *Antonio Gramsci: Beyond Marxism and Postmodernism*, London: Routledge.

Horsey, J. (2003) 'Canadian Peace Movement Gains Momentum', *Canadian Press Newswire*, 18 January.

Houtart, F. and Polet, F. (eds) (2001) *The Other Davos: The Globalization of Resistance to the World Economic System*, London: Zed Books.

Hoyles, A. (2003) 'Seen and Not Heard', *Resist: Official Zine of Globalise Resistance*, 9: 4.

Human Rights Watch (1999) *Systemic Injustice: Torture, 'Disappearance', and Extra-judicial Execution in Mexico*, New York: Human Rights Watch.

Hunt, M. (1987) *Ideology and US Foreign Policy*, New Haven, CT: Yale University Press.

Ikenberry, J. (2002) 'America's Imperial Ambition', *Foreign Affairs,* 81: 44–60.

Indymedia (2002) *Genoa Red Zone: 'Whatever Force Necessary'* (video), London: Indymedia.

—— (2004) 'Independent Media Centre', international gateway. Online. Available HTTP: <http://www.indymedia.org/or/index.shtml> (accessed 12 March 2004).

Infoshop (2003) 'Black Blocs for Dummies'. Online. Available HTTP: <http://www.infoshop.org/blackbloc.html> (accessed 7 October 2003).

International Confederation of Free Trade Unions (ICFTU) (2004) International Confederation of Free Trade Unions home page. Online. Available HTTP: <http://www.icftu.org/> (accessed 4 May 2004).

International Women's Health Coalition (IWHC) and Cidadania, Estudios, Pesquisa, Informacao, Acao (CEPIA) (1994) 'Appendix IV of the Proceedings of the "Reproductive Health and Justice" International Women's Health Conference', Cairo, 24–28 January. Rio, Brazil. Unpublished document.

IRIN News (2002), 'Focus on Mozambique: Poverty and Maternal Mortality'. Online. Available HTTP: <http://malawihere.com/viewnews.asp?id=744&recnum=1331&catid=> (accessed 24 April 2004).

Iyer, R. N. (1973) *The Moral and Political Thought of Mahatma Gandhi*, New York: Oxford University Press.

Jahan, R. (1995) *The Elusive Agenda: Mainstreaming Women in Development*, London: Zed Books.

Jazz (2001) 'The Tracks of our Tears', in Anon. (ed.) *On Fire*, London: One Off Press, 80–100.

Jensen, D. (2000) *A Language Older Than Words*, New York: Souvenir Press.

Johnson, B. (1999) 'Aimless, Feckless, Hopeless and Legless in Seattle', *Daily Telegraph*, 12 February.

Johnson, D. (2000) 'The Dwarfs Who Posture on the Shoulders of Giants', *Daily Telegraph*, 28 September.

Johnson, J. (1993) *Latin America in Caricature,* reprinted edition, Austin: University of Texas Press.

Judis, J. (2003) 'Over a Barrel: Who will Control Iraq's Oil?', *The New Republic,* 20 January: 20–3.

Kaiser, R. and Chinoy, I. (1999) 'Scaife: Funding Father of the Right', *Washington Post*, 2 May.

Kaldor, M. (2000) ' "Civilising" Globalisation: The Implications of the "Battle" for Seattle', *Millennium: Journal of International Studies,* 29 (1): 105–14.

Kaplan, E. (2003) 'A Hundred Peace Movements Bloom', *The Nation*, 6 January. Online. Available HTTP: <http://www.thenation.com/doc.mhtml?i=20030106&s=Kaplan> (accessed 6 March 2003).

Keller, B. (2002) 'The Sunshine Warrior', *New York Times Magazine*, 23 September.

Kelly, R. M., Bayes, J. H., Hawkesworth, M. and Young B. (eds) (2001) *Gender, Globalization, and Democratization*, Lanham, MD: Rowman and Littlefield.

Keysers, L. (1993) 'Women and Population Questions: From Rio to Cairo and Beyond', *Vena Journal,* 5 (2): 43–52.

Kiely, R. (2000) 'Globalization: From Domination to Resistance', *Third World Quarterly*, 21 (6): 1059–70.

King, M. L. (1986 [1958]) *Stride Toward Freedom*, San Francisco: Harper.

Kingsnorth, P. (2003) *One No, Many Yeses: A Journey to the Heart of the Global Resistance Movement*, London: Free Press.

Klare, M. (2003a) 'The Coming War with Iraq: Deciphering the Bush Administration's Motives', *Foreign Policy in Focus*, 16 January. Online. Available HTTP: <http://www.fpif.org/commentary/2003/0301warreasons.html> (accessed 3 March 2003).

—— (2003b) 'Blood for Oil: The Bush–Cheney Energy Strategy', in L. Panitch and C. Leys (eds) *Socialist Register 2004: The New Imperial Challenge*, London: Merlin: 166–85.

Klausmann, U., Meinzerin, M. and Kuhn, G. (1997) *Women Pirates and the Politics of the Jolly Roger*, London: Black Rose Press.

Klein, N. (2001) *No Logo*, London: Flamingo.

—— (2002) *Fences and Windows: Dispatches from the Front Lines of the Globalization Debate*, London: Flamingo.

—— (2003) 'Cut the Strings', *Guardian*, 1 February. Online. Available HTTP: <http://www.guardian.co.uk/Print/0,3858,4596386,00.html> (accessed 19 February 2003).

Knapp, D. (1999) 'Activists to WTO: Put People Over Profits'. Online. Available HTTP: <http://www.cnn.com/US/9911/29/wto.seattle.02/> (accessed 14 April 2004).

Koch, C. (2004) *The Day the World Said No to War: 02/15*, Edinburgh: AK Press.

Kolko, G. (1988) *Confronting the Third World*, New York: Pantheon.

Korbin, S. J. (1998) 'The MAI and the Clash of Globalizations', *Foreign Policy*, 112: 97–109.

Krause, J. and Remnick, N. (eds) (1996) *Identities in International Relations*, Basingstoke: Macmillan.

Kristol, W. and Kagan, R. (2000) 'Introduction: National Interest and Global Responsibility', in R. Kagan and W. Kristol (eds) *Present Dangers*, San Francisco: Encounter Books, 2–24.

La Feber (1989) *The American Age*, New York: Norton.

Lacher, H. (2002) 'Making Sense of the International System: The Promises and Pitfalls of the Newest Marxist Theories of International Relations', in M. Rupert and H. Smith (eds) *Historical Materialism and Globalization*, London: Routledge, 147–64.

Laing, R. D. (1967) *The Politics of Experience and The Bird of Paradise*, London: Penguin Books.

Landler, M. (2003) 'Meet the New Davos Man', *New York Times*, 2 February.

Landy, M. (1986) 'Culture and Politics in the Work of Antonio Gramsci', *Boundary 2*, 14 (3): 49–70.

Laniel, L. (2001) 'Drugs in Southern Africa: Business as Usual', *International Social Science Journal*, 53 (169): 407–14.

Lao Tsu (1972) *Tao te Ching*, new trans. G.-F. Feng and J. English, London: Wildwood House.

Lapid, Y. (1989) 'The Third Debate: on the Prospects of International Theory in a Post-Positivist Era', *International Studies Quarterly*, 33 (3): 235–54.

Lapid, Y. and Kratchowil, F. (eds) (1995) *The Return of Culture and Identity in International Relations Theory*, Boulder, CO: Lynne Rienner.

Laurence, J. (2003) 'Fears of Self-Harm Prompt Drug Curb for Young', *Independent*, 20 September.

Laxter, G. (2001) 'The Movement That Dare Not Speak Its Name: The Return of Left Nationalism/Internationalism', *Alternatives*, 26:1–32.

Lazreg, M. (2002) 'Development: Feminist Theory's Cul-de-Sac', in K. Saunders (ed.) *Feminist Post-Development Thought: Rethinking Modernity, Post-Colonialism and Representation*, London: Zed Books.

Le Bot, Y. (1997) *Subcomandante Marcos: El Sueno Zapatista*, Barcelona: Plaza y Janes Editores.

LeBrun, A. (n.d.) *Gynocracy Song*, trans. M. William, intro. W. Landstreicher. Online. Available HTTP: <http://www.omnipresence.mahost.org/annie.htm> (accessed 10 December 2003).

Lee, J. (2003) 'How the Protesters Mobilized', *New York Times*, 23 February.

Lee, T. (2003) 'Fairford Security', Reclaim the Bases! Online posting. Available email: email@reclaimthebases.org.uk (7 March).

Le Guin, U. (1974) *The Dispossessed*, London: Gollancz.

Lemann, N. (2002) 'The Next World Order', *The New Yorker*, 1 April. Online. Available HTTP: <http://www.newyorker.com/fact/content/?020401fa_FACT1> (accessed 1 October 2002).

Lenin, V. (1993 [1920]) *Left Wing Communism: An Infantile Disorder*, London: Bookmarks.

Levi, M. and Olson, D. (2000) 'The Battles for Seattle', *Politics and Society*, 28 (3) 309–23.

Levya-Solano, X. (1993) 'Lacandonia Babilonia en las postrimerias del siglo', *Ojarasca*, September: 23–8.

Lignes d'ATTAC (2001a) October, No. 14: 4.

—— (2001b) December, No. 16: 8.

Linklater, A. (1992) 'The Question of the Next Stage in International Relations Theory: A Critical-Theoretical Point of View', *Millennium: Journal of International Studies*, 21 (1): 77–98.

—— (1994) 'Dialogue, Dialectic, and Emancipation in International Relations at the End of the Post-war Age', *Millennium: Journal of International Studies*, 23 (1): 119–31.

—— (1996a) 'Citizenship and Sovereignty in the Post-Westphalian State', *European Journal of International Relations*, 2 (1): 77–103.

—— (1996b) 'The Achievements of Critical Theory', in S. Smith, K. Booth and M. Zalewski (eds) *International Theory: Positivism and Beyond*, Cambridge: Cambridge University Press, 279–98.

—— (1998) *The Transformation of Political Community*, Oxford: Polity Press.

Liscano, A. (1998) *Bolívar en Tres Perfiles*. México: Paradigma. Online. Available HTTP: <http://www.bolivar.ula.ve/cgi-win/be_alex.exe> (accessed 27 August 2002).

Lobe, J. (2002a) 'Hawks Deploy for Public Opinion War', Inter-Press Service, Washington, DC, 12 March.

—— (2002b) 'Neoconservatives Consolidate Control over US Mideast Policy', *Foreign Policy in Focus*, 6 December. Online. Available HTTP: <http://www.fpif.org/commentary/2002/0212abrams.html> (accessed 1 February 2003).

Maiguashca, B. (1994) 'The Transnational Indigenous Movement in a Changing World Order', in Y. Sakamoto (ed.) *Global Transformation: Challenges to the State System,* New York: United Nations University Press, 356–82.

Mann, J. (2004) 'The True Rationale? It's a Decade Old', *Washington Post,* 7 March.

Marcellus, O. (2003) 'Evaluation of the G8-Evian Mobilization ... And a Debate to be had on Violence', Caravan 99. Online posting. Available email: caravan99lists.riseup.net (2 August).

Marchand, M. (2003) 'Challenging Globalisation: Feminism and Resistance', *Review of International Studies,* 29 (3): 145–60.

Marchand, M. and Runyan, A. S. (eds) (2000) *Gender and Global Restructuring: Sightings, Sites, Resistances,* London: Routledge.

Marcos, Subcomandante Insurgente (1995) *Shadows of Tender Fury: The Letters and Communiques of Subcomandante Marcos and the Zapatista Army of National Liberation,* trans. L. Lopez, New York: Monthly Review Press.

—— (1997a) *La Historia de los Colores,* Mexico: Offset Industrial.

—— (1997b) 'The Fourth World War has Begun', *Le Monde Diplomatique,* September. Online. Available HTTP: <http://mondediplo.com/1997/09/marcos> (accessed December 2004).

—— (1998a) *Cuentos Para una Soledad Desvelada,* Mexico: Ediciones del Frente Zapatista de Liberacion Nacional.

—— (1998b) *La Historia de las Preguntas,* Mexico: Offset Industrial.

—— (1998c) *Relatos de El Viejo Antonio,* prologo de Armando Bartra, Mexico: Centro de Informacion y Analysis de Chiapas.

—— (1998d) 'Los Siete Arcoiris', in L. H. Navarro and R. V. Herrera (eds) *Acuerdos de San Andres,* Mexico: Era, 132–6.

—— (2001) *Our Word is our Weapon,* ed. J. Ponce de Leon, New York: Seven Stories Press.

—— (2003) 'The World: 7 Thoughts in May 2003', trans. Irlandesa. Online. Available HTTP: <http://iticwebarchives.ssrc.org/Z%20Mag/www.zmag.org/content/showarticle8a5e.html?SectionID=51&ItemID=3783> (accessed December 2003).

Marin, G. (2002) 'Beyond Porto Alegre...'. Online. Available HTTP: <http://www.forumsocialmundial.org.br/main.asp?id_menu=14_2_1&cd_language=2> (accessed 9 December 2002).

Marongiu, J.-B. (1995) 'Excès de Vitesse', *Libération,* 21 September.

Marshall, J. (1990) 'Structural Adjustment and Social Policy in Mozambique', *Review of African Political Economy,* 17 (47): 28–43.

Martin, G. (2003) 'Why is it all Quiet on the Western Front?', *The Big Issue in Scotland,* 20–26 March: 23–6.

Martin, J. and Neal, A. (2002) *Defending Civilization: How our Universities are Failing America,* Washington, DC: American Council of Trustees and Alumni.

Martinez, E. (2000) 'Where was the Color in Seattle? Looking for Reasons why the Great Battle was so White', *ColorLines,* 3 (1). Online. Available HTTP: <http://www.tao.ca/~colours/martinez.html> (accessed 2 February 2001).

Marx, K. (1867) Vol. 1, ch. 28, of *Capital,* Marx-Engels Internet Archive. Online. Available HTTP: <http://www.marxists.org/archive/marx/works/1867-c1/ch28.htm> (accessed 9 March 2004).

—— (1975 [1843]) *Karl Marx: Early Writings,* trans. R. Livingstone and G. Benton, New York: Vintage Books.

—— (1983 [1843]) 'A Correspondence of 1843: Letter to Arnold Ruge', in E. Kamenka (ed.) *The Portable Karl Marx*, London: Penguin, 92–6.

—— (1990 [1867]) *Capital (Volume 1)*, London: Penguin.

—— (1991 [1894]) *Capital (Volume 3)*, London: Penguin.

—— (1993 [1858]) *Grundrisse*, London: Penguin.

Maslow, A. (1973) *The Farther Reaches of Human Nature*, Harmondsworth: Penguin.

Massingue, M. (1996) 'Riding on a Crime Wave', *Southern Africa Political and Economic Monthly,* 10 (2): 12–13.

Matsinhe, V. (2000) 'Quando Tradição e Modernidade se Mesticizam nos Chapas da Rota Hulene-Xipamanine', in C. Serra (ed.) *Conflito e Mestiçagem*, Maputo: Livraria Universitária, 85–143.

May, E. (1993) *American Cold War Strategy: Interpreting NSC-68*, New York: St. Martin's Press.

McAllester Jones, M. (1991) *Gaston Bachelard, Subversive Humanist. Text and Readings*, Winsconsin, MA: The University of Wisconsin Press.

McCarthy, J. D. and Zald, M. N. (1977) 'Resource Mobilization and Social Movements: A Partial Theory', *American Journal of Sociology,* 82 (6): 1212–41.

McMurtry, J. (1999) *The Cancer Stage of Capitalism And its Cure*, London: Pluto Press.

—— (2002) *Value Wars: The Global Market Versus the Life Economy*, London: Pluto Press.

Media Transparency Project (2003a) 'Bradley Fighting Vehicle'. Online. Available HTTP: <http://www.meditransparency.org> (accessed 11 April 2003).

—— (2003b) 'The Lynde and Harry Bradley Foundation'. Online. Available HTTP: <http://www.meditransparency.org/funders/bradley_foundation.htm> (accessed 11 April 2003).

—— (2003c) 'John M. Olin Foundation, Inc.'. Online. Available HTTP: <http://www.meditransparency.org/funders/john_m_olin_foundation.htm> (accessed 11 April 2003).

—— (2003d) 'Scaife Foundations'. Online. Available HTTP: <http://www.meditransparency.org/funders/scaife_foundations.htm> (accessed 11 April 2003).

Melucci, A. (1989) *Nomads of the Present: Social Movements and Individual Needs in Contemporary Society*, London: Radius.

—— (1996a) *Challenging Codes: Collective Action in the Information Age,* Cambridge: Cambridge University Press.

—— (1996b) 'An End to Social Movements? A Reassessment from the 1990s', Paper presented at the Second European Conference on Social Movements (2–5 October), Vitoria-Gasteiz, Spain.

Mertes, T. (ed.) (2004) *A Movement of Movements: Is Another World Really Possible?*, London: Verso.

Meyer, M. K. and Prügl, E. (eds) (1999) *Gender Politics in Global Governance,* Lanham, MD: Rowman and Littlefield.

Milia, D. (2000) *Self Mutilation and Art Therapy: Violent Creation*, London: Jessica Kingsley.

Miller, A. (2001 [1979]) *The Drama of Being a Child*, trans. R. Ward, London: Virago.

Milstein, C. (2002) 'Another World is Possible ... But What Kind and Shaped by Whom?'. Online. Available HTTP: <http://www.nadir.org/nadir/initiativ/agp/free/wsf/another_world.htm> (accessed 15 December 2002).

Mindell, A. (1995) *Sitting in the Fire: Large Group Transformation Using Conflict and Diversity*, Portland, OR: Lao Tse Press.

Ministry of Planning and Finance (1998) *Understanding Poverty and Well-Being in Mozambique: The First National Assessment 1996–7*, Maputo: GOM, Eduardo Mondlane University, International Food Policy Research Institute.

Mittelman, J. H. (ed.) (1996) *Globalization: Critical Reflections*, Boulder, CO: Lynne Rienner.

—— (2000) *The Globalization Syndrome: Transformation and Resistance*, Princeton, NJ: Princeton University Press.

Mohanty, C. T. (2003) *Feminism Without Borders: Decolonizing Theory, Practicing Solidarity*, Durham, NC: Duke University Press.

Mohanty, C. T., Russo, A. and Torres, L. (eds) (1991) *Third World Women and the Politics of Feminism*, Bloomington: Indiana University Press.

Moldenhauer, O. (2002) 'Globalisierung von Unten: Attac – Eine Bewegung im Aufschwung', in C. Buchholz, A. Karrass, O. Nachtwey and I. Schmidt (eds) *Unsere Welt Ist Keine Ware: Handbuch fuer Globalisierungskritike*, Cologne: Kiepenheuer & Witsch.

Molyneux, M. (1985) 'Mobilization without Emancipation? Women's Interests, the State, and Revolution in Nicaragua', *Feminist Studies*, 11 (2): 377–89.

Monbiot, G. (2003) 'Stronger than Ever', *Guardian*, 28 January.

Monroe, J. (1823) 'Monroe Doctrine'. Avalon Project at Yale Law School. Online. Available HTTP: <http://www.yale.edu/lawweb/avalon/monroe.htm> (accessed 27 April 2004).

Montemayor, C. (1997) *Chiapas: La Rebelion Indigena de Mexico*, Mexico: Joaquin Mortiz.

Montgomery, D. (2002) 'The Peace Warriors', *Washington Post*, 10 December.

—— (2003) 'Seeking Symphony in Two Movements', *Washington Post*, 12 April.

Morris, B. (1994) *Anthropology of the Self: The Individual in Cultural Perspective*, London: Pluto Press.

Morton, A. (2000) 'Mexico, Neoliberal Restructuring and the EZLN: A Neo-Gramscian Analysis', in B. K. Gills (ed.) *Globalisation and the Politics of Resistance*, London: Macmillan, 255–79.

—— (2002) ' "La Resurrección del Maíz": Globalisation, Resistance and the Zapatistas', *Millennium: Journal of International Studies*, 31 (1): 27–54.

—— (2004) 'The Juggernaut or Jalopy of Globalisation? Reflections on the "Travelling Circus" of Anti-Globalisation Resistance', in H. Veltmeyer (ed.) *Development in an Era of Globalisation: The Macrodynamics of Social Change*, Aldershot: Ashgate.

Moser, C. O. N. (1993) *Gender Planning and Development: Theory, Practice and Training*, London: Routledge.

Mozambiquefile, Maputo: Agência de Informação de Moçambique, various editions.

Mueller, T. (2002) 'Gramsci, Counter-Hegemony and the Globalisation Critical Movement', *Studies in Social and Political Thought*, 6: 55–64.

—— (2004a) 'What is really under these cobblestones? Riots as political tools, and the case of Gothenburg 2001', *ephemera: theory and politics in organization*, 4 (2): 135–51.

—— (2004b) ' "Will the Destruction be Constructive?" Anticapitalist Riots in Search of the "Radical" ', Paper submitted for publication.

Murphy, B. (2003) 'Neoconservative Clout seen in US Iraq Policy', *Milwaukee Journal Sentinel*, 6 April.

Murphy, C. (1998) 'Understanding IR, Understanding Gramsci', *Review of International Studies*, 24 (3): 417–25.

Murphy, C. and Tooze, R. (eds) (1991) *The New International Political Economy*, Boulder, CO: Lynne Rienner.

Muzaffar, C. (1998) 'Cultures Under Attack: Key Issues', in M. Hassan (ed.) *A Pacific Peace: Issues and Responses*, Kuala Lumpur: ISIS Malaysia.

Naples, N. A. and Desai, M. (eds) (2002) *Women's Activism and Globalization; Linking Local Struggles and Transnational Politics*, London: Routledge.

Navon, E. (2001) 'The Third Debate Revisited', *Review of International Studies*, 27 (4): 611–25.

Negri, A. (1984) *Marx beyond Marx*, South Hadley, MA: Bergin and Garvey (1989, New York: Autonomedia).

—— (2002) 'Towards an Ontological Definition of the Multitude', *Multitudes*, 9, Online. Available HTTP: <http://multitudes.samizdat.net/spip/article.php3?id_article=269&var_recherche=negri> (accessed 20 February 2003).

Neufeld, M. (1995) *The Restructuring of International Relations Theory*, Cambridge: Cambridge University Press.

Newman, S. (2000) 'Anarchism and the Politics of Ressentiment', *Theory & Event*, 4 (3). Online. Available HTTP: <http://muse.jhu.edu/journals/theory_&_event/v004/4.3newman.html> (accessed 21 October 2003).

—— (2001) *From Bakunin to Lacan: Anti-Authoritarianism and the Dislocation of Power*, Lanham, MD: Lexington Books.

—— (2003) 'The Politics of Postanarchism', Institute for Anarchist Studies, 23 July. Online. Available HTTP: <http://www.anarchist-studies.org/article/articleprint/1/-1/1/> (accessed 23 November 2003).

New York Times (1992) 'A Rising Cost of Modernity: Depression', *New York Times*, 8 December.

Nhabinde, S. A. (1999) *Destabilização e Guerra Económica no Sistema Ferro-Portuário de Moçambique, 1980–1997*, Maputo: Livraria Universitária.

Nieves, E. (2003) 'Antiwar Groups Shifting Their Focus to Bush', *Washington Post*, 14 April.

Notes from Nowhere (eds) (2003) *We are Everywhere: The Irresistible Rise of Global Anti-Capitalism*, London: Verso.

Observatoire Geopolitique des Drogues (OGD) Report (2001) 'Part Five: Africa', in *Crime, Law and Social Change* 36: 241–84.

O'Brien, R., Goetz, A. M., Scholte, J. A. and Williams, M. (2000) *Contesting Global Governance: Multilateral Economic Institutions and Global Social Movements*, Cambridge: Cambridge University Press.

O'Connor, A. (2003) 'Antiwar Campaign Spreads Online', *Los Angeles Times*, 20 March.

Opel, A. and Pompper, D. (eds) (2003) *Representing Resistance: The Media, Civil Disobedience, and the Global Justice Movement*, Westport, CT: Greenwood Press.

Oren, I. (2003) *Our Enemies and Us*, Ithaca, NY: Cornell University Press.

Packer, G. (2003) 'Smart-Mobbing the War', *New York Times Magazine*, 9 March.

Paget, K. (1998) 'Lessons of Right-Wing Philanthropy', *The American Prospect*, 1 September. Online. Available HTTP: <http://www.prospect.org/print-friendly/print/V9/40/paget-k.html> (accessed 11 April 2003).

Palast, G. (2003) *The Best Democracy Money Can Buy: The Truth about Corporate Cons, Globalization, and High-Finance Fraudsters*, New York: Plume.

Panitch, L. and Gindin, S. (2003) 'Global Capitalism and American Empire', in L. Panitch and C. Leys (eds) *Socialist Register 2004: The New Imperial Challenge*, London: Merlin, 1–42.

Parrinder, G. (1977) *The Wisdom of the Early Buddhists*, London: Sheldon Press.

Pasha, M. K. and Blaney, D. L. (1998) 'Elusive Paradise: The Promise and Perils of Global Civil Society', *Alternatives*, 23 (4): 417–50.

Paulino, A. R. (2003) 'Criminalidade Global e Insegurança Local – O Caso de Moçambique', Paper presented at Colóquio Internacional: Direito e Justiça no Século XXI, Universidade de Coimbra (29–31 May).

Payutto, Ven. P.A. (1994) *Buddhist Economics: A Middle Way for the Market Place*, Bangkok: Buddhadhamma Foundation.

People for the American Way (1996) *Buying a Movement: Right-Wing Foundations and American Politics*. Online. Available HTTP: <http://www.pfaw.org/general/default.aspx?oid=2052> (accessed 11 April 2003).

Peoples' Global Action (1998) 'Manifesto'. Online. Available HTTP: <http://www.nadir.org/nadir/initiativ/agp/en/PGAInfos/manifest.htm> (accessed 9 December 2002).

—— (2001) 'Third Conference of PGA in Cochabamba, Bolivia, 16–24 September 2001'. Online. Available HTTP: <http://www.nadir.org/nadir/initiativ/agp/cocha/intro.htm#manif> (accessed 9 December 2002).

—— (n.d.) Peoples' Global Action home page. Online. Available HTTP: <http://www.nadir.org/nadir/initiativ/agp/en/index.html> (accessed 9 December 2002).

Perlman, F. (1983) *Against His-story, Against Leviathan! An Essay*, Detroit: Red and Black.

Peterson, V. S. and Runyan, A. S. (1999) *Global Gender Issues,* 2nd edition, Boulder, CO: Westview Press.

Pieterse, J. N. (ed.) (2000) *Global Futures: Shaping Globalisation*, London: Sage.

Pilger, J. (2004) 'American Terrorist', *New Statesman*, 12 January.

Pinkola Estes, C. (1993) *Women Who Run With the Wolves: Contacting the Power of the Wild Woman*, London: Rider Books.

Platt, T. and O'Leary, C. (2003) 'Patriot Acts', *Social Justice,* 30: 31 March.

Powers, T. (2003) 'War and its Consequences', *New York Review of Books*, 27 March. Online. Available HTTP: <http://www.nybooks.com/articles/16155> (accessed 30 April 2003).

Proceso: Seminario de Informacion y Analysis, Mexico City, various editions.

Project for a New American Century (PNAC) (1997) 'Statement of Principles', Washington, DC: Project for a New American Century. Online. Available HTTP: <http://www.newamericancentury.org/statementofprinciples.htm> (accessed 12 February 2003).

—— (1998) 'Letter to President William J. Clinton', Washington, DC: Project for a New American Century. Online. Available HTTP: <http://www.newamericancentury.org/iraqclintonletter.htm> (accessed 7 March 2003).

Purdum, T. (2003) 'The Brains Behind Bush's War Policy', *New York Times*, 1 February.

Rabelais, F. (1966) *The Histories of Gargantua and Pantagruel*, trans. J. M. Cohen, London: Penguin Books.

Rabinow, P. (1986) 'Representations are Social Facts', in J. Clifford and G. Marcus (eds) *Writing Culture: The Poetics and Politics of Ethnography*, Berkeley, CA: University of California Press, 234–61.

Rahula, W. (1959) *What the Buddha Taught*, New York: Grove Press.

Ramonet, I. (1997) 'Désarmer les Marchés', *Le Monde Diplomatique*, December.

Reagon, B. J. (1998) 'Coalition Politics: Turning the Century', in A. Phillips (ed.) *Feminism and Politics,* Oxford: Oxford University Press, 242–53.

Red Mexicana de Acción Frente al Libre Comercio (RMALC) (2002) 'ALCA'. Online. Available HTTP: <http://www.rmalc.org.mx/tratados/alca/alca.htm> (accessed 27 August 2002).

Reunión de Redes de la Campaña contra el ALCA (2002) 'NO al ALCA. Jornadas de Resistencia Continental contra el ALCA'. Online. Available HTTP: <http://www.nadir.org/nadir/initiativ/agp/free/imf/ecuador/txt/2002/jornadasquitoalca.htm> (accessed 27 April 2004).

Reus-Smit, C. (2001) 'Constructivism', in S. Burchill, R. Devetak, A. Linklater, M. Paterson, C. Reus-Smit and J. True, *Theories of International Relations,* 2nd edition, Basingstoke: Palgrave, 209–30.

Reuters (2003) 'Millions Join Global Protests of Iraq War', 15 February.

Rhythms of Resistance (2003) 'Who We Are'. Online. Available HTTP: <http://www.rhythmsofresistance.co.uk/?lid=56> (accessed 23 September 2003).

Riley, M. (2001) 'Anti-Globalisation Groups Prepare for Online Battle', *The Sydney Morning Herald*, 22 June.

Rilling, R. (2003) 'American Empire as Will and Idea: The New Grand Strategy of the Bush Administration', *Rosa-Luxemburg Stiftung Policy Paper* 2/2003, 1–12.

Robertson, R. and Khondker, H. (1998) 'Discourses of Globalization: Preliminary Considerations', *International Sociology,* 13 (1): 25–40.

Roder, U. (2003) 'Lechars Airport: Not Endless Discussion – Real Disarmament Now'. Online. Available HTTP: <http://tridentploughshares.org/antiwar/uroder.php> (accessed 5 January 2004).

Rodgers, J. (2002) 'Self-Perceptions: Mass Media, the Internet and the Framing of Political Activism', Paper presented at the International Studies Association annual convention (24–27 March), New Orleans, USA.

Rodino, V. (2003) 'They Chose Her as a Speaker for that Panel Because She Was Young and Female', *Resist: Official Zine of Globalise Resistance*, 9: 5.

Rosenberg, J. (1994) *Empire of Civil Society*, London: Routledge.

Rosenberg, M. (2002) 'World Social Forum Porto Alegre, Brasil, January 2002: Which Other World is Possible?', *WGNRR Newsletter*, 75: 1–4. Online. Available HTTP: <http://www.klaever.nl/open_document.asp?id=82&site_id=157> (accessed 14 April 2004).

Roszak, T. (1971 [1968]) *The Making of a Counter Culture: Reflections on the Technocratic Society and its Youthful Opposition*, London: Faber and Faber.

Rowbotham, S. and Linkogle, S. (eds) (2001) *Women Resist Globalization:* London: Zed Books.

Rowell, A. (1999) 'Faceless in Seattle', *Guardian*, 6 October.

Ruggiero, V. (2002) ' "ATTAC": A Global Social Movement?', *Social Justice,* 29 (1–2): 48–60.

Ruins, A. (2003) *Beyond the Corpse Machine,* Leeds: Re-Pressed Distribution.

Rupert, M. (1995) *Producing Hegemony: The Politics of Mass Production and American Global Power,* Cambridge: Cambridge University Press.

—— (1998) '(Re-)engaging Gramsci: A Response to Germain and Kenny', *Review of International Studies,* 24 (3): 427–34.

—— (2000) *Ideologies of Globalization: Contending Visions of a New World Order,* London: Routledge.

—— (2003) 'Anti-Capitalist Convergence? Anarchism, Socialism and the Global Justice Movement', in M. Steger (ed.) *Rethinking Globalism,* Lanham, MD: Rowman and Littlefield, 121–35.

—— (2004a) 'Globalising Common Sense: a Marxian-Gramscian (Re-)vision of the Politics of Governance/Resistance', *Review of International Studies,* 29 (1): 181–98.

—— (2004b) 'Class Powers and the Politics of Global Governance', in M. Barnett and R. Duvall (eds) *Power and Global Governance,* Cambridge: Cambridge University Press.

Rupture (2004) 'Mentalists', *Rupture,* February: 3.

Ryckmans, P. (1986) *The Chinese Attitude Towards the Past,* The Forty-seventh George Ernest Morrison Lecture in Ethnology, Canberra: The Australian National University.

Ryner, J. M. (2002) *Capitalist Restructuring, Globalisation, and the Third Way,* London: Routledge

Said, E. (1995) 'Orientalism', in B. Ashcroft, G. Griffiths and H. Tiffin (eds) *The Post-Colonial Studies Reader,* London: Routledge, 87–91.

St Clair, J. (1999) 'Seattle Diary: It's a Gas, Gas, Gas', *New Left Review,* 238: 81–96.

Salladay, R. (2003) 'Anti-War Patriots Find they Need to Reclaim Words, Symbols', *San Francisco Chronicle,* 7 April.

Sandoval, C. (1995) 'Feminist Forms of Agency and Oppositional Consciousness: US Third World Feminist Criticism', in J. K. Gardiner (ed.) *Provoking Agents: Gender and Agency in Theory and Practice,* Urbana and Chicago: University of Illinois Press, 208–26.

Saunders, K. (ed.) (2002) *Feminist Post-Development Thought: Rethinking Modernity, Post-Colonialism and Representation,* London: Zed Books.

Schlamp, H.-J. (2002) 'V-Männer im Schwarzen Block', *Der Spiegel,* 36: 76–8.

Schoch, J. (2000) 'Seattle – das war wie Mai 1968', *Tages-Anzeiger,* 26 January.

Scholte, J. A. (1996) 'Globalisation and Collective Identities', in J. Krause and N. Renwick (eds) *Identities in International Relations,* Basingstoke: Macmillan, 38–79.

—— (2000a) 'Cautionary Reflections on Seattle', *Millennium,* 29 (1): 115–21.

—— (2000b) *Globalization: A Critical Introduction,* Basingstoke: Macmillan.

Schumacher, E. (1973) 'Buddhist Economics', in H. Daly (ed.) *Towards a Steady-State Economy,* San Francisco: W.H. Freeman, 231–9.

Scott, A. (1990) *Ideology and the New Social Movements,* London: Unwin Hyman.

Sellers, J. (2004) 'Raising a Ruckus', in T. Mertes (ed.) *A Movement of Movements,* London: Verso, 175–91.

Sen, A. (2001) 'All Players on a Global Stage', *The Australian,* 16 May.

Sen, G., Germaine, A. and Chen, L. (eds) (1994) *Population Policies Reconsidered: Health, Empowerment and Rights*, Boston: Harvard School of Public Health.

Serra, C. (1999) 'Exclusão Social e Paradigma de Mondlane', *Estudos Moçambicanos*, 16: 119–26.

—— (2001) 'Tudo o que é Sólido se Esfuma', *Estudos Moçambicanos*, 18: 5–23.

—— (2003) *Em Cima de uma Lâmina – Um Estudo Sobre Precaridade Social em três Cidades de Moçambique*, Maputo: Livraria Universitária.

Shapiro, M. J. (1999) 'The Ethics of Encounter: Unreading, Unmapping the Imperium', in D. Campbell and M. J. Shapiro (eds) *Rethinking Ethics and World Politics*, Minneapolis: University of Minnesota Press.

Sharma, R. (2003) 'Debt Drives 86% Farmers to Suicide', *Hindustan Times*, 23 December. Online. Available HTTP: <http://www.hindustantimes.com/news/5822_506443,0015002000000106.htm> (accessed 29 January 2004).

Sharp, G. (1973) *The Politics of Nonviolent Action*, Boston: Porter Sargent.

Sharp, J. (1998) *Bordering the Future*, Austin, TX: State Comptroller.

Shaw, K. (2003) 'Whose Knowledge for What Politics', *Review of International Studies*, 29 (3): 199–221.

Shaw, M. (1994) 'Civil Society and Global Politics: Beyond a Social Movements Approach', *Millennium: Journal of International Studies*, 23 (3): 647–67.

Shiva, V. (1999) 'This Round to the Citizens', *Guardian*, 8 December.

Shot By You (2003) 'Blind Lead Stupid to Nothing', '2000 Anarchists Go on Rampage in San Francisco', Online. Available HTTP: <http://indymedia.org/news/2003/01/1562024_comment.php#1567370> (accessed 19 January 2003).

Showstack Sassoon, A. (1986) 'The People, Intellectuals and Specialized Knowledge', *Boundary 2*, 14 (3): 137–68.

Signs: Journal of Women in Culture and Society (2001) Special Issue on Globalisation, 26 (4).

Sistersong (2004) Sistersong home page. Online. Available HTTP: <http://www.sistersong.net/> (accessed 14 April 2004).

Sivanandan, A. (1999) 'Globalism and the Left', *Race and Class: A Journal for Black and Third World Liberation*, 40 (2/3): 5–19.

Sklair, L. (1994) *Capitalism and Development*, London: Routledge.

—— (2002) *Globalization: Capitalism and its Alternatives*, 3rd edition, Oxford: Oxford University Press.

Smail, D. (1984) *Illusion and Reality: The Meaning of Anxiety*, London: J.M. Dent.

Smelser, N. J. (1962) *Theory of Collective Behaviour*, New York: Free Press.

Smith, J. (2002) 'Globalizing Resistance: The Battle of Seattle and the Future of Social Movements', in J. Smith and H. Johnston (eds) *Globalization and Resistance: Transnational Dimensions of Social Movements*, Lanham, MD: Rowman and Littlefield, 207–27.

Smith, J. and Johnston, H. (eds) (2002) *Globalization and Resistance: Transnational Dimensions of Social Movements*, Lanham, MD: Rowman and Littlefield.

Smith, J., Chatfield, C., Pagnucco, R. and Chatfield, C.A. (eds) (1998) *Transnational Social Movements and Global Politics: Solidarity Beyond the State*, Syracuse, NY: Syracuse University Press.

Sontag, S. (2003) 'The Power of Principle', *Guardian*, 26 April.

Sorel, G. (1972 [1908]) *Réflexions sur la Violence*, Paris: Marcel Rivière.

Spivak, G. C. (1995) 'Can the Subaltern Speak?', in B. Ashcroft, G. Griffiths and H. Tiffin (eds) *The Post-Colonial Studies Reader*, London: Routledge, 24–8.

Starr, A (2000) *Naming the Enemy: Anti-Corporate Movements Confront Globalization*, London: Zed Books.

Staudt, K. (1998) *Free Trade? Informal Economies at the US–Mexico Border*, Philadelphia: Temple University Press.

Staudt, K. and Coronado, I. (2002) *Fronteras No Mas: Toward Social Justice at the US–Mexico Border*, New York: Palgrave USA.

Staudt, K., Rai, S. and Parpart, J. (2001) 'Protesting World Trade Rules: Can We Talk about Empowerment?', *Signs: Journal of Women in Culture and Society*, 26 (4): 121–57.

Steger, M. (2002) *Globalism: The New Market Ideology*, Lanham, MD: Rowman and Littlefield.

Stehli, I. (2000) 'Alice im Globalisierungsland', *Tages-Anzeiger*, 23 September.

Sturgeon, N. (1997) *Ecofeminist Natures: Race, Gender, Feminist Theory and Political Action,* London: Routledge.

Sullivan, S. (2001) 'Danza e Diversità: Copri, Movimento ed Esperienza Nella Trance-Dance dei Khoisan e nei Rave Occidentali' (On Dance and Difference: Bodies, Movement and Experience in Khoes_n Trance-Dancing – Perceptions of "a Raver"), *Africa e Mediterraneo Cultura e Societa,* 37: 15–22.

—— (2003) 'Frontline(s)', *ephemera: critical dialogues on organization*, 3 (1): 68–89. Online. Available as PDF file at: <http://www.ephemeraweb.org./journal/3–1/3–1index.htm> (accessed 26 April 2004).

—— (2004a) ' "We are Heartbroken and Furious!"(#2) Violence and the (Anti-) Globalisation Movement(s)', CSGR Working Paper, 133/04. Online. Available HTTP: <http://www2.warwick.ac.uk/fac/soc/csgr/research/workingpapers/2004/> (accessed May 2004).

—— (2004b) ' "We are Heartbroken and Furious!" Engaging with Violence and the (Anti-)Globalisation Movement(s)', CSGR Working Paper, 123/03. Online. Available HTTP: <http://www.warwick.ac.uk/fac/soc/CSGR/wpapers/wp12303.pdf> (accessed January 2004).

—— (2004c) 'New Social Movements, New Violence: Militancy, Militarisation and Masculinities in (Anti-)Globalisation Politics', Paper presented at workshop on 'Globalization of Political Violence', Prato, Italy (28–30 June).

—— (2004d) 'From Docile to Diffuse Bodies: Ekstasis as a Politics of Becoming', Paper presented at conference on 'Desiring Dissent: Bodies and/of/in Resistance', Essex Management Centre, University of Essex (5–6 May).

—— (forthcoming) 'Distributed Networks and the Politics of Possibility: Interpretations of what's New about the Form and Content of Glocal Anti/Post-Capitalism', CSGR Working Paper.

Sweeney, J. J. (2002) 'The New Internationalism', Speech to Council on Foreign Relations, New York (1 April 1998), in R. Broad (ed.) *Global Backlash: Citizens Initiatives for a Just World Economy,* Lanham, MD: Rowman and Littlefield.

Sylvester, C. (1994) *Feminist Theory and International Relations in a Postmodern Era,* Cambridge: Cambridge University Press.

Tai, H. (1989) 'The Oriental Alternative: An Hypothesis on Culture and Economy', in H. Tai (ed.) *Confucianism and Economic Development: An Oriental Alternative*, Washington, DC: Washington Institute Press, 6–37.

Takashina, S. (1996) 'The Heritage of Memory', *Japan Echo,* 23 (4): 70–7.

Tarrow, S. (1998) *Power in Movement: Social Movements and Contentious Politics,* 2nd edition, Cambridge: Cambridge University Press.

—— (n.d.) 'Beyond Globalization: Why Creating Transnational Social Movements is So Hard and When it is Most Likely to Happen'. Online. Available HTTP: <http://www.antenna.nl/~waterman/tarrow.html> (accessed 20 July 2000).

Taylor, M. (1997) 'Why no Rule of Law in Mexico? Explaining the Weakness of Mexico's Judicial Branch', *New Mexico Law Review,* 17 (1): 141–66.

Teivainen, T. (2002) 'The World Social Forum and Global Democratisation: Learning from Porto Alegre', *Third World Quarterly,* 23 (4): 621–32.

Tempest, R. (2003) 'Not your Parents' Protesters in Iraq Fight', *Los Angeles Times,* 15 February.

Thomas, L. (2002) 'Interview with Naomi Klein', *Feminist Review,* 70: 46–56.

Thompson, A. C. (2003) 'Anarchy in the USA: Black Bloc Antiwar Rioters Speak Out', *The San Francisco Bay Guardian,* 18 March. Online. Available HTTP: <http://www.sfbg.com/37/25/x_news_war.html> (accessed 8 October 2003).

Thoreau, H. D. (1966 [1848]) *Walden and Civil Disobedience,* New York: W.W. Norton.

Toje, A. (2002) 'Live to Fight Another Day? Non-Lethal Weapons and the Future of Violent Conflict', *The Norwegian Atlantic Committee.* Online. Available HTTP: <http://www.atlanterhavskomiteen.no/publikasjoner/andre/kortinfo/2002/10–2002.htm> (accessed 19 September 2003).

Tolstoy, L. (1967) *Writings on Civil Disobedience and Non-Violence,* London: Peter Owen.

Tormey, S. (2005) '"Not in my Name": Deleuze, Zapatismo and the Critique of Representation', *Political Studies,* forthcoming.

Totton, N. (2002) 'Foreign Bodies: Recovering the History of Body Psychotherapy', in T. Staunton (ed.) *Body Psychotherapy,* Hove: Brunner-Routledge, 7–26.

Touraine, A. (1985) 'An Introduction to the Study of Social Movements', *Social Research,* 52 (4): 749–87.

Transnational Institute (n.d.) Transnational Institute home page. Online. Available HTTP: <http://www.tni.org/> (accessed 4 May 2004).

Treneman, A. (2003) 'Peaceniks: the Unlikely Alliance', *The Times,* 21 January.

United for Peace (1993) United for Peace and Justice home page. Online. Available HTTP: <http://www.unitedforpeace.org/> (accessed 14 March 2004).

United Nations Conference on Trade and Development (UNCTAD) (2002) *The Least Developed Countries Report 2002,* Geneva: United Nations Publications.

United Nations Development Program (UNDP) (1999) *Human Development Report 1999.* Online. Available HTTP: *<http://www.undp.org/hdro/index2.html>* (accessed October 1999).

United Nations Educational, Scientific and Cultural Organisation (UNESCO) (1999) Operational Guidelines for the Implementation of the World Heritage Convention, World Heritage Committee 99/2 (March). Online. Available HTTP: <http://whc.unesco.org.opgutoc.htm> (accessed 9 March 2004).

United Nations Office for Drug Control and Crime Prevention (UNODCCP) (1999) *The Drug Nexus in Africa,* UNODCCP Studies on Drugs and Crime Monographs, New York: United Nations.

University of Sussex (2002) 'Protesting is Good For You, say Psychologists', Press release, 16 December. Online. Available HTTP:

<http://www.sussex.ac.uk/press_office/media/media270.shtml> (accessed 20 January 2004).

V-Day (n.d.) 'About V-Day'. Online. Available HTTP: <http://www.vday.org/contents/vday/aboutvday> (accessed 5 May 2004).

Vargas, V. (2002) 'World Social Forum: A Space of Our Own', *Dawn Informs,* May: 20–1.

Varney, W. and Martin, B. (2000) 'Net Resistance, Net Benefits: Opposing MAI', *Social Alternatives,* 19 (1): 48–51.

Vest, J. (2002) 'The Men from JINSA and CSP', *The Nation,* 2 September. Online. Available HTTP: <http://www.thenation.com/docprint.mhtml?i=20020902&s=vest> (accessed 13 March 2003).

Vidal, J. (1999) 'Real Battle for Seattle', *Guardian,* 5 December.

—— (2002) 'Florence Besieged by Army of Free Thinkers', *Guardian,* 8 November.

Viejo, E. (2003) 'Protecting the Movement and its Unity: A Realistic Approach', in Notes From Nowhere (eds) *We Are Everywhere: The Irresistible Rise of Global Anticapitalism,* London: Verso, 371–3.

Viner, K. (2000) 'Lessons to Be Learnt from "Luddites" ', *Guardian Weekly,* 5 November.

Vines, A. (1998) 'The Struggle Continues: Light Weapons Destruction in Mozambique', *Basic Papers – Occasional Papers on International Security Policy,* No. 25. Online. Available HTTP: <http://www.basicint.org/pubs/Papers/BP25.htm> (accessed 24 April 2004).

Virilio, P. (1977) *Vitesse et Politique,* Paris: Éditions Galilée.

—— (1995) *La Vitesse de Libération,* Paris: Galilée.

—— (1998) *The Virilio Reader,* ed. J. Der Derian, Oxford: Blackwell.

Vivekananda, S. (1964) *Teachings of Swami Vivekananda,* Calcutta: Advaita Ashrama.

Wacquant, L. (2001) 'The Penalisation of Poverty and the Rise of Neo-Liberalism', *European Journal on Criminal Policy and Research,* 9: 401–12.

Walker, R. B. J. (1988) *One World, Many Worlds: Struggles for a Just World Peace,* Boulder, CO: Lynne Rienner.

—— (1994) 'Social Movements/World Politics', *Millennium: Journal of International Studies,* 23 (3): 669–700.

—— (1999) 'The Hierarchalization of Political Community', *Review of International Studies,* 25 (1): 151–7.

—— (2000) 'International Relations Theory and the Fate of the Political', in B. Neufeld and M. Ebata (eds) *Confronting the Political,* Basingstoke: Macmillan, 212–38.

Washington Valdez, D. (2002) 'Death Stalks the Border/*La Muerte Acecha La Frontera*' (in Spanish and English), Special Report, *El Paso Times,* 23 June. Online. Available HTTP: <http://www.elpasotimes.com/borderdeath> (accessed 6 March 2003).

Waterman, P. (2000) 'Social Movements, Local Places and Globalized Spaces: Implications for "Globalization from Below" ', in B. K. Gills (ed.) *Globalization and the Politics of Resistance,* Basingstoke: Palgrave, 135–49.

—— (2002a) *Globalization, Social Movements and the New Internationalisms,* 2nd edition, London: Continuum.

—— (2002b) 'Reflections on the 2nd World Social Forum in Porto Alegre: What's Left Internationally?', Draft 29 April 2002, sent in email.

—— (2003) 'The World Social Forum and the Global Justice and Solidarity Movement: A Backgrounder', Draft 11 August 2003, sent in email.

Watson, M. (2003) 'Where do we go from Here? Notes on the Anti-Capitalist Movement after Evian', *ephemera: critical dialogues on organization*, 3 (2): 140–6.

Webb, C. (2003a) 'Mobilizing Online against the War', *Washington Post*, 11 March.

—— (2003b) 'Overseas, Internet is Rallying Point for Antiwar Activists', *Washington Post*, 12 March.

Weber, T. (1993) 'The Marchers Simply Walked Forward until Struck Down: Nonviolent Suffering and Conversation', *Peace and Change*, 18 (3): 267–89.

West, P. (2004) 'When Irish Eyes are Spying', *New Statesman*, 5 January: 20–1.

Whitaker, C. (2003) 'Notes about the World Social Forum'. Online. Available HTTP: <http://www.forumsocialmundial.org.br/dinamic.asp?pagina=bal_whitaker_ing> (accessed 30 June 2003).

White House (2002) *National Security Strategy for the United* States. Online. Available HTTP: <http://www.whitehouse.gov/nsc/nss.html> (accessed 19 December 2002).

White, S. K. (1991) *Political Theory and Postmodernism*, Cambridge: Cambridge University Press.

—— (2000) *Sustaining Affirmation: The Strengths of Weak Ontology in Political Theory*, Princeton, NJ: Princeton University Press.

Wichterich, C. (2000) *The Globalized Woman: Reports from a Future of Inequality*, London: Zed Books.

Wignaraja, P. (ed.) (1993) *New Social Movements in the South: Empowering the People*, London: Zed Books.

Wildfire (2003) *Apocalypse Now! An 'Uncivilised' Case against War*, London: Wildfire Collective.

Wilkin, P. (1999) 'Solidarity in a Global Age – Seattle and Beyond', *Journal of World Systems Research*, 6 (1): 20–65.

Willful Disobedience (n.d.) 'A Few Words: Developing Relationships of Affinity', *Willful Disobedience* 2 (12). Online. Available HTTP: <http://www.geocities.com/kk_abacus/vb/wd12fw.html> (accessed 24 September 2003).

Williams, I. (2002) 'Bush's Hatchet Man in the State Department', *Salon*, 10 May.

Williamson, J. (2003) 'The Washington Consensus and the Crises in Latin America', Seminar at Department of Economics, Warwick University (14 January).

Win Without War (2003) 'Our Mission'. Online. Available HTTP: <http://www.winwithoutwarus.org/> (accessed 30 April 2003).

Wolf, N. (1992) *The Beauty Myth: How Images of Beauty are Used against Women*, New York: Anchor.

WOMBLES (2003a) 'G8 Evian: June 1st–3rd, 2003. Lausanne Solidarity Declaration', *Love & Rage In the Dying Days of Capitalism*, 1: 32–5.

—— (2003b) 'Radical Dairy: A Review of a Social Centre, What is Community and the Need for Space', *Love & Rage In the Dying Days of Capitalism*. 1: 8–11.

—— (2003c) Back cover, *Love & Rage In the Dying Days of Capitalism*, 1: 39.

—— (2004) WOMBLES home page. Online. Available HTTP: <http://www.wombles.org.uk> (accessed 30 April 2004).

Wood, E. M. (2002) 'Global Capital, National States', in M. Rupert and H. Smith (eds) *Historical Materialism and Globalization*, London: Routledge, 17–39.

—— (2003) *Empire of Capital*, London: Verso.

Wood, L. J. (2004) 'Breaking the Bank and Taking to the Streets: How Protesters Target Neoliberalism', *Journal of World-Systems Research*, 10 (1): 69–89.

Woodley, G. (2000) 'The Battle for Seattle: Globalization and its Discontents', *Social Alternatives*, 19 (1): 26–9.

Woodroffe, J. and Ellis-Jones, M. (2000) 'States of Unrest: Resistance to IMF Policies in Poor Countries'. Online. Available HTTP: <http:/www.wdm.org.uk/cambriefs/DEBT/unrest.htm> (accessed December 2000).

World Bank (1998) *Rebuilding the Mozambique Economy: Country Assistance Review*, Washington, DC: World Bank.

—— (2003) *Mozambique: Country Assistance Strategy*, Washington, DC: World Bank. Online. Available HTTP: <http://www.worldbank.org/afr/mz/reports/CAS2003.pdf> (accessed 24 April 2004).

World Social Forum (2002) 'World Social Forum Charter of Principles'. Online. Available HTTP: <http://www.forumsocialmundial.org.br/main.asp?id_menu=4&cd_language=2> (accessed 15 December 2002).

Women's Global Network on Reproductive Rights (WGNRR) (1993) 'Reinforcing Reproductive Rights', Unpublished discussion paper obtained from Coordination Office.

—— (2004) 'Who we are'. Online. Available HTTP: <http://www.wgnrr.org/frameset.htm> (click on links to 'About WGNRR', then 'Who we are') (accessed 14 April 2004).

Wurtzel, E. (1999 [1994]) *Prozac Nation: Young and Depressed in America*, London: Quartet Books.

Yechury, S. (2003) 'Massive Protest Demonstration in Thessaloniki', *People's Democracy*. Online. Available HTTP: <http://pd.cpim.org/2003/0706/07062003_EU_summit.htm> (accessed 16 September 2003).

Ygarteche, O. (2000) *The False Dilemma: Globalization: Opportunity or Threat?*, trans. M. Fried, London: Zed Books.

Younge, G. (2003) 'Peace Movement Wraps Itself in Stars and Stripes', *Guardian*, 31 March.

Yuval-Davis, N. (1997) *Gender and Nation*, London: Sage.

Zalewski, M. and Enloe, C. (1995) 'Questions about Identity in International Relations', in K. Booth and S. Smith (eds) *International Relations Theory Today*, Cambridge: Polity Press, 279–305.

Zapatista Encuentro: Documents from the 1996 Encounter for Humanity and against Neoliberalism (1998) New York: Seven Stories Press.

Zapatista Net (1995) Zapatista Net website guide. Online. Available HTTP: <http://www.actlab.utexas.edu/~zapatistas/guide.html> (accessed 12 March 2004).

Zapatistas! Documents of the New Mexican Revolution (1994) New York: Automedia.

Zernike, K. and Murphy, D. (2003) 'Antiwar Effort Emphasizes Civility over Confrontation', *New York Times*, 29 March.

Zimbardo, P. G. (2004) 'A Situationist Perspective on the Psychology of Evil: Understanding how Good People are Transformed into Perpetrators', in A. Miller (ed.) *The Social Psychology of Good and Evil: Understanding our Capacity for Kindness and Cruelty*, New York: Guilford.

Index

eBooks

eBooks – at www.eBookstore.tandf.co.uk

A library at your fingertips!

eBooks are electronic versions of printed books. You can store them on your PC/laptop or browse them online.

They have advantages for anyone needing rapid access to a wide variety of published, copyright information.

eBooks can help your research by enabling you to bookmark chapters, annotate text and use instant searches to find specific words or phrases. Several eBook files would fit on even a small laptop or PDA.

NEW: Save money by eSubscribing: cheap, online access to any eBook for as long as you need it.

Annual subscription packages

We now offer special low-cost bulk subscriptions to packages of eBooks in certain subject areas. These are available to libraries or to individuals.

For more information please contact webmaster.ebooks@tandf.co.uk

We're continually developing the eBook concept, so keep up to date by visiting the website.

www.eBookstore.tandf.co.uk